The Four Deaths of Acorn Whistler

The Four Deaths
of Acorn Whistler

TELLING STORIES IN COLONIAL AMERICA

JOSHUA PIKER

HARVARD UNIVERSITY PRESS
Cambridge, Massachusetts
London, England   2013

Library of Congress Cataloging-in-Publication Data
Piker, Joshua Aaron.
  The four deaths of Acorn Whistler : telling stories in colonial America /
Joshua Piker.
     p. cm.
  Includes bibliographical references and index.
  ISBN 978-0-674-04686-3 (alk. paper)
  1. Acorn Whistler, d. 1752.   2. Acorn Whistler, d. 1752—Death.
3. Creek Indians—Kings and rulers—Biography.   4. Cherokee
Indians—Violence against—South Carolina—Charleston.   5. Southern
States—History—Colonial period, ca. 1600–1775.   6. Great Britain—
Colonies—America—Administration.   7. Great Britain—Colonies—
America—History—18th century.   I. Title.
  E99.C9A28 2013
  975.004'97385—dc23
     [B]   2012041388

For Francesca, as always
And for Naima, from now on

Contents

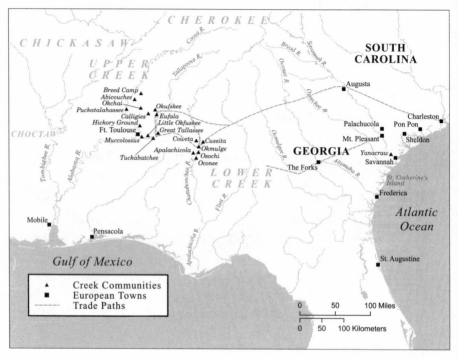

Acorn Whistler's World

Prologue

APRIL 1, 1752

$\mathcal{T}$HE DAY'S VIOLENCE was unexpected and thus all the more shocking. "About an hour before sunset," twenty-six Creeks fired on a party of twelve Cherokees. Initial reports that the Creeks "have Killed every one of them" or that "Ten . . . are destroyed" were wrong, but the carnage was still appalling. The attack clearly took the Cherokees by surprise. Three were killed "at the first volley; the rest fled, one of which was killed in the Chace, and one taken Prisoner"; at least two Cherokees were wounded. Later reports suggest that a fifth Cherokee died, and since there is no record of the prisoner ever being returned, he likely died as well. The numbers alone, moreover, cannot convey the brutality of the attack. A colonist who overheard the Creek barrage soon found "the head of an Indian lying in the road and near the side of it saw the body of an Indian lying." Another colonist reported that "one old Man had his Throat cut," while a second victim "was shot thro' the body, and his Head was cut off." All were "scalp'd." Twelve days afterward, one colonist labeled the incident a "Skirmish," but most adopted the term South Carolina officials were using by 9 p.m. on April 1: "murder."[1]

As brutal as the attack was, however, its location was worse. This was no frontier dust-'em-up, no ambush in the woods. Consider this: the Cherokee party was heading north, and the Creeks struck

1

from "behind," that is, from the south. If the Cherokees turned around at the sound of the Creeks' guns, the last thing they might have seen—besides the onrushing Creeks, of course—was the setting sun glinting off St. Philips Church, "the most elegant Religious Edifice in British America."[2] The Cherokees were, in other words, "within the Sight of Charles Town," in the heart of British South Carolina, on "The High Way" that ran up a narrow peninsula linking the colony's capital city to the mainland. South Carolina Governor James Glen had a penchant for hyperbole, but no one—Indian or colonist—quarreled with his assertion that "the Murder" happened "in the very Face of this Government . . . and, in a manner, in our Arms!" The more phlegmatic colonists labeled the attack an "insult" and "outrage," while the more melodramatic spoke of "the Heinousness of the Crime" that was "done in open Defiance and Contempt of the English." The Cherokees had no trouble agreeing, telling Glen that "your broad Path is sprinkled with the Blood of our People"; "the Mischief done . . . at his Excellency's Door" demonstrated, they said, that "the Creeks think Nothing" of the governor. Even Creeks came to recognize that the "Blood . . . spilt at your very Gates" was an "Insult and Injury" that "could not well be greater," an "Evil" that could not be ignored.[3]

And, in fact, the site of the attack was even more inflammatory than that. Think of those Cherokees facing north. When the Creeks attacked from the south and the Cherokees whirled around, did they turn to the right or the left? We cannot know, of course, but if they turned right, the first thing they might have seen—even before the Creeks—was Belvedere, Governor Glen's mansion. The attack took place less than "half a mile" from "Your Excellency's gate," close enough that his gravely ill wife surely heard the shots. Perhaps the Cherokees were not speaking metaphorically when they claimed that their people were killed "close by his Door"? Glen, who arrived home after the attack, awoke very early the next morning—he had summoned his council to a 7 a.m. meeting—to the news "that there were several bodys of Dead Indians . . . lying on the Path." The dead Cherokees were almost certainly on the land of Artimus Elliott, Glen's neighbor and a member of one of the colony's "great rice-planting families." And the living? They were seen a mile or two north, on the

"Plantation" of Joseph Wragg, a recently deceased "eminent Merchant" and longtime "Member of his Majesty's Council."[4] This was an exclusive neighborhood in which to stage a massacre.

Worse than the violence of the attack, though, and worse than the incongruity of its location, was the fact that all involved had taken steps to avoid just this sort of incident. The Creeks and Cherokees were at war in 1752, but these Creeks had been warned—explicitly, publicly, repeatedly—not to harm these Cherokees, and these Creeks had promised—explicitly, publicly, repeatedly—that these Cherokees were safe. The Creek and Cherokee parties first met by accident in Charleston on March 29. The Creeks had arrived the day before and were "encamped" by "the old School-House," where the Cherokees also intended to stay. This "Accident" almost "produced very ill Consequence," according to Glen, "for the Creeks seeing [the Cherokees] coming in imagined, I suppose, that they were coming to attack them and immediately took to their Arms." They "were on the very Point of firing on the Cherokees" when colonists intervened and "with much ado . . . prevented . . . Bloodshed."[5]

Two days later, on March 31, Glen met with the Creeks in the council chambers. He told them that "the Cherokees are our Friends, so that the killing any of them in our Settlements is the same as killing any of us" and "a Thing we could not have put up with." The Creeks' response reassured Glen: "they had made Peace with them and . . . they had Eat and Drank with them and exchanged Blankets and Smoaked together and shaken Hands." Glen knew enough of Indian diplomacy to recognize that exchanging food and clothes and sharing tobacco represented a powerful statement of goodwill. "In fine," he said, the Creeks "looked upon" the Cherokees "as Brothers, and gave me the strongest Assurances that they would not touch them." Better yet, the Creeks "promised" to end the ongoing Creek-Cherokee war by making "the Peace general, when they went home." Glen, in turn, told the Cherokees "that they might depend on it, that the Creeks would not hurt them." Given the bloody events of the following afternoon, it is not hard to see why Glen would later begin a story about April 1, 1752, by remarking, "But will you believe it, Friends and Brothers, or can you think it possible, what we are now to tell you?"[6]

The spokesman for the Creek party—the man who made all those pretty promises—was Acorn Whistler, a head warrior from the Creek town of Little Okfuskee. Four and a half months later he was dead, executed by his fellow Creeks to make amends for the April 1 attack. Beginning immediately after his mid-August execution, Creeks and Britons talked incessantly about Acorn Whistler's guilt and the meaning of his death, a conversation that only ended in the summer of 1753 when a new crisis pushed the Acorn Whistler affair into the background. Prior to that point, though, stories about Acorn Whistler made the rounds in Creek country, the British colonies, and Great Britain.

People interested in ending the Creek-Cherokee war sought to use the April 1 attack as an example of warfare's horrors and Acorn Whistler's execution as evidence of the Creek desire for peace. Other people, especially those personally connected to Acorn Whistler, instanced his execution as proof of their eagerness to resume relations with the groups victimized by the attack. Still others saw Acorn Whistler's execution as a chance not to renew old political ties but to create new ones, either by remaking their own society or by repositioning themselves within their societies' hierarchies of wealth and status. Whatever their goals, though, all of these people found it necessary to tell stories about Acorn Whistler's death. And whatever their goals, no one—not even Acorn Whistler's kinsmen and townspeople—took it upon themselves to use their story to defend his innocence. Generations of historians, taking their cue from the unanimity among Acorn Whistler's contemporaries, have blamed him for the April 1 attack.[7] In so doing, these scholars have unwittingly joined an old conversation, a centuries-long discussion that features the regular retelling of stories about Acorn Whistler. That these stories shape our histories more than two and a half centuries later tells us a great deal about their power, but the stories themselves tell us almost nothing about either what happened on April 1, 1752, or why Acorn Whistler had to die. There were, it turns out, many reasons to execute Acorn Whistler, but no one at the time truly believed that he died because he was responsible for the April 1 attack.

Consider, for example, that neither Acorn Whistler nor his followers were present when the Cherokees were killed. At the time of the attack, Acorn Whistler was, in his words, "about the town drinking." Moreover, he said, "our People were scattered here and there, and some on board of Ships" in Charleston's harbor. No one disputed these points; nor did they object when Acorn Whistler distinguished "our people" from "they" who "did it of themselves." Everyone knew from the very beginning that the attackers were all Lower Creeks. Acorn Whistler, by contrast, was an Upper Creek, as were his eleven followers. He was, then, on very firm ground when he declared "[t]his was done by the Lower Creeks and not by me."[8]

Better still for Acorn Whistler, he was not the Lower Creeks' leader. In fact, he barely knew them. The Upper and Lower Creek parties had traveled separately from Creek country to South Carolina, meeting by accident sixty miles from Charleston while both were visiting Sheldon, Lieutenant Governor William Bull's plantation. Acorn Whistler may then have persuaded the Lower Creeks to accompany his people, and he spoke for the joint party when they arrived in Charleston. But he was not granted leadership over the Lower Creeks until after April 1, 1752. That dubious honor was foisted on him as a post hoc promotion designed to smooth over plot problems in postmortem stories.[9]

Consider, as well, that neither Acorn Whistler nor his Upper Creek followers believed themselves to blame for the violence. In the aftermath of the attack, the Upper Creeks were, in their words, "very much scared" but did not act as if they were guilty, while the Lower Creeks were quite obviously guilty but not scared, or at least not for long. Thus, after killing the Cherokees, all the Lower Creeks immediately fled, leaving Charleston at such "a prodigious Rate" that militia dispatched four hours later to "go in pursuit" never caught up with them. Once safely away from Charleston, however, the Lower Creeks concluded the heat was off. They stopped at planter Henry de Sausseur's home on April 3 and stayed until April 6. While there, they bragged of attacking the Cherokees, offered to sell their prisoner for eight bottles of rum, and "express[ed] no manner of fear that they should be pursued."[10]

Acorn Whistler and all of his Upper Creeks, by contrast, remained in Charleston for almost twenty-four hours. While there, the Upper Creeks "utterly" denied "all Knowledge of the proceedings of ye Lower People." Of course, "they appeared all very much Concerned," but they did not flee until after meeting with Governor Glen in the afternoon of April 2. At that session, the Upper Creeks became alarmed when Glen stated that they would be disarmed and imprisoned until his suspicions were allayed; the colonists outside the room opining that "they all ought to be hanged" did nothing to ease the Upper Creeks' minds. And so, after leaving the council chamber, all the Upper Creeks but one took to their heels. Four men who stopped at Mary Surreau's Ashley Ferry house were captured that night, taken back to Charleston, admonished by Glen, and then released; three men and two women headed west to Pon Pon, where they rejoined those captured at the ferry. And one man simply disappeared.[11]

For his part, Acorn Whistler first went to ground for a week and then straggled into Lieutenant Governor Bull's house alone and "almost starved with Hunger and Cold." After receiving "Victuals and some Cloaths," he rejoined his Upper Creek party, but not before promising he would "hunt in those Parts, and then would return to Charles Town." He never did. Perhaps he learned from his people that there was no reason to do so? After all, Glen had told the Upper Creeks captured at the ferry that "if you should meet Acorn Whistler you should laugh at him for his Fear." He need not have run off because "[t]he English never punish the Innocent with the Guilty" and "never intend[ed] to resent upon the Upper Creeks the injuries done by the Lower Creeks only." Acorn Whistler's flight, then, had not changed Glen's conclusion about "the Upper Creeks," whose "Conduct has not only been blameless but commendable."[12]

That does not mean, of course, that Acorn Whistler was a saint. True, after his execution, a fellow Creek called him "as great a Man and Warriour as any in their Nation," and in his lifetime he was described as a "King" with seven towns under his "command" whose "love [of] Peace" had earned him the name "White King." But the details of Acorn Whistler's life belie those rosy assessments. He drank, sometimes to excess. He used violence as a political tool, frequently to excess. He was a relentless self-promoter, invariably to excess. In fact, the only person to claim that Acorn Whistler was a "White King" who ruled over seven towns was Acorn Whistler himself, and it is worth noting that in Acorn Whistler's Muskogee language only one letter separates *lak.cv* [acorn] from *lak.sv* [liar].[13] Those wishing to blame him for the assault, therefore, have some evidence at their disposal.

Acorn Whistler, for example, certainly knew of the Lower Creeks' plan prior to the attack. Under close questioning by Glen on April 2, Acorn Whistler first claimed ignorance of what the Lower Creeks had intended but then acknowledged "They asked me the Night before if I would joyn them," information that he neglected to pass along to the British because "I was very lame in my Knee. The Indians kicked me and I could not walk, and I was drunk as well as they." Besides, he said, "I did not think they would have done it after I refused it." Glen was unimpressed. "I am surprised how he can contradict himself so. . . . There is a great Difference betwixt saying that one forgot a Thing and of never knowing any Thing about it." Glen had a point, but it is also true that it is one thing to hear of a plan from drunken men while you yourself are drunk; it is something else entirely to participate in that plan while you are sober. And when Acorn Whistler sobered up, not only did he decline to participate in the attack but "as soon as I found" the Lower Creeks "were a going," he realized his refusal to join them had not scotched their plans; "I then run away & told the Interpreter" that the Cherokees were in danger. In other words, he did not exactly keep the Lower Creeks' secret under his hat.[14]

More damning, though, is the possibility that Acorn Whistler's involvement in the attack went beyond prior knowledge of Lower Creek plans. The assault may have been his idea. Or at least that is what Hiacpellechi, one of the Lower Creek attackers, claimed four months later: "Acorn Whistler was the Cause of all the Mischief that was done. . . . [I]t was by his Orders that they feigned a Peace with the Cherokees and when they went out of Town he told them that it would be good to kill them." Hiacpellechi's story, however, is shot through with lies and at least one half-truth. And, of equal importance, Hiacpellechi would have taken the rap if Acorn Whistler did not. As a kinswoman told him, "You too was one that was the Occasion of all this Disturbance, and . . . some of you must suffer Death for it." She cautioned that "you had better tell the Truth," but who could blame him for interpreting that advice as "Lie or die"? In other words, Hiacpellechi was not exactly an unimpeachable witness.[15]

Of course, less reliable people than Hiacpellechi have sent better men than Acorn Whistler to their deaths, and sometimes those deaths were well deserved. That does not seem to have been the case with Acorn Whistler, however. He was guilty of bad judgment, bad luck, bad timing, and perhaps even bad faith, but not murder. It is clear, in fact, that he became a scapegoat. The initial failure to tell Glen of the Lower Creeks' plans. The possible involvement in hatching those plans. The dead Cherokees at Glen's door. The shifting alibi. The flight from Charleston. The week spent in hiding. The failure to return to Charleston. There was just enough there—in the right light with the right spin from the right hands— to cost Acorn Whistler his life. But why did the "right" people go to all this trouble? Why make the effort to ignore some facts and distort others? Why, in short, was Acorn Whistler executed? And, of course, why should we care? Answering those questions requires listening to the stories that were told about Acorn Whistler's death.

Introduction

ACORN WHISTLER AND THE STORYTELLERS

*T*HE DETAILS of Acorn Whistler's execution are, to put it mildly, a bit unclear. We know that he was executed, that the executioner was his own nephew, and that the nephew was then killed to prevent him from naming his coconspirators. Put in terms of the who, what, where, why, when, and how elements of storytelling, this means that we know who and what. What else do we know? Where? Probably in Acorn Whistler's hometown of Little Okfuskee, although all we can say for certain is that "the News" of his execution "was brought to [the Creek town of] Tuckabatchees . . . the Distance from the Place where the said Indian was killed being 15 or 16 Miles." Little Okfuskee was about that far from Tuckabatchee. When? Probably on August 15, 1752, but possibly on August 14. Even those who considered the execution to be—no pun intended—a matter of life and death had to admit they were "not positive" about the "particular Day." How? We know only that great care was taken that Acorn Whistler not suspect a thing before "the Bussiness was done."[1] Why?

The reasons behind Acorn Whistler's execution can certainly be traced, in part, to the broader historical moment in which he died. Taken as a whole, in fact, the big picture is a remarkably unsettled one. The political truths, institutional structures, and international relationships that encompassed colonists, imperial officials, and Native Americans in 1752 were extremely fragile. At the time of Acorn Whistler's death, his fellow Creeks were at war with the Cherokees to the north, a war that centered on the Lower Creeks in what is now western Georgia, not on Acorn Whistler's Upper Creeks in modern-day Alabama. Some Creeks saw divisions like Upper vs. Lower as a problem and were working to create a true Creek nation; others remained committed to a version of local autonomy that privileged community and family. To the east of the Creeks were two British colonies, South Carolina and Georgia, which did not get along particularly well with each other but which could be counted on, in the event of a war, to unite against Spain's imperial outpost in Florida and France's representatives in Louisiana. In part because all involved knew that such a war was a matter of when not if, Britain's leaders back in London were reshaping imperial administration, a project that necessarily encompassed Britain's dealings with both its colonists' Indian neighbors and its colonists. That those colonists were themselves intertwined with Indian country and the international networks of the Atlantic world complicated matters considerably, as did the colonists' ambivalence about the fraught but critically important relationship between metropole and colony.

All in all, then, North America in the middle decades of the eighteenth century was a place where leaders who aspired to power invariably settled for influence, a world where plans quickly devolved into hopes, orders into requests, dominion into chaos. Whether such a situation offered daunting challenges or welcome opportunities varied from person to person, but no one escaped its implications. The stories about Acorn Whistler's death attest to the ways in which this environment of tension, violence, and transformative possibility influenced his fate. Again and again, the storytellers linked Acorn Whistler's execution to the macroscale realities of the day: international war and intranational rivalries, imperial reform and national consolidation, cross-cultural disagreements and transatlantic arguments, colonial intrigues and metropolitan politics. The early modern world was a dangerous place, and the stories told about Acorn Whistler's execution demonstrate that he was one of its casualties.

But if it is true that these storytellers were attuned to the macro, it is also true that none of them would have made the mistake of thinking that anything concrete, valuable, and enduring could be accomplished in the wider world without attending to details closer to home. Our storytellers, in fact, were students of the ordinary and scholars of the local. They knew the power of the personal, the quotidian, and the routine. Their stories about Acorn Whistler were deeply attentive to those microlevel realities, not because they were in danger of confusing a mustard seed with the kingdom of God but rather because they knew that great oaks from little acorns grow. At a distance of more than two and a half centuries, of course, it is tempting to subordinate acorns to oaks, or perhaps even to step back from the oak trees and look for the forest. Doing so has its value, but only if we remember the importance of individual trees and the acorns from which they sprang. Colonial Americans of all backgrounds knew that if their stories were to have any hope of success, they needed to encompass acorn, tree, and forest.

All of that is worth saying because if part of the reason that Acorn Whistler was executed can be traced to the big picture, then another part is rooted in a much smaller one. That is true, of course, in the most literal of senses since, as the prologue's discussion of the April 1 attack makes clear, Acorn Whistler's execution can be traced directly to a very specific event at a very particular place with a very limited cast of characters. But Acorn Whistler's execution was "micro" in another, more revealing sense as well. The big-picture realities of the day—the fluidity and uncertainty of the early modern world—meant that the individuals who saw to it that Acorn Whistler was executed and then told stories about his death were intimately familiar with insecurity, fear, and failure. They knew that no hard and fast line separated winners from losers in colonial British America, and they likewise knew that, in times of flux and chaos, telling the right story was more important than getting the story right. In a maelstrom of change and possibility, the right story, even if untrue, could change the world. Local narratives could render imperial agendas untenable; personal accounts could unsettle the plans of would-be nation-builders; news of the quotidian and the ordinary could fracture transatlantic networks. Not surprisingly, then, telling stories became—as my favorite storyteller later put it—"a refuge in time of need, the fourth Grace, the tenth Muse, man's best and surest friend."[2] Acorn Whistler was executed, in part, because of this volatile local environment. His executioners knew that microhistories could have global implications, but they also were all too aware that, whether they focused on the workaday or the world-historical, victories would be hard-fought, and even winners would settle for a good deal less than half a loaf.

ACORN WHISTLER, though, received neither loaf nor slice nor crumb. Understanding why that was so—and appreciating what his fate tells us about the world in which he lived—requires returning to the question of why he was executed. There is no simple, definitive answer. We can reconstruct the events surrounding the April 1 assault in some detail; we can situate those events quite firmly within both the larger geopolitical context and his executioners' more local milieu. But doing so will not give us a definitive answer, much less a simple one. Some questions, of course, do not have such answers, but that is not the problem here. The people who told stories about Acorn Whistler's execution have left us with four clear-cut, mutually exclusive answers, four reasons for why Acorn Whistler had to die, four narratives to explain his execution, four attempts to use his fate to reshape the world that he left behind. In a very real way, the storytellers have left us with four different deaths.

The four stories were the work of people drawn from different interest groups among Acorn Whistler's contemporaries. Each of the storytellers came to recognize that his or her plans in the present and hopes for the future were wrapped up with Acorn Whistler's execution. Start with Governor Glen, a representative of Britain's empire who was based in North America and who looked to Indian country for professional salvation as he struggled with the transition from an older, looser form of imperial administration to a more centralized mode of governance. In the story that Glen told, Acorn Whistler died an imperial death. Move on to Malatchi, a political and military leader of the Creek nation who spent the late 1740s and early 1750s crafting ever-more coherent and forceful ideologies of Creek unity and personal power. Malatchi made sure that, in his story, Acorn Whistler died a national death. Turn then to a set of Creeks from the town of Okfuskee, local headmen wedded to more traditional Creek understandings about the importance of family and the centrality of community. When they told the story of Acorn Whistler, his death was a local one. Look finally at Thomas and Mary Bosomworth, British colonists who sought connections with metropolitan homelands so as to create new forms of power, influence, and wealth on the colonial periphery. Their story set up Acorn Whistler for a quintessentially colonial death. These people all told stories about Acorn Whistler's execution, each of which simultaneously reflected their radically different perspectives on the world and agreed on a simple point: Acorn Whistler had to die.

That said, this simplicity—four sorts of storytellers; four stories; one ending—is itself a bit misleading because none of these storytellers worked in isolation. At this point in American history, stories from Creek country, colonial towns, and imperial capitals crossed oceans and cultural frontiers, producing new stories along the way. The stories told about Acorn Whistler's death show us debates and conversations that transcended the boundaries that we sometimes take for granted. We, who grew up learning distinct histories of Indians or colonists or imperialists, are predisposed to hear separate stories, to segregate the colony from the empire, the community from the nation, the Creeks from the British. The stories told about Acorn Whistler, though, bring us face to face with unfamiliar combinations; they show us a world that cannot be divided into tidy categories. Community *and* nation. Family *and* empire. Creek *and* colonist. Indian *and* British. Local *and* transatlantic. In Acorn Whistler's world, people with different cultural backgrounds, clashing political affiliations, and incompatible personal agendas perforce constructed intertwined narratives. These varied storytellers were regularly and routinely surfacing in each other's lives, everyday and ever-present realities that had to be accounted for in story after story.

That was the case because none of these storytellers was powerful enough to ignore the stories told by their contemporaries. Yes, each of our storytellers was influential and important. Glen was a European-trained lawyer and governor of Britain's richest colony on mainland North America. Malatchi was, by a fairly wide margin, the most powerful Creek of his generation. Okfuskee's headmen led the largest town in Creek country. Thomas Bosomworth was an Oxbridge-educated Anglican minister; Mary Bosomworth was descended on her mother's side from the leading Creek family and had a history of working closely with key British officials in Georgia and South Carolina. In the grand scheme of things, these were all powerful people. Compared to their contemporaries, they were enviably well placed and well connected, and they could each plausibly claim to have the ability to call upon the corporate power of at least one polity.

But they also had to contend with the realities of the early modern world, with its weak institutions, attenuated power centers, negotiated truths, and endemic fluidity. In such a context, attempts to impose a particular brand of order on the world were a constant feature of life, but those efforts—if they were to have any hope of success—necessarily relied on plausible stories, carefully cultivated relationships, and cautiously applied pressure. Would-be leaders who privileged brusque orders, biddable subordinates, and brute demonstrations of force did not last long. That Acorn Whistler was executed demonstrates that the messy mix of intimacy and intimidation could produce results. That four stories emerged to explain his death, though, suggests that results should not be confused with consensus, progress with victory. Colonial America, in fact, was much better at producing losers than winners.

That Acorn Whistler was not a winner is suggested by the fact that his fate pivoted on an April Fools' Day surprise, a coincidence that would have meant nothing to him—although his Anglo-American contemporaries likely commented on it—but which nonetheless adds weight to the impression that he was something less than fortune's favorite. More to the point, Acorn Whistler was executed, a fate most winners avoid. To be sure, some victims of the scaffold find that history treats them more kindly than did their executioners. The suffering of John Proctor and Rebecca Nurse in Salem has been redeemed on stage and screen; John Brown's soul goes marching on. That has not, however, been the case with Acorn Whistler. Historians have accepted his executioners' stories, and anyone seeking to double-check those stories will struggle to find the information that might permit such a project.

One person's defeat, though, was not automatically another's triumph. Colonial America did not work that way. Acorn Whistler's execution neither ended the debate between those he left behind nor short-circuited the quotidian and contentious process of trying to regularize their shared world. In the end, some of the storytellers were more or less happy with Acorn Whistler's death, but none of them could truly be said to have won the day. And yet winners write the histories, or so we are told. Who, then, writes the histories when no one wins? How should we write about a place and a time where the absence of winners was the norm, not the exception? And if the histories that we have from that place and time are based upon stories told by losers intent on being seen as winners, then how might that affect our understanding of colonial America?

So, TO SOME EXTENT, the reason that we have four stories about Acorn Whistler's death—and the reason he was executed at all—goes back to the agendas of the storytellers and the nature of the world they inhabited. But the other part of the answer to the "Why was he executed?" question centers on Acorn Whistler himself. We do not, it must be said, know much about the man. Prior to the 1752 crisis that took his life, he appears in the records only five times and only as a bit player in larger dramas. The nature of those appearances, though, makes it clear that, if we could ask Acorn Whistler's contemporaries why he was executed, their answers would likely range from "Why not?" to "Couldn't have happened to a nicer guy." Acorn Whistler, in short, had never given anyone important a pressing reason to defend him, but he had given many people real incentives not to do so. This personal history provided the raw material for the four stories later told about his death. His past became a reason storytellers could both agree that Acorn Whistler had to die and believe that they could tell persuasive stories about that death.

To understand those stories and Acorn Whistler's deaths, then, we need to know more about Acorn Whistler. Let us turn to those five appearances: 1741, 1744, 1746, 1749, 1750. And, truthfully, that

is overstating matters since 1741 and 1746 functioned as 1744's prologue and epilogue respectively, while 1750 was 1749's coda. Call it
two sets of appearances: 1741/1744/1746 and 1749/1750. Now, what
do they tell us about Acorn Whistler?

〜 IT WAS a measure of the man that, in Acorn Whistler's first
sustained appearance in the historical record, he was both unnamed
and misidentified. On July 28, 1744, twelve Upper Creeks were in
Charleston to discuss the Creeks' place in the long-running struggle
between Great Britain and France. At Governor Glen's invitation,
four headmen from the influential towns of Okchai and Okfuskee
had been escorted down by Alexander Wood, a British trader in
Okfuskee; "5 more Indians," including at least three Alabamas,
joined them unexpectedly in Augusta and came along to Charleston. The Alabamas were one of the three divisions in Upper Creek
country; Alabama towns tended to favor the French, while the
Okchais and Okfuskees' Abeika division tended to be pro-British.
The Upper Creeks arrived in Charleston on July 14, met with Glen
on July 25, and by July 28 it was time for the British to think about
which presents would be given to which Indian visitor. Glen's council decided that the "Headman of the Albamas called the Mad-Tur-
key" would receive, among other things, a coat, blue pants, and a
scarlet jacket; "two [other] Albamas" would receive similar (but less
prestigious) items.[3]

Very nice, except that none of these people were Alabamas. Later
in life, Mad Turkey lived in an Okfuskee village, and in 1744 he
likely was "head of" Little Okfuskee, a town in the third Upper
Creek division, the Tallapoosas. The other "Albamas"? No one
bothered to write down their names in 1744, but they were Acorn
Whistler and his brother, also (in Acorn Whistler's words) "Talapussee People" from Little Okfuskee. We know that Acorn Whistler was present in 1744 because, a year and a half later, he tried
to visit Charleston again. Glen denied him permission, writing
that it was "needless" for "Acorn Whistler or his People to come
down especially as he & his Brother were here to see me last year &
kindly entertained & received handsome presents from me." Since
the "two Albamas" in 1744 received identical presents (as would be

appropriate for brothers), and since no other Upper Creek party visited Glen in 1744 or 1745, Glen's reference to Acorn Whistler visiting "last year" could only refer to this party.[4]

That Acorn Whistler appeared in 1744 as an anonymous faux Alabama is fitting for several reasons. In the first place, his anonymity in 1744 extends into the present. We still know neither his personal name nor his title; all that survives is a nickname—"called by us the Acorn Whistler"—used by the British. Moreover, the British failure to record his name speaks to his relative insignificance. After all, the British noted names for three of his traveling companions in 1744, one of whom was unimportant enough that he never appeared again in the historical record while another did not reappear until 1774. Acorn Whistler could, it seems, disappear in even the slimmest of shadows. His lack of status likely led him to seek out potential patrons in the British colonies. He had been an uninvited member of the 1744 party, and when he returned for a second visit in 1746 only eleven other Upper Creeks had been down to see Glen even once.[5]

The lack of status that repeatedly brought Acorn Whistler to South Carolina, however, prevented him from being taken seriously once there. Thus, in 1746, Glen had him stopped before he arrived in Charleston since "I did not understand that he was sent by the nation," and he "brought no Talk from the beloved men of that Nation." Glen underlined the point just before the 1752 attack, telling Acorn Whistler that "I have observed that when the Head Men of this Nation come down, I never found that he came with them, but always by himself"; two years before, Glen called him "a Worthless fellow." As a result, Glen refused to accept Acorn Whistler's word on Creek affairs—"I do not talk to you as to the Nation"—and insisted on treating Acorn Whistler and his people "as private Persons." And yet, when Acorn Whistler did accompany Creek leaders, the British ignored him. He could apparently choose between traveling with other headmen (and being obscured by them) or traveling without those headmen (and being seen as illegitimate). What of the posthumous statements that Acorn Whistler was "one of [the Creeks'] greatest Men" and "as great a Man and Warriour as any in their Nation"? We could say that people were speaking kindly of the recently departed or trafficking in comforting fictions, but lying is more accurate.[6]

That said, though, there was a grain of truth—however small—in claims that Acorn Whistler was "great." After all, he carried a British commission. In fact, Acorn Whistler first appears in the historical record in April 1741 when South Carolina's secretary drafted an "Indian Commission" for "the Acorn Whistler on parchment under the Great Seal." The British gave commissions to Indians whom they wished either to reward or to court; Indians accepted commissions as tangible, displayable markers of British favor. Great men in Creek country carried commissions, but so too did some mediocrities who found themselves in the right place at the right time. Acorn Whistler was clearly one of the latter. He received a commission only because the Okfuskee trader Alexander Wood sent his name and that of another headman with ties to Okfuskee to South Carolina's lieutenant governor, along with the recommendation "that Commissions and Presents may be given to some Headmen in the Creek Nation, to encourage those People to remain attached to our Interests." Once the commissions were drafted, a British agent who happened to be going to Creek country delivered them. With that done, no British subject ever again mentioned Acorn Whistler's commission. But other Creeks knew of it, and it certainly empowered Acorn Whistler to accompany Wood and the Okfuskees to Charleston in the summer of 1744.[7]

As he met Glen, then, Acorn Whistler was a headman—perhaps the head warrior—of Little Okfuskee, a town of at most one hundred people. By Creek standards, that was a tiny place; Great Okfuskee was perhaps twenty times larger, and even unimportant communities generally had at least two hundred inhabitants. Moreover, even in this small pond, Acorn Whistler was not the biggest fish, as demonstrated by the British decision to present Mad Turkey with more valuable gifts. Acorn Whistler, though, could count on mustering a dozen followers whenever he visited Charleston, and he could depend on being treated with a degree of respect by those he met. He was not the "greatest" of men, then, but nor was he truly insignificant. He was just important enough for the lies that were told about his stature to be convincing. He could be presented to

Glen in 1744 as someone worthy of receiving more presents than a common warrior, and he could be memorialized as a great leader after his death. But he was not so important that his execution would present a long-term problem. He was the perfect fall guy.[8]

Acorn Whistler's status aside, it is significant that he was introduced to Glen as an Alabama. That was a lie, but a plausible one. Little Okfuskee truly was in Alabama country. The Alabamas were settled around Fort Toulouse—it was often called the Alabama Fort—the easternmost French garrison in the region and the guarantor of French influence in Creek country. How could Governor Glen, a man who had arrived in North America only seven months before, be expected to know that a community reportedly located "within two miles of the French Garrison" was not an Alabama town? Besides, this lie fit well with what Glen wanted to hear in July 1744. Glen had learned that Britain and France were once again at war, and he immediately determined that South Carolina would "distress and annoy the Subjects of the French King"—as London's orders required—by conquering Fort Toulouse. Of course, the colony would need help, and who better to ask than Alabamas from a town "settled right [next] to the French" fort who arrived in Charleston with Britain's traditional Okchai and Okfuskee allies?[9]

The ensuing talks were sensitive enough that "Ye Gov. did not think proper that the Conference should be taken in writing." Within two weeks, though, even Charleston's newspaper knew the gist: "the Upper Creeks . . . have resolv'd to commence Hostilities against the French." Maybe they had, but the attack did not happen. An Okchai headman's attempt to broach the topic to his fellow Upper Creeks produced "a small uproar," and there is no hint that Acorn Whistler and his fellow "Albamas" even mentioned the issue once they returned to Creek country. This unwillingness to follow through on such commitments suggests—and later events confirm—that Acorn Whistler's attachment to either Britain or France was a good deal less than firm. The British had reason, therefore, for singling Acorn Whistler out in 1741 as someone who needed the "encourage[ment]" that a commission represented "to remain attached to our Interests." To do Acorn Whistler justice, however, he came by his habit of playing the imperial field honestly. Not only

were the Creeks famed for "playing off" Britain against France, but
Acorn Whistler lived in a town located right on what the French
called the "ligne qui Separe nos Villages de cause des Anglais." He
would step across that line whenever it suited him.[10]

Acorn Whistler's willingness to play the French against the British and vice versa did not mean that he could do without Europeans and their goods. Few Creeks could. These items were highly
prized and energetically sought, and Acorn Whistler was a particularly ardent pursuer. Take, for example, the goods he received
during his 1744 Charleston visit: "a blew coat, britches of whetney
turned up with red, shirt, stockings, shoes, hat, flap, and boots,"
plus a gun, knife, blanket, check shirt, boots, and looking glass. He
also received a portion of the supplies given to the Upper Creeks
as a group: gunpowder, bullets, gunflints, and brass kettles. Given
that Acorn Whistler's people had just been described as "asking for
nothing better" than to have French traders assigned to their communities, and given that those same people were becoming convinced "that it is impossible for [the French] to supply them with
what they need," these British goods were certainly most welcome.[11]

Did something about Acorn Whistler's reaction to these goods
catch the eye of British officials? Is that why, in 1741, Acorn Whistler received not just a commission but also "Presents"? Is that why,
in 1746, Glen prohibited Acorn Whistler from coming to Charleston so as to prevent "ye Expence" attending "such a visit" from
"straggling" Creeks "who are too apt to come only for presents"?
Is that why, in 1750, when Glen described Acorn Whistler as "a
Worthless fellow," he did so while discussing the French habit of
"bribing" Indians? Whatever the case in 1741, 1746, and 1750, when
Glen and Acorn Whistler met in 1752, Acorn Whistler's material
demands were impossible to overlook: "I want a Saddle"; "We want
Wire for Rings to our Ears"; "I came down to get Necessaries"; "I
hope we are to have Presents"; "I want some Shot to kill Turkeys."
Glen, used to dealing with truly "great" men, could only respond, "I
am surprised to hear a Man of his Sence talk about such Tryffles."[12]

Glen missed the point. Acorn Whistler lacked subtlety and polish,
but he had enough "Sence" to know that the goods he sought were
not "Tryffles." Saddles and shot and such had important functions

in Creek lives; Acorn Whistler himself called them "Necessaries." Moreover, acquiring these things took a great deal of effort. The average Creek man hunted for a year or more to accumulate enough deerskins to purchase the goods Acorn Whistler received as gifts during his 1744 Charleston sojourn. Those same goods, of course, also served as tangible markers of social connections—of the ties that bound people together in mutually beneficial webs of exchange—and of political authority. In Creek society, headmen received gifts from foreigners, which they redistributed to their followers; and headmen, because they attracted followers, also attracted British traders (who brought more goods) and British officials (who gave more gifts). The headman-follower relationship within Creek country was thus linked to the foreign goods that accompanied the headman's relationship with non-Creeks.

It was those bonds with outsiders that Acorn Whistler sought to strengthen during his 1752 trip to Charleston. He needed to "come down to see the Governor and my Friends here" because he attracted neither traders nor officials, and thus had few followers. When he visited Glen in 1752, he noted that his town had no trader and that "Part of my Errand" was to ask the governor for one; he neglected to mention that Little Okfuskee's trader had died the year before, and no one else saw much potential in the town. To make matters worse, Acorn Whistler acknowledged that, "Of all the Presents we [the Creeks] had sent from Georgia, we [Acorn Whistler's people] had not 10 Bullets a Piece." He found himself, in short, in a classic double bind, needing gifts and trade to win followers but needing followers to attract gifts and trade.[13]

And then his Upper Creek party encountered the Lower Creeks at Lieutenant Governor Bull's house. Followers on the hoof. Instant respectability. So "the Acorn Whistler said," as a Creek recalled, "come down [to Charleston] with us, we shall make the more." So Acorn Whistler "perswaded them," as another Creek put it, "to go along with them and promised to get some Presents for them at his Request." So he asked, and asked, and asked for presents. And a trader. And some public token that would allow him to solidify his status as an influential man. By both Creek and British standards, it was a pathetic performance, one that earned him Glen's scorn

and a drunken kick from an erstwhile Lower Creek follower. It was
a performance that encouraged the Lower Creeks to disregard his
advice and attack the Cherokees. It was a performance indicating
that—his claim that "I command seven Towns" notwithstanding—
Acorn Whistler in 1752 was much closer to being the anonymous
faux Alabama of 1744 than a true Creek leader. It was a performance
that helped cost him his life.[14]

⌒ SOMETIME IN MID-JULY 1749, "a Gang of thirty Warriors
[were] sent to War by the French Captain" at Fort Toulouse, who was
"dayly givin[g] the [Creek] Indians Powder and Bullets for nothing
on that Account." These "Tallapoosas Albamons & some Abickous"
intended "to fall upon some of the Out Towns of the Cherokees."
French officials hoped that the resulting Creek-Cherokee war would
prevent Britain from mobilizing these two Native nations against
French Louisiana. Upper Creek headmen "did what they could" to
stop the warriors, and "most of them" were "persuaded to return."
The rest, though, "went against the Town of Hywasse, killed two
Cherokees, and brought their Scalps to [the Creek] Nation." The
leader of this party? The "Indian called Acroon Whistzler." The
"bad Man . . . called the Acron Whistler." "Acorn Whistler."[15]

Just Acorn Whistler being Acorn Whistler, right? Certainly, much
here seems familiar, including the mixed-bag war party of Tallapoosas, Alabamas, and Abeikas. In a world in which war parties generally
consisted of people who shared familial and communal ties, a "Gang"
that drew on all three Upper Creek divisions attested to both Acorn
Whistler's opportunistic, catch-as-catch-can approach to attracting
followers and his failure to impress other, more traditional constituencies. Relatedly, the fact that his war party quickly broke apart
under pressure from other headmen reinforces our sense that Acorn
Whistler's influence was ephemeral and easily counteracted. But,
as we already know, he was not entirely powerless. Some warriors
remained at his side, and even the Upper Creeks' leading headmen
concluded that his party "could not be stoped." Also recognizable,
of course, are the European gifts, what the Cherokees characterized as "Large Presents and ammunition." These goods evidently
both interested Acorn Whistler—who, Glen claimed, was "hired" or

"bribed"—and allowed him to assemble his war party. Again, no surprise there: Acorn Whistler's moments of greatest power depended
upon foreign sponsorship, either real or potential.[16]

That the foreign sponsor in question was France, however, seems
to represent something of a departure from precedent. After all,
Acorn Whistler received a British commission in 1741, and in 1744
and 1746 Acorn Whistler sought out the British; he would do so
again in 1752. By 1749, though, he was most definitely contributing
to what Glen labeled "the Intrigues of the French." Acorn Whistler continued to be *au courant* with French affairs until at least the
summer of 1750, when he informed a British trader that the Lower
Creek headman "Malatche had been at the Alabama Fort and invited
several of the Officers of that Fort to his Town."[17]

Still, this apparent lunge toward the French was not truly out of
character for Acorn Whistler. He did, after all, live near the French
fort, and he had seen his proposed 1746 trip to Charleston vetoed by
the British. More to the point, Acorn Whistler's relationships with
Europeans were clearly instrumental, not emotional. His willingness
to use French plans to further his own ambitions should not be surprising; nor should we be shocked that he worked to keep his British
options open. Thus, his 1750 report about activities at the French
fort was given to a Briton and concerned Malatchi, a man whose
"Behaviour," Glen believed, "for some time past has given great Reason to suspect he is too much inclined to the French."[18] At one level,
then, Acorn Whistler's 1749–1750 adventures simply make explicit
what was implicit in 1744–1746: when dealing with the British and
the French, loyalty and consistency were not his first priorities.

That said, however, Acorn Whistler's activities in 1749 and 1750
do bring into focus facets of his life that are unfamiliar and worthy
of discussion. Most critically, these two incidents reveal that, whatever his skills as a warrior, Acorn Whistler was no politician. In fact,
when it came to politics, he was terminally tone deaf. Acorn Whistler went to war against the Cherokees in 1749 just as a long-running effort to forge a Creek-Cherokee peace agreement was coming
to fruition. His war party set off a week after a public meeting to
discuss the agreement was announced, and, more provocative still,
Acorn Whistler and his warriors "past by" the peace conference, a

slap in the face to the assembled headmen, albeit one that backfired when they persuaded many of his men to abandon him. Those that remained, however, attacked the Cherokee town of Hiwassee. For Acorn Whistler of Little Okfuskee, that was a brazen move. His town's name bespoke a connection to Okfuskee, and everyone in Creek country knew that Okfuskees were leading the Creek effort to make peace with the Cherokees. The Okfuskees, moreover, were not negotiating with Cherokees in general; they were negotiating with Hiwassees.[19]

By the time Acorn Whistler's war party set out, Okfuskees and Hiwassees had staged ritual adoptions of each other's people, exchanged gifts of corn and conch shell, and promised to feed each other in the future. Hiwassee women had even sent "the King of the Oakfuskees a White Flag" to signal their mutual desire for peace. For a Creek to attack Hiwassee after all of that was like slaughtering a peace delegation. For a Little Okfuskee, however, doing so was even worse; it was the equivalent of ambushing his own relatives and townspeople. And all involved knew that this was true. The French recruited Acorn Whistler with just such a provocation in mind, and the Cherokees responded to his attack by renewing their war with the Creeks and making sure the Okfuskees suffered dreadfully. And Acorn Whistler's fellow Upper Creeks? They knew it too, but they apparently did not react until after the attack of April 1, 1752, gave them a chance to demonstrate the danger that Acorn Whistler incurred when he worked against community and family.[20] To put it mildly, Acorn Whistler had miscalculated.

Or had he? Perhaps he meant to anger those members of his family and community who sought peace with the Cherokees and alliance with the British? Perhaps. But if he cast his lot with the French and pro-war Creeks, then what are we to make of the 1750 incident in which he told the British of Malatchi's visit to the French fort? In the months prior to Acorn Whistler's report, Malatchi had destroyed the Creek-Cherokee peace effort, outraged Governor Glen, and sought closer ties with the French. Such a man would have been a natural ally for Acorn Whistler, who was also disaffected with the British, dealing with the French, and opposed to a Creek-Cherokee peace. And yet Acorn Whistler ratted Malatchi out to the British. It is hard to imagine that Malatchi was happy to learn that officials in South Carolina and Georgia knew the details of his French initiatives. Acorn Whistler had, in other words, found a way to anger Creeks of all political stripes—pro-peace and pro-war, pro-British and pro-French. The man had a tin ear.[21]

And a heavy hand. That is the other nugget we can take away from Acorn Whistler's 1749–1750 cameo. He was not adverse to using violence to advance his agenda, and his violent acts were not subtle ones. Acorn Whistler's claim that "They call me the White King for I love Peace" was not just false but risible. Even later storytellers intent on inflating Acorn Whistler's importance did not cloak him in the mantle of peace. After his death, when "They" called Acorn Whistler something besides "a very great Man," the word "They" used time and again was "Warrior," the social and spiritual antithesis of a peace-loving "White King." "They" certainly had their reasons, particularly his assault on Hiwassee. For a Creek, this was the worst sort of violence, a premeditated attack on a town whose recent diplomatic history should have ensured its people's safety. The rituals performed by Hiwassees and Okfuskees invoked spiritual powers associated with harmony and regeneration to create familial and communal bonds in the service of international peace. Blood spilled in anger canceled all of that out, as Acorn Whistler knew it would.

Acorn Whistler's contemporaries did not believe the Hiwassee attack was out of character. There are hints even before 1749 that Acorn Whistler could be dangerous. In 1744, after all, Glen *was* looking for military help when he welcomed Acorn Whistler's "Albamas" with open arms; and in 1746 Glen *did* fear that forbidding Acorn Whistler's second Charleston trip might lead him to "return to the nation with some disgust & and express some dissatisfaction." More concretely, the stories told about Acorn Whistler's actions in 1752 frequently invoked the violent nature of "this hot brained Madman." He was, we are told, a "very hott-headed, passionate Man" who was executed by his nephew, "whom he had used very ill some Time before . . . and had threatened to kill." "[B]efore he was Killed," Acorn Whistler "said he would go and Kill a White

Man, he did not care Whom, no not if he was the next man to the Governor he would Kill him as soon as he could in order to bring on a War between the English and the Creeks." Such a threat was believable because it "is generally granted that Acorn Whistler was the most dangerous Man in the whole Creek Nation." And so on.[22]

Some (perhaps all) of these people were lying, but lies need to be believable to work. It is, therefore, worth noting that Creeks, colonists, and British officials evidently thought that a statement bordering on "Acorn Whistler is a homicidal maniac" would suffice to explain the 1752 assault at Glen's gate. After all, the violence of April 1, 1752, resembled the 1749 assault on Hiwassee. In both incidents, Cherokees were killed by Creeks, trusts were betrayed, one-time enemies died at the hands of supposed friends, and places of safety were stained with blood. Was it just an accident that Acorn Whistler, the man responsible for the 1749 outrage, was in the neighborhood for the 1752 sequel? I believe that the answer is "yes," but then again I have neither a reason to want Acorn Whistler dead nor an agenda that could be advanced by his death. Others most certainly did.

⌒ THE EVENTS OF 1741, 1744, 1746, 1749, and 1750 had everything to do with whether Acorn Whistler could be executed in 1752, but they were not enough to warrant killing him. Even the attack on April 1, 1752, was not sufficient to have Acorn Whistler executed. In the end, Acorn Whistler died not because of his actions from 1741 to 1750 or the violence of April 1, 1752, but rather because of the intersection of his past and the needs of various storytellers. We should not be surprised. The old saying about sticks and stones notwithstanding, words can do more than break your bones. They can kill.

To understand the world that the storytellers sought to shape with their deadly words about Acorn Whistler, this book considers three types of narratives. There are, to begin with, the stories about Acorn Whistler's deaths told by Glen, Malatchi, Acorn Whistler's family and community, and the Bosomworths. Because these stories serve as the book's foundation, each is the subject of one of the book's four parts. Of course, whatever intrinsic interest these stories may hold, they focus on a man about whom even specialists in Creek history know little. Stories of this sort would not seem, at face value, to be worth the price of admission. Each story about Acorn Whistler's death, however, also speaks to a subject that transcends Acorn Whistler's fate. These range from the evolving nature of the British empire and the emergence of the Creek nation to the potency of Native models of local life and the ambiguities inherent in colonists' assertions of power. Each story about Acorn Whistler's death, in other words, has a subtext that motivated the storyteller and shaped the story's message. And while Acorn Whistler's death is not a particularly important topic, the subtexts most certainly are. They allow for the discussion of issues over which Acorn Whistler's contemporaries were willing to kill and which historians debate to this day. The subtexts—imperial, national, local, and colonial—are the book's second type of narrative.

And then there is the book's third type of narrative, the historian's tale, which centers on how these stories and their subtexts were linked even as they were being told. To appreciate this third sort of narrative, we have to remember that we can split the stories apart and isolate one subtext from another, but Acorn Whistler's contemporaries could not. They did not have the luxury of hearing the stories separately. Instead, each story emerged in dialogue with the others as Creeks, colonists, and imperial officials crafted tales about Acorn Whistler that inevitably addressed the other storytellers. The end result is odd—I sometimes describe this book as *Rashomon* meets *Last of the Mohicans*, with a dash of *Who Framed Roger Rabbit?*—and at times untidy, but so was the colonial American world that I seek to illuminate.

The four stories that follow offer competing versions of why Acorn Whistler had to die and what his death meant. All four stories were told in the aftermath of Acorn Whistler's death, and none of them are true. None of them, that is, provide a completely reliable answer to the question, "Why was Acorn Whistler executed?" That is as it should be. These stories were told by interested parties, and they were intended to produce results; they were not the objective reports of neutral truth seekers. All of which is to say that, if there is a truth to be found here, it is in the relationship between the stories, not in the stories themselves. Of course, that relationship is itself a tale, a tale about Indian country, the American colonies, the British empire, and the early modern world that encompassed them all. That tale, boiled down to its essence, asks us to turn our backs on clichés about winners and history, and to consider instead the ambiguity, negotiation, and conflict that characterized Acorn Whistler's intimately entangled and inescapably insecure world.

~ I
IMPERIAL

$\mathcal{G}$OVERNOR JAMES GLEN was in the frontier town of Ninety-Six on June 8, 1756, when he learned that he had become simply "Mr. Glen" a week earlier. His successor, William Lyttelton, had landed in Charleston on June 1. Because so few of Glen's personal papers have survived, we can only imagine how he reacted to no longer being addressed as "Governor" and "Your Excellency." Certainly, Lyttelton's arrival was no surprise. Glen had known for several years that he would be replaced; he had even given a farewell speech in 1754, after receiving "certain advice that another Governour may be soon expected." That certainty, it turned out, was unfounded, and Glen enjoyed two more years in office. But Glen's superiors in London had long ago made it clear that they found his performance unacceptable. Long exculpatory letters from Glen; wholehearted attempts at reform; energetic efforts to demonstrate his worth—nothing had changed their minds. So be it. Glen clearly thought they were wrong and that his "Government" had been a rousing success. Most likely, then, Glen greeted Lyttelton's "Notification . . . to Mr. Glen" that he "had no further power to give any direction concerning the Affairs of this Government" with the mixture of disappointment and relief that accompanies the arrival of long-awaited bad news.[1]

Most likely, as well, Glen heard of Lyttelton and thought of Indian affairs. After all, Mr. Glen failed to greet the new governor personally because Governor Glen had squeezed in one more trip to Indian country. Even had Glen not been "gone to the Cherokees" when Lyttelton arrived, however, Glen's thoughts might well have turned to Indians. He had long focused on Indian issues, believing that they represented "a very weighty & momentous concern . . . which may affect ye Trade of Great Britain, ye welfare & happiness of this Province, our Security & Safety, our Lives & Fortunes, & those of our Posterity, in a Word, our All." Moreover, Lyttelton's presence attested to the failure of Glen's efforts to impress his superiors, efforts which had centered on Indian affairs. As Glen told the Lord Commissioners for Trade and Plantations, "I have taken a good deal of Pains to arrive at some Knowledge in these matters, and . . . I have by my repeated Letters Endeavoured that your Lordships should be not stranger to them." To do otherwise would be "unaccountable Indolence and supiness in any . . . Governor." Glen was certain that he been neither indolent nor supine. Only a few months before Lyttelton arrived, Glen remarked that "As my Administration is now near a Close, there is no Part of it that I reflect upon with more Pleasure than the Pains I have taken in Indian Affairs." Even the members of South Carolina's House of Assembly, with whom Glen had frequently clashed, noted that "We must do your Excellency the Justice to say that You have applied a particular attention to them."[2] So, when Glen reviewed the accomplishments of his now-closed administration, he likely thought of Indians. Did he also think of Acorn Whistler?

Again, we do not know for sure, but if Glen was thinking of Indians, then it would have required an act of will not to recall this Creek, dead now almost four years. After all, Acorn Whistler had been a persistent presence in Glen's dealings with Indians. True, Acorn Whistler had been a second-tier headman from a third-tier town, a man whose death was more important than his life. And yet there was Acorn Whistler, again and again, surfacing at significant points in Glen's career. In Charleston during the summer of 1744, at Glen's first meeting with a large group of Indians. In Cherokee country during the summer of 1749, leading Creeks to war against the Cherokees and undermining Glen's efforts to forge peace. In Charleston yet again, in April 1752, first accompanying the murderous Lower Creeks and then fleeing Glen's suspicious questions and all-too-confining hospitality. And in Charleston one last time in the late spring of 1753, this time as a ghost, a disembodied presence hovering over a conference held to renew Creek-British relations and seal the elusive Creek-Cherokee peace. That 1753 conference, Glen now knew, was the high-water mark of his administration, the moment when it seemed that his plans for Indian affairs—and, not coincidentally, his career—were coming to fruition. Lyttelton's presence showed that both those plans and his political career had failed. Did Glen, hearing of Lyttelton's arrival, blame Acorn Whistler?

Not likely. Acorn Whistler was not important enough to blame. And, more to the point, Acorn Whistler had offered—however inadvertently—Glen the chance to reshape Indian affairs and thereby salvage his future in Britain's empire. No, Glen would not have seen Acorn Whistler's hand in Lyttelton's arrival. But it seems likely that Glen would have thought of Acorn Whistler. Glen's story about Acorn Whistler's death had been Glen's last chance to carve out an enduring place for himself in the British empire. Investigating that story offers us the opportunity to understand not just this storyteller but also the empire that Glen had served since he "kiss'd the King's hand" in 1738.[3]

Almost fifteen years later, on the eve of Acorn Whistler's last visit to Charleston, George II remained king, but the empire in which Glen worked was changing dramatically. Beginning in the late 1740s, the British empire became more imperial in the modern sense of the term—centralized, rationalized, efficient, hierarchical, militaristic, and expansive. The local autonomy and loose metropolitan oversight of colonial affairs that characterized Glen's early years in office vanished, as did official tolerance for governors who ignored their instructions and abetted colonists' assaults on the king's prerogatives. At the same time, "[b]ureaucratic adventurer[s]" began rethinking the constitutional relationships that bound Britain and the colonies; Protestant Britain's military and economic struggle with Catholic France emerged as an all-encompassing obsession; and Indians became, after midcentury, increasingly prominent in imperial plans.[4] Despite being ahead of the curve when it came to despising the French and appreciating the Indians' importance, Glen struggled to find a place in this new-model empire. His story about Acorn Whistler shows him trying desperately to fit in. But it also demonstrates how difficult that would be for Glen, a man whose attention wandered when it came to constitutional issues and who was habituated to looser, more localized forms of administration. Glen's story, then, allows us to observe the disruptive and disorienting nature of the shift in imperial culture.[5]

In doing so, though, we move beyond the spatial constraints characteristic of an imperial story. We do so because—as was true for many of his contemporaries—both Glen's struggle and his story were enmeshed with Indian country. As imperial officials on the ground in North America wrestled with centralizing directives from London, they found that Indian affairs allowed them to explore ways of melding traditions of imperial governance with innovative approaches to colonial problems. Glen's effort to demonstrate his own worth invoked older patterns of localized governmental autonomy, but it did so by working toward a newer, more centralized set of relationships. His story about Acorn Whistler was meant to end with the creation of an Indian alliance that he could deploy against the French to win North America for Great Britain. This plan showed Glen playing imperial politics at the grandest of levels, but he still thought in terms of local autonomy. The alliance, after all, would be the creation of one governor, would rely on his personal connections, and would center on his colony. Indian affairs, therefore, offered colonially based imperial officials like Glen the chance to have their cake and eat it too. They could be both independent actors and imperial centralizers, locally grounded but in the service of a potentially global empire. Doing so, though, meant moving out of the empire and into areas controlled by Indians. And, ironically, such a move triggered further metropolitan efforts at imperial reform, both to rein in the empire's colony-based enthusiasts and to deal with the fallout from their actions. Glen's energetic efforts to overcome his personal imperial crisis and find his place in the new-model empire brought him to Indian country. The story he told about Acorn Whistler's death was bound up with the exigencies of his own imperial struggle, and that struggle helped encouraged the continued modernization and centralization of Britain's empire.

~ 1

The Governor

$\mathcal{T}$HE DUKE OF BEDFORD, the head of Britain's Board of Trade, sent Governor James Glen two letters on March 12, 1751. Almost a year later, a few weeks before Acorn Whistler arrived in Charleston, Glen presented one of those letters to South Carolina's council. That letter is less significant for its content—orders about how to reimburse someone who had distributed presents to Creeks—than for the fact that it demonstrates that, somehow, Glen could still bring himself to read his mail from London. Doing so could not have been easy. Letter after letter brought harsh critiques from his superiors. Sometimes, these were brief but hard-hitting snippets, as with a single page that pronounced his actions to be first "very Irregular," then "unprecedented & Irregular," and finally "highly blameable." Bad as that was, the long letters were worse. One runs to thirty pages, chock-full of phrases like "this strange and very unreasonable Negligence," "your Inattention to our Orders," and "neglecting [your] Duty."[1]

As early as 1748, those superiors told Glen, "We much doubt whether any Instances are to be found of a Governor having" acted in ways "more inconsistent with his Instructions tending more to the Destruction of His Majesty's Prerogative and of all order of Government more subversive of the Constitution or more introductive

of . . . Mischiefs." Two years later, the same superiors complained
about having to complain about the same issues: "We have seldom
opportunity of Writing to you upon the affairs of Your Province
without being obliged at the same time to complain of some Departure from your Instructions and often of a Notorious Breach of Prerogative." The low point for Glen, though, must have come when
he read the Duke of Bedford's second letter of March 12, 1751, a
relatively brief note rife with familiar criticisms ("Indiscretion";
"unwarrantable Proceedings") but with a new and most unwelcome
moral: "it is highly probable His Majesty will no longer suffer you to
remain in your Government." No wonder that, as Acorn Whistler
headed for Charleston, Glen opted not to share that particular letter. The governor had no desire to advertise the fact that his career
hung by a thread.[2]

Glen's predicament was not entirely his fault. The acquaintance
who characterized him as "a Man of Universal knowledge" and the
historian who praised him as "a man of excellent ability" were too
kind, but Glen had many of the attributes we would expect to find
in a successful governor.[3] He was well-educated, with a solid understanding of British law and imperial history and a keen appreciation
for the hard work required to master complex issues. That diligence
was married to a genuine enthusiasm for all facets of his job—
administrator, politician, negotiator, strategist, public figure—and
such a high degree of decisiveness that it sometimes bordered on
imprudence. Still, if Glen could be reckless, he was also energetic,
active, and loyal. Of course, he hoped to profit from his office, but
his devotion to the well-being of Britain and its empire was readily
apparent. Glen was no dilettante, then, no placeholder, no empty
suit. He had his flaws, to be sure, but Governor Glen should have
been a success. That he was not can be traced in equal measure to
those flaws—which will become clear below—and to the nature of
the empire that he served. As British officials rethought imperial
governance, Glen found himself under ever-increasing pressure,
aware that his position was tenuous and certain that his plans for
redemption were achievable, but forever watching success hover
just out of reach. Glen's story about Acorn Whistler emerged out of
his struggle to close that gap, to reshape American affairs in such

a way that he could plausibly claim to be at home in Britain's new-model empire.

Glen's story comes first in this book because his decision to talk about the Acorn Whistler crisis made it either necessary or possible—depending on the circumstances—for the other storytellers to launch their own narratives. Precedence, though, is not the same thing as power. Glen's story came first, but it emerged out of weakness, and the governor would, in the end, be forced to modify his story more fundamentally than any of the other storytellers. Glen, in other words, got the narrative ball rolling, but then almost immediately lost control of the story. The reason that he did so begins with his position within the British empire, where the governor faced a series of challenges that were as much structural as personal.

⌒ THE IMPERIAL CHALLENGE that surfaces most frequently in Glen's letters centered on the system of patronage that drove British politics. At midcentury, politicians routinely traded offices and contracts for votes and support from kin and friends. No man rose to, or remained long in, high office without having patrons. In the 1730s, Glen played the patronage game well, parlaying a good birth, fine education, and several low-level offices into marriage to the daughter of (depending on whom you believe) either an earl or a baronet and good standing with the Earl of Wilmington, Lord President of the Privy Council. Wilmington may, in fact, have been (again, depending on whom you believe) the biological father of Glen's wife; he certainly, as Glen noted, "procured for me the Government of Carolina." The gossip about Glen's wife aside, that was how British imperial politics worked.[4]

By the late 1740s, however, Wilmington was dead and Glen's patronage networks were dying. As he put it, "[I] have been so long in this distant corner of the World as to know little of the concerns of the Great." Later, as Glen's career lay in ruins, his agent in London remembered that the governor had been "deserted by every body," and a South Carolina acquaintance noted that Glen "Earnestly wished" for a friend "at London" because such a contact would have allowed him to remain "Governor as long as he pleased." Without connections, even when warned of danger, Glen's options were limited. He could flatter, which he did without fail, praising one newly appointed secretary of state's "distinguished Parts" and "honest Heart," and another's "acknowledged Abilitys [that] add a luster to your high Rank." Or he could plead, which he also did regularly, asking a superior to be "taken under your powerfull Protection" and "beg[ging]" a contact to "inform yourself how I may most probably succeed in securing [an Earl's] favour." Or he could fall back upon his record, asserting that "I have endeavoured that my Behaviour and Conduct should be without Reproach," and describing himself as "a person . . . against whom there never was the least Complaint." Of course, Glen's record was hardly complaint- or reproach-free. Within the empire's patronage game, such transparently false claims must be understood as less a bluff than a sign that Glen knew he held a losing hand.[5]

Glen had another burden to bear, as well. He was Scottish in the English-dominated British empire. The merging of Scotland and England's parliaments in 1707 accelerated the already-pronounced Scottish tradition of participation in foreign affairs. Scots became mainstays in Britain's imperial service and Atlantic trade, with many seizing on empire as a concept that put all of Britain's peoples—Scots, English, Welsh—on the same level, each a part of the larger British imperial whole. Or at least that was the Scots' theory. The reality was messier. The English continued to distrust Scots and to assume that Britishness was simply Englishness writ large. Beliefs of this sort became particularly virulent in the wake of the Highland Scots' strong support for the 1745 invasion of England by Charles Stuart, a French-backed Catholic of Scottish descent with a strong claim to George II's throne. Glen himself quickly issued a proclamation rejecting this "most unnatural Rebellion . . . in favour of a Popish Pretender." Still, when Charles's army came within a few miles of taking London, even Scots like Glen recognized that many Britons viewed them as potentially disloyal.[6]

That Euro-Americans often shared these anti-Scottish prejudices underlines a third challenge confronting Glen. Within the empire, provinces like Scotland and the American colonies dealt not simply with the metropole that was London but also with each other. The resulting socioeconomic network resembled a spider's web more than a wheel's hub and spokes. For people like Glen, that web could easily lead to liminality. After all, by midcentury, Glen was a Scot with limited exposure to London and an increasing amount of experience in America. As such, he was an imperial official who was not a metropolitan, an agent of a London-centered imperial politics who lived out the "overlapping provincialisms" that characterized much of imperial society. Moreover, even as a provincial, Glen was betwixt and between. He was a Scot whose fate was wrapped up with South Carolina, a man who planned to return to his natal province—"My Voyage home"—but whose worldview began to center on another. Given that series of contradictions, is it any wonder that Glen had trouble finding his footing in the empire?[7]

Glen's liminality was a product of imperial geography, but his problems had a temporal dimension, as well. He faced obsolescence as Britain's paradigm of imperial administration and cadre of imperial administrators changed radically. In 1748, the officials charged with direct oversight of colonial affairs left office. In the process, Glen lost patrons and superiors who had praised successes and gently admonished failings. By contrast, Glen acknowledged, "I have not the smallest acquaintance" with the Earl of Halifax, who now headed up the Board of Trade, and Glen's plea to receive "protection" from the Duke of Bedford, the new secretary of state, relied on "hopes," not connections. Of equal importance, Bedford and Halifax were predisposed to be underwhelmed by Glen's governorship. Both stressed the need to strictly supervise colonial affairs; both believed wholeheartedly in protecting the Crown's authority; both expected colonial governors to follow instructions carefully and to file reports regularly. Colonial innovations were to be rolled back. Colonial legislatures were to be brought to heel. Whether we label these changes "the application of new administrative rigour" or the substitution of "a new *directive* mode . . . for the traditional *consensual* one," it is clear that Glen was dealing with a new political world.[8]

Glen's chances of making a successful adjustment to that new world were greatly reduced by the fact that Bedford and Halifax's ascendancy was, from Glen's perspective, spectacularly ill timed. Glen had gotten into the habit of ignoring key parts of the king's instructions, particularly those sections requiring Glen to send

London detailed explanations of provincial laws and to ensure that those laws did not take effect until London had approved them. So, when Glen's new superiors turned their attention to South Carolina, they found a backlog of poorly framed and inadequately explained laws. Unimpressed does not begin to cover their reaction. Bedford wrote in August 1748 to tell Glen of the Lord Justices' "high Displeasure" with him; "it is their Excellencies express Command, which they expect due Obedience to, . . . that you should strictly observe your Instructions in the future." For their part, in June 1748, the Lord Commissioners raked Glen over the coals about avoiding "dangerous" laws, being "more attentive to your Instructions," and "send[ing] us an Explanation of this Matter." Three more letters from the Lord Commissioners followed in July, October, and December, full of statements about the "very extraordinary" acts Glen signed, the necessity of sending "all such Papers as are mentioned in the said Instructions," and the "difficulty" they had reconciling Glen's claims with his "past Conduct."⁹

Worse still, soon after Bedford and Halifax took office, Glen's self-proclaimed mastery in Indian affairs was cast into doubt. Glen had invested a great deal of energy into winning the French-allied Choctaws over to the British interest. Success, he believed, "would have been . . . the greatest blow that ever the French received in America"; he also hoped to profit personally by secretly investing in the trading firm to which he awarded a monopoly on the Choctaw trade. It all worked well enough that one of Glen's last letters before Halifax and Bedford took power proclaimed that the Choctaws "are almost unanimously come over to us." Then the bubble burst. By October 1748, Glen found it necessary to report that "some Strange fatallity" had marred his plans. Over the next several years, Glen tried mightily to shift the blame and change the subject, but he succeeded only in hiding the most damning details, not in obscuring the big picture. French countermeasures, Choctaw politics, and the incompetence of the trading company Glen had relied upon produced a Choctaw civil war that both destroyed the Choctaw's pro-British faction and exposed Glen's schemes. The Lord Commissioners were furious. They "equally lament[ed] and blame[d] the want of due Care" in the matter, and called for "more Prudence &

Circumspection" from Glen. Someone, they were sure, was guilty of "Treachery or neglect." A year later they reminded Glen that "your own Character is very nearly concerned." By November 1750, the Lord Commissioners were writing to Glen that "We have had no such Explanations as We think Satisfactory from you, but We again tell you how much We desire and expect one."[10]

Finally, Bedford and Halifax's rise to power coincided with the implosion of Glen's relationship with South Carolina's House of Assembly, the popularly elected branch of the legislature. In the spring of 1748, the assembly and Glen exchanged a series of snippy messages over the former's attempts to reduce expenditures and question Glen's Indian policies. On June 29, Glen finally lost patience, first proclaiming that "Sarcasms are indeed unbecoming the Gravity and Dignity of . . . the Legislature," and then proroguing the assembly. The colony's council—appointed by the king and nominally Glen's allies—decried "so hasty and precipitate an Act," but Glen did not reconvene the assembly for nine months. He did, however, write a long, heartfelt letter to Bedford (with an almost identical copy to Halifax) about being "stripped naked of power." Glen's complaints ranged from the tangible (the legislature, not the governor, assigned the most valuable offices) to the symbolic (churches prayed for the legislature, not the governor), but they added up to one inescapable fact: "the whole frame of Government [is] unhinged. The Political balance in which consists of the Strength and beauty of the British Constitution being here entirely overturned."[11]

Glen had a point. Assemblies throughout the American colonies were steadily expanding their power at the expense of the Crown and the governors who ruled in its name; South Carolina's assembly was as aggressive as any. However, if Glen had a point, he also had a problem. Or, rather, three problems. He was fighting against an entrenched local tradition. He was on bad terms with the very legislators who would have to support his plans to lessen their power. And he was working for imperial administrators who viewed preventing colonial encroachments on the Crown's prerogatives as the *sine qua non* of effective governance. Bedford and Halifax, in essence, established a floor below which governors dared not fall in dealing with legislatures. Glen may have seen that floor as an unreachable ceiling.[12]

The rather daunting list of challenges confronting Glen—a patronless, liminal, obsolescent Scot beset by troubled relationships with both Indians and legislators—as he sought to preserve his standing in Britain's empire did not mean he was dead in the water in 1748. There were things Glen could do to mitigate these problems, and he did them with a vengeance. He was, for example, a relentless self-promoter, and never more so than when he was writing about Indian affairs. At various times prior to the Acorn Whistler crisis, Glen claimed that "there is not an Enemy Indian within a thousand Miles," that South Carolina's Indian allies were "more numerous . . . than all the other Indians in the British Interest in all parts of America put together," and that those allies "have given such solid proofs of their fidelity . . . as I am sure cannot be paralleled in America, I much doubt whether they can be equaled in History." After 1748, his superiors occasionally went to some trouble "[t]o shew how little this Praise is due to you," and sarcastically noted that claims to success "never parallel'd in America" faced "contrary accounts." Three years later, though, Glen's story of his triumphs in the Acorn Whistler affair repeated the same offending phrase—"it cannot be parallel'd in the History of America"—to the same set of skeptical superiors. Glen had evidently concluded that he needed to blow his own horn regularly and vigorously.[13]

Likewise, Glen refused to let anyone suspect this Scot of disloyalty. His letters were full of paeans to Britain and its leaders. And once the subject turned to Britain's struggle against France, Glen was, if anything, even more emphatic—the French were dangerous and had to be opposed at every turn. Their religion was characterized by "Bigotry & Superstition" that showed in its "Sanguinary & persecuting Principles." Their king was a man of "faithlessness and restless ambition." Their "Councils" were "long famed for their Secrecy." When Britain and France were at war, Glen crafted plans to end the French threat forever and regularly bragged that "I have clearly traced their footsteps & discovered their intrigues." When France and Britain were officially at peace from 1748 to 1756, Glen wrote that "I shall be Cautious of doing any thing inconsistent with the peace," but he never stopped making plans to "carry the War into the Enemys Country" or writing gleefully of Indian assaults on French interests. Glen's anti-French actions were so pronounced by 1750 that the assembly opposed one initiative by sarcastically "beg[ging] leave to acquaint your Excellency that His Majesty [is] now in Peace with the French King." Glen, though, obviously suspected that he had little to lose in staking out a more-militant-than-thou position.[14]

Glen could also, of course, defuse some problems by changing his ways. In the fall of 1748, for example, Glen suddenly deluged his superiors with the sort of information they had long sought—"Observations" on South Carolina's recently passed acts, a detailed letter about Indian affairs, and an even more in-depth letter about the need to reform the colony's political system. In the following years, Glen repeatedly sent reports that "contain very full Accounts of this Country," often accompanied by letters that were themselves dozens of pages long. In one case, Glen responded to a letter from the Lord Commissioners with two letters covering a total of fifty-two pages, plus numerous attachments. Not surprisingly, "I am ashamed of the length of this letter" became a regular refrain.[15]

Glen also began making a fetish of noting that, when it came to instructions from London, "I have carefully observed [them] of Late, and I shall continue to do so for the future." And, in keeping with both those instructions and his superiors' critiques, he became hypervigilant about colonial efforts to impinge on the king's rights. He repeatedly refused to sign bills that were "Invasions of His Majesty's just prerogatives," and he protested to his superiors that "I have never knowingly permitted the Prerogative of the Crown to be Intrenched upon, and where I have perceived that before my time there had been Incroachments upon it I have watched proper Opportunitys of bringing back things by little and little to right order." Doing so generated complaints from the assembly, which Glen offered to certify—"I am ready to put the Great Seal to them"—and send to London. Glen felt that his new policies were making the right enemies for the right reasons, and he wanted the right people in London to know it.[16]

From London's perspective, however, this new-and-improved Glen was disconcertingly like the old-style Glen. It was quite clear that he still was not on the same page as his superiors. In one notable case,

Glen reacted to harsh criticism from the Lord Commissioners by telling them that their words were "the more Mortifying" because "I was big with expectations of having my behaviour approved of." The Lord Commissioners could only respond with a rhetorical question: "was it reasonable to expect nothing but Praise and Approbation in answer to so melancholy a Relation [from you] of so many Unfortunate Occurrences, all arising from a Cause which it was in the Power of Your Government easily to have prevented?" Relatedly, Glen's reports and letters—while now regular and lengthy—were often off the mark. What must his superiors have thought, for example, when they sought concrete information about recent encroachments on British possessions, only to have Glen respond by meandering through sixteen pages of background information before commenting that "I fear I have wearied Your Lordships and that you think it high time I should come to the Subject of the Encroachments"? And what must Their Lordships have thought when Glen then spent ten more pages reviewing events from previous centuries before ending with barely a comment on contemporary events?[17]

In addition, even when Glen's reports were on target, he still managed to show that he was out of touch. The Board of Trade, for example, praised a 1749 report as very thorough, but they were appalled that Glen had asked the assembly to approve it. After all, the king had sought "the genuine sense" of the governor, not the legislature, "[a]nd as this Paper likewise contained matters of state extremely improper to be imparted to them, Your laying it before them was highly blameable." Glen, of course, had been on notice to rein in the legislature, and so seeking their approval was, at best, obtuse. But to brag about having done so—as he did in letters to both Bedford and Halifax—to the very superiors who had put him on notice made him look not simply clueless but intransigent.[18]

It did not help, moreover, that Glen proved himself to be a less-than-creative thinker when it came to constitutional matters. In October 1748, for example, Glen wrote convincingly of the crisis in his colony's political system, but the reforms he proposed were both remarkably minor—appoint more council members; rework election laws; redefine "quorum"—and surprisingly parochial. Glen was focused on South Carolina minutia, not on the broader workings of empire, and his preferred stance was as a defender, not a reformer. He excelled in panegyrics to the "Perfection" of Britain's constitution, labeling "Deviations from it" as "dangerous" and "Improvements" as "hardly possible." Such rhetoric neither satisfied London nor produced reform in Charleston. His superiors pushed him to translate his principles into progress, while Carolinians forced him to compromise those principles to stave off chaos. Those compromises won Glen time but not admirers. They prolonged his slide, but did not reverse it.[19]

By the eve of the Acorn Whistler crisis, in fact, there is every indication that Glen's superiors believed he was a lost cause. The Lord Commissioners sent Glen six letters between May 1748 and November 1750, the last of which was exceptional for both its length and its harshly critical tone. Then they stopped writing.[20] Likewise, the Duke of Bedford's last letter to Glen was the aforementioned second letter of March 12, 1751, the one that criticized Glen's performance and told him that he would likely be replaced. After that, Glen received only one letter addressed solely to him from a secretary of state until the one-sentence 1755 letter informing him of Lyttelton's appointment as governor. In other words, Glen's superiors first told him off once and for all, and then they quite literally wrote him off. To be sure, Glen still received the letters sent to multiple colonial governors. But politically, he was a dead man governing, with only the time of death left to be determined.[21]

The cause of death was, for his superiors, readily apparent: an "unaccountable" willingness to permit "improper Claims of Privileges and Rights" by colonists; an inability to exhibit "steady and disinterested Conduct"; and a "want of Integrity prudence temper & fortitude." We might go even further and say that Glen had the ability to spin gold into straw, to transform positives into liabilities. It is, however, worth recalling Glen's many finer attributes—intelligence, diligence, persistence, loyalty, curiosity—if only to make the point that, when someone like Glen could not adjust to the imperial situation, the challenges of empire were growing increasingly daunting.[22]

⌐ IT IS WORTH RECALLING one other thing, as well: Glen knew he was in trouble, but he did not believe he was doomed. Glen, in fact, had a strategy for resuscitating his career: he would put forward "one general Plan Uniting in a Bond of Friendship all Indians whatever Contiguous to any part of his Majestys Dominions and in Alliance with any of this Government." Glen was not the first to hatch such a plan. New York and Georgia officials had proposed uniting Britain's Indian allies several years before Glen arrived in South Carolina, and the idea that Carolina's Indian allies could be thrown against the French—or, if that failed, that the French might win over the Indians "and turn them all against our Settlements"— was widely discussed among South Carolina officials in the mid-1740s.[23] Glen, though, quickly made the idea his own.

By the spring of 1746, the notion that "all the Indians in Peace with us, may also live in Peace with one another" was a staple in the governor's speeches to southern Indians. Glen hoped such rhetoric would convince the Indians that the British were peace loving, but he made clear to his British and Euro-American correspondents that the real payoff would be the destruction of the French. If the Cherokees, Creeks, Choctaws, Chickasaws, and Catawbas united, "the French may not be able to stand before" them and their British allies. "[O]ur Mother Country has thereby an opening into the Heart of [French] Louisiana, our Enemies Country, and may easily, with the Assistance of the Indians drive them from thence." As he told the Lord Commissioners in February 1748, with the addition of a few British troops, "I am perswaded . . . that all Louisiana might be added to his Majesty's Dominions."[24]

Expelling the French receded from Glen's rhetoric after peace returned in 1748, but the Indian alliance remained. Glen now emphasized that such an alliance was primarily defensive in nature. It would allow the British to resist French efforts to create "a general Insurrection," and it would reassure the Indians that no one could "Lift a hatchet against so many powerfull nations so united and determined to stand by one another." Given Glen's feelings about the French, though, the offensive potential of the alliance was never far from the surface. Even in peacetime, Glen reminded his superiors that, had "a Cessation of Hostillitys" not aborted the plan, "not one Frenchman would have been left alive in all that Country." And as another war with France loomed in the early 1750s, Glen returned to the language of "uniting togeather" the Indians "like one Man against the common Enemy."[25]

Glen invested a great deal of energy in these plans, first brokering the Creek-Cherokee peace that he hoped would finally unite all of Britain's southern Indian allies, and then turning to negotiations between the southerners and various northern nations, particularly the Six Nations Iroquois. A 1749 Creek-Cherokee peace agreement fell apart, but Glen believed it would soon be restored, and he succeeded in reconciling some southern and northern groups. By 1750, his plans for the south encompassed "the Cherokees Creeks Chickasaws and Catawbas . . . the Notchees Euchees Peedes Cape Fears &c." A year later he added "such Part of the Chactaws as are in our Interest" and the Charaws to the list, and hoped that these "Southward[s]" would be united with "Northward[s]," including not simply the Six Nation Iroquois but also "the Dellaware and Susqueehanna Indians" and "all the different Tribes who may be in Friendship with them, particularly those on the Ohio River."[26]

It was an ambitious plan, and Glen had reason to think it might save his career, reasons that went well beyond the obvious but important point that creating such an alliance highlighted aspects of Glen's political persona—unswervingly loyal to Britain; rabidly anti-French—that he very much wanted London to notice. Indian relations, after all, represented an arena of imperial affairs in which Glen was well positioned to take the lead. As he explained to the Lord Commissioners, "the distance betwixt the Indian Countrys and England," the "uncertain" nature of "conveyance[s]," and "above all the Politicks of these People" meant Indian diplomacy was "not to be learned by reading, nor in any other way, but by an attentive and intimate observation, by occular inspection." Seeking "absolute directions" from London would not lead to "happy consequences." Indian affairs, then, offered room for freelancing and creativity.[27]

And yet Indian relations were an important aspect of imperial administration, and Glen's superiors knew it. Bedford's first letter to the governor had praised "your Care & Attention in cultivating a good understanding & Friendship with the Indians." Bedford and his colleagues soon had cause to reconsider Glen's performance, but they remained "extremely sensible of the great Advantages,

Addition[,] Trade and Strength which are derived to His Majesty's Colonies from a strict Harmony and Alliance with the neighbouring Indians." Well after Glen's alliance-building efforts were under way, the Lord Commissioners pressed him to reconcile "the Catawbaws and the Six Nations, it being greatly for the Security of the Colonies, that all the Nations of Indians in the English Interest should live in amity and be in Alliance with each other." Glen could not have said it better himself, and he was happy to include their language—almost word for word—in his commission to the agent charged with negotiating that particular peace treaty.[28]

London's interest in this Indian alliance points to two other reasons for Glen to hope that facilitating such a coalition might win him positive reviews from his superiors. Both focused on imperial reform. The alliance, in the first place, offered the possibility that Indians could be transformed into orderly, effective, compliant agents of empire. Glen's fantasies about Indians—"they come when we send for them, they go when they are bid, they do whatever is desired of them"; "more could not be expected from Subjects and Vassals"—fit with his superiors' fantasies about empire. If Glen's plan succeeded, the rationalized and centralized imperial administration envisioned by Bedford and Halifax would extend to Indian country, a possibility that promised not simply safer colonies and loyal allies but also territorial expansion and metropolitan control.[29]

The alliance, moreover, seemed likely to further London's quest for control in another way: it would help roll back encroachments on the king's prerogative. Since the mid-1730s, the assembly had used its power of the purse to dominate Indian relations, insisting on approving any proposal that required public funds and demanding to see all Indian-related papers. Indian affairs, however, were among the "matters of State" that Glen's superiors believed were beyond the legislators' purview. Glen's project of building Indian alliances allowed him to remind the legislators of that. As he told the assembly while trying to win over the Choctaws, "there are some things that are so peculiar a manner inherent in the Crown and so much its undoubted prerogative . . . that I am sure I should be blamed for insinuating that they could not be done without the General Assembly." Glen's Indian alliance, then, promised to reform both colonial politics and Indian relations. How could that fail to improve his standing in London?[30]

And given all that Glen had riding on this alliance, how could the attack of April 1, 1752, not seem like a complete disaster? Glen had hoped the accidental meeting of the Cherokees and Creeks in Charleston would lead to a renewed Creek-Cherokee peace agreement, but the dead Cherokees at his gate pointed toward a very different future, one in which South Carolina's most powerful Indian allies redoubled their assaults on each other. In that case, the southern foundation of his alliance network would crumble, and, Glen knew, it would "not [be] Easey to take any steps" to reconcile Britain's northern and southern Indian allies. Moreover, no matter how sincerely Glen protested "my great Surprize and Concern" about the attack, he feared that its timing and location hinted at "our knowledge and Connivance." It was possible, therefore, that the Cherokees would no longer see him as a trustworthy mediator in their talks with the Creeks. The attack, thus, threatened to make the alliance impractical in the present while undermining Glen's role in any future reconciliation.[31]

It was time to reevaluate. No wonder, then, that on April 6, Glen and his council decided to "take into Consideration the affairs relating to the Indians in order that a full and particular state thereof be . . . collected together & drawn up." Two weeks later, when two councilors proposed thirty-five points that required addressing, Glen pushed them to go even further and "Enlarg[e] their Enquiry about the state of the Indian Affairs." This reexamination of the very foundations of Glen's Indian policies was the logical consequence of "the Insults given this Government by the Lower Creek Indians and their murdering the four Cherokee Indians on the Path near Charlestown."[32]

The events of April 1, 1752, likewise undermined everything Glen had been telling his superiors about Indian affairs. The Creeks attacked while his thirty-four-page letter about Indian relations was on its way to the Lord Commissioners. As Glen knew, "very disagreeable Acc[oun]ts relating to the Indians" in South Carolina were "daily put into the Papers" in London. His letter served as an extended rebuttal, detailing the challenges he confronted,

his unwearied efforts to serve the king, and his many successes.
Of course, he returned repeatedly to his attempts to convince the
Indians "how proper it was for all Indians who called themselves
friends to the English to be friends with one another," discussing
his role in sealing relationships between Creeks and Cherokees,
Catawbas and Iroquois, Catawbas and Natchez, and the British and
all of the above. And Glen argued that his contributions had gone
unappreciated: "if the Person who has had the chief, in many cases
the sole, direction, the chief care too and labour in bringing these
things about . . . Permit me My Lords, to ask, were such a person to
entertain some fond hope or expectation of receiving a little Praise,
would he be unreasonable? Would it be unnatural?" Glen ended
by noting that he "helped to keep all these Indians united to His
Majesty," which "I hope Your Lordships will be of opinion is a real
Service, tho it makes no show, and altho no parading paragraphs
have been put in Newspapers about it." Of course, thanks to those
London newspapers, his superiors were primed to doubt his letter's
catalogue of good works and good news. And once they learned of
the April 1 attack, their suspicions would be confirmed.[33]

   That same attack, moreover, forced Glen into the familiar but
untenable position of failing to uphold the king's prerogatives in
the face of the assembly's encroachments. As part of Glen's personal
reform project, he had drawn a line in the sand: the assembly would
receive Indian-related documents only when he needed money for
an initiative, and then he would only send copies, not the originals.
The issue came to a head less than a month before the April 1 attack,
with the assembly demanding to see "all the Letters, Accounts, &
papers of every kind," and noting that these should be "the Original Papers." In return, Glen admonished their "unprecedented &
unparliamentary Language" and asserted his intention to protect
"the Just prerogative of the Crown." The end result: Glen stuck
to his guns and the assembly refused to make available the funds
he requested. Glen did not officially inform the legislators of the
April 1 attack until four weeks later, when he sent them a rousing
letter about both the "most extraordinary Event" and the assembly's
responsibility to allocate money so he could take steps to remedy
the situation.[34]

The legislators' response was telling. They harshly critiqued Glen's plans, complained of being "kept much in the dark" about "Indian Affairs," and scarcely deigned to mention money. Four days later, Glen caved, sending the assembly a letter proclaiming his intention to resist initiatives "contrary to the Prerogative of the Crown," along with two Cherokee letters, which "I recommend . . . to your immediate Consideration, I have therefore to save the Time of Copying sent the Originals." Even with that concession, though, the legislators refused to support his plans for redressing the Creek-Cherokee crisis, arguing that "this Government have several times made Peace between those two Nations, which always has been and therefore we imagine ever will be of very short duration." Glen was left to sputter that he would "pursue such Measures, and take such Steps as may best Conduce to our present Peace and future Security," but he knew that, thanks to the April 1 attack, he had lost one round with the assembly and was in danger of losing the entire match.[35]

For GOVERNOR GLEN, then, the attack of April 1, 1752, represented the sort of disaster that threatened everything he had worked for in Indian country, South Carolina, and the British empire. Glen's long experience with imperial and cross-cultural politics meant that a few dead bodies did not much worry him. But these bodies killed by those people in that place at this time? As a diplomat and lawyer, Glen knew how to spin out "what if" questions and counterfactual arguments designed to explore worst-case scenarios. He could, therefore, have dreamed up an even more alarming crisis, but it would not have been easy. The attack of April 1, 1752, was the kind of thing that kept a man up nights. And it might deprive Glen of more than sleep. The attack could end his career.

Or, if he could find the right story, that attack could be his salvation. Such a story would, at the very minimum, have to provide three things. First, the cover necessary to sweep aside the authority-sapping, death-by-a-thousand-innovations-and-intrusions obstructionism that characterized the assembly's relations with its governor. Second, the classic narrative arc—from daunting problem through steadfast action to triumphant conclusion—that would convince Glen's superiors in London that he had rescued British honor from Indian insults and forged imperial power out of colonial chaos. Third, the rhetorical formula that would persuade the Creeks that performing the role assigned them by his story was in their best interest. Glen's story, in short, had to resonate in Charleston, London, and the towns of Creek country in such a way that colonists would get out of his way, imperial officials would get off his back, and Indians would get with the program. And there was no margin of error because Glen's career was foundering even before April 1, 1752. The governor needed a story.

~ 2

The Governor's Story

WHETHER GOVERNOR JAMES GLEN looked to Indian country, London, or South Carolina on April 2, 1752, he saw trouble. Already a patronless Scot out of step with London's plans for imperial reform and out of favor with his superiors, he now faced a Creek-Cherokee crisis that endangered both his plans for an Indian alliance and his ability to rein in the assembly. Glen needed a story that would speak to Indians, imperial officials, and colonial legislators. He found one. And then he found another one. He told the first story in the early months of 1752 before dropping it and, in the late fall, picking up the second. Both stories attested to Glen's predicament; both were structured around his hopes for the future; and both centered on him. Glen wanted them to be heard as pieces of a larger, coherent story about himself and what he brought to the British empire. And yet, when it came to apportioning blame, redressing problems, and—most especially—dealing with Acorn Whistler, the stories could not have been more different. These points of disagreement mark the stories as "first" and "second," mutually exclusive narratives that most emphatically did not build on each other. The governor, in short, had a story, part of which involved obscuring how fundamentally his story had changed over time.

⁓ GLEN'S FIRST STORY featured a protagonist/governor who channeled his righteous anger into punishing those who consorted with Britain's enemies and threatened his Indian alliance. An early version, as recorded by a South Carolina clerk:

> the Governor took occasion to mention. . . . That the Creeks
> . . . had on all occasions favoured the French. . . . That they
> openly & avowedly visit the French & receive visits & pres-
> ents from them, and . . . the pains his Excellency some time
> ago took to reconcile & heal the differences between the Cher-
> okees, & the Creeks, and to make peace between them. . . .
> & tho a Second time They had been reconciled the Creeks
> again did violate the Peace, not shewing any the least regard
> or respect to this Government. [B]ut now are Come to such a
> daring pitch of Insolence as to Kill and destroy our Friendly
> Indians within our very Settlements and barbarously scalping,
> murdering & destroying those [Cherokees] who were called to
> come down, to Confirm a lasting and solid peace for ever[.]
> That such behaviour his Excellency was certain, would not be
> passed over with out a Proper resentment.[1]

The villain in this story? Well, the Creeks, of course, but which Creeks? Certainly not Acorn Whistler, as the date in the endnote makes clear. The governor was telling his story almost three months before the Lower Creeks in Acorn Whistler's party killed the Cherokees at Glen's gate.

There had, it turns out, been two different assaults, one on April 1, 1752, and another in mid-December 1751. Each incident involved a Cherokee party under British protection that was attacked by Creeks who were visiting South Carolina. And the governor evidently decided that the villain in his story would have to be respon-sible for both attacks. The twenty-six Lower Creeks who killed the Cherokees on April 1 were obvious candidates. After all, they claimed to have left Creek country to attack Cherokees. More sig-nificantly, they may have been in the neighborhood of the Decem-ber assault. The Cherokees who were victimized in December likely stayed at Susannah Burnett's "Saludy Old Town" house "upon the

Road" to Cherokee country. They were seen "at Mrs Burnett's," and she submitted bills "for the use of Indians" and "for the entertainment of Indians." Along with those two bills, though, was a third: "for dieting twenty six Indians." Could that have been the twenty-six Lower Creeks?[2]

Placing those Lower Creeks at Mrs. Burnett's house would put them not just near the Cherokees' lodgings but also near where they were attacked. The Cherokee killed in the December assault was shot while "Crossing a Foard in Company with Richard Smith, & other white men Traders"; this party had just left "Mrs. Burnett's," where they were "all preparing to pass the River." The killers were Lower Creeks. Immediately following the attack, the Cherokees wrote to Glen about their "Fear of the Coweaters which are upon the Path." Glen himself noted that the attackers "had been Lying in ambuscade and . . . fired on the Cherokee & Killed him, and then with daring insolence brushing by the Whitemen, there present, did without the least regard to them, before their eies in a most barbarous manner scalp the said Cherokee and Went off most audaciously calling out Cowetas." That word, "Cowetas," could refer to inhabitants of the Lower Creek town of that name, but it was also shorthand for "Lower Creeks" more generally.[3]

So, to recap: Lower Creeks killed the Cherokee; twenty-six Lower Creeks were on the warpath against the Cherokees; twenty-six Indians ate at Burnett's house; the Cherokee was killed not far from Burnett's house. Suggestive evidence, perhaps, but far from definitive. One thing is clear, though: Glen may have seen a connection between the twenty-six Lower Creeks and the December assault, but he was not interested in exploring that link. He preferred to focus, instead, on one word: "Cowetas." He liked it so much, in fact, that by late April 1752 he was doubling it, claiming that December's attackers had called out "Cowetas, Cowetas." Doubling that word took the onus off the twenty-six Lower Creeks, at least to some extent, because Glen knew they were from the town of Osochi, not Coweta. Acorn Whistler, an Upper Creek from Little Okfuskee, was also in the clear. That was fine with Glen. He had bigger fish to fry. Glen's story would center on the man he singled out as being "Especially" blameworthy in his January 3 speech: "Malachi of the Cowetas."[4]

Glen had long believed that "Malatchis Behaviour . . . has given too great Reason to suspect he is too much inclined to the French," but the Coweta moved to the center of Glen's personal rogues' gallery in early 1752. Starting on January 3, Glen excoriated Malatchi on three occasions, culminating in an April 29 letter to the assembly detailing Malatchi's machinations going back to Glen's early years in the colony. During the war with France, Glen claimed, Malatchi "was the chief Person who opposed" Glen's plan to capture the French fort in Creek country; he likewise "obstructed our Measures" to build a British fort there. Malatchi attended British conferences and accepted British presents, but "immediately . . . went over to the French Fort" and "betrayed every word that he heard here." More recently, "some French Officers" received a warm welcome at Malatchi's Coweta, where the French flag was raised, the British one forbidden, and France's emissaries "caressed . . . in an extraordinary manner" while Glen's agent was denied "common Necessaries . . . tho' he offered to pay for them."

To make matters worse, Malatchi opposed Glen's Creek-Cherokee peace effort, a consequence of listening to "the artful Deceivers" of France, who "are never so well pleased as when they see Indians, particularly those contiguous to and dependent on this Government, burning their Hands in each other's Blood." The Coweta headman refused to attend a 1749 conference Glen hosted, although he did promise to abide by the peace treaty that resulted. "When he . . . was fully apprized of what had been transacted in Charles town," however, "instead of agreeing to the Peace, he gathered together some Hundreds of the Lower Creeks and went against the Cherokees. . . . There he committed great Cruelties; destroying Man, Woman and Child; burning two of the Towns to Ashes, and even setting Fire to the [British] Trader's House." Malatchi was, in short, the "grand Ringleader of the French Party" and an inveterate opponent of Creek-Cherokee reconciliation.[5]

At the same time, Glen made clear that, "instead of shewing our Resentment" at this "long Catalogue of Offences," his government had responded with "kind Usage" and "Indulgence." No more. "[A]ll these [past provocations] together fall short of what has lately happened here." Even the "base, bold, and cowardly Act" of

December was eclipsed by the "atrocious Action" of April 1, which was so abhorrent that "it is needless to use Art [to embellish it], for that Nothing could make it appear blacker." Failing to respond forcefully was no longer an option. As Glen told the assembly, "[i]t is not consistent either with the Honour or Safety of this Province to permit it to pass with Impunity. If we do, we shall render our Selves cheap and contemptible in the Eyes of all the Indians—and thereby provoke, if possible, greater Injuries." Making the same argument to the Creeks, of course, was impolitic, but Glen informed them that "no Indian can hear" of the April assault "without Abhorrence and Indignation, and without being sensible of the Injury done the English, and of the Justice and Necessity of giving them Satisfaction." As he proposed to tell the Upper Creeks, "your Brothers, the Lower Creeks, must not dream that we are to pass over [the April attack] unpunished."[6]

Glen insisted not just on punishment but also on making it clear who deserved to be punished. His initial suspicions of Acorn Whistler and his Upper Creeks disappeared. There was no ambiguity in Glen's statement that "[Y]ou Upper Creeks [have] been, at all Times, and on all Occasions . . . faithful Friends and Allies to the English." Nor was there a hint of doubt when Glen told his militia officers that the Upper Creeks' "Conduct has not only been blameless but commendable." Nor did Glen express any uncertainty when he wrote the Cherokees that "not one of [the Upper Creeks] . . . had any Concern of the [April 1] Affair. Not one of them went away with the Others nor did one of the Lower Creeks remain here." In fact, Glen was so eager to absolve the Upper Creeks that he provided the Cherokees an alibi for the flight of Acorn Whistler's people ("I having then taken their Arms") and made it seem as if they remained in Charleston for three days after the attack rather than one. His letter to the assembly did not even mention Acorn Whistler or the Upper Creeks.[7]

The Lower Creeks, by contrast, were everywhere in that letter and everywhere guilty, the authors of both "this heinous Offence" and a number of "smaller Ones. . . . all of them deserving Censure, some of them Chastisement." So, too, is their guilt clear in Glen's proposed letter to the Upper Creeks, an alliterative list of the

"Instances" of Lower Creek "Ingratitude, Insults, and ill Usage." And on it went: Glen to the Cherokees ("the Lower Creeks, regardless of . . ."); Glen to the militia ("Many of the Lower Creek Indians . . . have been guilty of . . ."); Glen to the council ("ye Lower Creek Indians for having barbarously . . ."). Glen was careful to note that the "Guilty are but a small part of the Lower Creeks," but he also made clear that the rot started at the very top, with Malatchi, "Head Man of the Coweataw Town" who "bears a great sway in many of the other lower Towns."[8]

In fact, in April and May 1752, as Glen wrote and spoke about the two attacks, he mentioned only one Lower Creek by name: Malatchi. Six months before, Glen had noted that Malatchi was "called by some people the King and Emperor of the Creek Nation, but is in truth no more than headman of the Cowetas." Now, though, Glen could hardly stop talking about Malatchi and his power, at times even equating Malatchi's actions with those of the Lower Creeks as a whole. At other times, Glen was content simply to mention Malatchi and ignore everyone else. In either case, the message was clear: Malatchi's policies and predilections dominated Lower Creek country. The attacks of December 1751 and April 1752 were, according to Glen's first story, the logical outcome of Malatchi's actions going back to the mid-1740s.[9]

If Glen's villain was clear, however, Glen's course of action was not, and his initial efforts to craft a story line to redress Malatchi's villainy reflected this uncertainty. The December attack, he said in January, "would not be passed over without a proper resentment," a wishy-washy assertion that was hardly clarified by his March request that the Creeks "enquire into this Offence that it may be punished." He was no more precise in the immediate aftermath of the April 1 assault, writing to the Cherokees four days later that "all proper Measures will be taken to procure Satisfaction." By late April, though, Glen had begun to settle on a list of demands that would determine both his strategy and his first story. An April 28 letter that he proposed sending to the Upper Creeks listed three conditions the Lower Creeks must fulfill. Two had been suggested by the council: return the Cherokee taken prisoner on April 1, and "punish the Murderers . . . as the Prefidiousness and Baseness of the Act deserves." The third condition, though, was of Glen's own devising: "That they depute some of their Headmen to come to Charles Town, to beg Pardon of this Government" and "to give Security" that the "Immunities and Privileges" of "all our Friends and Allies" would not be violated.[10]

If that last demand sounds like Glen was moving toward using the crisis both to humiliate the Lower Creek headmen and to reinvigorate his Indian alliance, that is likely not an accident. A month later, Glen presented the council with a dozen letters, talks, and depositions about the Cherokee-Creek war, many of which mentioned the need or desire for peace. The council's response—send an agent "to demand the satisfaction mentioned, but that when the said satisfaction shall be obtained, he shall do all in his power to bring about a peace between the Creeks and Cherokees"—delighted Glen: "his Excellency said he would see the same Carried into Execution with all Imaginable execution." The nature of that "Execution"—and the shape of Glen's first story—became clear on June 24, when Glen presented the council with "Instructions" for an agent to the Creeks. Again, Glen followed the council's suggestions, but the directions were distinctly of his own devising. Glen and the council agreed on South Carolina's demands and the order in which the agent should present them to the Lower Creeks: execute some of the murderers; make restitution for goods stolen from British traders; make peace with the Cherokees. The council, though, did not mention Malatchi, while Glen put the Coweta headman at the center of the process.[11]

Go to "the Cowitas," Glen instructed the agent, and "immediately . . . repair to the House of Malatchi." Then, summon Chigelly, Malatchi's uncle. "[I]n the Presence of these two Head Men only," briefly discuss the December attack, "fully . . . expatiate" on the April assault, and then demand "that they deliver up the Cherokee whom they carried off from thence, if alive, and punish with Death some of the most considerable of these twenty-six." And if Malatchi and his kinsman refused? "[T]hen you are without Communicating your Business to any of the other Lower Creeks, to sett off to the Town of Ofuskee" and convince the Upper Creeks to support Glen's demands. Glen sugarcoated these bitter pills by referring to Malatchi and Chigelly's "Friendship" with the British and his desire "to mix Mercy with Justice," but Glen's purpose was clear. The goal was not to humiliate Malatchi. Yes, forcing him to execute fellow Lower Creeks for attacking their Cherokee enemies would be humiliating, but more importantly such an execution would represent a very public step away from Malatchi's long-running policy of rebuffing British plans and making war on the Cherokees. Glen knew that punishing Malatchi would not save his career. Domesticating Malatchi just might.[12]

Which brings us to the other critical component of both Glen's "Instructions" to his agent and the governor's first story: "make a Peace betwixt the Creeks and the Cherokees." The council simply asked the agent to "do all that in him lyes" to make peace. Glen, though, expected that the agent would negotiate "with Malatchi to gain him over from the French to ye British Interest, that so Peace may be brought about between the Creek and Cherokee Indians." Glen's instructions emphasized reminding the Lower Creeks of their commitment to abide by the 1749 peace treaty and highlighting that "the Lower Creeks forgettful of their Promises and Engagements soon after broke out War with Cherokees." In order to push the Lower Creeks into line with Glen's vision of an Indian alliance, his agent was to tell them that the British "had endeavoured to extinguish the Flame [of war] being earnestly desirous that all Indians who are in Friendship with them should live in Friendship with one another like Brothers. That you are now sent again to propose to them to be at Peace with the Cherokees, that I have made the same Proposal to the Cherokees who I am certain will agree to it, that if the Creeks make Peace with them and desire Peace [with] the Northern Indians, I will immediately send among these Indians, and hope to make Peace betwixt the Creeks and them also."[13]

Never mind that many of those claims were misleading at best. Glen had not proposed a peace agreement to the Cherokees in the last six months. When Glen had mentioned such an agreement prior to that, the Cherokees had not been enthusiastic, and that was before the Creeks started killing peaceful Cherokees who were under British protection. As for "Peace [with] the Northern Indians," Glen had recently written a letter despairing of the prospect of finalizing just such a peace. But neither the agent nor the Creeks needed to be bothered with those details. If the agent did his job and got Malatchi publicly on board—so that the execution of the Lower Creek murderers reassured Cherokee skepticism, recouped British honor, and renounced French plots—peace between the Creeks and Cherokees might just take hold. And if those southern nations were at peace, then negotiations with the northern Indians might yield concrete results. And if those results came soon enough, then Glen's career might be saved, a happily-ever-after ending to a well-told story.[14]

That story, though, had its problems, problems that come into focus when we examine to whom Glen was and was not telling his first story. Glen was not, for example, telling this story to London. From December 1751 to September 1752, Glen sent eight letters to the Lord Commissioners and one to the secretary of state. None of these letters so much as hint at Creeks killing Cherokees in South Carolina; none of them mention sending an agent to the Creeks. And none of the letters written in 1752 refer to Glen's effort to form an Indian alliance. This silence is all the more noteworthy because Glen did write about Indian affairs in these letters, mentioning the French reception at Coweta, the possibility that France would win over the Creeks and Cherokees, and the need to tie those Indians to Britain. But Glen studiously avoided both the immediate crisis triggered by the two attacks and his plans for the alliance. Perhaps the governor had learned a lesson from his earlier fiasco with the Choctaws? This time, Glen would put his plans into effect and wait until success was certain before informing his superiors. His story would be about victory, not crisis management. In the meantime, he set up the story by reminding his superiors that Malatchi's town was a problem, that the French remained a danger, and that Indians were valuable allies. But the story itself could wait.[15]

So, apparently, could those Indians. Within days after the April 1 assault, Glen stopped talking to Indians. The Cherokees received a letter dated April 5, and then nothing for months. The Lower Creeks received nothing at all, and the Upper Creeks not much more. Glen did meet with five of Acorn Whistler's Upper Creek followers—the four who were recaptured, plus the one who never fled—on April 4, telling them that "the Reason of detaining you here was that you might carry up a Message to inform the Upper Creeks of what had happened." The message they took home must have been a verbal one since there is no evidence of Glen sending a letter, and the Creeks next heard from Glen on July 24 when his agent arrived in Coweta. True, Glen did write a very detailed letter, dated April 28, to the Upper Creeks about the crisis, but it was never sent. The council recommended "that it would have more might" if it was delivered by "an Agent," a suggestion that Glen immediately embraced—the next day, he asked the assembly for the necessary funds—but that made Glen's conversation with the Creeks contingent on Glen's fraught relationship with the legislature. As a result, Glen was reduced to telling a story about Indians, rather than to Indians. He would soon have cause to regret that omission.[16]

In the meantime, Glen told his first story to South Carolina's officials. The people who initially heard it were the members of his council. They helped shape both the narrative (by suggesting demands) and its transmission (by suggesting an agent), but they were always supportive. They shared Glen's sense that the two attacks required a response, and they went along when Glen's plan centered on Malatchi and the Indian alliance. Glen's second audience, the assembly, was less accommodating. He did not want much from the assembly: provide money for the agent and then fade into the background. Thus, while he sent the assembly letters brimming with overwrought rhetoric about the attacks, Malatchi's perfidy, and the need for a vigorous response, he confined himself to the most general of generalities—one of his paragraphs mentions obtaining "Satisfaction," "suitable Satisfaction," and "full Satisfaction"—when discussing his goals. The assembly was underwhelmed. They wondered at Glen's surprise when "Savages" who "carry on all their Wars in the most treacherous and cowardly Manner" killed their enemies. They asserted that "the sending of an Agent among the Creeks for such Ends might probably bring on a War with that People." And they were "very certain" that the agent's travels "must be attended with . . . no inconsiderable Expence." In short, no sale, and no agent.[17]

By now, the problems with Glen's first story are likely becoming clear. Glen did not tell his story to the Creeks because he was waiting for an agent to do it for him. When the assembly denied him funds for the agent, Glen simply could not afford to take "No" for an answer. If he did, he would cede the management of Indian affairs to the legislature. And once that domino toppled, the rest would follow. No control over Indian affairs meant no agent; no agent meant no story in Indian country; no story in Indian country meant no Creek-Cherokee peace; no peace meant no Indian alliance; no Indian alliance meant no redemption back in London. No, Glen had to have an agent. But without assembly support, getting one would be difficult. That was the first problem. Getting a reliable one would prove to be impossible. That was the second problem.

The assembly adjourned on May 16, but not before Glen told them that "I shall take the Advice of His Majesty's Council, and shall pursue such Measures" with "regards to Indian Affairs" as would preserve the colony's safety. Nine days later, the governor and council settled upon a small fiction to advance Glen's larger story. They agreed that "the said Lower Creeks have Superadded Since [the assembly adjourned] the Robberys & plundering of our Traders in the Cherokee Country together with ye Fresh Insults and Injuries." The situation was "insufferable," but the colony's "Indian Law" allowed Glen to appoint an agent to deal with "Emergencys of this Kind." In other words, Glen intended to exploit the by-now routine Lower Creek attacks in Cherokee country to declare a new crisis, to use the new crisis to appoint the agent denied him by the assembly, and to present the assembly with both a fait accompli and the bill.[18]

The weakness of this approach became clear when Glen tried to recruit that agent. As a council member noted, "On so precarious a footing, no fit person can see it worth their while to turn their Backs suddenly upon their private Affairs to engage in such a service." The Commissioner of Indian Trade, William Pinckney, was the logical candidate, except that the assembly controlled his office, and Glen had accused him of "disobedience." Pinckney, citing "the duty of his office," declined. The council then proposed "Colonial Henry Hyrne . . . as a fit person to undertake the said Agency." Hyrne considered the offer for ten days, and then told the governor and council that "all Indians have a notion that [it] can never be wrong to kill their Enemies wherever they can find them"; he too declined. So did Robert Steele. The bottom of the barrel was in sight—a chronically indebted Anglican minister whose signal qualification for the agency was the fact that his wife would accompany him to Creek country.[19]

The Reverend Thomas Bosomworth was appointed agent on June 16, twenty days after Glen had tried to persuade the council to give his wife, Mary, the job. Glen had argued that "Mrs. Bosomworth[,] who by birth is a Creek and a near relation of Malatchi," was "a very proper Person to be sent into ye Creek nation to demand satisfaction." The council, though, "were of Opinion that the said Mrs. Bosomworth might be useful & of assistance to an Agent but not the only person that ought to be Employed on this Occasion." Neither Glen nor the council mentioned Thomas in this debate, although Mary insisted on the "Necessity of his proceeding with me to the Nation." When it became clear, however, that no other candidates were available, a compromise emerged: since the council would not accept Mary as agent, Thomas would get the job, with the understanding that Mary would accompany him.[20]

Glen had reasons to worry about both Bosomworths, but Mary, at least, had the necessary connections and linguistic skills. She could, Glen thought, win Malatchi to "ye British Interest" and secure a Creek-Cherokee peace. In fact, when Glen listed for Mary the tasks he "particularly" wanted her to perform, he mentioned only getting satisfaction "for the robbing of our Traders" and "Assisting the Agent in bringing about a Peace between the Creeks and Cherokees"; it was left to the council to reference the two attacks, for which she must get "the Lower Creeks . . . to make a proper Submission, to this Government by delivering up to punishment the guilty." Mary characterized this particular aspect of the job as "a very nice and difficult Point to be obtained," and reiterated that "the Advice and Cooperation of Mr. Bosomworth will be absolutely necessary for carrying these Matters into Execution." Within a month, she had her wish, Thomas had his instructions, and Glen's agent and Glen's agent's wife were preparing to leave for Creek country.[21]

Glen must have been relieved. He finally had someone to tell his story in Creek country, and, as we have already seen, the governor's instructions to the agent made clear that Glen's first story focused on persuading Malatchi to make amends to the British and make peace with the Cherokees. Glen may even have been happy with the choice of the Bosomworths. After all, he had pushed for Mary's appointment. Moreover, Mary and Thomas were close relatives of the Creek headman upon whom Glen's plans centered. Glen instructed Thomas to emphasize this connection. Tell Malatchi and Chigelly "that the near Relation you stand in to them makes you rely" upon their "Friendship"; tell them that the governor "could not have given a more pregnant Proof" of his regard for them "than by making Choise of you whom I knew to be so nearly allied to them to execute a Commission of such Consequence." Glen knew that kinship was critically important in Creek society, and he recognized the power in such appeals. Finally, Glen knew the Bosomworths had a real incentive to make his story a reality. If they "succeeded therein," they would receive a generous per diem, plus a flat fee; if they failed, they would receive just the fee, which would barely cover "Expences." And, in that case, Thomas's perilous financial situation would land him in debtor's prison as soon as he returned from Creek country—nothing like the threat of incarceration to focus an agent's mind on the task at hand. So perhaps Glen was optimistic.[22]

Or perhaps not. Perhaps Glen already recognized what hindsight makes clear: if ceasing direct communication with Indians and relying on an agent to speak for him was a mistake, anointing the Bosomworths as agents and entrusting them with his story was worse. When Glen accepted the council's recommendation that he appoint an agent instead of writing to the Creeks, he ceded control over his story to the agent. Glen's letters, had he sent them, would have arrived in Creek country full of recriminations and demands; they would have represented facts on the ground that could not easily be toned down or talked away. The Creeks could have dictated their own letters in response or sent ambassadors to Charleston for a meeting. In either case, though, Glen would have been at the center of the dialogue. Sending an agent, by contrast, meant that Glen's story was only a starting point for negotiations controlled by the agent. Once finished, he would present Glen with an agreement, one that the governor could reject only if he was willing both to anger the Creeks and to return his story to square one, with no agent and no prospect of getting a replacement. For Glen, therefore, relying on an agent was a blunder.

He then compounded this mistake by relying on the Bosomworths. Yes, they were Malatchi's kin, but wouldn't that give them incentive to help him find a loophole in Glen's demands? Yes, they needed money desperately, but mightn't that lead them to take whatever deal Malatchi offered and present it to Glen as the best they could get? Yes, they were potentially helpful intermediaries, but didn't Glen remember their reputation as "pernicious and self-interested" people "capable of doing much Mischief"? Glen had entrusted his first story to a couple with a dubious history and powerful personal and financial reasons to subvert his agenda. Did Glen recognize what he had done? One piece of evidence suggests that he did. After folding the story into the agent's instructions and watching the Bosomworths ride off with it, Glen never told the first story again. Instead, in the fall of 1752, he suddenly started telling a new story. In Glen's second story, Acorn Whistler had to die.[23]

STORIES CONVEY TRUTHS; stories convey lies. Many stories, of course, do both. Even those meant to be true are usually partial and incomplete, and even those known to be lies generally contain some truths. Glen's first story was most certainly slanted, but it was also solidly grounded in the truth as Glen understood it. Acorn Whistler really did have a good alibi. Malatchi really had opposed Glen's plans, sought out French support, and led the war against the Cherokees. The Indian alliance really did have the possibility of transforming regional geopolitics. Of course, Acorn Whistler's alibi was not airtight, Malatchi's actions looked pro-Creek rather than pro-French when viewed from Coweta, and the Indian alliance on its best day would never be anything but desperately unstable. But it is worth pointing out that Glen's first story, while marred by distortions and omissions, was solidly grounded in reality. Doing so helps us appreciate why Glen believed that story might produce results. Of equal importance, doing so helps us appreciate both how radically Glen's second story diverged from reality and how different his new story was from the original one. It is, in fact, at the intersection between divergence and difference that we can begin to see how very desperate Glen was, how very important the story-telling process had become to him, and how very thoroughly he had lost control of his story.

Glen's second story retained important elements of his first one. Most critically, both stories were characterized by carefully constructed absences. In his first story, Glen went to some trouble to remove Acorn Whistler from the mix, first by assuring everyone that Acorn Whistler was innocent and then by focusing on Lower Creek depredations. In the second story, Glen worked equally hard to remove the Bosomworths from the narrative so that Glen did not have to share the limelight. Glen's November letter to the Creeks, for example, referenced "an Agent"—no names, please!—in the first two sentences, and then dropped him entirely. Likewise, in writing to London in December, Glen mentioned "the Gentleman whom I employed in this affair" and "an Agent," but made clear that it was Glen himself who was "directing the Agent in all his proceedings, and in every word he was to say." Just to be on the safe side, Glen saw to it that the supporting documents he sent to London were as Bosomworth-free as possible. Thus, despite his promise to "send Your Lordships a minute detail" of the Acorn Whistler crisis, Glen delayed passing along Thomas's report and made sure that it arrived both buried within a flurry of legislative journals and after the minutes of a Glen-dominated 1753 Creek conference—minutes that, not incidentally, Glen edited to remove Thomas's major contribution. The second story was to be about Glen, even if it was fundamentally at odds with Glen's first story.[24]

The second story poured out in November and December 1752 as Glen wrote a series of letters after he received Thomas's journal and letter (dated October 11). Those documents from Glen's agent announced Acorn Whistler's execution and proclaimed that "Affairs are at last brought to such an Issue as I hope will be satisfactory to your Excellency." Whether or not they were—and it is hard to take Glen's claim that he read the documents "with Satisfaction" as anything other than the beginnings of his second story—Glen quickly jettisoned his first story. That narrative had focused on Malatchi. The governor's new story centered on the now-dead Acorn Whistler, a man whom Glen's first story had pushed into the background. Suddenly, Glen began promoting the recently departed.[25]

Acorn Whistler became, in Glen's second story, one of the Creeks' most influential and powerful leaders. The Cherokees learned from

Glen that Acorn Whistler had been "a noted Headman" and "one of the greatest men in the Nation." Glen's superiors, likewise, were told that Acorn Whistler had been "one of the principle headmen, and greatest Warriour in that Nation." The Creeks, of course, knew better, and so they were presented with a more restrained version— Acorn Whistler-as-"Ringleader"—but Glen made sure to underline that Acorn Whistler "had many Friends both in the Upper and Lower Nations and many Warriours at his Command." So what if Acorn Whistler had never had a host of warriors at his beck and call? And so what if the Creek clan system meant that every Creek had "Friends" all over Creek country? Exaggerating the number of Acorn Whistler's followers and making a social commonplace seem exceptional was the price Glen had to pay for setting his sights on Malatchi but settling for Acorn Whistler. Such craven opportunism might be overlooked if Glen could make Acorn Whistler into something he never had been: a great man.[26]

And a flawed one, deeply and disturbingly flawed. If Glen's second story was to work, Acorn Whistler could not appear to have been someone who made a mistake or was in the wrong place at the wrong time. He needed to be, as Glen told the Lord Commissioners, "treacherous and at the same time barbarous." Thus, Glen noted that, on April 1, Acorn Whistler ignored "the Caution that I had given them the preceding day" and broke his "positive promises made to me in the Council Chamber, that morning." Then, although Acorn Whistler "had been the Contriver and Director [of] all the Mischief," he "and some others . . . stayed behind and pretended that They were Innocent and Ignorant of that Base Transaction." He was, quite simply, a "Master Worker of Mischief," "the Director of this Disorder," "the Spring & fountain from which these troubled Waters flowed." And that was Acorn Whistler's good side. Pushed to the wall, Glen declared, Acorn Whistler became a "hot brained Madman." The dead Cherokees at Glen's gate represented only a trickle compared to the "Rivers of Blood" that would have flowed had he not been executed. After all, Acorn Whistler "had lately proposed . . . to murder the English Traders in the [Creek] Nation," a "Wicked Plan" that threatened "Innocent Lives." No wonder "his own Friends" said that he "deserved Death and that the sooner he had his Deserts the Better being too dangerous a Man to be permitted to Live."[27] Acorn Whistler was, in short, violent, treacherous, powerful, and—thanks to Glen—dead. A nice way to begin a story.

Glen's goal, however, had never been simply to get satisfaction for the two Creek assaults on Cherokee visitors to South Carolina's soil. His first story had been designed to culminate in an enduring Indian alliance, built upon a Malatchi-supported Creek-Cherokee peace. Glen's second story was intended to produce the same ending, but here Malatchi's role would be markedly different. The Coweta headman emerged in this latter story not as a recalcitrant Francophile who had to be strong-armed into seeing the light but rather as a willing partner, a powerful leader, and a true friend. Such a transformation required that Glen be willing to lay it on thick. He was.

Thus, Glen told the Creeks of Malatchi's "greatness of Soul, the Justness of his sentiments and the Suitableness of his Actions." Malatchi, the Creeks learned from the governor, had been the lead investigator in seeking out the guilty, the man who "Searched," "Looked," and "Considered." Then, Malatchi became prosecutor and judge, the person who "Convinced," "proved," and "declared." "How glorious is such Behaviour for Malatchi[.] . . . How friendly to the English[.] How Salutory to his own Nation[. H]e therefore deserves to be Esteemed Valued and Loved by both English and the Creeks." The Cherokees, who had suffered severely at Malatchi's hands, had reason to doubt all of the above, and so Glen's letter to them was more restrained, an exercise in the third-person plural, not singular: "they" (Creeks), not "he" (Malatchi), had executed Acorn Whistler and agreed to peace. Likewise Glen's initial letter to London was too full of Glen to have any room for Malatchi, but by June 1753 Glen was writing to the Lord Commissioners to disregard his earlier criticisms of "King Malatchi" because "I have since been undeceived by better authority." Malatchi "is now looked upon by all his own People as the greatest Leader they ever had." He possessed "the Dignity of a King" and "Admirable Sense." "There are other considerable Men in that Nation, but he is really the Chief, and is Chiefly to be noted by us."[28]

Malatchi, thus, emerged as a fitting Indian counterpart to Glen, the second story's protagonist and prime mover. Depending on the audience, Glen's new narrative about himself changed slightly, but Glen never left the spotlight for long. Thus, to the Creeks, Glen presented himself as their "Loving Friend & Brother" who only sought "Satisfaction" when "unpardonable offences . . . made it necessary." It was Glen who "directed" the agent and laid out "Demands," but it was Malatchi who determined guilt and carried out the sentence. With that messiness out of the way, Malatchi faded from the story, and Glen went back to talking about himself, and peace. "I rejoice that you have accepted the proposals of Peace betwixt you and the Cherokees"; "I have sent to the Cherokees to acquaint them therewith"; "I hope it will be done Early in the Spring." Glen was, in brief, the sort of man who punished "Wrongs and Injuries," passed along "Commendation," praised "Friendship," and protected "the Innocent and Good."[29]

The Cherokees, likewise, were reassured by Glen of "of my Particular Regards for you" and of "my Sincere Friendship." And the Cherokees, of course, heard a lot about Glen. He reviewed his long history of taking "Pains and Trouble" to make peace, and made it clear that, while Acorn Whistler's April 1 assault may have spilled "the Blood of our Friends the Cherokees," Glen's people had also suffered. Thus, the Creeks had to "satisfy us"; Acorn Whistler died "as a Satisfaction to the English." With that done, Glen returned to the role of peacemaker between the Cherokees and the Creeks, who—he informed the Cherokees—"have accepted of the Proposals of Peace which I sent . . . and have sent me Word That Whenever I give them notice They will meet the Cherokees and Ratify the Peace in a more formal Manner in my Presence."[30] The Cherokees, in other words, were told that Glen was both reliable and essential. Like the Creeks, they could count on Glen and, more importantly, they could not do without him.

Glen saved his best effort, however, for his superiors. They needed to know the obstacles he had overcome and the scope of his triumph. Of course, that meant finally informing London of the Creeks' recent violence in South Carolina and highlighting the damage Britain sustained from it. He did so by collapsing the December 1751 and April 1752 assaults into one event during which the Creeks "murdered 6 Cherokees, contrary to the Treaty betwixt the Creeks and us, contrary to the Caution that I had given them the preceding day, contrary to their positive promises made to me in the Council Chamber, that morning." Glen did not mention that the name of Malatchi's hometown became a war cry, but he made sure to note that the attack "was the height of Insolence to us having been perpetrated in the very eye of the Government hard by Charles Town, and while we in a manner held the Cherokees in our Arms."[31]

Glen also made it clear that, bad as this attack was, it was but a small part in two broader struggles. The first was with "the French," who "rekindled the War betwixt our Friends, the Creeks and Cherokees," and then "instigated" further violence. The second was with the assembly, which "absolutely refused" to recognize "the evident necessity of demanding satisfaction" and argued "that it was impossible to expect satisfaction, and that it was out of our power to take it." Opposition of this sort, though, only made Glen's subsequent actions more laudable. He defied the assembly's defeatism. He sent an agent with detailed "Instructions under my hand and Seal." He procured from the Creeks both "satisfaction to the English for the blood of their Friends the Cherokees shed at Charles Town" and a commitment "to a peace betwixt them and the Cherokees." He had, in short, "once more happily succeeded in extinguishing [a French-induced war], contrary to the expectations of most people in this Province, and in a way so Honorable for the English, that I hope Your Lordships will pardon me, if I once more make use of the words, that it cannot be paralleled in the History of America."

Glen's second story, then, reworked some fairly unpromising material into a narrative that argued that Acorn Whistler had been punished, Malatchi was working for peace and the British interest, and Glen had facilitated both developments despite obstacles foreign and domestic. And the larger Indian alliance? It remained Glen's grail. "[W]e are," he told the Cherokees, "extremely Solicitous to preserve peace amongst all our Friendly Indians . . . that we may be all Linked together in one Chain of Friendship." In fact, Glen believed that his second story put such an alliance within reach and that—as he told the Lord Commissioners about the Creek-Cherokee peace—"matters will be . . . put upon such a foot that for the future all their differences will be referred to me."[32] The importance that the governor ascribed to negotiating those differences and crafting an enduring Indian alliance emerges most clearly in an extraordinary series of letters written by Glen on November 15, 1752. I have quoted extensively from those to the Creeks and Cherokees because they show Glen telling his second story to those nations, but consider them now in the broader context of Glen's proposed Indian alliance.

The letters, as presented in the council journal, began with a very brief note to Thomas Bosomworth saying, essentially, well done and come home "immediately." Glen wanted his story back. Four more letters show why. To begin with, Glen to the Creeks, in which Glen extolled the resolution of the Acorn Whistler affair and the Creeks' willingness to make peace with the Cherokees. Then, Glen to the Catawbas, in which he instructed the Catawbas to abide by their promises and told them not to antagonize the Cherokees because the Creeks and Cherokees would soon be at peace. Then, Glen to the Six Nations Iroquois, in which he praised them for making peace with the Catawbas, emphasized his role in bringing that agreement about, and ended with an impassioned plea for peace between the northern and southern Indians. Finally, Glen to the Cherokees, in which he summarized his efforts to halt the Creek-Cherokee war, reviewed the Acorn Whistler affair, asserted the Creek desire for peace, and linked such a peace to an alliance encompassing the Catawbas, Chickasaws, and "Northern Indians." The Iroquois and Cherokees, moreover, were reminded "how Different has been the Behaviour of the English" from that of the French.[33]

In other words, just as Glen began telling his second story, he revitalized his efforts to smooth over relations between the southern Indian nations and to make peace between those people and Britain's northern Indian allies. He even laid the groundwork for turning this alliance against the French. It was a solid day's work by anyone's standards. As Glen told the assembly, "all who understand anything of those matters and who love their Country must rejoice to see Measures successfully pursued that have a tendency to raise its Reputation and encrease it's Credit amongst the Indian Nations, and to preserve, promote and perpetuate Peace with them." Acorn

Whistler was dead, but Glen had reason to think that his Indian alliance—and his career—suddenly looked viable.[34]

It would, however, be a mistake to lose track of the fact that Glen's second story was fundamentally a defensive one. Making the best of a bad situation is not the same thing as being in a good one. Consider Glen's effort to push the Bosomworths into the background. Doing so was an absolute necessity if Glen was to hide his lack of control over events. Once Thomas and Mary left Augusta, Georgia, on July 13, Glen neither heard from nor wrote to anyone connected to Creek country until a letter from Thomas arrived in late October. The difference between what Glen expected the agent to accomplish in those three months and what Thomas actually accomplished accounts for the distance between Glen's first and second stories. And that distance can itself be used as a rough measure of the degree to which Glen lost control of his story when it encountered stories told by Creeks and colonists. Likewise, consider Glen's harsh language about the assembly's resistance to his plans. When Glen wrote to the Lord Commissioners, he had just finished fighting—and losing—a pitched battle with the assembly over a particularly egregious encroachment on the king's prerogative. Glen not only capitulated to his legislative adversaries a few days prior to writing to London about Acorn Whistler, but he also disguised his surrender via what a historian has labeled "extraordinary tampering" with the assembly's journals. Glen's second story, then, did not end his problems, and those problems were hardly confined to Indian country.[35]

Indian country, though, remained Glen's best hope for solving those problems. Thus, Glen sent an agent there with his story, even though he had real reasons to doubt the agent's loyalty and ability; and thus Glen retreated in the face of assembly pressure on some issues, but fought back against their efforts to dictate Indian policy. If Glen was going to rescue his career, he needed to control Indian affairs. His stories were, finally, stories about control over Indians—over one Indian man (first Malatchi and then Acorn Whistler), over that man's people, over their relationship to other Indians, and over those Indians' relations to Britain. Control of this sort offered Glen the chance to demonstrate that he could contribute to and shape—if not control—Britain's imperial future. Indian country and its people were, Glen thought, destined to play an important role in both Britain's imperial rivalry with France and Britain's colonial administration of Americans. And so too was Governor Glen, if his stories about Acorn Whistler were to be believed.

Of course, simply returning to the arrival of William Lyttelton as Glen's replacement demonstrates that Glen's hopes came to naught. His stories did not work as he intended. Given that Glen was right about the Indians' importance in Britain's struggle with France, it is ironic that affairs in Indian country ended any hopes Glen had for his political career. His efforts to retain control of the embryonic Indian alliance after 1752 led him to resist the efforts of other imperial officials who sought to mobilize South Carolina's Indian allies. Instead of winning North America for Great Britain and praise for himself, Glen found that he was criticized on both sides of the Atlantic for putting his colony's needs ahead of Britain's military priorities. Glen was simply too locally focused and too wedded to provincial initiatives to become a modern imperialist.

Rather than being persuaded by Glen's stories, his superiors turned to Edmond Atkin, a longtime member of Glen's council with a penchant for sending devastating critiques of Glen's Indian policies to London. In fact, as Glen's second story crossed the Atlantic, Atkin submitted a detailed "Account" that linked Glen's Choctaw fiasco of the late 1740s to "the present miserable Posture of our Affairs among . . . *all* [Indians], owing to the like wretched Management of them for several Years past." Two years later, Atkin gave Lord Halifax an even more detailed "Report" and a "Plan" for "A General Regulation" of Indian relations. Atkin advised that "Direction of Indian Affairs . . . be taken into his Majesty's own hands, and executed under his Royal Instructions" by officials who would deal with "the Indians for the future." Soon thereafter, Atkin was appointed the southern colonies' Superintendent of Indian Affairs.[36]

Glen had, of course, hoped to put himself in just that position, albeit informally. His failure opened the door for an adversary with an even more ambitious plan for centralizing Indian relations and projecting imperial power. It is tempting to argue that Atkin's own story about Glen, arriving in Whitehall just before Glen's second story about Acorn Whistler, ended any possibility that Glen's superiors would allow themselves to be persuaded that Glen's approach had merit. Certainly, the Lord Commissioners pushed aside Glen's story, pausing to note only that his letter was "relating to Indian affairs" before turning to other matters. There is no evidence that any of Glen's superiors subsequently commented on his story.[37]

The ironies of Glen's situation, however, go well beyond Atkin's rise and his possible role in silencing Glen's story about Acorn Whistler. Glen was, after all, a committed imperialist who was undone by his inability to transcend his provincial mind-set. Moreover, Glen had shaped his story around the goals of Britain's new-model empire and had made Indian country part of the imperial reform project, only to have his example remind London that the logic of imperial reform meant that Indian relations should be under direct royal control. Finally, in the name of expanding imperial power and preserving his own place in the empire, Glen had started the process that led to Acorn Whistler's death and had eagerly reworked his story to focus on that death, only to see his own career sacrificed to further British ambition and metropolitan oversight. As Glen discovered, projecting imperial power into Indian country did not always go as planned, no matter what story you told.

~ II
NATIONAL

$\mathcal{W}$E HAVE NO WAY of knowing for sure where Malatchi was when the five Cherokees were killed on April 1, 1752. He was in his hometown of Coweta on June 3, 1751, for a talk between Georgia's agent and the Lower Creeks, and he had been "near the Cherokee Old Towns" for "some Time" on July 20, 1752. For the 412 days between those sightings, however, all we have are general statements that "Malatchi did thus-and-such at some point," plus frequent references to what Malatchi did in years past or might do in the future. That gap in the records is worth noting. After all, we are not talking about an easily overlooked figure like Acorn Whistler. Malatchi was a man whose influence in the region rivaled—perhaps exceeded—that of Governor Glen. Yet Malatchi is often invisible to us.[1]

To make matters worse, even when we can glimpse Malatchi, it is hard to trust what we see. That July 20, 1752, report of his whereabouts, for example, comes to us not from Malatchi, and not firsthand or even secondhand but thirdhand, from a person who spoke to someone who spoke to someone who saw Malatchi. That the report comes in the form of a written English-language summary of a translator's summary of spoken Muskogee is also worth noting, as is the fact that the writer in question had a less than ironclad commitment to accuracy and truth. There is, in short, always someone standing between us and Malatchi, and even on those occasions when the sources offer us Malatchi's own words, the tangled lines of transmission and fears about misrepresentations remain. For a book that hopes not simply to see Malatchi but also to hear him, that is quite clearly a problem.

That said, though, issues of obfuscation, transmission, and translation dog any historical project. Modern-day Creeks build narrative histories around this truth. Thus, a Creek story might end, "They are doing exactly what I said, she said, it was said." This technique specifies a series of speakers both to highlight the narrative's layers and to invoke connections between present and past. Likewise, eighteenth-century Britons, who were continually beset by conflicting stories and unfamiliar sources, worked out informal standards to validate narratives. They relied on factors such as whether someone was a trusted eyewitness who could describe minute details about layout and movement in a sworn deposition, and they made a point of distinguishing between firsthand reports, secondhand hearsay, and more distant rumors. Each of these traditions, moreover, recognizes that a person or event—no matter how famous—is not an open book. As a Creek storyteller relaying a tale "destined to never be obliterated from . . . memory" put it, "a good story, however ancient, is always new." Both historical traditions offer models for coming to terms with the inevitable weaknesses of the sources available for a person like Malatchi.[2] It is also worth noting that, while much of Malatchi's history is unrecoverable, we have a great deal of information about Creeks more generally. That knowledge allows us both to interrogate assertions about Malatchi and to extrapolate from the known to the unknown.

Besides, not knowing where Malatchi was on April 1, 1752, is hardly the end of the world. Of much greater importance is his reaction when he discovered what happened that day. The twenty-six Lower Creek attackers likely arrived back in their town, Osochi, by mid-April, after lingering in South Carolina until at least April 6. Malatchi's town, Coweta, was only about a dozen miles from Osochi, and a war party bringing in scalps and a live prisoner was big news. Malatchi certainly heard of their arrival. They were followed soon after by Acorn Whistler, who had rejoined his Upper Creek followers on April 9 on the road to Palachucola, South Carolina, where he "had left his Horses" several weeks before. There, they crossed the Savannah River and picked up "a Road Leading . . . to the lower Creek Nation." Once in Creek country, Acorn Whistler spoke to Malatchi, who learned that the Creeks had "kill[ed] their Enemies," "the Governor loved the Cherokees," and Glen was furious. How did Malatchi respond? He went to war against the Cherokees.[3]

On the one hand, doing so was entirely appropriate. Cowetas had been fighting Cherokees since 1715, when the Cherokees massacred a Coweta-led delegation seeking an alliance. A decade later, Malatchi's father and predecessor as Coweta's leader swore "we [will] have Nothing of Makeing a peace with Cherokeys . . . nor never shall . . . while there is a Cowwataid Liveing." Malatchi's uncle likewise promised "he never wou'd make Peace with the Cherokees," and Malatchi himself "looked upon the Cherokees as the Agressors." The war waxed and waned over the years, but it heated up dramatically in

1749, with Malatchi leading Lower Creek war parties that destroyed two Cherokee towns and "burnt" nine Cherokee captives. For the Cowetas, the war remained "very hott" in mid-April 1752, a fact reflected in a Cherokee's response to Glen's plea for peace: "The Coweaters slights your Talks." In revenge, Cherokees facilitated Iroquois raids on the Lower Creeks. In February, the Iroquois captured "one Coweta" and took a scalp—possibly from a Coweta—while preparing to send a larger war party and telling the British that "they will not make Peace . . . on any Terms" with "a Nation . . . called Caw, we, tas." With a background like that, of course Malatchi "thought no Harm in what" the twenty-six Osochis did on April 1. And, of course, when "a Friend" of his "was killed by the Cherokees just by" Coweta in May or early June, he went "out to War."[4]

On the other hand, however, there was nothing natural or inevitable in Malatchi's reaction to the news of the April 1 attack. Other responses were certainly possible, and those alternatives help us understand the significance of Malatchi's decision to go to war. Compare, for example, Malatchi's decision to incorporate the April 1 attack into his ongoing war against the Cherokees with Glen's recognition that the day's events represented a potential deathblow to a tottering peace plan. For Glen, the attack was a crisis; for Malatchi, it was almost a nonevent. More revealing still, compare Malatchi's response in the spring of 1752 with the way Malatchi claimed, a year later, that he had responded. By late May 1753, the April 1 attack no longer fit with Malatchi's agenda; he now publicly blamed it on "the Faults of a few private Men," whose "Evil" actions he "neither consented to or approved of." And so, Malatchi claimed, "when I was informed of what had happened" at Glen's gate, the notion of going to war against the Cherokees never crossed his mind; instead, Malatchi's thoughts turned immediately to providing the British with "Satisfaction." The nonevent had become—retrospectively, at least—a problem. The different approaches to the April 1 attack—Malatchi vs. Glen; Malatchi in 1752 vs. Malatchi in 1753—tell us a great deal about Malatchi's place in the world and the story he would tell about Acorn Whistler.[5]

In the spring of 1752, Malatchi viewed the April 1 attack from a position of strength that Glen could only envy. Malatchi was a

well-established headman of the leading town in the most powerful Indian polity in the region, a man with impeccable family connections, an exemplary military record, and a hint of supernatural
power. Quite the contrast with Glen, the patronless Scot plopped
down in an American province of an English-dominated empire.
Malatchi, moreover, had demonstrated a real flair for imperial
relations. He had strong ties to French Louisiana and, to a lesser
extent, Spanish Florida, plus a functional (if increasingly tense)
relationship with British Georgia and South Carolina, neither of
which had previously been willing to cut off his people's access to
British goods for fear of driving him into the arms of France or
Spain. Quite the contrast with Glen, the governor whose signature
imperial initiative—win over the Choctaws from the French—had
cratered and whose standing within his own empire was in free fall.
Finally, within Creek country, Malatchi had shown himself to be
a creative and innovative politician in the service of both Creek
nationalism and personal ambition. Following in his father's footsteps, Malatchi had declared himself "Emperor" and was working
to weld the Creeks' fractious towns, regions, and ethnic groups into
a coherent and effective nation. Quite the contrast with Glen, the
reluctant centralizer whose rearguard actions in response to provincial encroachments on royal prerogative were neither ingenious nor
successful. Perhaps, then, it makes sense that we do not know where
Malatchi was on April 1, 1752. We might expect that a day that gal-
vanized a desperate British governor did nothing of the sort to the
confident Creek emperor.[6]

And yet the changes in Malatchi's story by May 1753 show that
the governor was not without influence and the emperor was very
far from all-powerful. Malatchi could initially afford to treat the
April 1 attack as business-as-usual, but he could not ignore Glen's
story about that attack. Once the governor started telling his story,
his problems became Malatchi's problem. The sticking point for
Malatchi was Glen's decision to stake his governorship on forcing
Malatchi to punish the Lower Creek attackers and make peace with
the Cherokees. That decision threatened to put the vulnerabilities
of both the emperor and his nation on display. The Creek nation
was a newly imagined, faction-ridden, and ephemeral construct, a

political innovation that lacked popular legitimacy, coercive power, and functioning institutions. Malatchi's claim to leadership within this all-but-fictive polity was stronger than that of any of his contemporaries, but that says more about their weakness than his strength. The nature of Creek politics at midcentury made "Creek Emperor" seem as oxymoronic as "Creek Pope." Both the role that Malatchi claimed, then, and the polity that he invoked were more aspirational than actual. As a result, his place in the world depended on a series of careful balancing acts between perception and reality. Glen's story—by putting Malatchi in a position where he might have to act as an emperor on behalf of a nation—put a heavy finger on several finely calibrated and critically important scales.

Consider, for example, what Malatchi learned from Glen's story. The governor was furious? Fine, but he could not be allowed to become angry enough to cut off British trade with the Creeks. Otherwise, Malatchi's Creek supporters might find themselves a new leader who could guarantee access to European goods. The British thought Malatchi had the power to control his followers and punish wrongdoers? Fine, but they could be allowed to ask for only the least controversial of demonstrations. Otherwise, Malatchi would quickly bump up against the limits set by Creek traditions regarding chiefly authority and coercive force. The British believed that Malatchi held the keys to peace with the Cherokees? Fine, but that particular lock had to be opened with care. Otherwise, Malatchi's Creek rivals, headmen with well-established ties to the Cherokees, would push the emperor into the background. The governor had recruited Malatchi's cousin Mary Bosomworth and her husband Thomas to speak for him? Fine, but that meant Malatchi had to take their talks seriously. Otherwise, he risked turning his back on both the family connections that undergirded his authority and the two people who had regularly reminded Britain of his power. All of which is to say that Glen's story suddenly gave Malatchi a very good reason to care about what had happened on April 1, 1752. Glen's story, in fact, persuaded Malatchi to tell his own story.

Watching Malatchi craft that story offers us the opportunity to understand not just this particular storyteller but also the nation he was struggling to create and hoping to lead. Malatchi's mix of national and personal agendas left him open to pressure from Glen, but it also led him to realize that the Acorn Whistler crisis could serve as both a turning point in Creek national development and a tool for enhancing his own authority. The right story would allow Malatchi to solidify his relations with the British while simultaneously pushing the Creeks toward a more centralized political system and marginalizing his Creek rivals. The right story would convince the British that things that were as yet relatively insubstantial—the Creek nation and its emperor—were real, and then use the British belief in those things to call them into being. If that sounds like magic, well, Malatchi was twin-born—he was often called "The Twin"—and Creeks believed that twins had supernatural powers. But, in truth, the right story would be more confidence game than magic act. Base the right story on a plausible fiction; back it with real but woefully insufficient resources; attract more resources from others; use those resources to make the right story real. Right, in short, would make might.

That Malatchi's story put him in this position is worth highlighting because of what it tells us about nation-building, Native and Euro-American alike, in the colonial era. When someone as powerful as Malatchi resorts to smoke and mirrors, we are reminded of the enormous difficulties that accompanied the emergence of the nations we now take for granted. These nations were neither primordial polities nor divine gifts. They were human constructs rooted in the concerns and cross-cultural conversations of the late colonial period. Native nationalists worked at the intersection of a more traditional Native politics and the demands and opportunities presented by their Euro-American neighbors; Euro-American nationalists worked at the intersection of a more traditional colonial and imperial politics and the demands and opportunities presented by their Indian neighbors. For each people, the process of creating a nation was enormously contentious, and every step toward nationhood was tentative and provisional.

Malatchi certainly knew this. After all, the Creeks watched their Choctaw neighbors wage a bloody civil war from 1748 to 1750, and Malatchi worried that if the Creeks were forced to back either the British or the French in war, then "it would occasion the spilling of

Blood" and the Creeks "would no longer be a people."[7] The Creeks staved off civil war, but only until 1813. Their Euro-American neighbors were less fortunate. The United States was forged in the civil war of 1775–1783 and refined in the Civil War of 1861–1865. The Creeks, too, fought a civil war in the early 1860s, as did several of their fellow Native nations from the Old South. And all of these civil wars—Native and Euro-American alike—took place within America's most successful nations; all of these civil wars were fought by people who lived in either the so-called Five Civilized Tribes or under the aegis of Manifest Destiny. These civil wars were not, in other words, an aberration. Founding Fathers like Malatchi needed to be confidence men because the nations they envisioned were so insubstantial and contentious. That was the reality of American nation-building.

∼ 3

The Emperor

𝓜ALATCHI WENT TO WAR against the Cherokees in the late spring or early summer of 1752. That he did so speaks to both his assets and liabilities at the time. On the one hand, this war was part of a long-running power play by his family and community. Since the early years of the eighteenth century, his father, Brims, and his uncle, Chigelly, had worked to focus Creek-European relations and Creek politics on Coweta and themselves. They had been remarkably successful by Creek standards, but the project was far from complete. Malatchi's 1749 decision to ratchet up the Cherokee war placed himself and his townspeople at the center of regional geopolitics. It was a bold move.

In September 1749, the Upper Creeks had agreed to peace with the Cherokees, an initiative sponsored by Governor Glen and cautiously endorsed by Chigelly. Malatchi overrode Chigelly, ending the fragile peace and reminding all concerned that he and his people could make or break alliances at will. Malatchi, moreover, linked his war to an effort to solidify his ties with the French, a relationship that enhanced not only his power but also his reputation as a person capable of reshaping international affairs. And, best of all, these initiatives worked, particularly the war. A half century later, Cowetas were still showing visitors where Cherokee "captives were tied and

. . . received their doom," while a British trader later remembered that the Creeks "defeated [the Cherokees] so easily, that in contempt, they sent several of their women and small boys against them." True or not, Malatchi's forces essentially depopulated Lower Cherokee country and won rich new hunting grounds for the Creeks. His 1752 venture, then, was simply more of a good thing for a man who had gambled on a controversial war and won.[1]

And yet, on the other hand, there were signs that Malatchi's gains were fragile. To begin with, after 1749, Malatchi presided over a regional, not a national, war, one that pitted Lower Creeks against Lower Cherokees. The Upper Creeks and Upper Cherokees raided each other at several points, but both parties sought to limit the damage and confirm a lasting peace. Thus, in July 1750, the Upper Creeks stated that "we all agree to be at Peace and Live like Brothers with the Upper Cherokees," who confirmed in April 1751 that "the Upper Creeks . . . we look upon as Friends." Those same Upper Cherokees, however, complained that "we are now at War with the Covetas . . . and the Lower Creeks, who . . . are daily doing us some Mischief," while those same Upper Creeks hoped that "the Twin [Malatchi] and several of the Head Men of the Lower Towns" would "Embrace the Opportunity of the Peace as we have done." Acorn Whistler, then, had a point when he responded to the April 1 attacks by saying, "The Lower Creeks have served us so before and when we have made Peace with the Cherokees, they have knocked it in the Head, and made War again." Malatchi's war, in short, worked against Creek national unity.[2]

That same war also severely strained Malatchi's already tense relationship with the British. It is tempting to conclude, in fact, that Malatchi simply overplayed his hand in the years between 1749 and 1752. South Carolina officials came to believe that "Malatchis Behaviour" and that of "the Coweta and [their neighboring town of] Cussetta . . . should be Resented by this Government"; "he should receive a check" for his "pernici[ou]s Practices." Georgia's leaders agreed that "Malatchi and his People" deserved "a severe Rebuke," although they were reluctant to support Glen's preferred solution of "withdrawing the trade." That disagreement notwithstanding, by May 1751, the colonies' diplomatic offensive left a French official fretting that the British had "overthrown . . . the influence of the Emperor of Kawitas, who they knew was on our side." The Frenchman overstated British leverage, but not British goals. Malatchi was nearing a straw-that-broke-the-camel's-back moment with his British neighbors.[3]

Because the documents reveal so little about what Malatchi was doing and thinking in the spring of 1752, however, we cannot be certain about his perspective on these problems. He understood that the Upper Creeks did not support his war. Did that worry him? He was aware of British anger. Did it lead to some restless nights? The only solid piece of evidence that we have—Malatchi went to war against the Cherokees—suggests the answer to both questions is "No." His participation in the war party seems to be a classic "Stay the course!" moment, the act of a man confident in his strategy and secure in his power.

Perhaps, though, it was not that simple? Perhaps Malatchi's war party signified less doubling down than killing time? Perhaps he was engaging in a relatively low-risk, small-scale raid for personal reasons—his friend had just been killed, after all—while he figured out how to deal with the fallout from his war? There is no way to know for sure. What is clear, however, is that Malatchi found himself in a position at once enviable and dangerous. No one else could pretend to be the emperor of the Creek nation, but if his own claim to the title was to be more than pretense then he had some work to do at home and abroad.

⌒ To APPRECIATE the worst-case scenario inherent in Malatchi's deteriorating relationship with the British, consider two memories about his death. In 1759, three years after Malatchi died, Ishempoahi of Coweta—the uncle/advisor/regent of Malatchi's son—claimed that "Malachi on his death bed recommended to his Son to be at a good understanding with the English French & Spaniards but in particular with the English who are the chief support of our nation." In 1768, Ishempoahi provided a slightly different version of the same scene: "with [Malatchi's] last Breath, he recommended to his People, to hold the English fast, as their truest friends, and most capable to serve them."[4]

Ishempoahi's memory was not playing tricks on him. Malatchi truly believed that the Creeks needed the British. In fact, Malatchi eventually claimed to send Acorn Whistler to his death because "it was better that his Life should be taken than that they should break off all Friendship with the English by which Means many innocent Persons must suffer." There are, of course, numerous ways innocent people can suffer, but Malatchi was almost certainly thinking of what we would call economics. Exchanging deerskins and services for British goods was as important to the Creek economy as the agricultural fields surrounding their towns. French and Spanish supply networks were unreliable at best; as Malatchi put it, "we did not want war with the English as we are all sensible that neither French nor Spaniards are so able to supply us with goods for our Skins as they." Malatchi, in life as in memory, had reason to privilege the British.[5]

But the situation was more complex than that. Consider another deathbed scene, this one narrated by Malatchi himself in 1746: "His Father (the old Emperour Brim) had charged him before he died never to suffer white Blood to be spilt on his ground." A Carolinian in attendance gave Malatchi's speech a happy spin, explaining that the Creeks worked "above all to preserve a good understanding with all white People, English, French, and Spaniards." The next year, though, Malatchi again invoked "the Words of my Father" to show the fear that motivated this policy: "the English were come from the East, to settle upon our Lands, the Spaniards towards the South, and the French toward the West. And he said, I wish you may not see the day when they will be taking your Lands from you, and making Slaves of your Wives and Children." Malatchi, in fact, followed in Brims's footsteps and led a Creek faction that sought to ward off dependence on any European power—and the dispossession and slavery that might follow—by cementing ties to them all. In practice, however, even Creeks like Malatchi who juggled European alliances knew the British were their economic lifeline. The British could be managed. They could be played off each other— Georgia vs. South Carolina; traders vs. officials—and reminded that the Creeks had other European friends. They could even be made angry, albeit carefully and temporarily. But alienating the British completely was out of the question.[6]

Walking that line was something Malatchi struggled with his entire life. The second time he appears in the historical record, Georgia's agent dismissed him as "Intirely in the French interest," and similar characterizations—"a French Friend from his Childhood"; "closely attached to the French Interest"; "This good and faithful ally of the French"—followed him everywhere. That both the French and the British made such claims is worth noting, but so too is the fact that, at times, Malatchi's ties to the British were quite strong. In 1740, for example, a Georgia official claimed that Malatchi's "Good-will to the English, is not to be questioned"; he was a person "whose Fidelity we could rely on." Three years later, South Carolina's lieutenant governor hosted him in Charleston and "ordered . . . presents to be delivered him." Malatchi was not, then, irredeemably in the French camp, but he was struggling with some intractable questions. With the British, where did arm's length end and out of touch begin? With the French, where did attentive end and adhesive begin? How do you say "no" to a wealthy adversary and an impecunious friend? Given that the Creeks' economy depended on British goods and Malatchi's vision of the Creeks' diplomatic system depended on not taking sides in the Franco-British rivalry, answering those questions required careful thought. A mistake could cost someone dearly. There is, in fact, every reason to think that Malatchi's missteps in his dealings with the British helped cost Acorn Whistler his life.[7]

Malatchi's problems with the British intensified when his insistence on retaining ties to the French clashed with Glen's militant francophobia. Their initial meeting, in Charleston in late October 1746, was cordial enough, with Malatchi accepting Glen's "commission"—a document attesting to its bearer's British bona fides—and Glen honoring Malatchi by asking him which other headmen merited their own commissions. Then, over the course of the next four days, things went to hell. Glen pushed the Creeks to join the British in attacking the French fort in Upper Creek country; failing that, Glen hoped the Creeks would let the British build their own fort there. Some Upper Creeks granted Glen permission to build a fort, but the proposals alarmed Malatchi. He characterized the governor's "Talk" as "cross," and was appalled—"I did not know what to think"—when

Glen's arm-twisting included a threat "to send his Traders out of my Nation." The conference ended with "Malatchi only not consenting" to the proposed British fort, and only "Mallatchi's town [was] excepted" from receiving a portion of the ammunition that Glen used to buy land for the fort. Malatchi returned to Creek country and immediately informed the French of Glen's plans.[8]

The fiasco at Charleston left Malatchi's relationship with Glen in tatters. Malatchi spent the next year issuing threats in response to both the British military exercises he had seen while in Charleston and the rumors that "the Governour was raising an Army of 500 Men, to march into my Nation without my Consent." Assuming that Glen would recall the traders, Malatchi "gave orders that all my people should make themselves Bows and Arrows" as "we should then have no other Weapons," and a British trader reported hearing Malatchi declare that "if Carolina sends up any Forces to attack the French Fort, tho' the Governor goes with them, he will meet them in the Woods and tell him to return[. I]f he will not he must take what follows." Such talk died down as it became clear that Glen was not raising an army, but in the spring of 1748 several British traders still felt it necessary to reassure South Carolina that the report that "Malachi . . . was coming down with 3000 Men is entirely false." The following summer, Malatchi refused an invitation from Glen to finalize a Creek-Cherokee peace in Charleston, preferring to go first to Savannah and then, a few months later, to war against the Cherokees. Glen was beside himself, of course, but Malatchi hardly seems to have cared. He did the bare minimum to reassure Glen that "we shall not undervalue the Talk you sent us," while also informing him that "the Cherokees tell nothing but Lies" and that peace depended on the Cherokees coming cap-in-hand to Coweta. That was in July 1750. Malatchi did not send another word Glen's way until it was time to discuss Acorn Whistler's death.[9]

As Malatchi contemplated Acorn Whistler's fate, he certainly took into account the fact that his own connections with Georgia were, if anything, in even worse shape than his ties to South Carolina. By the mid-1740s, seemingly every possible point of contact between Malatchi and Georgia's leaders had become a sore point. The Creeks who lived near Savannah? Malatchi accused Georgia of despoiling their land and claiming that, because they were Indians, "their Evidence signified nothing." Malatchi's kinswoman, Mary Bosomworth, who had served as Georgia's interpreter and Indian liaison since 1733? Malatchi was furious that Georgia denied her reimbursement claims and refused to recognize her control of lands deeded her by the Creeks. General James Oglethorpe, Georgia's de facto leader until the early 1740s and reputed friend of the Creeks? Malatchi accused him of both reneging on his promises and, even more seriously, "impos[ing] upon us" by drafting "a Paper to take away our Lands and not let us know anything of it." In other words, it was no surprise that, by December 1747, Malatchi was "ready to believe what the French said" about Georgia's desire for Creek land and Creek slaves. He "every day expected to hear that . . . a War would begin."[10]

Issues came to a head at a Savannah meeting in August 1749, when the agendas of the Bosomworths, Malatchi, and Georgia's leaders collided. Malatchi was reported to have felt "very much Slighted" even before the conference began, and the accusation by Georgia officials that he had "two Tongues" did nothing to smooth things over. We do not have to accept the Georgians' characterization of his talks as "fraught with dangerous and ill natured insinuations"; nor do we have to credit their assertions that "Malatchi appeared so angry as to foam at his Mouth." It is clear, though, that Malatchi was incensed. "I was," he remembered, "received in a very rude and uncivil Manner, more like Enemies than Friends," and he responded in kind. Several colonists "received considerable Damage by Malatche and his People," and Creeks referred to "Melatchee's bad Talk" about the "the White People" being "cross"; that fall, a trader reported Malatchi's claim "that the white People wanted to make War with them." Malatchi, in fact, believed "the English had thrown him away" and that Georgia had "pitched upon" another Lower Creek "to command the whole Nation, and told him that . . . he (Malatchi) was a French Man and did not love the English." Seeking to sum all this up, Malatchi referred to "the bad Ussage we have since met with from the People of Georgia." He died without ever returning to Savannah or attempting to patch up this particular relationship.[11]

For Malatchi, a would-be leader of a people who depended upon British trade, the state of his relations with Georgia and South Carolina by the late 1740s should have been worrisome. Like Governor Glen at roughly the same time, Malatchi seemed to be facing problems wherever he turned. Unlike Glen, however, there is absolutely no evidence that Malatchi was concerned. Quite the contrary. Malatchi seemed to go out of his way to stick his finger in the eyes of both Georgia and South Carolina, and relations with those colonies immediately went from bad to worse. What could have led Malatchi to be blatantly provocative? The answer, in our terms, is that he was thinking outside the box. Malatchi believed that he could bypass the neighboring British colonies and deal directly with London, thereby winning the freedom to oppose South Carolina and Georgia's initiatives—including those directed at his French contacts in Louisiana—while retaining his people's connections to Britain itself. He could, in other words, strengthen his father's system of playing the British off against the French by expanding the playing field. If the strategy worked, many of his intractable British vs. French problems would disappear.

We first see signs of the new strategy in late 1746, when Malatchi suddenly started calling himself Opiya Mico, a title he would use repeatedly over the next half-dozen years. "Mico" refers to the civil leader of a town; the British usually (mis)translated it as "King." "Opiya" is a bit more complicated. It literally means "seeker, one who is looking for something," but it connotes both distance and spiritual power. When combined with "Mico," "Opiya" referenced the widespread tendency among southeastern Indians to reward those with the ability to engage productively with distant and dangerous forces. Malatchi was not the only Coweta, much less the only Creek, to be called Opiya, but the fact that he sought not simply to span the Atlantic but also to remake the Creeks' diplomatic world made him an especially appropriate Far Off Mico.[12]

The title's implications became clear the following year when Malatchi, speaking as "Opiya Mico," presented a talk that harshly criticized both Glen and Georgia's leaders. Malatchi delivered this speech in Georgia, but not in Savannah, the colony's capital, and not to the president and assistants, the colony's leaders. Instead,

Malatchi went to Fort Frederica, the home of a regiment of British soldiers, and he spoke to Lieutenant Colonel Alexander Heron, "Commander in Chief of all His Majesty's Forces" in the area. His choice of venue and audience was no accident. Malatchi had very critical things to say about the colonies and colonial officials, and he elected to say them to Britain's man at Britain's fort. How he chose to frame that criticism was even more indicative of his goals as Opiya Mico.[13]

He began by reminding Heron that "It pleased the Great God above . . . to move the heart of the Royal King to send You over" and care for both "his White people" and "us Indians." Because of the God-to-king-to-colonel pedigree, Heron naturally sought "to live in peace with us" and "did not mind the Lies and bad Talks about us." With the larger supernatural and transatlantic context established, Malatchi could detail his concerns with Georgia and South Carolina—a project that consumed fully 75 percent of the speech—and then return to praising Britain's king and hinting at the need for a direct king-to-Creek relationship. Once "we have the good Talk from the Great King," Malatchi noted, then "we and the English should live like Brothers together." To further this connection, Malatchi singled out "the Great King's Son . . . one of the Greatest Warriors in the World." In a move that any Creek would recognize as initiating a relationship that combined alliance with friendship, Malatchi sent Prince William "this Pipe of Peace with the Arms and dress of my Forefathers." By so doing, Malatchi hoped to obtain "Justice and redress [for] our Grievances," of course, but he also sought to push aside colonial officials. Malatchi was playing imperial politics on an Atlantic scale.[14]

Creeks knew, however, that effective international diplomacy combined words and gifts with personal contacts. And so Malatchi's imperial ventures in the late 1740s and early 1750s featured attempts to send an "Agent to transact their Affairs in England." That was, in large measure, what he saw in the Bosomworth family. Thus, in his 1747 speech, Malatchi noted that "I desire that Mr. Abraham Bosomworth . . . may be sent to the Great King with this Talk of mine." Abraham was Mary's brother-in-law and an officer in the Frederica garrison who had served as Colonel Heron's Creek agent.

He claimed to have received "the title of the Great Warrior" while in Coweta and that he was "greatly esteemed by Malatchi." Heron acceded to Malatchi's request and sent Abraham to London as the Creeks' "beloved Man." There, he met with the Duke of Bedford and helped convince King George to authorize an especially large shipment of presents for Georgia and South Carolina's Indian allies.[15]

Abraham returned in 1749 with both the presents and a letter from Bedford to Glen recommending "Mr. Abraham Bosomworth . . . as a very fit Person to be Agent on the part of the Governor Council and Assembly of South Carolina for the distribution of the Presents." Glen was in no position to refuse, knowing as he did "the Consequence to this Province of having the favour and friendship of his Grace." Of course, when Abraham, in his words, "did afterwards at different times attend the several Distributions of the said Presents," Malatchi would have seen the benefits of enlisting metropolitan power to put pressure on colonial officials. Georgia's leaders, in fact, claimed that Malatchi "reported in every Town in the Upper and Lower Creek Nation that Mrs. Bosomworth through her Interest with the Great King had procured them presents and that her Brother Abraham (whom she sent to him) had brought them over the Great Water." They were likely wrong about Mary's role in this. Malatchi, after all, was Far Off Mico, and he had no reason to credit Mary since he himself sent Abraham to England. But their recognition that Malatchi had forged ties to Britain and its king, and believed he had profited from doing so, was astute.[16]

Malatchi, moreover, did find a way to use Mary in this project. Mary and Thomas planned to visit England to press her claims against Georgia, a development Malatchi encouraged. Malatchi visited Savannah in 1749, in part, to see Mary off on her transatlantic trip. While in Savannah, Malatchi approved a document that "authorized and Impowered" Mary to negotiate the Creeks' land issues with "His Majesty King George or his Great Men and Councellors over the Great Water." A year later, Malatchi signed a similar proclamation, one that began by noting the Creeks' "frequent Complaints" to colonial officials, especially "the Magistrates of Savannah," who "refused to hear our Talk." The document then affirmed twice over that Mary had the power to negotiate for the

Creeks with the king "over the Great Water." As Malatchi later put it, "we . . . advised her to go to the great King, and relate the whole Affair to him, and to make our Complaint." Because these documents also proclaimed Mary to be the Creeks' "Princess," historians have treated them with a healthy skepticism. Malatchi likely did the same, but the problematic nature of Mary's claims should not blind us to the fact that Malatchi put her to work in the service of Far Off Mico's larger goal: bypass Britain's local representatives and open a channel to London. Significantly, in both documents, the first title provided for Malatchi is Opiya Mico.[17]

In the process of dealing directly with London and its king, however, Malatchi became not simply Opiya Mico but also the emperor of the Creek nation. That status was the domestic payoff of the foreign power harnessed by, and the Atlantic possibilities created by, Far Off Mico. Thus, in his 1747 speech to Heron, the first thing that Malatchi "desire[d]" Abraham Bosomworth to tell "the Great King" was "that I am now Emperor of the Creek Nation" with "2000 fighting Men under my Command" and "the Care of their Wives and Children." Heron was impressed enough that he referred to "Malatchi the Emperours Arrival." The next week the Lower Creek headmen in Frederica signed a "Declaration to all Subjects of the Crown of Great Britain" proclaiming Malatchi "to be our Rightful and Natural Prince" with "full Power and Authority . . . to Transact all Affairs relating to our Nation"; two deeds that Malatchi signed soon after referred to him as "Emperour." Two years later, during the Savannah confrontation, the document that deputized Mary to act for the Creeks while in England identified Malatchi as the "Rightfull and natural prince of the upper and lower Creek Nations." The 1750 version referred to him simply as "Commanding King," two variants of which appeared on a pair of 1750 land transfers; one of those deeds also called him "Malatchi Opeya Mico Rightful and Natural Prince of the said Nations." Variations in phrasing aside, each of these documents adopts exactly the same form when referring to Malatchi: first his name, then his title as Far Off Mico, and finally a nation-ruling, European-inspired designation, be it prince, king, or emperor. We do not have to accept that Malatchi truly had attained imperial power to recognize the cultural resonance of linking a powerful personal name (Malatchi) with a title (Opiya Mico) implying that foreign connections buttressed national leadership (emperor)[18]

It was not a coincidence, then, that Malatchi's efforts to bypass Georgia and South Carolina happened just as he came out as emperor. For the Bosomworths, declaring that Malatchi was emperor was simply a means—they needed a VIP on their side— to the end of victory in their struggle with Georgia. For Malatchi, though, the situation was more complicated than the phrase "means and ends" allows. On the one hand, he welcomed the power (an end) that the title emperor implied, but on the other hand he intended to use that power (now a means) to unify the Creek nation (a different end). However—on the third hand?—even that oversimplifies matters since a properly constituted Creek nation (now a means) would further its leader's power (an old end). Malatchi envisioned, in short, a feedback loop in which power and polity, emperor and nation, were reciprocally created. Each was a means; each was an end. And to make the situation more complicated still, the emperor-nation loop was itself the hoped-for outcome (an end) of another feedback loop (a means). That circuit encompassed a Far Off Mico whose overseas connections allowed Malatchi to plausibly claim to be emperor, which made him more valuable to the British, who would therefore be more likely to act in ways that enhanced his power. And so on.

All of that likely calls to mind expressions such as "house of cards" and "If we had ham, we could have ham and eggs, if we had eggs." And, to some extent, fair enough. We must recognize, however, that Malatchi had solid reasons for committing himself to this convoluted plan. The intractability of the French-British rivalry and the reality of the Creeks' dependence on Britain, combined with his own increasingly dicey relationship with Georgia and South Carolina, left him with questions that had no satisfactory answers. Reaching across the ocean changed the conversation in such a way that allowed him to at least envision success. Given the options he confronted, that was no small accomplishment. We should recognize, as well, that those options were even less appealing than I have acknowledged because, to this point, I have only considered his dealings with Europeans. In doing so, I have almost certainly reversed Malatchi's own priorities, and I have quite clearly downplayed the challenges faced by a man who first became the emperor of the Creek nation when he dealt with Europeans, a comparatively easy audience. He had a tougher crowd waiting for him at home in Creek country, which was no surprise given that he was not the first emperor in a nation that was not a nation and did not have an emperor.

⌒ WHEN WE TURN to Creek country, the difficulties Malatchi faced are immediately apparent. True, his father had been called emperor by various European powers at various times, but that title says more about European hopes and fears than Creek political reality. The exercise of authority in Creek country, in both Brims's day and Malatchi's, was nonexclusive, noncoercive, and decidedly nonimperial. As a Carolina agent put it in 1708, "One can hardly perceive that they have a king, at all, for the Chiefs of Each Village . . . are only heads of small Townships. . . . Nothing [is] more contemptable than the authority of these chiefs." He went on to call each town "a sort of petty republick," a phrase echoed almost sixty years later by two British officials, who noted that the "Nature of the Indian Government, which is, so many united Republics, leaves a vast Competition for Power amongst them, and produces a number of Leading Men, who, each has his Weight in the direction of their Affairs." Other observers said such similar things—"The Indians . . . have no such titles or persons, as emperors, or kings"; "The power of their chiefs, is an empty sound"; "[the mico] has not the least shadow of executive authority"—that an eighteenth-century Creek claiming to be emperor inevitably invites bad jokes about new clothes.[19]

Malatchi certainly had no trouble finding Creeks who pushed back against even his most cautious assertions of power. In 1749, for example, some of his fellow Lower Creeks stated that "Melatchee had no superior Right to Them or any other Chiefs in the Nation," while other Lower Creeks said "they would throw away his Talk and believe him no more." The next year, "the Cheifs of this Nation disown[ed] . . . Malatche's Power" to unilaterally resolve a land dispute, and five years later "the Head Men and Warriors" refused to support Malatchi's "Promises," saying "they were Kings in [their] own Towns as well as he was in his." Likewise, when Louisiana's governor asked the Upper Creeks "to recognize this emperor [Malatchi] as their great chief," they "refused to do this, claiming that one chief over each village was enough."[20]

None of this, of course, shocked Malatchi, who came of age watching his father struggle with identical issues. Thus, when it was time to explain how Acorn Whistler was executed, Malatchi noted that "I did not think it would be advisable in me to take the whole upon my own shoulders; I thought it would be more prudent to consult with the beloved men, it being a custom with us to consult with our beloved men upon all affairs of importance." Of course, Malatchi's agenda was more complicated than he let on, and so his apparent willingness to share decision-making power was only part of the story. But the speech is worth noting because it shows that Malatchi, whatever his ambitions, was not in position to speak imperial power to Creek cultural truth. Malatchi's goals would have to be realized within a tradition that had no room for emperors.[21]

Nor, truthfully, for nations. To be sure, the Creeks recognized large-scale political units that were based on shared history, geographical proximity, and common interest. They distinguished Creeks from Cherokees, Upper Creeks from Lower Creeks. They knew that Upper Creeks were more likely to act in concert with Upper Creeks than with Lower Creeks, and they assumed that Creeks resolved debates with other Creeks via consensus and compromise, not with the warfare they sometimes used to settle disputes with non-Creeks. The Creeks also recognized, however, that these were fundamentally unstable, ad hoc polities. Membership was not fixed; institutions were not regularized; power was not centralized; procedures were not codified. Patterns of interaction, while real, were nevertheless contingent, dependent on a continual process of alliance-building and relationship maintenance that was rooted in local loyalties and personal connections. That always-in-process, never-carved-in-stone nature of Creek politics was a central obstacle to Malatchi's agenda. Coalition-building came naturally to Creeks; nation-building did not.

Take, for example, a passage from a 1739 letter from Georgia's James Oglethorpe: "Chigilly and Malatchee the Son of the great Brim, who was called Emperor of the Creeks by the Spaniards, insist upon my coming up to put all things in order, and have acquainted me that all the Chiefs of the Nation will come down to the Couetta Town to meet me, and hold the General Assembly. . . . All the Towns of the Creek Nation, and of the Cousees and Talapousees . . . will come down to the Meeting." It sounds quite impressive—emperor, nation, general assembly—but if "All the Towns of the Creek Nation" were meeting, who were those "Cousees and Talapousees"? They were Upper Creeks. Were they part of the "Nation"? The short answer is "Yes." A better one is "Yes, but. . . ." Yes, the Upper Creeks were part of the nation, but the issues to be discussed at the meeting with Oglethorpe were not nearly as important to the Upper Creeks as they were to the Lower Creeks. Knowing that, the Upper Creeks faded into the background, allowing Malatchi and his uncle to promise a "national" meeting, when "regional" was more accurate, and permitting Malatchi and his uncle to devise "national" policy on a local issue. Although Oglethorpe did not know it, he was being invited to a meeting of stakeholders, not national leaders.[22]

In the end, no Upper Creek attended the conference with Oglethorpe. As a result, they felt only minimally bound by what was agreed to there, particularly in regard to the decision to cede some land to Georgia. When pushed to the wall, however, they agreed that the Lower Creeks could alienate the lands in question because, as an Upper Creek headman named Gun Merchant later explained, "Malatchi was a very Great man [and] they did not want to have any further disputes between the two nations [that is, the Upper and Lower Creeks]." Moreover, as Glen noted, "Lands are generally deemed to belong to that part of the Nation next to which they lye," and Gun Merchant acknowledged "it was but a little Way from [the Lower Creek] Towns to Georgia" while "he lived at a great Distance," and his people "knew nothing about" the land in question. Other circumstances and other issues would invoke a different set of interests and call forth a differently configured constellation of "national" leaders. Thus, even as Gun Merchant attested to Malatchi's greatness and grudgingly supported his land cession, he rejected the suggestion of "the Twin, and other Head Men of the Lower Creeks" that the Creeks postpone a visit to South Carolina. The "Lower Creeks might go when they pleased," Gun Merchant said, but he "was determined to sett out without Loss of Time." Perhaps that was why Malatchi distinguished between "The Upper Towns" and "all my People in general"? The nature of "nation" in Creek country meant that sometimes the latter included the former and sometimes it did not. Defining the nation's contours was like trying to pin jelly to a wall.[23]

"Nation," in fact, was even slipperier than that—and thus Malatchi's agenda faced even more profound challenges—because the default Creek mode of self-identification was distinctly local. Thus, when Acorn Whistler told Glen "I command seven Towns," the obvious point—Liar!—is less interesting than the fact that Acorn Whistler's effort at resume enhancement focused on towns. A year later, Creeks again foregrounded towns—and again lied—when they claimed that they were tricked into signing a deed by Georgia's agent, who told them "that the intent and meaning was only to know the names of the Head Men of every Town in the Nation that the People of Georgia might know to whom to send their Presents." Implicit in this alibi were two claims: gifts from another culture were given directly to Creek towns, and headmen identified themselves with their communities. Both claims, in fact, were unassailable, and thus the lie was believable. The Creek nation was, at its core, a world of towns. In the words of one observer, "Every town is independent of another. Their own friendly compact continues the nation."[24]

Malatchi almost literally could not open his mouth without dealing with this basic fact. Expressing his ambitions for himself and his people in Muskogee, his native language, without recurring to the town was impossible. Thus, when Malatchi wanted to say "nation," he said (i)tálwa, the same word he used for "town." "King" or "emperor," in Malatchi's terms, was mí:kko, the leader of a town. A literal translation of his word for "kingdom," oh-mí:kk-itá, would be "town leader above a town leader," and the root of "to rule" was, again, mí:kko. As late as 1825, when a bilingual clerk was codifying Creek law, he rendered "National Council of the Muskogee Nation" as ma.skó.ki itálwa talwa-âlki, which could easily be misread as "Muskogee Town Townspeople." Even today, Muskogee speakers refer to the Creek Nation's principal chief as (i)talwa-âlki im-mí:kko, and the president of the United States is known as wacina-mí:kko, the white Americans' town leader. Given all of that—and given that Malatchi's people had, as a trader put it, "no words to express despotic power, arbitrary kings, oppressed, or obedient subjects"—it is hard to imagine Malatchi agreeing with the Spaniard who proclaimed that "Language is the perfect instrument of empire." If Malatchi was to emerge as the emperor of a united Creek nation, he would do so despite the Muskogee language, not because of it.[25]

Still, that said, Malatchi did have reason to believe that certain Creek political traditions offered him the chance to convince Creeks that his vision of the future was in keeping with their shared past. Creek politics, for example, was not confined to an out-of-kilter federalism featuring an insubstantial nation ruled by all too substantial towns. A range of political affiliations called Creek people to push beyond the local and the communal. Regional blocs—Upper and Lower Creeks—were very much a part of Creek life, and ethnogeographic divisions (the Abeikas, Tallapoosas, and Alabamas) were likewise fixtures among the Upper Creeks. These blocs and divisions encouraged Creeks to identify as something other than townspeople; they enjoined a degree of compromise and accommodation as towns negotiated their respective concerns; and they promoted the emergence of a leadership cadre with a constituency and a policy focus that transcended town interests. In the right hands, entities of this sort could become building blocks for a nation. Those hands would also find that the Creek moiety system provided raw material for nation construction. Creeks assigned each town to a "fire," red/war or white/peace. Towns who shared a fire were "my friend"; towns belonging to the other fire were "my enemy or opponent." These moieties helped to structure everything from international diplomacy and warfare to attendance at key religious ceremonies and participation in ball games. Malatchi could, in theory, call upon these traditional connections as he sought to turn rhetoric about national unity into reality.[26]

And, of course, he could call on family connections, a set of personal networks that, while not explicitly political in nature, did play a profound role in Creek politics. British observers frequently noted that thus-and-such a headman "has a great Family & of course a good deal of Influence"; one even suggested that Muskogee speakers wishing to express the idea of despotic rule had to cobble together an expression like "bad war chieftains of a numerous family, who inslaved the rest." Family, in both cases, meant clan, the social center of Creek life, just as town was the political center. Each Creek was born into his/her mother's clan, and each Creek therefore started life with a web of connections throughout Creek country. Acorn Whistler, for example, had clan ties to individuals in—at the minimum—the towns of Little Okfuskee, Coweta, Cusseta, Atasi, Okfuskee, and perhaps Hitchiti. Unlike the Cherokees' system, each Creek clan was not present in each town, and the Creeks had dozens of small clans, not the seven large ones that structured Cherokee society. Still, among the Creeks, clan membership determined issues ranging from leadership of towns to responsibility for revenging a wrong. The clan system ensured that Malatchi had kinsmen throughout Creek country predisposed to look favorably upon his initiatives. Even with their help, "inslaving" was not an option, but nationalizing was a possibility.[27]

Allies in Creek country, though, were every bit as likely to have been made as born. Malatchi, thus, could draw on Creek traditions of turning potential rivals into influential supporters. Creeks recognized formally consecrated bonds that ran the gamut from fictive kinship to instrumental friendship. These could be relationships based upon the exchange of symbolically resonant items and pledges of goodwill, much like the bond Malatchi proposed with Britain's Prince William. Or these could be ties brought into being by the reciprocal exchange of favors, as when Malatchi requested in 1746 that Glen provide commissions for Cusseta's Warrior King and Okfuskee's Mad Warrior, both of whom—six years later—wound up supporting Malatchi's story about why Acorn Whistler had to die. Such ties were quite obviously of value to any ambitious Creek headman, and, to make this tradition of networking even more useful still, these relationships were not confined to individuals. Corporate groups, too, were understood to create bonds with each other, a process that usually began with a community ritually adopting another community's headman, who served as a mediator between his hometown and his adopted one. The towns would then, as a Creek origin story put it, "have a chief in common." Although our sources all too often do not allow us to track these sorts of ties, it is clear that these town-to-town relationships could be long lasting. Malatchi's Coweta, for example, was closely linked to the Upper Creek town of Tuckabatchee from the late seventeenth century into the twentieth century, and other Creek towns had comparable ties. These were, perhaps, the raw material for larger, more regularized polities.[28]

WHAT, THEN, does it all add up to? What are we to make of Malatchi's situation in the spring and early summer of 1752? Quite obviously, he faced some daunting challenges. At home, his goals for personal power and national unity flew in the face of long-standing Creek practices. Abroad, the constant and contradictory demands generated by the British-French rivalry, his people's economic dependence on Britain, and his own increasingly toxic relations with Georgia and South Carolina threatened to undermine his ability to play the Europeans off against each other. All that is clear. It is also clear, however, that Malatchi had solid reasons for hoping that he could overcome these challenges. His plan to sideline his colonial neighbors in favor of transatlantic British contacts offered the promise of significantly increasing both his power and his diplomatic options. His knowledge of Creek culture and society gave him hope that he could mobilize personal connections and traditional large-scale corporate groups to overcome the Creeks' ingrained localism and antiauthoritarianism. And, of course, Malatchi's plans for reaching beyond Creek country for power were intimately connected to the possibilities he saw for changing Creek politics, and vice versa.

And so? My sense is that Malatchi was in a delicate position in April 1752, expecting his plans to bear fruit but aware that failure was a real possibility. The good news, from his perspective, was that he was playing with house money. If his schemes collapsed, he would go back to being an influential headman from a distinguished family in a town that was critically important to a powerful Native people. Or, to put it another way, failure is relative. Malatchi, unlike Glen, was not going to be fired or recalled in disgrace. The bad news? It would not, Malatchi knew, take much to derail his plans. There were simply too many moving parts, too many things he could not control.

And so, he was careful. He met with Acorn Whistler. He either talked to or heard about the Osochis. As he put it, "I considered within myself what would be the Consequence" of the April 1 attack. And he decided that the consequences would be minimal. No need to call off the Cherokee war. No need to reach out to anyone—Native or European—who might have been offended by the assault at Glen's gate. The attack simply was not a big deal. And then, suddenly, it was. In fact, the best measure of exactly how delicate Malatchi's position was in the spring of 1752 is the speed with which he changed his mind about the events of April 1. By August, it was clear that he needed a story.[29]

~ 4

The Emperor's Story

ON AUGUST 11, 1752, Malatchi called the Warrior King of Cusseta and Otassee King into his house. He hoped to convince them that the twenty-six "young Fellows [from Osochi] had never . . . done the Mischief if it was not by Order of . . . Acorn Whistler," who "was answerable for all their Actions even by the Laws of their own Nation." To clinch the argument, Malatchi told the two headmen about his meeting with Acorn Whistler in the aftermath of the April 1 attack. Thomas Bosomworth's summary of Malatchi's speech is worth quoting at length:

> He (Malatchi) then related to them all the bad Talks the Acorn Whistler gave to him when he came up from Charles Town, That the Governor had taken away all the Indians' Arms, and wanted to kill them; that he was obliged to fly for his Life naked like a Slave, and might have perished in the Woods. That he was now got Home into his own Country, and that he never would forgive the English as long as he lived. That he would burn his Commission and would have Satisfaction before long, and made use of all the Arguments in his Power to induce him (Malatchi) to kill all the English in the Nation directly.

Malatchi then noted that, when asked what they had done to provoke the British, Acorn Whistler "replied Nothing at all, but kill
their Enemies, which he told the young People to do and it was
very good, but the Governor loved the Cherokees and wanted to
kill them for it." Acorn Whistler, according to Malatchi, ended by
threatening "that he would kill some white Man himself, and then
[the Creeks] would all be obliged to make War."[1]

Some aspects of Malatchi's August 11 account ring true. Lower
Creeks had killed Cherokees; Glen had gotten angry and taken the
Upper Creeks' guns; Acorn Whistler had fled and suffered hardships in doing so. These things truly had happened, and it is easy to
imagine Acorn Whistler telling Malatchi all of this. And the rest?
Lies. From Acorn Whistler believing Glen wanted to kill "them"
and Acorn Whistler ordering the attack to Acorn Whistler intending to kill "some white Man" and bring on a Creek-British war—
all lies. And all, quite clearly, lies told by Malatchi about Acorn
Whistler, not by Acorn Whistler to Malatchi.[2] To accept Malatchi's
statements of August 11 as gospel is to miss the significance of his
conversation with the two Creek headmen. His speech during that
meeting was advocacy, not testimony. Malatchi was not setting the
record straight about an earlier chat with Acorn Whistler. Instead,
on August 11, Malatchi began telling his story about why Acorn
Whistler had to die.

This narrative was actually Malatchi's second story about the
April 1 attack, not his first. Malatchi, like Glen, was willing to
abandon one plotline when a more promising one became available.
Once Malatchi started telling his second story, however, he stuck
to it, although he invoked it with varying degrees of intensity as his
needs changed and his appreciation for the story's problem-solving
possibilities increased. Malatchi's problems, to be sure, were not of
Acorn Whistler's making, but Malatchi came to realize just how
useful a story about Acorn Whistler could be in solving them. That
solution had a price, of course, and Malatchi had to weigh its costs
and benefits. Thus, before telling the story on August 11, he sat
"some time in a very thoughtful Posture." And then he summoned
the two headmen and began to speak. A few days later, Acorn Whistler was dead. On August 11, 1752, Malatchi had decided that he

could live with his story's price. He was right. As time went on, in fact, it began to seem more and more like a bargain.[3]

ↄ It is relatively easy to demonstrate that Malatchi lied on August 11. His assertions on that day contradict what we know about Acorn Whistler's past and future. More difficult, however, is recognizing why we should care. The answer, at its most basic level, is that investigating these lies is necessary for understanding both Malatchi's first story and his second. Because Malatchi's first story emerged during that 412-day period when he is almost invisible in the documentary record, much of what we "know" about this period of his life comes from his second story. In order to understand Malatchi's first story and what it meant when he moved on to the second, we must recognize how the second story misrepresents both Acorn Whistler and Malatchi. Documenting Malatchi's lies on August 11, in other words, opens up the possibility of hearing Malatchi's first story.

To begin with, Malatchi lied about Acorn Whistler's life prior to late April 1752. Acorn Whistler was not, for example, in position to "Order" the twenty-six Lower Creeks to do anything. True, Acorn Whistler was a head warrior. True, the Lower Creeks were a war party. But the Creeks were not a modern military, where any commissioned officer can give orders to any private soldier. In Creek society, generic headmen did not order around generic warriors. Rather, headmen with particular relationships with specific warriors were sometimes in position to exercise a certain conditional authority over those warriors. Malatchi knew this as well as anyone. In fact, two months after Malatchi claimed that "the Laws of their own Nation" made Acorn Whistler "answerable" for the "Mischief . . . done by the young People," Malatchi himself characterized "young People" as "very ungovernable," and claimed that "the Head Men particularly himself" were "unjustly blamed" for their "mad Actions."[4]

And leaving aside the issue of a headman's power in the abstract, there was another very specific reason why Acorn Whistler could not control the twenty-six "young Fellows" from Osochi. By the standards of Creek culture, Acorn Whistler was not the leader of their war party. Acorn Whistler, after all, met the Osochis by happenstance in South Carolina. Thus, he had not recruited them in their town; he had not supervised their purification ceremony before setting out; he had not brought the sacred bundle that permitted success on the warpath; he had not insisted that they follow the rules that went with accompanying such a relic. Acorn Whistler had not, in short, taken the necessary steps to acquire a war leader's power. No surprise there since his Upper Creek party was not on the warpath. The fact that Acorn Whistler's party included women showed that quite clearly; Creek men on the warpath avoided Creek women because they could nullify male spiritual power. The Osochis, then, had no reason to listen to Acorn Whistler, and so, in the end, they did not. When Malatchi claimed to be shocked—shocked!—at this turn of affairs, he was not only lying but also betting that the British would be too enmeshed in their own hierarchical military traditions and too ignorant of Creek culture to notice. Needless to say, that was a winning bet.[5]

Malatchi won another bet about Acorn Whistler's past when he gambled that no one would notice that Acorn Whistler did not say that Glen "wanted to kill them," a phrase Malatchi twice put in Acorn Whistler's mouth. By the time Acorn Whistler met with Malatchi, Acorn Whistler knew full well that Glen was not blaming any Upper Creeks for the attack. Glen had said as much to five of Acorn Whistler's followers on April 4. Acorn Whistler met up with those men on April 9. Their news—of Glen's speech, of the guns and ammunition he gave them, and of his efforts to capture the Lower Creeks—combined with the food and clothing Acorn Whistler received from Lieutenant Governor William Bull would have convinced Acorn Whistler that he had dodged a bullet. To be sure, he might have told Malatchi that he had initially feared Glen's response to the attack and that the governor doubted his alibi. But the "them" in danger, Acorn Whistler knew, were not his people but Malatchi's Lower Creeks. Everyone else knew it too. As a British trader put it, he "never heard any News or the least Talks or Suspicion of [Acorn Whistler's] being to be killed."[6]

Malatchi's August 11 speech not only misrepresented Acorn Whistler's past, though. It also tendentiously misread his future— the period between their late April meeting and Acorn Whistler's mid-August death. In the few months of life remaining to Acorn Whistler, he showed no sign of "kill[ing] some white Man" and triggering a war with Britain. Instead, he may have sent Glen "good Talks," and he certainly dropped back into a series of routine relationships with Britons who traded in his neighborhood. Thus, in late spring, he visited John Spencer's house near Muccolossus, and spoke to Spencer and Moses Nunes, a Tuckabatchee trader. Both men not only escaped with their lives but also apparently never knew that, according to Malatchi, they were in mortal danger. At roughly the same time, Acorn Whistler spoke to Timothy Mellan of Fushatchee, and in mid-July Acorn Whistler asked Richard Blake to carry "a Message . . . to Mellan at Augusta about building some Houses for him in the Nation." Again, there were no casualties, hardly a surprise since these utterly prosaic activities reveal no hint of murderous intent. More likely, Acorn Whistler was simply, as Blake suggested, "alive and well" and reimmersed in his domestic routine—trading and home-building, politicking and socializing. Not exactly the future one would expect from Malatchi's version of Acorn Whistler's April speech.[7]

If Malatchi's version of Acorn Whistler's speech is riddled with lies, then what did Acorn Whistler tell Malatchi about April 1? My guess: something fairly close to the truth. I say that both because Acorn Whistler had very little to gain by lying at that point and because of how Malatchi behaved after speaking with Acorn Whistler. So, what Malatchi likely heard from Acorn Whistler went something like this. The twenty-six Osochis killed the Cherokees despite being told not to. Glen was furious and initially suspected Upper Creek involvement; thus Acorn Whistler fled. But Glen came to realize that the blame lay with the Osochis. Acorn Whistler probably even expressed anger with Glen for doubting his word and forcing him to flee ignominiously. What Acorn Whistler certainly did not say, though, was that he was responsible for this mess and that he intended to compound the problem by starting a war.

Malatchi's response, as we have already seen, was likely "no big deal." Perhaps he might have initially hoped that blame for the April 1 attack would fall on Acorn Whistler's Upper Creeks, which might force them to join Malatchi's war with the Cherokees. But if

what the Upper Creeks said was true—and they had presents from
Glen to back up their story—then Acorn Whistler and his followers were off the hook. In that case, the April 1 attack was simply
another Lower Creek victory in the Cherokee war. And Governor
Glen's anger? Malatchi knew, on the one hand, that Glen had been
furious with him since 1746, and, moreover, that Glen's displeasure
had been exacerbated by the "Cowetas" attack on Cherokees who
were under British protection the previous December. On the other
hand, Malatchi recognized that he and his people had prospered
despite Glen's anger, and Malatchi believed that, as Far Off Mico,
he had marginalized South Carolina's governor.

Glen's response to the December 1751 attack, in fact, likely encouraged Malatchi to dismiss the April attack's significance. In a March
20, 1752, letter that would have arrived among the Lower Creeks a
few weeks before Acorn Whistler and Malatchi met, Glen wrote the
Creeks of his "Asstonishment and Resentment" upon hearing of the
December assault. But he asked only that "as we are your Friends
you will enquire into this Offence that it may be punished," and he
suggested "caution[ing] your People from coming into our Settlements"; Glen signed the letter "your loving Brother." The December 1751 attack could, of course, be tied directly to Coweta. If Glen
responded so ineffectually to that attack, if Glen expected so little
of Malatchi when his own people were involved, if Glen continued
to invoke the language of friendship and kinship—if all of this was
true, then how could Malatchi fail to conclude that the fallout from
the events of April 1 would be minimal? This too would pass, and
probably sooner rather than later. It is, therefore, appropriate that,
in the months after Malatchi's meeting with Acorn Whistler, we do
not hear anything concrete from the Coweta headman about April
1. Those months of silence, in a sense, are the essence of Malatchi's
first story. He apparently thought little of the April 1 attack, and
said less.[8]

To be sure, given the nature of the documents, Malatchi may
have spent the summer of 1752 consumed by worry and ranting
against some combination of young Creek men in general, young
Osochis in particular, and Acorn Whistler most especially. But it is
extremely unlikely. Echoes of Malatchi's belief that there would be

little fallout from the April 1 attack can be heard in his decision to go to war against the Cherokees. More concretely, Malatchi exhibited a remarkable confidence, later that summer, that any feathers ruffled on April 1 could be smoothed over quickly and easily. Thus, when he returned from the warpath on August 3 and found the Bosomworths in Coweta bearing a talk from Glen, he expressed "Joy and Friendship" but put them off for three days while he dealt with more pressing matters. "[I]t was," he said, Creek "custom when they returned from War to relate all their Transactions to the Head Men and other Ceremonies of Physicking, &c. to be undergone." Plus, he had to give the "necessary Orders" for Coweta's upcoming Green Corn Ceremony. Malatchi was not misrepresenting his people's traditions or his responsibilities, but nor was he displaying any sense that a crisis was brewing.[9]

And over the next week, as it became clear that April 1's attack could not be swept under the rug, Malatchi showed every sign that his first story left him utterly unprepared for Glen's demands. His confusion and hesitation attest to the distance between what he expected to hear and what the Bosomworths were telling him: "punish with Death some of the most considerable of the Offenders" for the "Crime" of "stain[ing] the white People's beloved Ground with Blood." When Mary and Thomas met privately with Malatchi and Chigelly on August 6 to deliver that demand, the two headmen "paused a considerable Time, and an Air of deep Concern was very visible in their Countenances." Malatchi, in fact, remained silent and let Chigelly deliver first his response—"to kill their own People for killing their Enemies was what he could not understand"—and then their joint conclusion that it was "a very hard Sentence." Only after a long, passionate speech by Mary did Malatchi speak, and then only to say "that it was a Matter of such great Consequence that they did not know what Answer to give." They would, Malatchi said, consult "with all the head Men" at a Lower Creek meeting already planned for August 10. He was both playing for time and looking for cover.[10]

That meeting "in the Coweta Square" produced more of the same. It opened with Malatchi and Chigelly informing their colleagues of Glen's talk; it closed—after "they sat in Council all Day and all

Night"—with a group visit to the Bosomworths and the declaration that "all their united Wisdom could not determine what Answer was best to be given to the Demand." The Bosomworths responded with "all the Arguments in my Power" (Thomas) and "a very long and pathetic speech" (Mary) before an Osochi attacker finally fingered Acorn Whistler as "the Cause of all the Mischief." Even then, Malatchi did not speak, and the other headmen could only declare "that they left it entirely to Malatchi." It took both another meeting later that day and Thomas's badgering—"I hoped he would make no Hesitation"; "I desired to know his final Answer"—to break Malatchi's silence and move him away from his first story.

And still he did not move far. "Malatchi replied that any Satisfaction should be given but shedding of Blood which he thought a very hard Demand and complained very much of our Partiality to the Cherokees." In particular, Malatchi asked why Cherokees went unpunished for killing a Creek in Savannah, another Creek at "the white Man's door in Augusta," and two British traders in Creek country, while Creeks went to their deaths for killing Cherokees. If that sounds like both a less-than-complete abandonment of the first story and part of a broader Creek effort "to excuse the Crime," the Bosomworths agreed. The end result was "Disputes on both Sides too tedious to be related," culminating in Mary's ultimatum: "some of them must suffer Death . . . or all the Traders would immediately be ordered out of the Nation." And still Malatchi had to think "some Time" before he sent for the two headmen, "both of them very near Relations of the Acorn Whistler's," and started telling a new story. It was no longer possible to argue that the April 1 attack was unimportant, and it was no longer politic to acknowledge that he had once believed exactly that.[11]

⌒ IN SUDDENLY BLAMING Acorn Whistler, did Malatchi abandon his first story? Or did he erase it? Although Acorn Whistler would have considered the question to be of secondary importance, the distinction matters. Verb choice, in this case, goes to the heart of how and why Malatchi crafted his stories. "Abandon" is an act of weakness; "erase," an act of (relative) strength. "Abandon" implies bending to reality; "erase," shaping that reality. "Abandon" retreats and writes off; "erase" revises and writes over. I have described Malatchi as both a confidence man and a powerful man. I have described both the obstacles in his path and the assets at his disposal. I have described his position as both dangerous and enviable. Given that mix, it will come as no surprise to learn that I believe he both abandoned and erased his first story. More to the point, I believe that he did so in exactly that order, and thereby demonstrated first the very real limits on his power and then his growing realization that his second story could be a political godsend. Within months after abandoning his first story on August 11, Malatchi's second story had put him in a strong enough position that he could erase his first story and put some substance behind the notion that there was both a Creek nation and a Creek emperor. Perhaps we should have expected as much. If necessity is the mother of invention, just imagine the ingenuity that desperation might produce.

Malatchi certainly had reason to feel desperate on August 11. It was one thing to be on bad terms with his British neighbors, but it was something else entirely to learn that this relationship was on the verge of imploding. Glen, via the Bosomworths, was flatly stating that failure to grant "Satisfaction" would "be looked upon . . . as an open Declaration of War." Malatchi could not afford to ignore such rhetoric. His nation would splinter in the face of a war with Britain. Nor could Malatchi risk finding out if Mary's final threat—"all the Traders would immediately be ordered out of the Nation"—was a bluff. The emperor's support would decline alongside his people's economic prospects. And if the thought of disregarding the message was unappealing, so too was the thought of dismissing the messengers. The Bosomworths had been critical in Far Off Mico's efforts to bypass the neighboring British colonies, and Thomas now bore King George's commission attesting to his "especial Trust and Confidence in [Thomas's] Loyalty and Fidelity." In reading this commission to Malatchi and talking of a trip to England, Thomas reminded Malatchi that Far Off Mico's transatlantic connections would wither away without the Bosomworths. Simply in terms of the British, then, Malatchi's future on August 11 seemed to promise some combination of armed conflict, trade embargo, and severed contacts.[12]

The situation in Creek country was no less alarming because Glen's accusations were, from a Creek perspective, laughably ignorant. It would not be easy for Malatchi to convince his people that the governor had a case. Creeks knew that the attackers had not "stain[ed] the white Beloved Town with . . . Blood." The Lower Creeks had waited until the Cherokees left Charleston and thereby forfeited the Beloved Town's protection. Creeks also knew that the attackers had not committed the "Crime" of "murthering the Cherokees." The Lower Creeks had simply killed their enemies, which was the purpose of their expedition and the province of warriors. Chigelly had put it exactly right almost two decades earlier: "if we meet with any of the Cherikees we or they must die." Even describing the April 1 attack as—in Glen's words—"contrary to the solemn Promises of the Offenders themselves" was too simple by half, a misrepresentation that conflated a temporary truce made at the insistence of one's host with an enduring peace sanctioned by one's headmen and sanctified by regular symbolic exchanges. There was, then, little in Creek culture to support Glen's charges, a fact that made his insistence on spilling "the Blood of some of the Offenders" seem not simply misguided but murderous.[13]

And had Malatchi found a way to overcome Creek perceptions about Glen's ends, there remained the nagging problem of his own means. Malatchi could not execute the Osochis without the support of Osochi's leaders and the attackers' families. As a Creek said about a later murderer, "all the other Towns say that his Relations are in this Town and that we were the only people that ought to have him kill'd." To make matters worse, the attackers were Malatchi's "Relations," a tie of "Flesh and Blood" that profoundly complicated life for a headman whose authority depended upon the support of his powerful family. If Malatchi ignored the will of town and clan, his own life would have been in danger because an unsanctioned execution was murder, which the dead men's families were obliged to revenge.[14]

Adding to Malatchi's problems—and moving from cultural rules to social networks—his ambitions meant that he needed the support of Osochi, the very town he would have angered by demanding the attackers' executions. If he was to attain truly national power, towns like Osochi—the friend town of his town's friend town—had to fall in line. Osochi, though, had a history of being less than enthusiastic about Malatchi's leadership. Five of its headmen did sign the 1747 document declaring Malatchi "our Rightful and Natural Prince," but Osochis also led the Lower Creeks who were dissatisfied with Malatchi after the 1749 Savannah confrontation. That twenty-six Osochis—more than half of the town's warriors—joined Malatchi's war against the Cherokees was a welcome sign, but Malatchi could not take Osochi's support for granted. He had no intention, there-fore, of finding out what would happen if he sacrificed some Osochi kinsmen for participating in a war that he himself had championed.[15]

Of course, implicit in this discussion of Malatchi's relations with his fellow Creeks and the British is a basic but important point: any story that Malatchi told about the events of April 1 had to con-vince two distinct audiences, neither of which was predisposed to accept the other's assumptions. It was a classic rock-and-a-hard-place moment, and Malatchi had only himself to blame. He had sys-tematically used his ties to Britain to leverage his power in Creek country, and vice versa. The result was an impressively broad set of connections, an unprecedented degree of influence, and the promise of more to come. Malatchi, though, was too good a politician not to recognize that a quo might accompany these quids, that his two constituencies might make incompatible demands on him, that he might one day move from having two bases to having two masters. Salvaging the gains he had made and preserving the possibility of future advances meant telling a story that each side could swallow, if not relish. That story did not have to be true, which was fortunate because Malatchi had already tried something like the truth in story number 1. Now, it was time for story number 2.

Malatchi's second story had one signal virtue: it gave both the Creeks and Glen what they asked for. Glen received a bloody apol-ogy. The Creeks received respect for their customs and protection for people who had done nothing wrong. There was, of course, a catch. The blood came from the wrong person, and Creek tradi-tions were invoked to effect a decidedly nontraditional execution. The sugar that made these bitter pills go down was Acorn Whis-tler. Malatchi gambled that some combination of Glen's obvious suspicion of Acorn Whistler, the tendency of officials back in Britain to assume that a leader like Acorn Whistler had more power than he actually did, and a governor's need to present his superiors with a victory would lead Glen to accept a solution that featured live Osochis and a dead Acorn Whistler. At the same time, Malatchi also gambled that, if he went through traditional Creek channels, he could persuade his people to accede to the execution of a man who was as vulnerable as a Creek headman could be. Acorn Whistler, after all, lived in an unimportant town, used violence to undermine his people's peace initiatives, and was involved—no matter how tenuously—in an incident that threatened to destroy the Creeks' relations with the British. Malatchi bet, in short, that he could tell a story that would satisfy both sides, but only if he used Acorn Whistler to square the circle.

Malatchi began his second story by simultaneously abandoning his first story (and thereby bowing to Glen's assertion that the April 1 attack was a problem) and summoning two of Acorn Whistler's relatives to hear the second story (and thereby bowing to Creek customs about clan responsibility for punishing malefactors). In the new story that Malatchi trotted out, the problem was not that Cherokees had been killed—"they thought no Harm in what [the attackers] did"—but that young Creeks had been lured to Charleston, denied knowledge of the governor's speech forbidding an attack on the Cherokees, and then set upon those very same Cherokees. In other words, Malatchi told the two headmen that the Creeks present in Charleston could be neatly divided into two groups: "the innocent" and "their Relation (the Acorn Whistler)," who "ought to have known better, as he heard the Talk from the Governor, and should have taken care that no Mischief was done." In failing to do so, Acorn Whistler had insulted and angered the British.[16]

With that established, Malatchi could then launch into his series of lies about what Acorn Whistler told him during their April meeting. Individually and as a whole, these lies furthered the impression that Acorn Whistler had harmed the British in the past and that, since "he never would forgive the English as long as he lived," worse was yet to come. Malatchi followed that up with two powerful arguments. Acorn Whistler would be even more dangerous once "he came to hear of the Demand" that someone be executed to make amends for the April 1 attack. And as Acorn Whistler "himself had acknowledged that he was the Cause of the young Fellows committing the Crime for which Nothing but Blood would make satisfaction, it was better that his Life should be taken than that they should break off all Friendship with the English." The next move, Malatchi said, was clear: "as he was their Relation it was their Business to do that," and with "all possible Haste."[17]

It was a beautiful story, one that contained a little something for everyone. Glen received not only a direct acknowledgment that the Creeks had insulted him and his colony on April 1 but also blood satisfaction. Even better, Malatchi offered Glen not the heads of a few inconsequential warriors but the life of their leader, who Creeks suddenly started referring to as "a great Man." Malatchi knew that Glen would see through Acorn Whistler's promotion to greatness and leadership, but he suspected that he had given Glen enough for the governor to claim victory. Glen had, after all, received everything he wanted except the right body, and Malatchi covered that oversight by publicly stating that, in this regard, Glen had traded up.[18]

The Creeks, likewise, had to come to terms with Acorn Whistler's dead body, but they too found much to appreciate in Malatchi's story. Malatchi, for example, redefined the problem so that Creek beliefs about attacking the Cherokees were reinforced. At a time when some Lower Creeks were "in great Rage and Fury about the Demand that is made of their Lives . . . for killing their Enemies," Malatchi changed the subject from dead enemies to insulted allies. And then he picked culturally appropriate people to deal with the problem. The two headmen Malatchi summoned to hear his second story had political ties to the towns at the center of the crisis. Otassee King lived in the community closest to Acorn Whistler's Little Okfuskee, and the Warrior King of Cusseta lived across the river from Malatchi's Coweta. Involving these men meant invoking their towns, which helped to legitimize the proceedings. More importantly, though, the two headmen were Acorn Whistler's kinsmen. That relationship was critical because, as Chigelly told them, "You are his own Flesh and Blood. Either of you or any of his own Relations may kill him and who has any Thing to say to it?" Malatchi, thus, made sure that these two headmen arranged the details themselves. They adjourned to Cusseta, where they picked Acorn Whistler's nephew as the executioner and gave him a plausible cover story: "his Uncle was mad and wanted to kill him" because of an earlier dispute "on Account of some Woman." Otassee King then went to Upper Creek country to contain any fallout, and Malatchi sent "a Relation of the Acorn Whistler belonging to the Cowetas" to help out. From a Creek perspective, the right people were handling the problem in the right way. That would go a long way toward ameliorating the fact that Malatchi's second story insisted that the wrong man be executed.[19]

The brilliance of Malatchi's second story should not, however, blind us to the weakness of its storyteller. Remember that Malatchi began the second story by abruptly abandoning his first one. The new story he proceeded to tell was fundamentally a conservative one. It depended entirely on traditional connections—on kinship, community, and personal ties among the Creeks, and on relations with the neighboring British colonies. Gone were the national-level processes an emperor might have deployed; gone, too, were the transatlantic ties a Far Off Mico might have relied upon. Malatchi was playing defense here, not offense. He was looking to cut his losses, not to field-test his more expansive claims. And even though he was in a defensive crouch, Malatchi still worried that he had stuck his neck out. That would change over time. In fact, the history of the second story ends with Malatchi retaking the initiative and advancing his political ambitions. But, in the aftermath of telling his second story on August 11, the chance of that outcome must have seemed vanishingly small. Malatchi was, quite simply, terrified.

His fear leaps out of the records from August 11—"he was afraid"; "there is real Danger"; "all possible Haste"—and seems to have intensified the next day when he learned that Acorn Whistler's relatives had assigned the role of executioner to the nephew. "Both Malatchi and Chiggilli seemed much afraid of some Miscarriage in the Execution, and blame [the two headmen] for trusting a Matter of so much Consequence to a Boy for Fear he should [reveal] the Cause of his Uncle's Death." Malatchi communicated that fear clearly enough that "the Man that was first sent to instigate [Acorn

Whistler's] Nephew to kill him" responded to Acorn Whistler's execution by killing the nephew to shut him up; as Malatchi put it, he "Fear[ed] that [the executioner] being a young Man, and in order to take the Odium of the Action from himself, should be foolish enough to declare that he was sent on to kill the Acorn Whistler." Malatchi's own reaction to hearing that Acorn Whistler was dead went unrecorded, but the arrival of that news on August 19 coincided with Malatchi's decision to go on a two-day "drunk," which rendered him incapable of conducting public business. He then skipped a meeting of "all the Head Men of the Lower Towns" on August 24, and let Chigelly take the lead at an August 31 "Consultation." There, it was decided to send the Bosomworths and two Lower Creeks—but not Malatchi—to the Upper Creeks so as to convince Acorn Whistler's kinsmen "of the Justice and Necessity of his Death." It was Chigelly—not Malatchi—who "made a long and excellent Speech" telling the party bound for the Upper Creeks "how they should act," and it was Chigelly—not Malatchi—who removed a potentially unreliable Cusseta headman from the party and substituted a Coweta leader. Malatchi kept quiet and stayed that way until late September. It was a most un-emperor-like performance by a man whose story had produced this crisis.[20]

Malatchi's fears were well founded. To begin with, his second story could well have triggered the very conflict with the British that he sought to avoid. In the few days between August 11 and Acorn Whistler's death, Malatchi believed that "there is real Danger of [Acorn Whistler] doing Mischief if the Talk [about his guilt] should reach his Ears, which would unavoidably make War with the English." Malatchi had, in other words, given Acorn Whistler a reason to attack the British, who were now publicly demanding that he be executed. Acorn Whistler was dangerous not (as Malatchi's second story would have it) because he had always been angry at the British but because Malatchi's second story made him fear for his life. And after Acorn Whistler's execution, Malatchi knew, the situation became even more dire. As Malatchi and Chigelly cautioned the Bosomworths on August 12, "if it should immediately be known" that the British were behind Acorn Whistler's death "before all the Head Men . . . can meet to consult about it, it is their Opinion that his Relations will certainly take Revenge upon" the British. Malatchi and his allies needed to retain control of the narrative by keeping Acorn Whistler's relatives pacified until the second story could be told in the appropriate diplomatic context. Then and only then did they have a chance to avoid an all-out war. That Malatchi thought this dicey proposition was his best option speaks volumes about the desperation that prompted his second story.[21]

And that was particularly true because Malatchi's worries did not end with the possibility that Acorn Whistler's relatives "might have took Satisfaction upon the white People." Malatchi had his own skin to think about as well. As Thomas Bosomworth noted, "the Indians were very industrious to conceal those Persons who [were] any Ways instrumental in this Man's death for Fear of their own Lives." Otassee King and the Warrior King of Cusseta, the headmen who first heard Malatchi's story on August 11, had warned him that, while they supported Acorn Whistler's execution, he had "many Relations . . . that might not be of the same Opinion." What must Malatchi have thought, then, when he learned on August 30 that Acorn Whistler's "Freinds were so enraged [at his death] that they burnt [his] Town and left it"? How would Malatchi have reacted when, two days later, Acorn Whistler's son arrived in Cusseta "and accused the King of that Town as the *Author* of [his father's death], and demanded the life of a Cussitaw Fellow, an adopted Relation of the King's, for Satisfaction"? That destroying a dead man's possessions and accepting—as Acorn Whistler's son eventually did—"some Present" in lieu of blood revenge were traditional Creek responses to murder would have been cold comfort for Malatchi. It was also traditional, after all, for relatives to kill someone like Malatchi who was "answerable" for their loved one's death.[22]

Malatchi's role as storyteller meant that he had more reason than anyone to be afraid of retaliation, and his efforts to stay out of sight are particularly striking. He did not resurface until after a late September conference in Tuckabatchee produced not only multiple statements by Acorn Whistler's relatives that they "were very well contented that he should suffer Death" but also a conference-wide consensus regarding "the Reasonableness and Justice of the Acorn Whistler's Death." And even after this public acceptance of his second story, Malatchi took care, as he and Chigelly said, "not . . . to speak any Thing before the Relations of the Acorn Whistler that might renew their Grief and Sorrow for his Death."[23]

That caution notwithstanding, however, the Tuckabatchee conference's explicit embrace of Acorn Whistler's fate allowed Malatchi to resume his public political role. Indeed, his actions in early October demonstrate that he thought the crisis was over and that his second story had worked. Thus, rather than avoiding meetings, he hosted one in Coweta on October 4. Rather than getting drunk and dodging responsibility, he took steps to prevent alcohol from interfering with public business. Rather than foisting unpleasant tasks on other towns and families, he accepted their declarations "that whatever Malatchi should do in Regard to the publick Affairs . . . they would stand by and confirm." Most tellingly, rather than let others speak for him, he reemerged as the Lower Creeks' leader. At the October 4 conference, he opened the Creek speeches by reminding everyone that "whatever he should act or do, in regard to public Business, that it should be looked upon as firm and valid." He then stepped back and let Cusseta's Warrior King testify that Acorn Whistler's "own Relations . . . thought it was good that his Life should be taken." With that statement as cover, Malatchi immediately took over the meeting. No other Creek spoke.[24]

When Thomas Bosomworth asked why Acorn Whistler's nephew had been killed, Malatchi answered that this "innocent" man died to ensure his silence until the matter could be explained, a sacrifice to the Creeks' desire that "all past Injuries be forgiven and forgot, and a new Chain of Friendship made, which would continue forever." In the service of that goal, Malatchi then addressed Glen's other two concerns, making sure to emphasize his own power and influence: "he would take care to see [the British traders' horses] restored," even if he had to reach into "different Towns" to do it; and as "the Upper Creek Nation had entirely left [the issue of peace with the Cherokees] to his Determination, the whole Lower Creek Nation should comply with every Thing the Governor desired." To confirm all of this, "Malatchi offered his Mark," the only Creek to do so. Beside that mark, Thomas wrote "Malatchi, Opia Mico and commanding King of the Indian Nation." Malatchi was back.

Malatchi, in fact, clearly believed that his second story had put him in position to make some demands of Glen. At an October 11 meeting with Thomas and Chigelly, Malatchi insisted that the British stop making "Captains and great Men" of Creeks "who had no Right to command." Georgia, he said, had tried appointing someone in his stead, an effort that "made [Malatchi] hitherto the more indifferent in Matters that concerned" the British. Malatchi and Chigelly went on to say that "as they had punished their People with Death for Satisfaction to the English, they hoped the Governor would punish the white People for the Crimes they were guilty of": wife stealing, horse thieving, trespassing, "and ussing [Creeks] very ill when they are in Liquor." They closed by gesturing to the new reality Malatchi's second story had made possible, sending "their Complements to your Excellency" and drinking "your Health . . . and a lasting Friendship with the English." All in all, it was classic Malatchi: using his ability to get things done in Creek country to make British connections, which he then used both to redress the complaints of his Creek people and to ensure that other Creeks could not make their own British connections. He had long ago mastered this sort of maneuver.[25]

And yet it is important to recognize that, in seeking to benefit from the success of his second story, Malatchi was not simply returning to the status quo ante Acorn Whistler. True, Malatchi invoked British contacts, but, thanks to his second story, these contacts were suddenly based in the colonies, not the metropole. For the first time in years, he was calling on his British neighbors and no longer relying on the vagaries of transatlantic networks. That reality likely explains why Malatchi ceased calling himself Far Off Mico after the October 4 meeting at Coweta. With Acorn Whistler dead and Malatchi's second story ascendant, the man formerly known as Far Off Mico could see a more secure path to personal influence and national unity. It led to Charleston, not London.[26]

Malatchi's efforts to follow that path are visible almost literally from the moment he left the October 11 meeting with Thomas and Chigelly. That afternoon, Thomas learned that a Chickasaw had killed a British trader in that Upper Creek town of Breed Camp. The murder, Malatchi realized, offered him a golden opportunity to build upon his second story and further enhance his relationship

with Charleston. As he later told Glen, "Immediately upon my hearing of" the murder, "I concluded that it was best to give [you] . . .
Satisfaction . . . before it was asked." In so doing, Malatchi demonstrated how much had changed in his world since he started telling
his second story about Acorn Whistler. Now Malatchi had solid reasons for anticipating Glen's desires, and now Malatchi could frame
his willingness to procure the necessary satisfaction as the logical
continuation of his efforts, as laid out in his second story, to respond
to Glen's concerns during the Acorn Whistler affair.[27]

Thomas certainly linked the two events, writing that the
"Behaviour of the Creeks" after the trader's murder "was a Consequence flowing from the Demand made upon them [during the
Acorn Whistler affair], and the Satisfaction given by the Death of
one of [the Creeks'] own Head Men which was a sufficient Incentive to them that other Nations should comply with the like just
Demands of Government." In fact, though, the equation Thomas
that laid out—We Creeks killed our man; now you Chickasaws kill
yours—did not do justice to Malatchi's position. The real issue, from
his perspective, was not that the Chickasaws execute the guilty party
and give satisfaction to the British as the Creeks had, but rather that
Malatchi should be seen as making them do those things. If that
happened, then not only would Malatchi have aided his friend the
governor but Malatchi would also have further obscured his first
story's refusal to punish anyone for the April 1 attack. The parallels
between the Chickasaw incident and the Acorn Whistler affair, in
other words, allowed Malatchi to use his actions in the former to
erase any hint of vacillation that he might have shown in the latter.[28]

And if that prospect was not incentive enough to involve himself in the Chickasaw incident, Malatchi knew that obtaining satisfaction from the Chickasaws would be easy, at least compared to
the outcome he had engineered during the Acorn Whistler crisis.
After all, the Chickasaw's victim was an ally who was killed in a
trader's house in Creek country, not an enemy killed on the road
in South Carolina. In this case, Creek customs and British desires
matched up nicely; there would be no messy debate about Cherokees who were off limits and Creeks who were on the hot seat. Even
better, the murderer was not a Creek; he was, in Malatchi's words,

"One of the Chickesaws who live in our Nation." His town, Breed
Camp, was a Chickasaw outpost in the northwest corner of Upper
Creek country. It was a relatively ephemeral place, inhabited only
for twenty years as a way station to protect British traders who were
bringing the guns and ammunition that allowed the Chickasaws
to ward off their French and Choctaw enemies. In keeping with
the Breed Camp Chickasaws' tenuous foothold in Creek country,
they did "not concern themselves in the Creek Affairs," and their
Creek hosts viewed them as both not-quite-Creek and, in Malatchi's
words, as "younger Brothers."[29] For Malatchi, then, the Chickasaw
incident was the Acorn Whistler affair all over again, only with a
much greater chance of success and no personal danger whatsoever.

And so Malatchi "promised to accompany" Thomas "with a Resolution that" British demands "should be complyed with," even
though the trip would take them through the Upper Creek towns
of his leading rivals. Once there, Malatchi pushed the Upper Creeks
to support Thomas's demands. He called meetings, and, in one case,
closed one down when it deadlocked. He told the Upper Creeks of
the "strict Orders" he had given, and issued a "preremptory Message"
to the Chickasaws. He made speeches "shewing the Reasonableness
and Necessity of [the Chickasaws] granting the Demand and the
Consequences they might expect if they refused"; at several points,
he came close to "compell[ing] them by Force of Arms to give Satisfaction." And once the Chickasaws had complied, he "made a long
Speech" to them as their "elder Brother," reminding them that they
were "settled by Permission in the Creeks' Country" and threatening "to send for a Number of Warriors" if the problem resurfaced.[30]

Then, Malatchi returned to Coweta, stopping off at Tuckabatchee
to relate "all our Proceedings in the Upper Town." Tuckabatchee,
of course, had hosted the September conference at which the Upper
Creeks publicly approved of Acorn Whistler's execution, and Malatchi, of course, had failed to attend that meeting, even though Tuckabatchee was "a Friend Town to Coweta" and its nearest Upper Creek
neighbor. His speech at Tuckabatchee at the end of the Chickasaw
incident, therefore, served to underline a theme of his entire Upper
Creek journey: Malatchi's weakness during the Acorn Whistler
affair was a thing of the past. He was now a force to be reckoned

with throughout Creek country. In fact, Malatchi quite obviously felt that the Chickasaw incident offered him the chance to act as, when viewed in the right light, an emperor on a national stage.[31]

Of course, even Malatchi knew that his trip had not truly been an unalloyed example of imperial power on a national scale. Yes, he had called meetings, made speeches, and issued preemptive messages, but always in conjunction with the leading Upper Creek headmen. Yes, he had issued orders, but only to the Lower Creeks. Yes, he had made threats, but only to Chickasaws. Yes, he had forced the Chickasaws to give satisfaction, but the dead man was—yet again—not the murderer but rather the murderer's uncle, who had "sacrifice[d] his own Life for" his nephew. Moreover, a contemporary Creek who subjected Malatchi's itinerary to a close reading would have noticed how Malatchi's power waxed and waned depending on where he was at the time. The traditional sociogeography of Creek country— who could speak where with what degree of authority—structured Malatchi's efforts to deploy power. The British might see him as the unchallenged leader of an ever-more united nation, but the Creeks knew better.[32]

Still, if Malatchi's trip could be interpreted in different ways by different audiences, that was simply the residue of Malatchi's long-standing habit of using his position in Creek country to enhance his standing with the British, and vice versa. And once Malatchi returned to Coweta, the process continued, most notably with the December 8 arrival of Glen's letter accepting Acorn Whistler's death as satisfaction for the April 1 attack. Malatchi was "highly satisfied" with Glen's response, and no wonder. Glen not only embraced Malatchi's second story but embellished it, exaggerating Malatchi's role in Acorn Whistler execution. This was the letter, moreover, in which Glen praised Malatchi's "greatness of Soul" and stated that he "deserves to be Esteemed Valued and Loved by both English and the Creeks." And just as valuable were Glen's promises to address the Creeks' complaints, which Malatchi had raised on October 11.[33]

Malatchi was not shy about spreading this good news. He first called a meeting for Cowetas and Cussetas, where "the Contents of the Letter were interpreted Paragraph by Paragraph," and then "he ordered the Cussetaw King to call a Meeting at the Town of the Parachucklaws" so as "to communicate the same to the Rest of the Lower Creeks." Malatchi was, once again, using support from one constituency to enhance his status with the other. Acorn Whistler was dead, Glen was happy, and the emperor was back in the saddle, and all because of Malatchi's second story.[34]

～ SIX MONTHS LATER, a newspaper reported that "upwards of 100 Indians from the Creek Nation" led by "Malatchi their Emperor" arrived in Charleston. Glen, writing in the third-person self-promotional, noted that the Creeks were there because "all differences" with the Cherokees had been "happily composed by the Good Offices of the Governor and a Peace made by his mediation. And both Parties having agreed to ratify it in his presence King Malatchi and . . . the Headmen of the upper and lower Nation accordingly set out from their own Country." Malatchi had other ideas. During his stay, he would deliver his grudging, conditional approval of a truce; but that was not why Malatchi was in Charleston. Instead, he would use this visit to Glen's capital to lend substance to the newspaper's offhand remark about the emperor and his nation. His second story would be the centerpiece of that effort.[35]

Malatchi had neither been to Charleston nor met with Glen for a half-dozen years. For much of that time, the two men had been adversaries rather than allies. Malatchi's second story about Acorn Whistler both emerged as a result of that tense standoff and provided its resolution. Malatchi arrived primed to tell it again if it became necessary, which it did, in large part because Glen insisted on bringing up Acorn Whistler. Glen's opening speech began with a nod to the events of April 1 and then went on to review both that attack and the December 1751 one. Faced with Glen's statement that "I desire to have it from your own Mouths a public Declaration of what has been done in the Matter," Malatchi responded by asserting his loyalty to "our Friends the English." Because of that relationship, "I did not expect to hear that our Nation had been accused for the Faults of a few private Men, or that the Head Men would have been blamed for it." And then Malatchi told his second story once again, adding some detail and, more importantly, giving this story an effective new structure.[36]

Malatchi's discussion of who was responsible for the Acorn Whistler affair took the shape of a diamond. He started from the tip with
"I," widened first to "we" and then even further to the passive voice's
no-one-and-thus-everyone before contracting back to "we" and,
finally, to "I." The story began, "when I was informed of what had
happened" on April 1, "I soon saw that it would not be passed over
or put up with, and I concluded that you [Glen] would certainly send
to demand Satisfaction." Of course, "I was not at all surprized" to
see Thomas; "I knew the Bussiness he was come upon." And, even at
this early date, "I was pretty clear in my own Opinion that it was just
and necessary to give this Satisfaction." Toward that end, "I thought
it would be more prudent to consult with the beloved Men," and "I
acquainted" the Creek beloved men of the issue's "Consequence."

And then, as Malatchi's story drew closer to Acorn Whistler's
death, he dropped "I" and moved from the diamond's tip toward its
middle by speaking of "we the Creek leaders." As his story moved
from investigating what had happened to finding out who was to
blame and determining what to do about it, Malatchi noted that "we
found," "We found," "all of us thought," "we turned our Thoughts,"
"we found," and "We therefore thought." Until, suddenly, just as
Acorn Whistler's fate hung in the balance, Malatchi moved away
from "we" to the diamond's widest point. There, he adopted the
all-encompassing passive voice for one critical sentence: "He
accordingly was put to Death." With that accomplished, Malatchi
could return to "we thought," "we did," and "we looked upon" to
describe the effort to manage the execution's fallout. And, finally,
Malatchi ended with "I": "there remains Nothing further for me to
say upon that Head, and therefore I hope our Friendship with the
English will stand upon the same good Footing as heretofore." The
diamond was complete. It was elegant, but why bother?[37]

Malatchi's diamond-shaped second story worked for him in three
distinct ways. The personal dimension is easiest to see. The diamond allowed him to emphasize, and sanitize, his own role. With
this narrative, Malatchi completed the process of erasing his first
story and, with it, any lingering ambiguity about his part in the
Acorn Whistler affair. In Charleston, Malatchi never so much as
hinted that he had treated the April 1 attack as a nonevent; nor did

he suggest that he had been blindsided by Glen's demands and had to be pushed into making satisfaction. His first story, and the hesitation it engendered in his initial response to Glen's story, had been completely erased. Malatchi had, he now claimed, taken the lead in recognizing the problem and creating the context for its solution. And, in the end, it was Malatchi who closed the book on the incident, stating that no more was left to say and reminding everyone of the enduring Creek-British friendship. According to Malatchi's second story, the emperor was in control, and he always had been.

But the story Malatchi told in Charleston was as much national as personal, and the diamond allowed Malatchi to give the nation its due. In this narrative, Malatchi did not claim that he had killed Acorn Whistler. Glen had given him room to do so when he described Malatchi as the investigator, prosecutor, judge, and jury in an earlier letter to the Creeks, but Malatchi was having none of it. In fact, he significantly downplayed his own role in pushing for Acorn Whistler's death by neglecting to mention his critical August 11 meeting with Acorn Whistler's relatives. Instead, Malatchi's reliance on "we" functioned to place his own power within the broader context of a unified Creek nation endowed with a set of well-established traditions, an ability to police itself, and a mature deliberative body. In so doing, he knew that he would appear all the more powerful—the foresightful and cautious leader of a nation with reliable and effective customs of leadership. According to Malatchi's second story, the emperor ruled over a true nation.

And the third thing that Malatchi's diamond-shaped story did for him? We can see it in both the structure of the story and in his use of the passive voice. Call it "the cross-cultural." The narrative form that Malatchi employed was perfectly adapted to his long-standing habit of speaking to two audiences—British and Creek—at the same time. The diamond itself referenced the structure of traditional Creek oral histories, the "I said, she said, it was said" form that I discuss above. In both, the first-person singular finds support from another person or group, and both are then buttressed by the all-encompassing passive. The Creeks in Charleston would have understood, and appreciated, this story. And so, too, would the British. They would have cared little for the diamond, but its constituent parts had real meaning for them. The British were, for example, primed to focus on the actions of a leader, the subject with which Malatchi both opened and closed his story. And the British were likewise predisposed to recognize the national institutions and traditions signified by all those *we*'s. The manner in which Malatchi told this story, in short, worked cross-culturally.

And so, too, did his use of passive voice: "He accordingly was put to Death for that Offence." No one killed Acorn Whistler. Everyone killed Acorn Whistler. Take your pick. For Malatchi, the use of passive voice set up a case of "Heads, I win; tails, I win." Creeks, colonists, and British officials were guilty or innocent together. Saying so, of course, further distanced Malatchi from the violence that he had feared when he debuted his second story. How could a Creek-British war break out if everyone was to blame for Acorn Whistler's death? How could he himself be in danger if no one was to blame for Acorn Whistler's death? More centrally, however, spreading the blame or sharing the alibi had the significant advantage of reminding all present that they were implicated in Acorn Whistler's fate. After all, Malatchi had been pushed by Glen, badgered by the Bosomworths, and assisted by Acorn Whistler's kinsmen. This had been a cross-cultural affair from start to finish.

It was appropriate, therefore, that Malatchi found a British man to tell his story for him: Glen. Malatchi spoke many more times at the meeting, but he never again mentioned Acorn Whistler or the April 1 attack. Glen, by contrast, could not shut up about those subjects. The day after Malatchi spoke, Glen described Malatchi's speech as "very wise," accepted the way the Creeks "punished" the guilty, and stated "that Affair is never more to be spoke of." Except, of course, that Glen returned to it in that day's closing speech, when he not only praised the Creeks for giving the British satisfaction but also invoked the 1749 efforts of "the Indian called the Acorn Whistler" to subvert the Creek-Cherokee peace. And then, on the conference's third day, Glen noted that the Cherokees "can hardly give entire Credit to your Promises of Peace, after some of your People so lately murdered their Country Men near Charles Town in Breach of a solemn Promise." The governor, though, would tell the Cherokees that the attack was the work "of a wicked Head Man," that "your Nation had publically disclaimed any Knowledge" of it, and that his "own Relations" agreed he should be "put to Death for that Offence and the whole Nation unanimou[s]ly approved of it." Glen was singing Malatchi's tune, and Malatchi was happy to listen, especially since he was in the process of getting everything he could possibly want from the Charleston visit.[38]

Malatchi's success during the conference, in fact, was so complete that personal victories that would normally rate as important triumphs—pushing Glen to intercede in the Creeks' dispute with Georgia; winning Glen's promise to represent Mary Bosomworth's land claims "to the Great King"; being permitted by Glen to "distribute" the Creeks' presents "to those that you shall think most worthy" of them—fade into insignificance. More important by far were the many moments when Malatchi presented himself as the Creeks' leader and was treated as such by the British. He was, in Glen's words, "the Head and Mouth of the Nation," the Creeks' "Head King . . . and happy is that Nation that has such a Head." And, as a result, the conference played out as an extended, public, one-on-one negotiation between governor and emperor. Glen said as much on several occasions. He would listen "if any other Head Men have any Thing to add . . . though Malatchi has spoke very fully." And when someone else did talk, Glen remarked that "I have given great Attention to all that has been said, but chiefly to what was spoken by the King," while also noting that "the other Person" spoke "without any Direction from the Nation." Malatchi's was the voice that mattered.[39]

Malatchi was, of course, happy to further that impression. When several Upper Creeks interrupted a typical governor-emperor set piece to make their own demands, Malatchi dismissed them: "They ought . . . to be considered as Children, and no Regard to be paid to any Thing they have said; they in a very rude and abrupt Manner broke in upon my Discourse without any Power or Commission from me or the Nation." He then assured Glen that "the several Matters that have been talked over and agreed upon betwixt your Excellency and me shall stand. It is the only true Talk, and shall be ratified and confirmed. Every Thing else is to be considered as Wind."[40]

Glen supported him to the hilt. First, Glen "commended Malatchi's Behaviour, and told him that he did not know how to reward the Trouble he had taken in his own Country." Then, Glen remarked that Malatchi's horse was worn out and gave him "a handsome riding Horse," which Glen followed with a "Snuff box" from his own pocket for Malatchi to keep "as a proof of the personal Friendship between them." Finally, Glen "took a Ring from off his Finger with a Stone and Seal, and told Malatchi, that as he was the chief Person upon whose Intelligence he could rely, he hoped that he would from time to time correspond with him, and inform him of the true state of his Nation; and that he might know that the Letters came from himself, and were written by his direction, he made him a present of that Ring and Seal, and desired that all the Letters that he sent, might have that Impression upon them."[41]

South Carolina's clerk described the ring as a "Token of Friendship and Confidence," and wrote that "Malatchi was highly pleased, and returned the Governor many Thanks." Who could blame him? Glen had made a gesture that combined the personal and political in an eye-catching way. Imperial power was made of stuff like this, as was the ability to rule a nation. And so, the next day, "King Malatchi having convened all his People sharply reprimanded such of them as had behaved ill and made them ashamed of what they had said and afterwards made so equal a division of the Presents that ever one was perfectly pleased." Or so the clerk tells us.[42] Given the nature of Creek politics, the reality was certainly messier—less unified, less harmonious, less hierarchical. Malatchi was not yet emperor; the Creeks were not yet a nation. But, from Malatchi's perspective, progress was being made. His story about Acorn Whistler had worked.

~ III
LOCAL

$\mathcal{A}$CORN WHISTLER'S TOWN, Little Okfuskee, was not an important place. Founded as an offshoot of Okfuskee in the late 1720s or early 1730s, Little Okfuskee never rivaled its mother town's influence. Perhaps rivalry was not, however, Little Okfuskee's point? It is possible that Okfuskees founded Little Okfuskee to secure a stake in the expanding trade between the British and the Choctaws. In the 1720s, Okfuskee hosted the trading post that was at the center of British efforts to bring the Choctaws into their commercial empire. Little Okfuskee was situated near the path between Okfuskee and Choctaw country, and it thus may have served as a marker of Okfuskee's investment in this new trade route. The Okfuskees, in fact, established similar villages—the first before 1711 and five more in the 1760s—on the eastern path linking the Creeks to the British; they might very well have done the same thing on the western path to the Choctaws.[1]

Or perhaps rivalry *was* the point of Little Okfuskee? After all, Okfuskee was a prominent British ally in Upper Creek country, while an Upper Creek described Little Okfuskee as "settled right [next] to the French" at Fort Toulouse. Little Okfuskees dealt with the French garrison. How else could Acorn Whistler have gained French support for his 1749 attack on the Cherokees or learned the details of Malatchi's 1750 visit to the fort? Relatedly, Little Okfuskee first appears in the historical record in 1733, just after the Okfuskees publicly demonstrated their pro-British orientation in Charleston. Perhaps, then, Little Okfuskee was founded by pro-French Okfuskees who objected to their townspeople's decision to privilege Britain over France?[2]

Or perhaps Little Okfuskee's founders simply wanted to leave their options open and pursue relations with both the British and the French? Those Europeans struggled mightily for trading posts in Little Okfuskee's neighborhood during the town's early years, and the town's location suggests that it was well placed to profit from that competition. The first map showing the town depicts four Creek communities clustered closely around Fort Toulouse. Little Okfuskee was not among them, but it was at the forefront of a group of six towns just a little further away, likely right on the boundary that a roughly contemporary French map labels as "ligne qui Separe nous Villages de cause des Anglois." A later census places Little Okfuskee sixteen miles from Fort Toulouse, not exactly right next to the French but certainly in the portion of Creek country where neither the British nor the French dominated.[3]

If Little Okfuskee was founded by a pro-French or neutralist faction of Okfuskees, that would explain why, unlike Okfuskee's villages on the eastern path, Little Okfuskee was never described as part of Okfuskee. Creeks distinguished between a *talwa* (town) and a *talofa* (village); a talwa often encompassed and controlled several spatially distinct talofas. Little Okfuskee was an independent talwa, while Okfuskee's eastern settlements were dependent talofas. And not only was Little Okfuskee independent, but it also was not part of Okfuskee's division. The Upper Creeks grouped themselves into three ethnogeographic units: Tallapoosas, Abeikas, and Alabamas. Little Okfuskees were Tallapoosas; Okfuskees were Abeikas. In sum, Little Okfuskee was an autonomous town, not a subordinate village of Okfuskee; it was in the Tallapoosa division, not in Okfuskee's Abeika division; and it was located so as to allow easy contact with the French, not with Okfuskee's British allies. Circumstantial evidence, to be sure, but taken as whole it suggests a distant relationship between Little Okfuskee and Okfuskee.[4]

In fact, Little Okfuskee's strongest ties were to Okfuskee's rival, Muccolossus, a powerful Tallapoosa community, and its headman, Wolf. In 1758, Wolf was "Chief" of Muccolossus "and of four or five other little Towns," including Little Okfuskee; a dozen years before, Wolf referred to "the other Towns of which he was headman," all of which "lay"—as did Little Okfuskee—"very near the [French] Fort." Wolf and his town often opposed Okfuskee's initiatives, with relations becoming so bad that Okfuskee's Red Coat King called Wolf "mad" while Wolf both "laid the blame" for a sensational outbreak of violence on Red Coat King and "proposed to the Upper Creeks to join and cut off" Okfuskee. If the Little Okfuskees allied themselves with Wolf and Muccolossus, then that would be more circumstantial evidence that Okfuskee and Little Okfuskee were not close.[5]

Whatever motivated the Little Okfuskees to leave Okfuskee and whatever the subsequent relationship between the two towns, it is clear that Little Okfuskee failed to thrive. If its inhabitants hoped

to profit from Britain's Choctaw trade, then they were undone by
the imperial rivalry and Choctaw factionalism that doomed that
exchange network. Or, if the Little Okfuskees intended to cozy up
(to one degree or another) with the French, then they were undone by
France's marked inability to supply even its more important Indian
allies with the necessary goods and services. And so Little Okfuskee
remained a tiny town, with a "low and unhealthy" location, "broken
land" down to the river, and "broken pine barrens back of that." The
most optimistic estimate—Acorn Whistler's own—said it was home
to "about" twenty "Gun Men," approximately one hundred people.
Other estimates went as low as ten gunmen, roughly fifty people.[6]

That those people so rarely surface in the documentary record
suggests that the town was not just small but also insignificant.
How else to explain the fact that only two colonial-era cartogra-
phers bothered to note Little Okfuskee's location? Why else would
mapmakers of the time have shown "Great Oakfuskee" and "Les
Affasqués Abékas" (Okfuskee) but not "Little Oakfuskee" and Les
Affasqués Tallapoosas (Little Okfuskee)? Why else would Little Okfuskee find itself on South Carolina's 1761 list of "Names
of Places inserted in [traders'] Licenses" that were "not Towns"?
Why else would Acorn Whistler's Little Okfuskee be commemo-
rated only by a creek named "Ofuckshe" while another town come
to be known as Little Okfuskee Old Town? Even the best-known
twentieth-century reproduction of the 1733 map depicting Little
Okfuskee shows a village icon where Little Okfuskee was located,
but neglects to provide the town's name. A more recent attempt at
chronicling all Indian communities in preremoval Alabama con-
fuses Acorn Whistler's Little Okfuskee with a later village of the
same name while erroneously claiming that "No map source" exists
for the town. Little Okfuskee was that kind of place.[7]

No matter how unimpressive, though, Little Okfuskee and its
connections were pivotal to the Acorn Whistler affair for the very
simple reason that towns and town-based relationships were at
the center of Creek sociopolitical life. Creeks privileged the local
to a degree that can disorient people used to thinking in terms of
nation-states. That emphasis on local ties, of course, encompassed
more than community. Family was also a critical component of

eighteenth-century Creek local life, particularly for structuring political relations within a community. But the historical record's limitations mean we will never have anything other than an abstract sense of what this meant for particular people living in a particular community in the colonial era. Those limitations reflect European ignorance and bias, but they also can be traced to how Creeks presented themselves. Creeks active at the intercommunity and international levels routinely self-identified as members of particular communities, not of families or clans. Unlike their northern Native contemporaries, when Creeks practiced politics outside of their communities, they very rarely claimed to be representing their families, and they almost never signed documents with clan symbols. As a result, my sources are filled with community references but contain only rare hints about families. It is, thus, par for the course to know that Acorn Whistler was a Little Okfuskee but to have no idea about his clan identity.

All of which points us toward a critical fact: family was an issue in Creek politics, but not the central one. Relations between communities and nations were family inflected, not family based. If Creek politics was a language, family provided the accent but community was the syntax. Individuals and corporate groups drew on family for both technologies (descent; adoption) to establish relationships and a vocabulary (brothers and fathers; mothers and daughters) to describe those relationships. Those bonds, however, knit together either communities or their representatives, and those relationships were emphatically community centered. It was the communities' interests that structured the course and content of those relationships, and the communities' leaders—self-consciously and publicly acting as such—were the ones who formed those ties, maintained them, and, if necessary, broke them. As a result, our ignorance about Acorn Whistler's family life is unfortunate but not debilitating. The simple fact that he had a clan (as all Creeks did) tells us a great deal about the family-related events of 1752. If we did not know Acorn Whistler's town, however, we would be at sea, unable to make sense of the local story about why he had to die.

Understanding that story requires recognizing that "local" does not imply "small-scale" or "nearby." This local story centers on the personal and political ties invoked by family and community, but, for Creeks, those bonds were not confined to people who lived in the neighborhood. Clan ties extended throughout Creek country, and even an apparently small-scale geographic entity like a community was an expansive thing. Town-based relationships bound people who lived far apart. For example, Okfuskee was on the Tallapoosa River, but Okfuskees also lived in talofas sixty miles east on the Chattahoochee River, closer to Malatchi's Coweta than Okfuskee. These villagers remained Okfuskees because of their continued participation in the rituals enacted in Okfuskee's square ground, particularly those focused on the town's sacred fire. And, in fact, Okfuskees extended their community east beyond the Chattahoochee to the Atlantic. Among Creeks, "Oakfuskee and Charles Town was always reckoned as one"; their inhabitants were "one People and one Fire." Of course, Okfuskees were well aware that Charleston's people had no intention of participating in Okfuskee's rites. But the Okfuskees also knew that community metaphors and communal feelings—if not community identity—could encompass the British town dwellers in South Carolina's capital.[8]

What unified this Creek system and what made it work was a commitment to engaging the world through "local" processes: the intimate, face-to-face, personal relations invoked by family and community and extended—depending on the issue at hand and the desires of those involved—to people in other places. Those relationships were phrased in terms of family and community bonds linking individuals and corporate groups, and so they were recognizably extensions of the relations that structured Creek daily life. "Local," then, references not just family and community but also familial and communal; it implicates not just the "real" bonds linking kinspeople and townspeople but also the "fictive" ones that created new relatives and recognized expanded communities. "Local" is necessarily tied to place but it is also broadly expansive. In using the word in this way, I follow the example of Creeks who sought connections with distant others through the same processes they used when near hearth and home.

Within Creek country, there were, of course, many local stories about why Acorn Whistler had to die. The Osochis had a story, as did the Cowetas; but I can recover neither because Osochi appears so rarely in the records, and Malatchi so dominates those records that his narrative eclipses that of his Cowetas. And Little Okfuskee? Its people had their stories—How could they not?—but I have almost no clue what they were. The stories told by the people most modern Americans would recognize as Acorn Whistler's "real" family and community are lost. There is, though, a story that can be both uncovered in the records and tied to Acorn Whistler's local connections. It centers on Okfuskee, but like all Creek local stories, it draws on far-flung family ties and community relationships. And this Okfuskee story almost certainly overlaps with those told in Little Okfuskee because neither Little Okfuskee's status as a Tallapoosa talwa near the French fort nor its ties to Wolf of Muccolossus were enough to remove Acorn Whistler's town from Okfuskee's local networks.

Exploring this local story brings into focus the concerns of Creek people at midcentury. It suggests that their central worry had relatively little to do—at least initially—with Europeans. We are used to reading Indian histories that foreground culture conflict with Europeans, aggression by Europeans, and dispossession at the hands of Europeans. That Okfuskee's eighteenth-century town site now sits at the bottom of the Lake Martin reservoir and modern-day Okfuskee is in Oklahoma, over seven hundred miles west of its people's flooded square ground, suggests that those more familiar histories do not lie. Those histories, though, do not do justice to this local story because they ignore the critical fact that, at this point in their history, the Creeks were powerful, confident people who had long since found ways to incorporate the Europeans into their town-based system of diplomatic and political maneuvering.

This local story about Acorn Whistler, then, most definitely includes Europeans, but they appear in the narrative in much the same way as the Cherokees do. For these Creek storytellers, their Native and European neighbors were allies to be managed or rivals to be dealt with. In either case, their actions could be profoundly threatening to certain Creek interest groups—that is, to specific local networks—but the Creeks had no reason to believe that either set of neighbors endangered the Creek system's fundamental integrity. As a result, while no Creek at midcentury dreamed of ignoring the Europeans, no Creek would make these newcomers the protagonists in Creek local stories. That place was reserved for fellow Creeks, and especially for a family and community's traditional rivals in other Creek families and communities. There was, in short, little in Creek experience to suggest that local stories should center on anything but local variables—on the storytellers' local networks, on their rivals' own local connections, and on the ways those competing systems of local alliance and affiliation were effected by the issues of the day.

What of Creeks like Malatchi who sought to subsume the local within larger, nation-like structures? The local storytellers interpreted such ambitions through local lenses. Malatchi's project was seen in Okfuskee as a Coweta power grab, both because the Okfuskee storytellers were predisposed to see the world that way and because Malatchi used his Coweta-based local networks to facilitate his national project. But if Malatchi's plan could be seen by the Okfuskees as a variation on a familiar theme, that did not mean that these local storytellers found his plans unthreatening. It did mean, though, that Malatchi could be beaten at his own game. Malatchi's attempt at mobilizing local networks to aggrandize power and influence could be neutralized or defeated by crafting new stories that called upon other local networks. Doing so would be challenging at a practical level, but it would not present Okfuskee's local storytellers with an existential challenge. This was the way they expected their world to work.

If all that sounds like the local story of Acorn Whistler's death was less fraught than the imperial or national one, I agree. Unlike Glen or Malatchi, the local storytellers were charting a course within an established system, not trying to craft a new one. It is tempting, in fact, to describe these localists as "conservatives" or "traditionalists," but labels of that sort obscure more than they reveal. These storytellers participated in a system of social organization that privileged fluidity and innovation. Okfuskee vs. Coweta was a relatively recent development, as was the Okfuskee-Charleston bond. New rivalries and new alliances would, the local storytellers knew, emerge over time because such relationships were at once real and transient—grounded in the enduring reality of family and community but subject to the machinations of individuals and the shifting agendas of corporate groups. As a result, Creek "traditionalists" deployed traditions that emphasized creativity, and Creek "conservatives" sought to conserve flexibility. Creeks knew that human agency mattered, that people—in conjunction with rituals and symbols that called on other-than-human powers—could reshape their world. In fact, this emphasis on creative traditionalism rooted in local understandings goes a long way toward explaining the fact that Okfuskee and other Creek talwas endure as meaningful sociopolitical units into the modern day. The sun did eventually set on the British empire, and it never rose on Malatchi's version of the Creek nation. But sacred fires—in Creek cosmology, local manifestations of the sun—still burn in talwas throughout Creek country.[9]

~ 5

The Family and Community

ONE OF THE UPPER CREEKS who profited from Acorn Whistler's 1744 visit to Charleston was Dog King of Eufaula. He did not accompany the Little Okfuskee, but he still received a looking glass from the British traders who escorted the Creek diplomats home. That party included three Little Okfuskees and the "Chief of ye Oakfuskees." It was, in short, an Okfuskee-heavy group, and the gift that Dog King of Eufaula received because of their journey speaks to the entangling and expansive nature of Okfuskee's local networks. Dog King was an Okfuskee headman in the 1720s and early 1730s, routinely representing the town in its dealings with outsiders. Suddenly, in 1734, he began to appear in the records as a headman from Eufaula, a town five miles from Okfuskee.[1] Even in his new talwa, however, Dog King's life remained intertwined with Okfuskee. Some of this stemmed from garden-variety neighborhood issues—as when Okfuskee's trader, Alexander Wood, shot Dog King's cattle—but Dog King also remained part of Okfuskee's political world. He was, for example, in contact with a British officer based in Okfuskee, and he visited Charleston with Okfuskee's "King" and "Head Warrior" in 1739. Dog King died just before the Okfuskees' 1749 trip to Charleston, but his son (also a Eufaula) accompanied the Okfuskees. The mirror that Dog King received in 1744, then, was simply the material residue of a sociopolitical fact: Dog King left Okfuskee, but he remained enmeshed in its local networks.[2]

The same was true of Dog King's contemporary, Acorn Whistler. At a distance of more than two hundred and fifty years, his relationship to Okfuskee is somewhat opaque, but certainly it went well beyond simply living in that talwa's namesake. Consider that Acorn Whistler was likely what we would call middle-aged in 1752, senior enough to command men and tell James Glen that "I am now old and cannot hunt as I used to do," but junior enough to be almost universally described as a war leader and to have Glen respond to his claims of decrepitude by noting that "He does not seem to be so old. I do not see one gray Hair upon him." Acorn Whistler's age matters because, if he was middle-aged in 1752, then he was not born in Little Okfuskee, a town founded just twenty to twenty-five years before. Little Okfuskee people "brought their first fires" from Okfuskee, and so Acorn Whistler likely was born an Okfuskee. He may have lived there for several decades.[3]

It is entirely appropriate, therefore, that the few glimpses that we have of Acorn Whistler show him acting in Okfuskee's shadow. Thus, we first notice Acorn Whistler when Okfuskee's trader, Alexander Wood, recommended that Acorn Whistler and his fellow Okfuskee expatriate Dog King receive British commissions. Three years later, Acorn Whistler accompanied at least one Okfuskee headman to Charleston only a few months after South Carolina officials arranged for Wood—who chaperoned Acorn Whistler's traveling party—to build Fort Bull in Okfuskee. Five years after that, Acorn Whistler's deadly intervention in the 1749 Creek-Cherokee negotiations short-circuited an Okfuskee-led peace initiative and killed Okfuskee-allied Hiwassees.

And in 1752? As we will see later, Okfuskees were intimately involved in every stage of the crisis that followed the April 1 attack. For now, though, it is enough to note that even seemingly minor details from Acorn Whistler's 1752 trip point back to Okfuskee. Take Jeremiah Knott, who Glen hoped would escort Acorn Whistler's people back to Creek country. Knott traded in Okfuskee and gave "Provisions" to the 1749 Okfuskee party "on the Road" home; several years later, Glen wrote that another Upper Creek party that included Okfuskees "may probably be prevailed upon" to come to Knott's house. Knott's brother-in-law and the "Patroon" of his "Trading Boat" was John Baxter, another Okfuskee trader, and Knott's partner was Alexander Wood, Okfuskee's fort-building, commission-procuring, cattle-shooting trader. Or take William Bull, who Acorn Whistler visited on the way to Charleston and who provided him with supplies after he fled South Carolina's capital. Okfuskee's Fort Bull was named for William when he was lieutenant governor because, as he put it, "I did propose, and prevailed with" the Upper Creek headmen to approve the project; four years earlier, he gave rich presents to Okfuskee's mico and head warrior. All of which suggests that Acorn Whistler had not succeeded—if he tried at all—in extricating himself from Okfuskee's local world.[4]

And that was a problem for the Okfuskees because people looking at Acorn Whistler could easily see Okfuskee. Yes, Okfuskees could argue that connecting the aforementioned events in Acorn Whistler's life to their town required ignoring some mitigating factors. Acorn Whistler received his 1741 commission at the intercession of Okfuskee's British trader, not its headmen. Acorn Whistler joined the 1744 party of his own accord, not at Okfuskee's invitation. Acorn Whistler's 1749 attack on the Cherokees was most emphatically not sanctioned by Okfuskee. Acorn Whistler's intended escort, Jeremiah Knott, lived on the road to Augusta, and so he did not accompany Acorn Whistler's Upper Creeks, who went home via Palachucola. Acorn Whistler's benefactor, William Bull, also hosted—as the various stories in this book demonstrate—Creeks from Cusseta, Tuckabatchee, Osochi, and Yuchi in 1752. It took a certain amount of creativity, Okfuskees could note, to make these incidents point to Okfuskee. Anyone seeking to do so was orienting discrete pieces of evidence in one direction when each piece could, in another's hands, easily point somewhere else.[5]

For the Okfuskee storytellers, though, the problem was that they were surrounded by creative people who had both motives for telling stories that tied Acorn Whistler to Okfuskee and access to the facts necessary to craft convincing tales. And, to make matters worse, the events of April 1, 1752, gave those people even more reason to emphasize that relationship. In other words, the local story told in

Okfuskee would have to deal with an inescapable fact: Acorn Whistler was not an Okfuskee in 1752, but he was Okfuskee's problem.

⟨ UNDERSTANDING THAT LOCAL STORY requires reorienting ourselves regarding the basic facts of the April 1, 1752, attack. Up until now, I have repeatedly said that Osochis attacked Cherokees at Governor Glen's gate. The Okfuskee storytellers would not have described the attack in that way. They would have granted each statement of fact, but they would have thought that, in harping on these details, I missed the point. From their perspective, these details provide, in turn, too much information, not enough information, and the wrong information. For these local storytellers, what needed to be said was that Lower Creeks attacked Estatoes on White Ground. Taking the time to consider each of those facts allows us to understand the perspective these Okfuskees brought to the Acorn Whistler crisis.

"Lower Creeks"

To be sure, when the Okfuskees who told this local story first heard of the attack, one of their initial questions likely was "What town did the attackers come from?" Once they learned the answer, though, they almost certainly started referring to the Osochi perpetrators as Lower Creeks. After all, Okfuskee had no formal relationship with Osochi, and no rivalry either. For Okfuskee and its offshoots, Osochi was simply a middling-sized Lower Creek town. Its people were best described as Acorn Whistler did: "the Lower Creeks" or "the Lower People." Anything more was, in this case, too much information.[6]

If the attackers had been from Coweta, the Okfuskees' reaction would have been markedly different. Coweta was important enough that Creeks everywhere paid attention to its people's doings, and Okfuskees were particularly attuned to news about Coweta. Okfuskees and Cowetas were rivals, a fact of life that was an accepted part of the region's political landscape. Perhaps the rivalry began with the Creeks moiety system. "White" Okfuskee opposed "Red" Coweta, with the result that Okfuskees who participated in Coweta's initiatives tended to be war leaders, not the town's civil headmen; Coweta's war and peace leaders followed a similar pattern when dealing with Okfuskee. Or perhaps the towns' antipathy stemmed from geography, with Okfuskee serving as the Upper Creeks' eastern gateway while Coweta occupied the same place in Lower Creek country. The path linking the Creeks to the British colonies split in two before reaching Creek country. The northern or "upper path" was often called the Okfuskee Path, while the "lower path" was the Coweta Path. Creeks disagreed about which should be privileged. Those who claimed that the path "from Charlestown to the Couaties" was "the Old White Path" were not popular in Okfuskee, whose people were deeply invested in the notion that their path was Old and White.[7]

Whether the Okfuskee-Coweta rivalry stemmed from geography or social structure, however, the tension between the two towns was enduring. As a result, Okfuskees habitually monitored Coweta and worked to counteract Coweta initiatives. In 1723, for example, Okfuskees refused to listen to Cowetas who claimed to be passing along South Carolina's talks, and those same Okfuskees told South Carolina's leaders about the Cowetas' anti-British statements. Later that decade, three Okfuskees signed a talk blaming Chigelly of Coweta for the death of a British trader while Coweta's Long Warrior brought a scalp to Okfuskee and taunted the "Head Warr King Okefuskeys" that it was from "One of your own Family," killed at Britain's behest. At the same time, Okfuskees and Cowetas disagreed over how to respond to South Carolina's demands that they attack the Yamasees. Okfuskee's Dog King joined another headman in sending "very severe Messages down . . . to the Cowetas . . . threatening them that if they did not comply with their Promises to the English [to make war on the Yamasees] that they would oblige them to do it. Telling them that they had several times brought the Tallipooses and Aubickaws into trouble by their Roguish doings, but that they would take care of them for the future."[8]

Relations between the towns continued in that vein for a century—so long, in fact, that the rivalry became self-perpetuating, grounded as much in historical grievances and personal animus as in the realities of geography or the dictates of Creek social structure. Thus, on the eve of the American Revolution, Cowetas boycotted three conferences called by Okfuskee's Handsome Fellow, who then refused to attend "a Fourth Meeting at the Cowetas." The next year, Cujesse Mico of Okfuskee told a British agent both that "we are not concerned with the Cowetas" and that the Upper Creeks in general did not "desire to have any Thing to Say to the Cowetas." His grandparents' generation would have sympathized, and his grandchildren's generation carried the rivalry forward. One of the latter, in fact, took the lead in executing a Coweta headman in 1828.[9]

Given that history, it should come as no surprise that, as the Acorn Whistler crisis unfolded, it was widely understood that both Okfuskee and Coweta had to be courted to ensure success. That fact was reflected, for example, in the 1751 decision of Georgia officials to send the Creeks two flags, "One to the Oakfuskees the other to the Cowetaw." Likewise, the next year, the Lower Creeks demanded that the Cherokees "will send two of their People as Hostages for the Peace over to the Cowetas and another to the Oakfusskees," while Okfuskee's Red Coat King insisted in 1753 that peace depended on the Cherokees giving the Creeks two captives, "one to be sent to the Cowetas and the other to the Oakfuskees." These gifts and demands can be read as an acknowledgment that Cowetas and Okfuskees did not work or play well together, of course, but they also attest to the fact that neither town would cede precedence to the other. Okfuskees and Cowetas, in short, kept an eye on each other. If the attackers on April 1, 1752, had been Cowetas, then Okfuskees most certainly would have taken notice.[10]

The attention Okfuskees paid to Coweta extended to the Cowetas' allies, particularly their nearest and dearest Upper Creek partners, the Tuckabatchees. Okfuskees knew that, in Okfuskee Captain's words, "Tuccobatchey . . . is a Friend Town to Coweta." Like Coweta, Tuckabatchee was a red town. Moreover, like Coweta, Tuckabatchee relied on the lower path; in fact, Creeks who argued that the Old White Path went from Charleston to Coweta invariably stated that it went "from thence to ye Taukabatchees." Okfuskees knew that involving Tuckabatchee in an initiative helped to win Coweta's support, and no Okfuskee was shocked when Cowetas and Tuckabatchees looked out for each other's interests. The relationship was enduring enough that a Creek noted in 1901, "It is taught to the young people from the cradle, as it were, to keep this friendship sacred. These two towns never oppose each other in anything." And the relationship was intimately intertwined with the towns' dealings with "the English at Charleston" because, as a Tuckabatchee headman noted, "Coweta first took them by the hand, and [Tuckabatchee] next."[11]

That assertion hinted at another reason Okfuskees believed Tuckabatchees had to be watched: their tendency to claim precedence in dealings with the British. As Tuckabatchee's mico emeritus put it in 1759, "It was I & my Warriours that used always to go down to Charlestown, and make up any Differences between the White People & us." Mad Dog of Tuckabatchee made the point even more clearly: "This Town was always looked upon as a Friend Town to the English. [I]t was this Town that made the Peace with them, whatever others pretend to." Okfuskees, familiar with these boasts, knew what it meant, therefore, when the one member of Acorn Whistler's Upper Creek party who did not flee Charleston turned out to be Folutka of Tuckabatchee. Glen praised Folutka for "the Confidence he has put in the English," but the governor was, as usual, being Anglocentric. Folutka had confidence in Tuckabatchee, its history, and the relationships its people could call upon when necessary.[12]

Okfuskees knew that Folutka was wrong, if not about his safety in Charleston then about the meaning of Tuckabatchee's history. Okfuskees were certain that their talwa enjoyed pride of place in the Creeks' dealings with Charleston. They said as much repeatedly— which explains Mad Dog of Tuckabatchee's statement about "whatever others pretend to"—and they had solid reasons for doing so. Okfuskee was, after all, a white town. As such, it was an appropriate partner for Charleston, which Creeks and colonists alike routinely described as a white town in its own right. In addition, Okfuskee's location on the upper path and on the Upper Creeks' eastern frontier gave its people unmediated access to, and a strong historical connection with, Charleston. As an Okfuskee headman put it, "I have always desired that the Path [] white from the Oakfuskees to Augusta and from thence to Charles Town, which [is an old] Town [and] we always had one [fire?]. This is not a new Friendship, it was from [the] Time [that] Charles Town was settled on the Edge of the

Marsh, when it was allowed by our Fathers that the white people should build a Town there & that we their Children should be one people." For reasons historical, political, and geographic, Okfuskees were, in a very real way, "at home" in Charleston.[13]

In fact, one of the strongest arguments Okfuskees could have made about their lack of responsibility for Acorn Whistler was that he fled Charleston. From an Okfuskee perspective, that was the sort of thing Osochis did and Tuckabatchees should do, but not Okfuskees. That Folutka of Tuckabatchee did not flee demonstrated that his town and its Coweta friends required watching. But the Osochis? Of course they behaved badly while in Charleston and then took to their heels. What, the Okfuskees might have asked, did you expect from Lower Creeks?

"attacked Estatoes"

If referring to April 1's attackers as Osochis gave Okfuskees more information than they needed, then describing the victims as "Cherokees" deprived Okfuskee's local storytellers of necessary data. Put simply, it mattered that the Cherokees in question were "chiefly" from Estatoe. That town "had long preserved kinship with the Creeks as a kind of insurance against aggression." This policy was embodied by Estatoe Mico, the son of Okfuskee's leading headman. His title showed that he had been adopted by the Estatoes to represent their concerns to the Creeks, a role that fused kinship connections and corporate identities. In keeping with those relationships, he took part in the Okfuskee-led delegation that traveled to Charleston in 1749 to make peace with the Cherokees, whose representatives included a headman linked to Estatoe. It is not clear what part the two men played in the ensuing negotiations, although Glen noted that Estatoe Mico's father, Red Coat King of Okfuskee, "had the greatest hand in bringing about the Peace." That was entirely appropriate since peace was built upon the sort of bonds—at once communal, familial, and international—that united Estatoe and Okfuskee.[14]

The 1749 Creek-Cherokee peace was, of course, dead on arrival, done in first by Acorn Whistler's attack on Okfuskee's allies in the Cherokee town of Hiwassee and then by Malatchi's more sustained campaign against the Lower Cherokees. Estatoe suffered horribly in the rekindled war, most notably in May 1750 when "between 4 and 5 Hundred of the Lower Creeks" burned half the town and "kill[e]d most of the Men." By 1752, the town's situation remained grim enough that the townspeople killed outside of Charleston on April 1 were the least of the Estatoes' worries. Writing to Glen to acknowledge his letter regarding that attack, an Estatoe headman joined with the leader of a neighboring town to tell Glen that "we have lost" thirty-three more "of our People" and that "We expect every Night that we shall be killed before Morning." For his part, Estatoe's British trader wrote that "I can't see how they will be able to plant themselves a Morcel of Provisions" because the "Enemy is so hard on them"; he was "afraid that they can't stand it much longer." Estatoe was in danger of breaking apart.[15]

The war also made itself felt in Creek country. Okfuskee's losses rivaled those of any Creek town. A Cherokee war party killed an Okfuskee "of a great Family . . . not far from the Town" in 1750, and then Cherokees killed "some Okfusskee Men" the following summer. Three more Okfuskees died at Cherokee hands in the winter of 1751–1752, and the Cherokee's northern Indian allies did their own damage. One raiding party took "two Scalps" and captured an Okfuskee "fellow and his Wife and Child"; the father and child were rescued, but the townswoman died in the attempt. At the same time, Okfuskee's hunters were driven in from their traditional hunting grounds near Cherokee country, leaving the Okfuskees to deal with the economic consequences of "Poor Hunts." No wonder that, just before the April 1 attack, Glen recalled that Okfuskee's Red Coat King had "compared War to a Wood on Fire. He said at first it might be extinguished, but if permitted to spread far and wide, it consumed all before it." Okfuskee had been badly singed by this war, and Estatoe was all but consumed by it.[16]

These tragedies, however, were not enough to destroy the Estatoe-Okfuskee relationship, although we can—at this distance—discover only hints of their interactions. While Acorn Whistler was in Charleston, for example, a Chickasaw headman asked two Estatoes to carry a talk to Estatoe and its neighboring town; he promised to finalize peace and "send a Runner to the Okfuskees" once the

Cherokees fulfilled their obligations. Four years later, two Okfuskee headmen on their way to Charleston chose to deliver a talk in Estatoe. One of those Okfuskees was either Estatoe Mico or his brother, and in echo of the bonds invoked by that title, a British trader who dealt with Okfuskee seems to have befriended a British trader based in Estatoe. Perhaps that friendship was merely a coincidence, but for the people living in Estatoe Mico's hometown in the 1750s Estatoe was not just another Cherokee town. As a result, we can be certain that soon after an Estatoe headman complained that the April 1 attack had "sprinkled" the "Path . . . with the Blood of our People," Okfuskees would have discussed what that Estatoe blood signified.[17]

To make matters more alarming for Acorn Whistler's family and community, they knew that the surviving Estatoes would have reported not just the attack but also the events leading up to it. While in Charleston, Acorn Whistler's party and the Cherokees participated in a ritual featuring an adoption-like process. The Creeks and Cherokees exchanged clothing and food before shaking hands and smoking together "in the most Solemn Manner." In doing so, they followed "the usuall method that they who are strangers use in contracting Friendships dureing their Travells." Such relationships, especially if solemnized by the "exchange [of] the clothes then upon them," were valued. One trader noted that "they cherish" such "friendship" and "in general, will maintain it to the death," a perspective nicely summed up by a Cherokee's statement that "you are his Brother indeed for he was naked and you cloathed him." Rather than embracing these personal bonds, however, the Lower Creeks drew on these traditions to set up the April 1 attack. They caught up with the Cherokees on the path, claimed to be "Friends and Brothers," and "pulled the Feathers off their own Heads and put them on the Heads of the Cherokees." And then, with the Cherokees "imagining no kind of Guile or Knavery," the Lower Creeks parted with them, "came softly back," and opened fire.[18]

Acorn Whistler's family and community certainly knew that, rhetoric about cherishing friends aside, these things happened. Relationships formed by human agency could be annulled by human agents; Creek tradition sanctioned both the creation of enduring bonds and the severing of those ties. Okfuskees also knew, however, that breaking such relationships was a politically charged act, the kind of thing you did only in the most pressing of circumstances and only when you needed to send a message that could not be misinterpreted. The Estatoes could very easily have read the April 1, 1752, attack as delivering just such a message—"We Okfuskees have severed our ties to you, our former friends at Estatoe"—but the Okfuskees, of course, had no such point to make in the spring of 1752. They must have been anxious about what the Estatoes would make of the news from Charleston.

Acorn Whistler's involvement gave his local connections yet one more reason to worry about the dead Estatoes. After all, Acorn Whistler's 1749 expedition against Hiwassee meant that he had a history of killing Cherokees linked to Okfuskee. Acorn Whistler's responsibility for that assault was widely acknowledged. The Cherokees—who knew enough about the Hiwassee raid's backstory to accuse the French of bribing the Creek attackers—presumably understood that he was to blame. Likewise, the Estatoes who survived the April 1 attack had seen that Acorn Whistler spoke for the Creek party in the Charleston adoption ceremony; they would have brought his name back to Cherokee country. And, if by some chance they did not, Glen's letter telling the Cherokees of the April 1 attack began, "A few Days ago a Creek Headman of the Town of Little Oakfuske called by us the Acorn Whistler arrived here." There was, thus, every reason for Okfuskees to worry that the Cherokees would associate Acorn Whistler—and, by extension, the people in his local world—with the Charleston ceremony, the treacherous attack, and the dead Estatoes. For the Okfuskees, the fact that April 1's victims were not just Cherokees but Estatoes promised to turn a skirmish into a crisis.[19]

"on White Ground"

The location of the April 1 attack further underlined the danger Acorn Whistler's family and community suddenly confronted. The issue was not the proximity of Glen's house, although that was awkward, regrettable, and—given their ties to the British—something the Okfuskees could ill afford to ignore. At its core, though, the attack was not about Creek-British relations because the Lower

Creeks struck only after the Cherokees left the safety of South Carolina's beloved town of Charleston. Doing so moved the violence into the realm of Creek-Cherokee relations. And once that was the context, the story of the attack told by Acorn Whistler's family and community would have emphasized that Lower Creeks killed Estatoes at the spot where the 1749 Okfuskee-led peace delegation had camped and exchanged ceremonial visits with the Cherokees. Acorn Whistler's family and community, in other words, would have immediately recognized that blood had been spilled on White Ground.

How do we know that the Estatoes were killed at such a symbolically resonant spot? The April 1 attack took place on Burnham Grant, which bordered Glen's Belvedere estate and had been owned, in the early 1740s, by Nicholas Burnham. In 1741, Nicholas married Elizabeth Smith. They had no surviving children, and neither did any of Nicholas's five siblings, except for his sister Mary. Nicholas was dead by March 1747. His will left his "Estate both Real and Personal" to his nieces, Mary's young daughters, Margaret and Mary Elliott. Their father, Artimus Elliott, took over Burnham Grant in their names, making it Elliott property. The payoff for this excursion into Burnhamiana is that the 1749 Creek party led by the Okfuskees stayed "at Mr. Elliotts Pasture" while visiting Charleston, and Artimus Elliott was paid "for entertaining Indians on Charles town neck."[20] The Creeks' Cherokee negotiating partners in 1749 also camped nearby—to be precise, at Sarah Amory's New Market Plantation, a mile and half south of Elliott's pasture. Amory's husband had been a Cherokee trader, and Cherokees had camped on their land since at least 1740. Both Creeks and Cherokees clearly had a history in this neighborhood.[21]

It is, therefore, easy to imagine that, on April 1, 1752, the Estatoes were very comfortable on the public road. They walked by the old Cherokee campsite at New Market where some Estatoes had stayed in 1748. Perhaps they stopped to lay a pebble on a kinsman's grave—several Cherokees "died [of illness] at Mrs. Amorys" during the 1749 conference—before deciding "to rest and refresh themselves" where the Creeks had camped in 1749, a familiar spot and a safe one. It is easy to imagine, moreover, that the Lower Creeks knew "Mr. Elliotts Pasture" well enough to set an ambush for their new friends.

And, finally, it is easy to imagine that the Okfuskees were appalled when they learned of the Lower Creeks' desecration.[22]

No one recorded what transpired between the Creeks and Cherokees at "Mr. Elliotts Pasture" three years before the Estatoes died there in 1752, but such sites were critical components in ceremonies performed for the twin purposes of relationship-forming and peacemaking. Consider, for example, the Cherokees' experience during that 1749 conference with another group of attendees, the Catawbas. The Cherokees and Catawbas camped three miles apart outside of Charleston. Then,

> Messages were sent on both Sides, to signify their Desire of living in Friendship, and renewing their Peace. Their Messengers being returned to their respective Chiefs, both bodies march'd with the greatest Solemnity, and so slow, that they were three Hours going a Miles and a half each. When they were approach'd pretty near each other, the principal man of each Body, stript himself as naked as he was born, went forward, and embraced the other, and after a serous Discourse, standing hand-in-hand each put on the other's Clothes, which was followed by a great shout from both Nations. Then both Bodies join'd, and march'd in great Order, the Chiefs at their Head, down to the Camp of the Cherokees, where they all din'd; the next Day the Cherokees din'd with the Catawbaes at their Camp.

In other words, these two Native groups met halfway between their respective campsites, conducted an adoption ceremony on this neutral ground, and then exchanged ceremonial visits—"in great Order"—at the other's temporary home, where they sealed the relationship by exchanging food.[23]

The 1749 Creek and Cherokee ceremonies at "Mr. Elliotts Pasture" are unrecoverable, but the Okfuskees and Hiwassees had been engaged in intense symbolic exchanges for months prior to arriving in Charleston. Those exchanges built on a tangible geographic fact—the path linking their nations left Creek country at Okfuskee and arrived in Cherokee country at Hiwassee—and were embodied by the Okfuskee who was Tasata of Hiwassee's adopted "Son."

The Okfuskees began the gift giving by sending their townsman's Hiwassee father a conch shell. Creeks used these shells to hold a ceremonial beverage that functioned as both "the ultimate expression of hospitality" and a "social cement"; Okfuskees later named a village after this type of shell. Accompanying this powerful symbol was an Okfuskee present of "Corn & water million seed," which the Hiwassees planted. Tasata then told the Okfuskees that he "Expects that you'll be as good as your word to come and eat part of them with us as also anything that we have." And to complete the move away from war, the "Women of his Town" sent "the King of the Oakfuskees a White Flag [so] that when you and your People take hold of it you may think of him that his heart is straight towards you all and Expects that yours is the same."

Less than two months later, Okfuskees, Hiwassees, and their allies met outside of Charleston. This was their first chance to conduct rituals face-to-face, exchange clothing, and share food—all necessary steps in the creation of enduring personal and communal relationships (and the international peace that would flow from them). The Charleston meeting was also, not incidentally, the Okfuskees' first chance to console the Hiwassees about their losses from Acorn Whistler's attack earlier that summer, and to reassure their Cherokee kinsmen and friends that they deplored his actions. Components of these activities—conducting, exchanging, eating, consoling, and reassuring—certainly took place in "Mr. Elliotts Pasture." For those Okfuskees who cared about the relationships created in 1749, spilling blood there three years later was unforgivable.[24]

～ STEPPING BACK from this reexamination of the April 1 attack's details, the picture that emerges is a tidy one. In 1752, Okfuskees had clearly defined rivals and reliable allies, long-standing habits and identifiable predispositions. There was a logic to their past, a structure to their present, and a trajectory for their future. That is not, however, the whole story. In the middle of the eighteenth century, life in Creek country was many things, but it was not tidy. Okfuskee was no exception. Understanding the perspective of Okfuskee's local storytellers requires acknowledging that their world was not neat and orderly. To some extent, this messiness litters the ground we have covered, although I have not highlighted that fact. But what else to call the decisions by Dog King and Little Okfuskees' founders to leave Okfuskee? To be sure, I cannot be certain what motivated those decisions. Were these colonizing ventures or secessions? If—as I suspect—it was the latter, were the partings amicable or not? Whatever caused the moves, however, they point toward the need for a more nuanced view of Okfuskee, for recognition that it was not a stable, homogenous place.

In 1752, Okfuskee was every bit as complicated and fluid a community as it had been when Dog King and the Little Okfuskees left town a generation earlier. Okfuskees moved away from each other, pursued options that distinguished them from their townspeople, and told different stories.[25] Such is the nature of human society, of course, but it is worth acknowledging here because—unlike with Glen or Malatchi—we are dealing with storytellers, plural. The local story told in Okfuskee about Acorn Whistler was woven out of many stories. These disparate narratives only merged together later, and then tentatively and partially. We do not, in other words, have to accept Sartre's dictum that "Hell is other people" to recognize that storytelling within a family and community was a messy business.

The messiness inherent in the Okfuskee's local story was exacerbated by the fact that even Okfuskees who never moved to other towns or villages were not confined to their home talwa. Individuals left Okfuskee for a variety of reasons, came back, and brought disorder with them. Consider another bit of untidiness which I have, again, mentioned but not underlined: in 1746, Malatchi requested that Glen give a British commission to Okfuskee's Mad Warrior. I discussed the request as an example of Malatchi deploying Creek traditions of alliance-building. Fair enough, but, in light of this chapter's discussion of the Okfuskee-Coweta rivalry, too simple by half. And, to further the messiness, this 1746 incident was not the first time a Coweta arranged for an Okfuskee to receive a British commission. In 1723, Malatchi's elder brother "delivered to the Oakfuskee King the Commission that was sent for him," even as other Okfuskees blackened this Coweta's name to South Carolina's governor. In reaching out to traditional rivals, both the commission-procuring Cowetas and the commission-receiving Okfuskees pursued avenues for forging alliances and acquiring influence that their townspeople had either rejected or overlooked. Creek political science allowed for creativity of this sort, but there is no escaping the fact that such initiatives unsettled and complicated a community's life.[26]

In 1723, for example, as Okfuskee King received the Coweta-procured commission, Dog King of Okfuskee pointedly said that he "did not hear [the Coweta's] Talk." Five years later, it was Dog King who threatened the Cowetas that he would force them to live up to their promises to the British. Was Dog King's departure from Okfuskee a few years after that determined by the fact that Okfuskee's "King" had accepted a Coweta's gift? Likewise, in 1752, Okfuskee Captain—who had recently stopped being known as Mad Warrior—became the town's first headman to publicly support Malatchi's story about Acorn Whistler's execution. Were his actions in 1752 determined by the commission he received courtesy of Malatchi in 1746? The answer to both questions is "No." But change the verbs in each question from "determined" to "influenced" and the answers shift to "quite possibly" (for Dog King) and "almost certainly" (for Okfuskee Captain). All of which means that the Okfuskees' local story was inevitably complicated by their townspeople's willingness to seek allies in unlikely places.[27]

And every now and then, the town as a corporate group acted in ways that demonstrated that, in the Okfuskee world, structure and habit coexisted with strange bedfellows and one-off alliances. Take Okfuskee's relations with the Lower Creek town of Cusseta. There was little to suggest that these two towns would be allies. Cusseta was Coweta's closest neighbor, and "the Cussetuhs and Cowetas were one fire." Like Coweta, moreover, Cusseta was a red town that relied on the lower path, and Cowetas and Cussetas frequently—although not invariably—worked together. Structurally, geographically, and politically, then, there was not much for Okfuskees to work with in Cusseta's case. And yet Okfuskee and Cusseta were allies for generations.[28]

Okfuskee-Cusseta ties may have begun with clan connections among the towns' headmen. In later years, each town selected its micos from the Bear Clan and its "second men" from the Wind Clan. Whether the townspeople did the same in the eighteenth century or not, the Okfuskee-Cusseta bond surfaced in a wide variety of contexts during Acorn Whistler's lifetime. In the 1720s, for example, Cussetas and Okfuskees adopted complementary positions in the Creek debate over attacking the Yamasees, and both towns were seen by imperial officials as particularly pro-British. When Cussetas and Okfuskees did disagree in 1727 over a Cherokee peace, Okfuskees still relayed Cusseta's concerns to the Cherokees. The Cherokees, in fact, were familiar enough with the towns' relationship by 1725 that they made plans "to goe [to war] against Okefuskee and Cusetaw." By the early 1740s, Cusseta and Okfuskee had headmen named Red Coat King, a title which was confined to these two towns and hinted at the widespread tradition of exchanging clothes to seal friendships.[29]

And as with the Okfuskee-Coweta rivalry, the Okfuskee-Cusseta bond outlived Acorn Whistler. During the American Revolution, for example, Okfuskees and Cussetas worked together to rally pro-American Creeks, a process that led them to describe their communities as "Friend Towns" and that involved Cussetas claiming Handsome Fellow of Okfuskee as a "Relation." In fact, the Okfuskee-Cusseta bond extended into the nineteenth century, as can be seen most clearly in the title carried by an Okfuskee head warrior: Cusseta Tuskeinchau. That honorific, of course, attested to his role in linking Okfuskee, his natal community, to the people of Cusseta, who had adopted him. And as significant as that relationship sounds, it actually went much, much deeper. Cusseta Tuskeinchau of Okfuskee was the brother of the Okfuskee who referred to Cusseta as a friend town during the Revolution; the nephew of the Okfuskee who Cussetas claimed as a "Relation"; and the grandson of Red Coat King, Okfuskee's mico and perhaps the adopted kinsman of Cusseta's own Red Coat King in the 1740s. Both Cusseta Tuskeinchau's title and his family's history, in short, were enmeshed in Okfuskee's long-standing relationship to Cusseta.[30]

The enduring nature of that bond lifts us from the messiness of Okfuskee's world and returns us to structure, habit, and, finally, order. The Okfuskee-Cusseta relationship was ad hoc, even messy;

but that did not mean that it was, in Creek terms, disorderly. For Okfuskee's local storytellers, fluidity and tradition were not mutually exclusive concepts, and neither were creativity and stability. These Okfuskees knew that no alliance between towns was unassailable, that no bond between individuals was unbreakable. They understood that what endured were not particular relationships but rather the social processes that Creeks embraced and the social categories that Creeks privileged. Communities, families, and friends came together and broke apart in certain predictable ways. They always had; they always would.

All of which is to say that the Okfuskee storytellers understood that their world was structured by concepts that were consistent and neat, even as they knew that the sociopolitical milieu called into being by those concepts was neither. Cusseta and Okfuskee were not natural allies, but that did not make their long-lasting alliance unnatural. Coweta and Okfuskee were always rivals and, at times, came close to being enemies, but Malatchi of Coweta and Okfuskee Captain could be friends. Okfuskee and Hiwassee were friend towns, but Okfuskees might one day have reason to kill Hiwassees. Reasonable Creeks could embrace these seeming contradictions because they understood that their social system relied on protocols and traditions, not laws and holy writ.[31]

Those same reasonable Creeks brought those same habits of mind to bear on the Acorn Whistler crisis. By any reasonable application of Creek categories for ordering the world, Acorn Whistler was not an Okfuskee. But no reasonable Okfuskee would have argued that the town could afford to ignore the messiness inherent in the events of April 1, 1752. Acorn Whistler was connected to both Okfuskee and the Lower Creeks who killed Estatoes on White Ground. And because of those connections, the Okfuskees would need a story.

~ 6

The Family and
Community's Story

$\mathcal{M}$ALATCHI DID NOT initially see the April 1 attack as a problem. The Okfuskees did. How could they not? Acorn Whistler, a man whose biography tied him not only to Okfuskee but also to recent efforts to kill Okfuskee's Cherokee friends, arrived in Charleston with a party of Creeks. They first took part in an adoption ceremony with Cherokees from Okfuskee's friend town of Estatoe and then ambushed those same friends at the spot where an Okfuskee-led delegation had recently conducted ceremonies of friendship and peace with the Cherokees. And then Acorn Whistler and his people fled. Only the sunniest of optimists could argue that those facts did not add up to an alarming situation for Okfuskee. A war with the Cherokees that had already brought death and hardship to the town would now get hotter.

If the contemporary records are to be believed, however, the Okfuskees did not start telling stories about the crisis until Okfuskee Captain spoke at the Tuckabatchee conference of September 21, 1752. The Creek talks on that day began with a statement by the mico of Little Okfuskee's neighboring town confirming that, after the British demand for satisfaction was made at Coweta, "it was agreed at the Cusetaw Town by his own Relations that the Blood of the Ac[orn] Whistler should be spilt for Satisfaction to the English."

Then, Okfuskee Captain told his story. Here it is, in its entirety: "his own Relations and a very great Man had suffered Death for Satisfaction to the English, and that he was very contented that he should suffer Death, in order to prevent those Tears that must have flowed in Case of a Breach of Friendship with the English which he hoped would never happen." And that, apparently, was the first thing the Okfuskees had to say about the April 1 attack. That was their first story, if the records are to be believed.[1]

There is, however, no reason to think the records are accurate. After all, those same records suggest not only that the Okfuskees' first story emerged almost six months after the April 1 attack but also that Okfuskees had nothing whatsoever to say about any topic during those months. The only document from April 1 to September 21 that references Okfuskees speaking comes from the pen of James Glen, whose instructions for Thomas Bosomworth quote Red Coat King's speech comparing war to a forest fire. But Red Coat King made that speech prior to April 1, 1752, which brings us back to the ridiculous image of the Okfuskees sitting silently in their square ground for months on end. No, the Okfuskees certainly began telling a story (and, quite possibly, more than one) about the April 1 attack as soon as the news of it reached town. And it is equally certain that Okfuskee Captain's September 21 version was not the story initially told in Okfuskee. What we hear on September 21 is the beginning of one version of the townspeople's second (or third? or fourth?) story, not their first. For that first story, we must examine the silences.[2]

Doing so requires taking April 1's events and their fallout, putting them into dialogue with what we know of Okfuskee's past and future, and extrapolating. It is not the most satisfying of processes. If the Okfuskees' larger story is worth hearing, however, then we have no choice but try to recover its first iteration by means of educated guesswork, always keeping in mind two things. First, that the alternative to informed inference is pretending that the Okfuskees sat in silence for almost six months. Second, that guesses, no matter how well grounded, can never replace the Okfuskee storytellers' own words. Their absence lingers, reminding us of how truly flawed our records are.

Look back over that speech by Okfuskee Captain and you will notice another absence: the Cherokees. Okfuskee Captain emphasized ties to the British, but he did not mention the people killed on April 1. We can be pretty confident that, in mid-April 1752, Okfuskees would not have told the story in this way. Within a few weeks of the April 1 attack, every Okfuskee would have known that Estatoes were killed on White Ground. The townspeople would also have been aware that Acorn Whistler was present in Charleston, appeared to lead the Creek party, and had a history of attacking Okfuskee's Cherokee friends. And, of course, no Okfuskee had to be told that Okfuskee had been at the center of Creek-Cherokee peace initiatives for years, and that the townspeople still hoped to forge such an agreement. By mid-April 1752, these were the key facts being talked about in Okfuskee. Taken together, they suggest that the Okfuskees' first story regarding the April 1 attack centered on their relationship to the Cherokees. Or at least that is my guess.

As Okfuskee Captain's speech demonstrates, that story would change. On August 16, news of Acorn Whistler's execution reached Okfuskee. The townspeople must have realized almost immediately that they had misread the situation and focused their first story on the wrong people. The long-term problem they faced was not Cherokee revenge but Coweta ambition and British bad faith. The Okfuskees' second story would have some very pointed things to say on those subjects. That story could not save Acorn Whistler, of course, and that likely did not bother the Okfuskee storytellers. They could believe that Acorn Whistler did not deserve death—they could even be furious that he was executed—and still not miss having him around. In life, Acorn Whistler had been a thorn in their collective side. In death, he left the Okfuskees to deal with angry Cherokees, inattentive Britons, and resurgent Cowetas. That trifecta endangered the local networks that secured the Okfuskees' place in both Creek country and the region as a whole. And so the headman whom Malatchi and Glen blamed for the April 1 attack became expendable, as did his reputation. The second Okfuskee story that emerged from this crisis would waste as few words as possible on that man. The Okfuskees intended to restore the status quo ante Acorn Whistler. The price for doing so was his blood and his good (sic?) name.

⌒ GIVEN THE HISTORICAL RECORD'S HOLES, it makes sense to begin discussing the Okfuskees' first story with two subjects the Okfuskees likely did not talk much about in the immediate aftermath of April 1. The first I have already mentioned: the British. Glen and his colony would have entered into the Okfuskees' first story to some extent because of the attack's location, but the Okfuskees would not have been too worried about the British reaction. Yes, Acorn Whistler was involved; and, yes, Acorn Whistler was an Upper Creek with ties to Okfuskee. But the attackers were Lower Creeks, and Glen's April 4 meeting with the Upper Creeks who were brought back to Charleston absolved Acorn Whistler's people of responsibility. Moreover, Glen's letter about December 1751's Coweta assault on the Cherokees likely arrived in Okfuskee just as the townspeople learned of the April 1 attack. In that letter, Glen blamed the "Lower Towns People" for the "Offence" of attacking Cherokees in South Carolina's settlements. The Okfuskees had every reason to think he would do the same with regard to April 1's sequel, and—as we have seen—they were right. Thus, from an Okfuskee perspective, it made sense to let the Lower Creeks worry about Glen and the British. The Okfuskees' story could focus on local matters.[3]

The other subject that Okfuskee's first storytellers likely passed over quickly was the Lower Creeks. My guess is that April 1's carnage did not immediately set Okfuskee tongues to wagging about those people. Although the Okfuskees would have discussed the attackers and their appalling tactics, no Okfuskee would have been shocked to hear of Lower Creeks killing Cherokees, and especially not Lower Cherokees like the Estatoes. The Lower Creeks and Lower Cherokees were at war, after all, and Lower Creeks had almost destroyed Estatoe two years before. All of which is to say that, when Okfuskees initially told a story about these incidents, Lower Creek involvement and Lower Creek guilt could be assumed, not explained or dwelt upon.

Instead, the townspeople's first story focused on April 1's implications for their relations with the Cherokees. They knew that, thanks to the events of April 1, a war that had already claimed too many Okfuskees was about to get worse. They were right. Approximately two weeks after the April 1 attack, Cherokees ambushed thirteen Okfuskees traveling to Augusta; twelve Okfuskees died. Another "Man [was] killed at the Oakfusskees" at roughly the same time. Add in the three Okfuskees scalped by Cherokees just before April 1, and the fortnight as a whole became Okfuskee's deadliest until 1814, when the Battle of Horseshoe Bend revealed Andrew Jackson's facility with ethnic cleansing. By mid-April 1752, then, Okfuskee was filled with mourning families and worried leaders. Anyone who tried to argue that the attack outside of Charleston was not a problem would have been lucky to be laughed out of town. The first story told in Okfuskee about April 1, therefore, emphasized the Cherokee crisis confronting the town and its families. Because their local networks extended into Cherokee country and South Carolina's capital, international war became the topic of the day. Of that we can be reasonably certain.[4]

What the Okfuskees actually did about the Cherokee situation is less clear. Apparently, they did not respond to their losses by going on the warpath. Okfuskee Captain later claimed, "I have kept my Warriours at Home, notwithstanding we lost many of our Friends by which Means I have got the ill Will of many of my People"; Red Coat King likewise remarked that "the young People . . . want War," but he claimed that he could "restrain them." His ability to do so may have stemmed from the townspeople's knowledge that some Cherokees desired peace. Thus, the trader who reported the destruction of Okfuskee's Augusta-bound party simultaneously noted that the "Cherokees sent in to the Upper Creeks to make a Peace."[5] Did the Okfuskees also send messages or diplomats to the Cherokees? Did they reach out to the Estatoes and Hiwassees? There is simply no way to know.

What is clear, however, is that Okfuskee stopped losing people to Cherokee war parties by the time Acorn Whistler arrived back in Upper Creek country. After mid-April 1752, only one report mentions an Okfuskee killed by Cherokees, and, for reasons that I will discuss in a moment, that report is not particularly credible. The Okfuskees' surprising immunity from attack meant that, when

Okfuskee Captain spoke in Tuckabatchee that fall, Okfuskees no longer centered their story on the Cherokees. Their worst fears about the Cherokees had not come to pass. And they now had something new to worry about: Acorn Whistler's execution. Their first story had not left them well prepared to deal with that development.

That is not to say that the Okfuskees' first story had ignored Acorn Whistler. It certainly had not. His personal history and his actions in Charleston, after all, helped to transform a small-scale incident into a deadly crisis. As a result, just as Okfuskee's local storytellers were talking about the Cherokees in their first story, so too were they talking about Acorn Whistler. The question, though, is whether the Okfuskee storytellers initially believed that Acorn Whistler was implicated in the Estatoes' deaths and deserved to be punished. My guess? Yes and no. Yes, the Okfuskees thought Acorn Whistler had a hand in the attack. The parallels between the April 1 attack and Acorn Whistler's 1749 assault on Hiwassee were simply too striking to ignore. To be sure, on April 1, Acorn Whistler had not pulled the trigger himself, but the Okfuskee storytellers would have been hard pressed not to conclude that he had used the Charleston adoption ceremony to set up the Estatoes. Or perhaps he had encouraged the Lower Creeks to fall on their new friends. Or perhaps he had neglected to give the British a timely warning of the Lower Creeks' plans. Or perhaps all of the above. Whatever the case, the Okfuskees' first story probably had some harsh things to say about Acorn Whistler's actions on April 1.

But, no, the Okfuskees did not think that Acorn Whistler deserved to be punished. His hands were not entirely clean, but that did not make him guilty. The Okfuskees, instead, would have seen Acorn Whistler as an accessory to people who were themselves guilty as hell. The storytellers, after all, had no reason to think that Lower Creeks needed any prodding to attack Estatoes, and the storytellers likewise knew that Acorn Whistler was in no position to give orders to the Lower Creek attackers. To the extent that heads deserved to roll, then, the Okfuskees believed that Acorn Whistler's was not one of them, a conclusion that explains why Acorn Whistler's actions after he returned home were not those of someone who feared punishment at the hands of his family and community. The Okfuskees had no real incentive to advocate for the man, of course, but they also had no real reason to argue that he should suffer for April 1's violence. They certainly did not expect that he would be executed.

Confirming that guesswork about how Acorn Whistler was treated in the Okfuskees' first story requires briefly turning away from Okfuskee and focusing on Thomas and Mary Bosomworth. Their speeches and actions in August and September 1752 reveal a great deal about how Acorn Whistler figured in the Okfuskees' first story. The Bosomworths clearly believed both that the Okfuskees could be counted upon to oppose any effort to punish Acorn Whistler and that his death left them angry and dangerous. The Bosomworths never said as much, but they left us three clues suggesting that they knew that, in the aftermath of Acorn Whistler's execution, controlling the fury of his family and community was an absolute necessity. Tracing how the Bosomworths tried to do just that allows us to watch them reacting to the Okfuskees' first story about Acorn Whistler. We cannot hear that story directly, but we can observe the Bosomworths and get a very good sense of what Acorn Whistler's family and community had been saying about the man in the immediate aftermath of April 1.

The place to begin is on August 13, the day after Acorn Whistler's nephew was chosen as the executioner, when the Bosomworths sent a letter from Coweta to "Ross and Germany at the Oakfuskees." Its recipients were Okfuskee's British traders; one of them, James Germany, was the son-in-law of Okfuskee Mico. No one bothered to record the letter's contents, but I suspect that the gist was "Heads up" and "Prepare those Okfuskees you can trust." Its bearer learned of Acorn Whistler's death, and brought the news to the dead man's family in Okfuskee. Of that family, only the Little Okfuskees' immediate reaction has come down to us, but that was violent enough—"enraged"; "burnt the Town"—to suggest that the Bosomworths were right to be cautious. The Okfuskees themselves did not burn anything. Perhaps the letter allowed someone like Okfuskee Captain to head off any violent displays? But the Bosomworths knew the Okfuskees would be outraged that a kinsman linked to their town had taken the fall for the Lower Creek attackers. That the Bosomworths did not see fit to send a letter to any other Upper Creek town is our first clue to exactly how angry the Okfuskees' contemporaries feared they might become.[6]

A second clue pointing to the Okfuskees' anger at Acorn Whistler's death—and thus to their first story's sense that he did not deserve to die—can be found in the Bosomworths' marked unwillingness to go anywhere near Okfuskee while the Acorn Whistler crisis remained unresolved. Glen's instructions to Thomas were very clear about the role Okfuskee should have played in this affair. Thomas was to present Malatchi and Chigelly with the governor's demands; if they did not comply, Thomas must immediately "sett off to the Town of Ofuskee." Of course, Glen thought Malatchi's Lower Creeks were responsible for the April 1 attack; if that was the case, then the Okfuskees—as Charleston's friends and Coweta's rivals—would support Glen's demands. The Bosomworths knew he was right. If the "Satisfaction demanded" included punishing the Lower Creek attackers as Glen insisted, then Okfuskee was the logical place to go. If, however, Glen might be offered Acorn Whistler's blood instead, then the Bosomworths knew better than to go to Okfuskee, whose people had every reason to view that offer as an outrage.[7]

So, when Chigelly and Malatchi refused to respond immediately on August 6, Thomas contented himself with remarking that "This Answer put me a little at a Stand how to act in Conformity to my Instructions . . . to proceed directly to the Oakfuskees." Instead of following orders, he allowed himself to be persuaded by Mary's assertion "that all our Hopes of Success was entirely founded upon the Interest and Authority of" Malatchi and Chigelly, who would "naturally" be "disgust[ed]" if the Bosomworths left for Okfuskee. In that case, Mary said, their "only Resource would . . . be the Interest of the Upper Creeks." She went on to note that those Upper Creeks "would not concern themselves . . . in Opposition to" Coweta's headmen, but her energetic effort to avoid Okfuskee suggests she had her doubts about that.[8]

The Bosomworths, in fact, were so intent on avoiding Okfuskee at all costs that they did the same thing a month later. When the Bosomworths arrived in Upper Creek country for the September conference to explain Acorn Whistler's execution, Mary refused to go further than Tuckabatchee, claiming that "it would be much better to give the Talk out in this Town than to proceed to the Oak-fuskees." She noted that "The Discovery of the Cause of the Acorn Whistler's Death would be a very ticklish Point, and it would be necessary to have some Friends to stand by us in Case of the worst; that the leading Men of [Tuckabatchee] are her own Relations and secured in our Interest." And she pointed out that Wolf of Mucco-lossus, Malatchi, and Chigelly had all said "they should stop . . . at the Tuccobatchees to give the Talk there"; she did not bother to note that none of these headmen were on good terms with Okfuskee. In response, Thomas again mentioned his instructions "to proceed to the Oakfuskees," but Mary stated emphatically "that Nothing could be done at the Oakfuskees, which could not as well or more effec-tually be done here." And she had a point, as long as what needed to "be done" was getting the Upper Creeks to approve the execution of an innocent(ish) man with ties to Okfuskee. That simply could not "be done" at Okfuskee, but it could be accomplished in Tucka-batchee, forty miles by trail—and even further emotionally—from Okfuskee. That town's angry inhabitants were not the right audi-ence for a story about Acorn Whistler's guilt.[9]

Thomas presented himself as reluctantly acceding to a fait accom-pli—"Reasons and Necessity together obliged me to conclude to give the Talk . . . here [at Tuckabatchee]"—but he provides us with the final clue that the Bosomworths knew that the Okfuskees were furi-ous about Acorn Whistler's death. He wrote in the journal that he would send to Glen that "Red Coat King of the Oakfuskees" missed the Tuckabatchee conference because his "whole Town [was] gone out to War for Satisfaction for a Woman that was killed." When an accomplished liar like Thomas found himself having to tell such a dumb lie, it suggests the lengths to which the Bosomworths went to avoid engaging with Okfuskee's angry people, whose first story had left them unprepared to accept Acorn Whistler's execution with equanimity.[10]

Thomas had to lie because Red Coat King's absence at Tuck-abatchee was too eye-catching to ignore. "Red Coat King" was a nickname, but a powerful one. It referenced both Creek views about using clothes to establish relationships and South Carolina's habit of giving red coats to only the most important Indian headman. The nickname's implications were borne out by one of this Okfuskee's titles, Fanni Mico, an honorific given to only the most trusted of cross-cultural intermediaries. His other title, Okfuskee Mico, attested to his influence in one of Creek country's most powerful and diplomatically active towns; he had likely been Okfuskee's mico for a quarter century. Add those titles and the nickname together and it comes as no surprise that this man was at the center of his town's relationships with both Charleston and the Cherokees. Glen had praised his leadership in the 1749 Creek-Cherokee peace negotiations, described him as "my good Friend," and quoted him in Thomas's instructions. Thomas knew Glen would wonder why Red Coat King avoided a meeting in which Creeks discussed the punishment inflicted on a Little Okfuskee accused of killing Cherokees and insulting the British. Thomas had every reason to believe that Red Coat King's people were furious that Acorn Whistler died in lieu of the Lower Creek attackers, but telling the governor that Red Coat King boycotted the Tuckabatchee meeting was a nonstarter. So Thomas lied.[11]

The Cherokee attack that supposedly necessitated Red Coat King's absence never happened. Thomas is the only person to mention it, and the female victim would have been the only Okfuskee killed by Cherokees between mid-April 1752 and the American Revolution. But leaving those issues aside, we can be certain that Thomas lied because Red Coat King would not have gone "out to War." Three years before, Glen's interpreter described the Okfuskee leader as "Old," and in November 1752 Red Coat King called himself "an old Man" who "could do Nothing but talk." Moreover, Red Coat King was Okfuskee Mico, a man whose talk would, in his words, "always be for keeping of Peace." Creek towns had war leaders to guide their people on the red path; in Okfuskee, that man was Okfuskee Captain. If the townspeople had all gone out to war, Okfuskee Captain would have taken the lead, not Red Coat King. But Okfuskee Captain actually attended the Tuckabatchee meeting. Thomas, in short, would have us believe that Okfuskee's elderly civil headman led the town to war while its head warrior attended a peaceful conference. The Okfuskees knew better, and so did Thomas. When Red Coat King would not talk to South Carolina's representative, something was very wrong in Okfuskee. And when Thomas Bosomworth was forced into such a blatant lie, it is clear that he believed that the Okfuskees' first story had not featured a guilty Acorn Whistler heading inexorably to a well-deserved death.[12]

All of which is to say that we can make an educated guess regarding the broad contours, if not the small-scale details, of the Okfuskees' first story. The townspeople initially focused their attention on the Cherokees, and while they would have criticized Acorn Whistler, they did not believe his actions merited death. That story, however, lost its salience as Cherokee attacks on Okfuskee ceased. And the story itself vanished almost entirely in the face of both Glen's first story and Malatchi's second. Glen's insistence that someone be punished for the April 1 attack and Malatchi's insistence that said someone was Acorn Whistler meant that the Okfuskees' first story was untenable. The Okfuskees did not have to like that fact—and their anger in late August and early September suggests that they did not like it one bit—but to continue telling their first story would be to court all manner of unpleasant outcomes.

After all, the Okfuskees' Charleston friends had decided—judging from the actions of Glen's agents—to accept the fiction that Acorn Whistler was guilty. If the Okfuskees insisted he was not, then they risked angering their most important European ally. Moreover, the Okfuskees' Coweta rivals were enthusiastically agreeing with the British. Malatchi's town had the backing of several prominent members of Acorn Whistler's family, including the head warrior from Okfuskee's friend town of Cusseta; and Cusseta itself had been heavily involved in the decision to execute Acorn Whistler. If the Okfuskees stood against this tide, they risked handing Coweta a diplomatic triumph and endangering Okfuskee's own community and family-based networks. And, finally, the British and Cowetas would soon start telling the Cherokees that a man linked to Okfuskee had been punished for killing the Okfuskees' Estatoe friends. If the Okfuskees continued to deny Acorn Whistler's guilt, then they risked having the Cherokees conclude that perhaps the Okfuskees—who had not punished Acorn Whistler in 1749 either—were not as peacefully inclined as they claimed to be.

Why take those risks? Acorn Whistler was already dead. The Lower Creek attackers were already off the hook. Better, by far, to calm down and back away from the first story. Accept Acorn Whistler's death and use it as a way to reassert Okfuskees' local verities. Although it took the Okfuskees almost a month after Acorn Whistler's execution to come to terms with the situation, it was time for another story.

∽ WE FIRST HEAR the Okfuskees' second story in Okfuskee Captain's speech at the September 21 conference in Tuckabatchee. He began with familial sacrifice. Two of "his own Relations" had "suffered Death," including "a very great Man." The Okfuskee's vocabulary underlined the family's pain—"suffered Death," rather than simply "killed"; "his own," rather than simply "his"—as did his willingness to exaggerate Acorn Whistler's (not exactly "very great") status. Then, Okfuskee Captain explained why the family put up with this pain: "for Satisfaction to the English," of course, but also "to prevent those Tears that must have flowed in Case of a Breach of Friendship with the English." British demands, then, had caused their friends in Okfuskee Captain's local world to suffer, and to avoid further suffering—on their part, to be sure, but also on the part of the Creeks as a whole—Okfuskee Captain's people had accepted this blow. And Okfuskee Captain emphasized his personal support for this decision, noting that "he was very well contented that" Acorn Whistler "should suffer Death"—that phrase again!—because "he hoped" a break with the British "would never happen."

The combination of suffering, sacrifice, and enduring friendship made for a very brief story, easily the shortest of the speeches made by Acorn Whistler's relatives at the Tuckabatchee conference. And, in a classic dog-that-did-not-bark moment, the Okfuskee Captain's speech was as notable for what he did not say as for what he did. To begin with, Okfuskee Captain appeared at the conference under the guise of his town-based title, but he never claimed to speak for the town, the family, or, in fact, for anyone but himself. Members of Acorn Whistler's family from other towns did so. Second, Okfuskee Captain described Acorn Whistler's death as necessary, but he never said it was just. Members of Acorn Whistler's family from other towns did so. Third, Okfuskee Captain spoke of pain and suffering, but he never hinted at retribution. A member of Acorn Whistler's family from another town did so. And, finally, Okfuskee Captain referred to the deceased as "a very great Man" and "he," but he never mentioned Acorn Whistler by name. A member of Acorn Whistler's family from another town did so.[13]

That these things could be said but Okfuskee Captain chose not to say them is significant, as is the fact that Okfuskee's leading warrior spoke while Okfuskee Mico stayed home. Those details allow us to flesh out the Okfuskees' second story a bit. Clearly, it was not a cheerful one. Consensus within the town was elusive, leaving a war leader who spoke only for himself in the place of a mico who would not speak—on this subject, at least—for his town. And even Okfuskees like that war leader who viewed Acorn Whistler's execution as essential did not see it as fair. Debate within the town notwithstanding, Okfuskees would not attack the British over Acorn Whistler's death, but they believed that their British friends had pushed them into a corner and their fellow Creeks had forced them to take one for the team. They had suffered so that others, including those who actually merited punishment, would not. And that suffering meant that they had a right to expect that things would go back to normal. Acorn Whistler was the problem? Acorn Whistler was dead. Problem solved. It was time, the Okfuskees believed, to speak of other things—of friendship, mutuality, and Okfuskee's long history of peacemaking.

In the future, other Creeks would refer obliquely to Acorn Whistler from time to time; other Creeks even broke with tradition and spoke the dead man's name. Okfuskees—as far as the records show—never referred to him again, not even indirectly. Why would they? Why would the Okfuskees want to be reminded of the crisis that man helped to create, of the anger his death produced, and of the solution forced upon them by craven friends and opportunistic rivals? The Okfuskees wanted to move on, and they had reason to think they could do so. After all, at the Tuckbatchee conference, when Okfuskee Captain and Acorn Whistler's other relatives endorsed his execution, Thomas Bosomworth then "commended the Behaviour of the Upper Creeks, when last in Charles Town (excepting the Acorn Whistler)," and said that "the Satisfaction" given "would confirm the high Opinion the Governor always entertained of their Wisdom and Justice." The governor would, according to Thomas, "be very glad to see them either at Augusta or Charles Town in order to make a new Chain of Friendship with them." That was exactly what the Okfuskees hoped to hear. No town, after all, had given the British more, been friends with them longer, or had a better claim to being at home in Charleston. Their second story had been told so that those facts could return to the fore.[14]

Thus, when Thomas Bosomworth finally made it to Okfuskee on November 5, 1752, his meeting with Red Coat King was cordial. The Okfuskee mico "highly approved" of Thomas's efforts with the Chickasaws at Breed Camp. More importantly, however, Red Coat King also "highly approved" of Glen's Cherokee peace plan. Glen, according to Red Coat King, "acted like a common Father to all Indians, and wanted them to live like Brothers together." Okfuskee's mico promised wholehearted support for Glen's effort, and "he hoped these was a Prospect of the Continuance of it." He also noted that the town's "young People" wanted war and that restraining them would be difficult if more Okfuskees were killed, but he allowed himself to be satisfied by Thomas's pledge that, if the worst should happen, "the Governor would see Justice done."[15]

Red Coat King had reason to accept those promises and to feel reassured. Glen's agent had finally arrived in Okfuskee. Thomas had first "Paid my Complements" to Okfuskee's mico and then spoken primarily about peace with the Cherokees, an issue that not only was vitally important to the Okfuskees but which also allowed them to actively and publicly support their Charleston friends' plans. Red Coat King even adopted Glen's preferred phrases (a British "common Father"; Indians who "live like Brothers") to express his approbation. And, best of all, no one mentioned Acorn Whistler. Taken as a whole, Thomas's time in Okfuskee must have left his hosts believing that, thanks to their second story, they had started to recover the position they held prior to the April 1 attack. Okfuskees were once again on their home turf, literally and figuratively, discussing a Cherokee peace in Okfuskee's square with their British friends in a mutually respectful way.

Other developments, though, suggested that the Okfuskees' second story was not working. The fallout from the Acorn Whistler crisis could not be pushed into the background so easily. The second story, for example, had not stopped Malatchi and the Cowetas' efforts to forge bonds with the British at Okfuskee's expense. The Okfuskees would have worried about this issue from the moment the Bosomworths set up shop in Malatchi's house and started referring to "our Friends from the Cowetas." Okfuskees knew that Coweta and Charleston had never been close, that Malatchi and Glen had been approaching daggers drawn for several years, and that people claiming to be Cowetas had attacked a Cherokee in South Carolina in December 1751. Yet Thomas and Mary—acting in Glen's name—ignored that attack and offered the Cowetas and their fellow Lower Creeks absolution in exchange for a Little Okfuskee's blood. Britain's representatives seemed bound and determined to let Cowetas control the satisfaction-giving process while sidelining Charleston's traditional friends in Okfuskee.[16]

The Okfuskees' willingness—as expressed in their second story—to sacrifice Acorn Whistler to preserve their ties to Charleston seemingly had no effect on the Coweta-Charleston rapprochement. In the aftermath of the Tuckabatchee conference, Malatchi was suddenly riding through Upper Creek country to deal with the death of a British trader and generally acting as if he had a special relationship with Charleston. That Glen's agents would facilitate this was bad, but Glen's own words were worse. His November 15, 1752, letter to the Creeks not only referred to Coweta as "the first town in the Nation" but rang with praises of "King" Malatchi. Only after Glen finished extolling Malatchi's "greatness of soul" and insisting that he "deserved to be Esteemed Valued and Loved by both English and the Creeks" did the governor finally mention an Okfuskee, and then only as part of a list of Creek headman whom he looked forward to seeing. Even there, Malatchi and Chigelly were the first two names Glen thought of; Red Coat King was the seventh. If that was what Charleston took away from the Okfuskees' second story, Red Coat King and his people were in trouble.[17]

And the same was true when the Okfuskees considered their relations with the Cherokees. Again, Coweta was moving onto Okfuskee's diplomatic turf, and, again, the Okfuskees must have been flabbergasted. Cowetas and Cherokees fought; Okfuskees and

Cherokees negotiated. That was how it had been, with a deviation now and then, since 1715. But in the fall of 1752, the Cowetas began a diplomatic offensive. By November, a Cherokee from Hiwassee was using the words "Cowetas" and "Peace" in the same sentence, and then going on to speak of "Hopes" and "Quietness." Soon thereafter, two Cowetas came to the hunting camp of "the Estertoe Warrior" to say "that now it was Peace"; generations later, Cherokees remembered these Cowetas as "messengers of peace." Then Cherokees notified Glen that "a Warrior of the Cowettas had been at [the Cherokee town of] Chotee . . . that he was received as a Brother, and that now the Peace . . . was concluded." And that was followed by a letter from Malatchi regarding the eight Cherokees "who came into my Town," the five who remained in Coweta, and the Coweta "Townspeople now in the Cherokees." These diplomats, moreover, were not just visiting each other. Malatchi's people were taking part in adoption ceremonies. In fact, the Coweta "received as a Brother" at Chota started a tradition of Cherokees bearing Coweta titles and Cowetas bearing Cherokee titles. No wonder a nineteenth-century Cherokee described "the Cowetas" as "the principal actors in re-establishing . . . peace," and no wonder he noted that the Cowetas had earned "the right of nominating a beloved mediating chief of this [Cherokee] nation, who are generally called Coweta Kings." Both right and title had their roots in the Cowetas' diplomacy that began in the months after Acorn Whistler's death.[18]

Coweta's new friendships with the Cherokees and Charleston, of course, threatened to make the Okfuskees' own local networks redundant, perhaps even obsolete. By the spring of 1753, the Okfuskees' alarm was palpable. None of this was what the Okfuskees had in mind when they swallowed hard and accepted Acorn Whistler's execution. They responded with a forceful invocation of their town- and family-based connections and a carefully calibrated demonstration of anger. In the process, they put Malatchi on notice that his plans would not go unchallenged, but they also demonstrated to their Cherokee and British friends that ignoring Okfuskee was not an option.

Sometime in the spring of 1753, Okfuskees decided that they would assert—publicly, explicitly, outspokenly—the points their second story had initially subordinated to the rhetoric of suffering and sacrifice: Okfuskee's history of peacemaking and its many alliances imposed certain obligations on the townspeople, including acquiescing in Acorn Whistler's execution; but that history also entitled them to expect that their friends would live up to their own obligations, including reciprocating when Okfuskees made a gesture of goodwill like acquiescing in Acorn Whistler's execution. Somehow, the Okfuskees' second story had not quite gotten those points across. The Okfuskees would pare the story down, hone its moral, and try again. If the subject of Acorn Whistler was raised, they would respond, but they would not mention him themselves. They would, instead, talk of peace and friendship. But they would also remind all concerned that they were not even remotely happy, and they would vigorously confront efforts to snub their leaders, marginalize their town, and ignore friendship's responsibilities.

The venue for this new-model second story was the Charleston conference in late May and early June 1753. Glen and Malatchi envisioned the meeting as a chance to wrap up the loose ends of the Acorn Whistler crisis and reap the rewards that their agreed-upon solution promised. The Okfuskees had their own agenda, which they signaled by sending seventeen men to Charleston. No other core Creek town sent more than seven representatives, and most sent only one or two. The Okfuskees in Charleston included the town's mico, its two leading warriors, and "the Head Man" of Sugatspoges, Okfuskee's largest talofa. No other town sent more than two headmen. The Okfuskees' turnout was impressive enough, in fact, that Thomas Bosomworth did what he could to obscure it. He presented Glen with a list of "Creeks now at Charles Town" that described six Okfuskees as inhabitants of Sugatspoges, which Thomas neglected to mention was part of Okfuskee. He likewise neglected to mention the talwa of two headmen, both of whom happened to be Okfuskees. An incautious reader of Thomas's list, thus, would think that Okfuskees were only moderately well represented. This was, of course, not the first time Thomas had misrepresented Okfuskee's participation at a conference. And as with his lie about Red Coat King's boycott of September's Tuckabatchee conference, Thomas was doing what he could to interfere with, and tone down, the Okfuskees' story. Despite himself, however, Thomas's list shows us how very seriously the Okfuskees took this diplomatic mission.[19]

Even more than that, though, the list suggests that Okfuskee's diplomats had no intention of putting their most diplomatic foot forward. Other Creek towns sent four "Women of Note," but the Okfuskees sent only men, thereby passing up a chance to mark their mission as an unmistakably peaceful one. Moreover, those men were led by Red Coat King, not by Fanni Mico. Of course, those two titles were held by the same man, but his choice of which title to deploy on this occasion was not just semantics. Twice before he had arrived in Charleston at the head of a large, multitown Creek delegation; both times he called himself Fanni Mico. In doing so, he claimed a particularly privileged adoptive relationship with Charleston, the sort of tie that made his town Britain's key friend in Creek country. In 1753, though, Fanni Mico was nowhere to be found. And, in keeping with his absence, Red Coat King made no speeches in Charleston, much to the surprise of some Upper Creeks. One headman noted that "We thought indeed that the Red Coat King might have spoke something, but he is very old," while another remarked that "I was in Hopes that that old Man (pointing to the Red Coat King) would have spoke to the Matter." Fanni Mico, though, was not in Charleston, and Red Coat King stayed silent, allowing the town's warriors to speak in his stead. The Okfuskees were not planning to play by the usual rules.[20]

If that was the Okfuskees' plan, what they heard at the conference could only have reinforced their conviction that the time had come for a more aggressive posture. The four-day meeting featured everything the Okfuskees' second story was intended to ward off. Acorn Whistler was an ever-present conversational theme. Glen lavished praise, favors, and gifts on Malatchi, who put himself forward as the Creeks' leader. The situation, in short, was exactly what the Okfuskees must have feared. And so the town's war leaders pushed back hard. In doing so, they attested not simply to the Okfuskees' investment in their own local networks but also to the enduring relevance of the Creeks' local truths. Those verities could be relied upon, even in the face of collusion between a European empire and a would-be Creek emperor. The Okfuskees' were worried and angry, but they also believed that truth will out—not the truth about Acorn Whistler, whose unjust execution the Okfuskees did not bother to mention, but rather the truth about how the local world worked and what happened when its tenets were violated.

The Okfuskees waited until the conference's second day to begin speaking. After Glen and Malatchi had batted around Acorn Whistler's demise, Glen's plans for Creek peace with the Cherokees, and Malatchi's complaints against Georgia; after Glen told the Creeks that he looked upon Malatchi as "the Head and Mouth of your Nation" but would now listen to "any of the other Head Men"; after Wolf of Mucculossus said "What Malatchi has now said is our Talk" and hinted that Red Coat King was perhaps too old to speak—after all of that, Handsome Fellow of Okfuskee took the floor. This "Head Warrior" began with a bow to peace: "As your Excellency recommended to us to be at Peace with the Cherokees, we came down with a free Heart, and are glad to see your Excellency." And then Handsome Fellow proceeded to remind Glen, gently but firmly, of the facts of political life in Creek country.[21]

The Creeks, the Okfuskee said, had not sent down the leader of their nation. There was no such person, and the leaders, plural, that the Creeks did send were there *for*—not rulers *of*—their people. Thus, Handsome Fellow told Glen, "here are the Head Men for our Nation, here is the King [mico/Malatchi], and here is the Red Coat King of Okfuskee."[22] These "two great Men"—as he called them later in his speech—"agree to Peace or . . . order War," and because "they are Men of such great Prudence . . . we agree to what they desire us." Moreover, the views of "all the Head Warriours" merited consideration, even though they "readily complied with every Thing you desired," and Handsome Fellow himself had to be consulted, even though he promised never to "stand out against any good Talks." The "Peace," in short, was "agreed to not as being your Desire only," much less Malatchi's, "but [because] the Head Men all considered that the Thing was Good in itself." That is why "The Kings and beloved Men are come down with one Heart . . . and, we, the Warriors, are come down to escort them." This was remedial Creek political science, but Handsome Fellow evidently thought that Glen needed to hear it. And it certainly did not bother this Okfuskee—Red Coat King's son—that Malatchi had to listen as well.

With those truths on the table, Handsome Fellow could then return to the subjects that were Okfuskee's strength: "You are pleased to observe that the first Thing to be done is to renew the Treaties between us, and it is chiefly upon that Account that we came down." The Okfuskee headmen could not resist denying that his people were responsible for any blemishes on that relationship—"We hope we never have violated any Treaty"—but the larger point was that their friendship was "now renewed. The Day shall never come that it shall be said that we had any thoughts of throwing away the English, but that there shall be allways a strict Friendship between us." In fact, "it shall be my constant Opinion that Nothing bad can come from the English"—and then a subtle qualifier—"notwithstanding any little Stories that may be told as to the Affair of Peace with the Cherokees." That was as close as any Okfuskee would come to mentioning Acorn Whistler. Hinting that "little Stories" had been a problem was worth doing, however, because it underlined how very committed Okfuskees were to their own story, which centered on peace with their friends in Charleston.

But not necessarily with the Cherokees. The Okfuskees had paid a price for the "little Stories" of the past. Now, Glen and Malatchi had to face a reckoning of their own. The governor would not get his Creek-Cherokee peace agreement, and Malatchi would not get the last word on the issue, despite claiming "I have considered within myself" four times in his speech preceding Handsome Fellow's. Thus, right after Handsome Fellow mentioned those "Stories" about Cherokee affairs, he stated that "notwithstanding the King [mico/Malatchi] has express himself fully on that Affair before, yet I shall speak a Word of it." Where, he wanted to know, were the Cherokees? As any Okfuskee would, "I was rejoiced to hear that we were to meet, and was in Hopes of seeing the Cherokees here, and I should be glad to know the Reasons why they are not come." Even had Cherokees been present, though, nothing could be decided now because the Creeks in Charleston "do not know how Matters are at Home, but I hope we shall hear good Accounts when we return, and our Nation expects to have good Accounts from us of what we came about." Cherokees had lied, telling Glen that "the Creeks always break the Peace"; Cherokees were "always the Aggressors." And so, Handsome Fellow stated, the Okfuskees would wait until they got home to decide on peace with the Cherokees. Glen wanted a Creek-Cherokee peace? Glen would have to wait. Malatchi had "considered within myself" about the peace? Malatchi would have to consider within Okfuskee's square.[23]

And then Handsome Fellow stuck the knife in again, from a different angle. Malatchi, after all, had just ended his speech by airing his anger at Georgia over a personal issue—the colony's treatment of "My Sister, Mrs. Bosomworth"—and Glen had just promised to represent Malatchi's concerns to Georgia's leaders. And so the Okfuskee ended his own talk by raising a personal matter: "the Trade [prices] should be lower." And not just on a few things. He listed fifteen items and the prices "We want," all of which represented significant markdowns: guns at 12.5 percent off current prices; blankets, shirts, hoes, and shoes at 25 percent off; bullets at 40 percent off; gunflints, gunpowder, earrings, knives, and scissors at 50 percent off.[24]

Glen must have been as shocked by the direct nature of the Okfuskee's request—"I am now to say something to your Excellency"—as by the unprecedented magnitude of the discounts requested. And Malatchi must have been as affronted by Handsome Fellow's offhand reference to the Coweta's earlier speech—"the King has spoke what was necessary upon other Heads"—as he was appalled by the Okfuskee's willingness to push him aside with the statement that "what I am to speak is without the Derection of any Head Man. It flows chiefly from myself, being a Head-warriour, and the Rest of the Head Warriors here present." An Okfuskee, in short, made demands on the governor who lived in Charleston, and an Okfuskee told Coweta's leader that he had not represented the concerns of a key constituency. And then that Okfuskee sat down without so much as a "please" or an "excuse me."

In style and substance, it was an extraordinarily assertive speech. But it did not work, and the Okfuskees probably had not expected it to. Glen immediately answered Handsome Fellow by promising to give "great Attention . . . chiefly to what was spoken by [Malatchi]," although he would "take notice of what was said by the other Person." That "notice," however, consisted of all but refusing to lower prices before thanking the Creeks for "agree[ing] to a Peace with the Cherokees," which they had not, in fact, agreed to. Then, Glen aired some of Okfuskee's dirty laundry: "It is very true the Cherokees accuse you as the first Breakers of the Peace, and perhaps not altogether without Reason." He proceeded to tell the story of how "the Indian called the Acorn Whistler . . . went against the Town of Hywasse and killed two of the Cherokees," all "to spoil the Peace." The Cherokees, Glen noted, "put up with the Loss of those two men."

Glen did not explicitly say that Okfuskee's ties to Acorn Whistler meant that the Okfuskees had no right to complain about the Cherokees, but no one could miss his point. And Glen did not say that the Okfuskees should accept the loss of two men (Acorn Whistler and his nephew/executioner) for the sake of peace, but no one could miss that point either. Just to be certain, however, Glen ended with "a short Story of what happened in the Cherokees within these few Years": "A noted Head Man" put to death by "one of his own Relations" with the active support of "the whole Town," and all for "Satisfaction to the English." It was, in short, the Acorn Whistler affair, only without the resistance from the malefactor's family and community. That, Glen said, "is the Way to preserve Friendship between us." The Okfuskees' more pointed second story had simply encouraged Glen to tell his own second story again.[25]

Even leaving aside Glen's unwillingness to consider price reductions and his tendentious misconstrual of the Creeks' point about the Cherokee peace, it would be difficult to pick the part of the governor's speech most likely to infuriate the Okfuskees. Laying the blame for the 1749 Creek-Cherokee war on Acorn Whistler's small-scale raid while ignoring how Malatchi had, as Glen put it the previous year, "gathered together some Hundreds of the Lower Creeks and went against the Cherokees"? Implying that the Okfuskees should shut up about the deaths of Acorn Whistler and his nephew and support Glen's demand for satisfaction while ignoring that the Okfuskees had already done so? Lecturing Okfuskees on how to preserve friendship with the British while refusing to acknowledge both the town's long history of doing just that and

Handsome Fellow's assertion that "there shall be allways a strict Friendship between us"? There were any number of things here to set the Okfuskees' teeth on edge.[26]

The speeches the next day were no better. Glen lectured the Creeks on the responsibilities of friendship before twice gesturing at Acorn Whistler ("a wicked Head Man") to explain why the Cherokees had not come to Charleston and ending by asserting that British traders must not be "Hurt and Ruin[ed]" by price reductions. Malatchi, for his part, praised Glen's "fatherly Care," promised that the Creeks "are willing . . . to ratify the Peace [with the Cherokees] in any Manner that your Excellency pleases," and returned to his long complaint about Georgia's treatment of Mary Bosomworth. Malatchi concluded by stating that "All that has been said by the Warriour [Handsome Fellow] concerning the lowering of Goods was chiefly with a View to make our young People at Home easey; but as I perceive the Proposal will not take . . . I shall say no more upon that Head," except to desire that price of bullets be reduced. Glen barely had time to obtain the consent of the traders in attendance before the Okfuskees brought the meeting to a screeching halt.[27]

Handsome Fellow "rose up" and, as Malatchi put it, "in a very rude and abrupt Manner broke in upon my Discourse." Doing so was a cardinal sin in Creek diplomatic protocol, and the Okfuskee compounded the insult by directly contradicting Coweta's headman: "We hope that the Abatement of all the Artickles requested will be agreed to." And then the Okfuskee turned on Glen, stating "I do not know what we have done that we should not have as much Favour shewn to us as to the Cherokees," who were allowed to purchase goods at prices even cheaper than those "we have desired." An "Abatement," he said, was necessary for all concerned. For Okfuskee's headmen, who "would have good News to tell our People when we go Home." For Okfuskee's people, who needed something "to lighten their Hearts and make them merry." And even for Glen, who would find that better prices "would cement and finish all the good Talks we have had with your Excellency." Why did Okfuskee's headmen need to bring home good news? Why did their people need to have their hearts lightened? Why did Glen need to confirm good talks with longtime friends? Handsome Fellow did not say.

Glen had been talking about Acorn Whistler and the responsibilities of friendship for days. Let the governor sort it out for himself.[28]

And the Okfuskees were not done. When Glen responded by reminding Handsome Fellow of all the trade-related things "I have already told you," he found himself face-to-face with Okfuskee Captain. The town's head warrior very quickly reviewed his pro-British credentials. "I have been honoured with a Commission from your Excellency, and have endeavoured to do my Duty and discharge the Trust reposed in me." Doing so meant angering his own warriors by keeping them at home while "we lost many of our Friends." But he had been dogged by bad luck: "some Accident or other always Disappoints my Endeavours." And so the man whose most recent public endeavor had been speaking up in favor of Acorn Whistler's execution asked Glen "to appoint some other in my Place." While "I shall always do the English all the Service in my Power," he was resigning his commission.[29]

It was a powerful rebuke to Glen. As Okfuskee Captain told the governor two days later, "among us, when a beloved Man, or a Warrior gets a Name, it always remains with him, and I look upon your Commission to be of the same Nature." Rejecting a commission—like rejecting a name—was to delegitimize a relationship; to do so during a conference of Creek headmen and South Carolina officials was to rub salt in the wound. And Okfuskee Captain was not confronting just Glen. Malatchi, after all, had vouched for the Okfuskee and persuaded Glen to issue the commission Okfuskee Captain was now returning. Coming as it did on the heels of Handsome Fellow's blatant show of disrespect for the Coweta headman, this move by the one Okfuskee who had publicly supported Malatchi's story about Acorn Whistler was a none-too-subtle reprimand for the would-be emperor. Even Thomas Bosomworth, whose habit of downplaying Okfuskee actions has been amply documented, referred to the "public Manner that the Offence was given." Malatchi ("very rude") and Glen ("rude and unmannerly") could only agree. The Okfuskees had finally gotten their second story's point across.[30]

The result was chaos. After Okfuskee Captain spoke, "many Warriours went out of the Room seemingly displeased [with Glen] and left their Presents behind." Glen reassured the Okfuskee leader of his "esteem" and asked him to "keep your Commission," but to no avail. "The Captain immediately went out of the Room leaving the Commission upon the Table and laying down the Present of Cloaths, &c. that had been delivered to him." And then a moment later, "several of the other Warriors and young men left the Room without taking any of the Presents with them, and making some Noise as they went out." They left "lying . . . in the Council Chamber" not only the gifts they had received but also "the other Presents that were intended to be distributed." It was all quite unprecedented, but not unexpected for anyone paying attention to Okfuskee's local truths. Neglect and abuse had been met first with reminders and requests, then with incivility and demands, and finally with rejection and departure. Ignoring the townspeople's story had consequences.[31]

Malatchi and Glen recognized the insult for what it was, but they had too much riding on the conference to knuckle under to the Okfuskee challenge. As we have seen, Malatchi apologized for "some of our People," characterized the disruption as the work of ignorant "Children," and assured Glen that any other voices were "as Wind." Glen responded by criticizing the insult to "His Majesty's Presents" and "paternal Love," praising Malatchi to the skies, and showering the Coweta with gifts. From an Okfuskee perspective, however, none of that was surprising, and all of it was beside the point. It is hard to imagine that the townspeople believed that Malatchi and Glen would, upon being confronted and embarrassed, suddenly see the light and begin to behave appropriately. On the contrary, the Okfuskees were simply putting down a marker. They intended to bring Glen back to his senses and Malatchi back to earth, but those were projects that could not be accomplished in a day. For now, it was enough to disrupt and discomfit, to remind and rebut. The hard work of repairing Okfuskee's relationship with Charleston and reestablishing Okfuskee's place within Creek country could now begin.

That process started two days later, on the conference's final day. The Okfuskees apologized to Glen. The records show that two Creeks sought to make amends. One, identified only as "Indian Chief," admitted he had been "at Fault," asked the governor "to forgive what is past," and stated that "I look upon your Excellency as a Father, so I hope you will forgive me." The nature of the previous days' confrontations strongly suggests that Indian Chief was Handsome Fellow, as does the reaction of the next Creek speaker, who pointed out Handsome Fellow's father, Red Coat King, and remarked that "I was in Hopes that that old Man . . . would have spoke to the Matter." It did not happen. The Okfuskees believed that it was not yet time for their mico to reengage with the governor.[32]

Okfuskee Captain apologized instead. He acknowledged that "I desired to resign the Commission which I had from your Excellency," but said that he meant "no Disrespect to the Governor or beloved Men" and noted that the uproar in the Council Chamber had made it impossible to "express myself." When Glen asked him to "take back your Commission, and continue as you hitherto have been, a good Friend to the English," Okfuskee Captain was happy to do so. In the process, he equated a British commission with a Native naming ceremony, asserted the enduring nature of the bond each created, and promised to "continue a true Friend to the English until the Day of my Death." These were exactly the subjects—relationships grounded on powerful ceremonies, rooted in time, and sustained by loyalty—that the Okfuskees believed should dominate their conversations with the British. They must have been pleased at Glen's words, and they would have been overjoyed to discover that the commission Okfuskee Captain took back was actually a new one. Symbolically, it had been renewed by Glen. That was a hopeful sign.[33]

Note, though, that Red Coat King left Glen's council chamber without uttering a word that made it into the historical record. That absence surely reflects the Okfuskees' sense that their ties with Charleston were not back to normal. For now, warriors would lead. But the seventeen Okfuskees who left Charleston must have believed that it was just a matter of time before the mico with the red coat and white pedigree could appropriately resume conversations with his Charleston friends. Note, as well, that the Okfuskees left Charleston without committing to peace with the Cherokees. Throughout that summer, Okfuskees would make some very specific demands of both Glen and the Cherokees before the townspeople would agree to cease hostilities. Their old friends in Charleston and Cherokee country still had some work to do before returning to the Okfuskees' good graces.[34]

And, finally, note that the Okfuskees' apologies were all directed to Glen, not Malatchi. In fact, the Okfuskees would not even travel with the Coweta if they could avoid it. Glen had recommended that the Creeks "keep in a Body to the Nation," but as Red Coat King later told him, "we parted and Malatchi and his People went the Lower Path, and I and my People went the Upper Path." The Okfuskees had no intention of following Acorn Whistler's trail through Coweta to Upper Creek country. Instead, they headed straight for Okfuskee, following the Old White Path and arriving— in Red Coat King's words—"safe [in] our Towns." Doing so simply made sense. Let Malatchi take the Coweta Path and write to Glen of "arriv[ing] safe in my own Nation." The Okfuskees believed that they had just given him a lesson in both how that "Nation" worked and the challenges awaiting anyone who presumed it was "my own." Local stories had power. Family and community mattered.[35]

~ *IV*

COLONIAL

$\mathcal{A}$CORN WHISTLER WOULD have survived the 1752 crisis if it had not been for Thomas and Mary Bosomworth. Of course, it was Malatchi's willingness first to accept the fiction of Acorn Whistler's guilt and then to push Acorn Whistler's kinsmen into planning the execution that sealed the Little Okfuskee's fate. But it was the Bosomworths who offered Acorn Whistler to Malatchi, and they did more than anyone else to ensure that Acorn Whistler would take the fall for the April 1 attack. In fact, the evidence suggests that Acorn Whistler was their preferred fall guy even before they accepted Glen's offer to be agents to the Creeks. Mary knew that Glen wanted the heads of several of the Osochi attackers and that, as she told Glen in early June, "the Satisfaction this Government thinks itself Honour bound to demand will be a very nice and difficult Point to be obtained." Or, put another way, Mary knew that Glen's other potential agents were right: the Creeks would not execute the men guilty of the April 1 attack, and it "would not be very safe for an Agent to ask." Mary and Thomas accepted the job anyway. They did so for two reasons. They were desperate—more on that below—and they knew that, while the Osochis were out of reach, the Creeks just might execute someone else. The Bosomworths, in short, left Charleston with Acorn Whistler in their sights.[1]

That fact explains why the Bosomworths were so threatened by reports that after Acorn Whistler fled Charleston on April 2 he stopped by to see them. There is no proof that such a visit took place, although the path from Palachucola (where Acorn Whistler left his horses in mid-March) to Lower Creek country (where Acorn Whistler met with Malatchi in mid-April) passed through the Bosomworths' trading post at the Forks; the Bosomworths were trading for deerskins that spring.[2] Whether or not the Bosomworths met Acorn Whistler in April 1752—and my guess is that they did not—Thomas was worried enough about the accusation that, in November 1752, he had the trader Moses Nunes sign an affidavit swearing that Acorn Whistler had told him that he "never came near Mrs. Bosomworth's House or spoke to her"; a month later, John Spencer, another trader, signed a similar affidavit at Thomas's request. And then, in January 1753, Thomas forwarded those affidavits to Glen, along with a letter that mentioned the "many Slanders and absolute

Falsehoods" concocted by his enemies, particularly "that the Acorn Whistler . . . came to our House in Georgia."[3] Of course, by that point, the Bosomworths had succeeded in having Acorn Whistler executed, and so Thomas and Mary naturally wanted to beat back rumors linking them to him. The odd thing, though, is that the Bosomworths were beating back those rumors well before there was any reason to do so—well before, that is, anyone was accusing Acorn Whistler of murdering those Cherokees.

Acorn Whistler was not publicly named as the mastermind of the April 1 attack until August 11. But on July 3, a few hours before the Bosomworths left Charleston for Creek country, Thomas wrote Glen about "entirely false" reports "that the Indian called the Acorn Whistler had lately been at our House in Georgia"; "neither of us have seen the Acorn Whistler for some Years past." The next day, the Bosomworths met Lachlan McGillivray, the Indian trader reportedly spreading the worrisome rumor. According to Thomas, "I taxed Mr. McGilvray with it, and he absolutely denied that ever he heard the Acorn Whistler say that he had seen either me or Mrs. Bosomworth after the Affair of murthering the Cherokees." Thomas happily recorded the trader's statement in the journal he would send to Glen.[4]

That journal entry and July 3's letter were written just after Glen had cleared Acorn Whistler and the Upper Creeks of any taint of guilt. When Mary met with Glen on June 2, "his Excellency took occasion to mention to her the many and repeated Insults & injuries done by the Lower Creek Indians," and Thomas's instructions from Glen both blamed the April 1 attack on "the six and twenty Lower Creeks" and called for the Creeks to "punish with Death some of the most considerable of those twenty-six." Those same instructions "commended the Behaviour of the Upper Creeks, and particularly those 12 who were in Charles Town, and refused to have any Hand" in the April 1 attack. By early July, therefore, Acorn Whistler was in the clear, except in the Bosomworths' minds.[5]

It comes as no surprise, therefore, to learn that the Bosomworths were responsible for the sudden appearance of the Acorn Whistler-as-mastermind story. Mary did her part in Coweta on August 11. Acorn Whistler was accused at the end of that day's Lower

Creek meeting by Mary's "Relation," Hiacpellechi of Osochi. Hiacpellechi spoke only after Mary called him in front of the head-men, "Address[ed] herself to him," and asked "who it was that first begun" the "Disturbance" on April 1. With Mary staring him in the face, Hiacpellechi piled half-truth upon lie upon yet another lie, each falsehood increasing Acorn Whistler's burden of guilt. When Hiacpellechi finished, "Mrs. Bosomworth then told the Head Men that they ought to consider who was the most criminal for some of the most considerable must suffer Death." Thomas followed up in his journal, working to give the accusation against Acorn Whistler the veneer of legitimacy by explaining that Hiacpellechi had been present at the day-long conference, but "all the while sat undiscov-ered in the Room" until Mary called on him.

The Bosomworths had created a dramatic little moment, but it was quite clearly a set piece aimed at shifting the burden of guilt from the Osochis to Acorn Whistler. It is impossible to imagine that, at a "Private Conference" called to consider the Osochis' April 1 attack, an Osochi participant in that attack spent a day lurking in the back-ground unnoticed and un-consulted. The meeting, after all, took place not in Coweta's spacious townhouse but in Malatchi's personal home, where the room in question was at most twenty feet by fifteen feet. The audience in Malatchi's "Hut"—as a visitor had described Coweta's "Kings House"—knew who was in that small room, and so they found Hiacpellechi's appearance and accusation neither sur-prising nor persuasive.[6] John Ladson and Lachlan McIntosh, the traders who witnessed the incident, thought so little of it that their affidavit describing the meeting does not mention Hiacpellechi or Acorn Whistler. More to the point, the Lower Creek headmen in attendance refused to condemn Acorn Whistler, instead dumping the matter in their host's lap. Malatchi, for his part, "replied that any Satisfaction should be given but shedding of Blood," and it took "many Disputes" to convince him that Acorn Whistler must die. Still, Malatchi did finally come around, and Acorn Whistler was finally killed. And thus, despite telling a story that strained—per-haps even herniated—credulity, the Bosomworths had their man.[7]

The Bosomworths' success in this regard demonstrates that, from the very beginning, they were different from this book's other storytellers in three key respects. In the first place, the Bosomworths enjoyed the luxury of consistency (if not veracity). The other storytellers had to adjust to the "fact" that Acorn Whistler was guilty, and so they had to tell more than one story. Not the Bosomworths. If we take July 3rd's letter and July 4th's journal entry as the beginning of their tale, then the Bosomworths' story always featured a guilty Acorn Whistler. That narrative drove other storytellers to abandon their initial stories and adopt new ones. Second, the Bosomworths were not forced to tell a story by the Acorn Whistler affair. They elected to involve themselves in the crisis, lobbying to become Glen's agents and then devoting a year of their lives to the task. The other storytellers, by contrast, found that being involved was a command performance, although they realized this at different times—immediately, in Glen's case; by early August, in Malatchi's case; by mid-August, in the Okfuskees' case. A crisis for the other storytellers, in short, was an opportunity for the Bosomworths, and events that forced the other storytellers to repudiate out-of-date narratives allowed the Bosomworths to tell a simple, consistent story. And a self-congratulatory one. After all, a third perk of choosing to get involved and being "right" about Acorn Whistler all along was the ability to portray oneself in a flattering light. The Bosomworths' story would show them to be problem-solving diplomats deploying their Anglo-Creek connections so that a guilty man was punished. No one else could tell a story like that.

The differences setting the Bosomworths apart are worth enumerating because they help us to realize that Mary and Thomas came to the Acorn Whistler affair from a different place—literally and figuratively—than the other storytellers. The Bosomworths were neither truly British nor truly Creek. They were connected to Britain and to Creek country, but they and their story were distinctly colonial. In saying that, of course, I realize that neither Thomas nor Mary—to say nothing of the union of Thomas and Mary—are the sort of people who jump to mind when we think "colonial America." The voluminous literature on Mary tends to focus on evaluating her identity and explaining or eviscerating her more risible claims to status and land-ownership. Thomas usually figures in these histories as an ambitious and unscrupulous Englishman whose quest

for riches led him to embrace first holy orders and then a potentially
rich Indian widow. And once married, scholars tell us, Thomas and
Mary Bosomworth drew on her powerful Indian connections and
his first-class European education to lay claim to most of Georgia
and to hold the British southeast hostage to their ambitions.[8] None
of that fits well with the standard definitions of "colonial." After
all, if we take "colonial" to mean "early," then Mary's Anglo-Creek
heritage and the Bosomworths' Anglo-Anglo-Creek marriage were
hardly typical of early Americans. And if we understand "colonial"
to mean "precursor to the United States," then the Bosomworths'
reliance on a combination of European knowledge and Indian power
and their repeated interference in the process of colonization seem
to work against the developments that led to the United States.

If, however, we recognize that "colonial" refers less to a time
period or a process of national incubation and more to a distinc-
tive set of relationships, then applying that adjective to the Bosomworths' story makes sense. Colonial relationships could be political,
social, economic, intellectual, or cultural—and often they were
compounded of each of those elements—but they were always spatial and hierarchical, with the colonist living both at a distance
from the mother country and in a place that was subordinate to
the homeland. Colonists looked at once around them and over
their shoulders, taking in both their local area and their situation
vis-a-vis home. The lived experience of colonialism, then, could
be enormously destabilizing, which explains why scholars have
written of colonial elites who "frequently oscillated between Old
World and New World forms" and of colonial authors who looked
"both homeward to the seat of imperial culture and outward to the
localities that would remain for them subordinate." The colonial
experience, though, also offered individuals opportunities to craft
novel but effective forms of power. Colonial societies were always
works in progress, with a seemingly endless number of possibilities for ambitious nobodies to rise to prominence. Moreover, the
imperial system in which colonists lived encouraged self-promotion
because early modern empires were riven by clashing agendas and
competing identities, hobbled by distance and inefficiencies, reliant
on negotiation and consent for daily governance, and confronted

by rival empires and the ever-present need for reform. The Bosomworths were very much creatures of this world, and the story they
told was distinctly colonial.[9]

The Bosomworths sought to secure wealth and influence by posi-
tioning themselves as the people best able to harness the potential-
ities of colonial life. Thus, they routinely situated themselves in a
colonial setting and referenced power that came from the mother
country; they regularly insisted that their actions here were justified by their influence there. What made this colonial two-step
work so well for them was that they could look over their collective
shoulder to two different homelands. Mary was born in Coweta to
a Creek woman of Malatchi's clan, and she maintained her Creek
ties throughout her life; Thomas was born to a less exalted English
family but made himself into "a Young Gentleman" of "good Character and behaviour." Either was a force to be reckoned with, and
their marriage would seem to have been a match made in colonial
heaven. Mary was strong in Creek country and the neighboring
Euro-American backcountry areas, just where Thomas was weakest;
and Thomas was strong in the genteel circles of Anglo-America and
back in England, just where Mary was weakest. Or at least that was
the theory, and that was the story Mary and Thomas tried to tell.[10]

The reality was—as colonial realities generally were—a good deal
messier. One problem was that Mary was not truly strong in Creek
country. To be sure, she had influence via her family and her own
ability to distribute resources, but—notwithstanding her periodic
statements to the contrary—she could never mobilize large numbers of warriors, never speak for a united Creek nation, and never
act as that nation's princess or queen. What she could do, though,
was claim that she could do those things, as long as she made that
claim while in British colonial capitals or in London. The other
problem was that Thomas was not truly strong in British circles.
His heavy debts, erratic career choices, and marriage to a woman of
Creek descent meant that he could neither act as a British gentlemen
nor exercise real influence in Britain's corridors of power. What he
could do, though, was claim that he could do those things, as long
as he made that claim while in Creek country. In other words, Mary
could be seen as truly powerful only by those standing outside of

Creek country, and Thomas could be seen as influential only by those standing on the margins of Britain's empire.

During the Acorn Whistler affair, then, Mary came to the fore when dealing with British officials. In that context, she could safely assert her claims of influence in Creek country while Thomas faded into the background. When in Creek country, by contrast, Thomas took the lead publicly, asserting his ability to speak for Britain while Mary—who was more influential in Creek country than Thomas was in British circles—generally worked her more traditional connections in his shadow. It was a very delicate dance. Success required gesturing to the right set of hypothetical strengths while hiding real weaknesses, and then moving to a new place, donning new costumes, and gesturing toward different strengths while hiding different weaknesses. Done right, this dance positioned the Bosomworths as colonial people capable of drawing on the very real power of two old worlds. And because the Bosomworths at their most nimble could plausibly invoke those two power centers, they enjoyed certain luxuries as storytellers. If someone moved very carefully, then, the colonial position was one of tremendous influence. But it was so very easy to make a misstep since, in the colonial world, even seeming luxuries and apparent strengths brought with them potentially debilitating liabilities.

So—to return to the Bosomworth's three luxuries discussed above—yes, the Bosomworths could tell a consistent story, but actually doing so proved extraordinarily difficult. Thomas tried to tell that story once in October 1752 and then twice more in January 1753, a process of reiteration and reframing that he justified by noting that "there is a Complication of Facts and Evidence produced in different Parts of my Journal which may not appear so clearly at one View." The end result was so unsatisfying that in the years to come, even as the Bosomworths regularly wrote up detailed overviews of their past initiatives, they never again tried to retell their Acorn Whistler story. And, yes, the Bosomworths could choose to involve themselves in the Acorn Whistler crisis. But of all the storytellers, the Bosomworths entered that crisis in the worst shape, "Besieged," as Thomas put it, "with Difficulties and Distresses on every Side" and well-nigh overwhelmed with, in Mary's words, "the present Melancholy State of our Affairs." The Bosomworths, then, drew on two old worlds during the Acorn Whistler crisis, but they did so because their "Affairs" suffered from being securely rooted in neither. Finally, yes, the Bosomworths could chose their own role in their story, but they also had to talk about themselves because that was what they were selling—their personal histories, personal connections, and personal influence. Other storytellers could fall back occasionally on institutions and structures to move the narrative along, and other storytellers did not regularly interrupt their stories to defend their reputations by beating back harmful rumors, rebutting malicious lies, and undermining inconvenient truths. The Bosomworths' presentation of self, by contrast, frequently devolved into an extended exercise in what Mary described as her "Right of Complaining." Winners sometimes wrote colonial history, but so did whiners.[11]

The Bosomworths, then, had one story to tell, but doing so was difficult and only partly because their story was based on a lie about Acorn Whistler's guilt. More fundamentally, the Bosomworths struggled with the realities of the colonial condition. They confronted a world where possibilities and pitfalls were intertwined. In the right context, being colonial could mean inhabiting a very advantageous position, one with access to both an established center of power and an emerging world of transformative possibility. Being colonial, though, was more often a decidedly mixed blessing. Mary and Thomas are best understood in that context. They were products of the colonial world, people whose agendas, actions, and stories were profoundly shaped by the hierarchies and geographies of colonial life. In fact, because the Bosomworths both enjoyed more avenues of advancement and faced more crippling obstacles than their contemporaries, they embody a particularly instructive version of the colonial condition.

We know that, in the area of North America that became the United States, the pressures and possibilities of colonial life eventually led to independence, nationalism, and the creation of a settler empire with colonial relationships of its own. Those same pressures and possibilities in the same area, though, were more likely to lead to other, less familiar and less exalted outcomes. Most colonial stories from the seventeenth and eighteenth centuries led not toward independent nationhood but rather deeper into colonialism. Certainly, that was true of the Bosomworths' story. When it comes to the colonial experience, therefore, the Bosomworths may look to us like odd outliers, but it is the cultural and political descendants of the people whose colonial stories led to independence who are the true anomalies.

~ 7

The Colonists

$\mathcal{J}$OSEPH WRIGHT, "INDIAN TRADER," stated in a deposition that he had served as interpreter for the Bosomworths' conference with the Creeks at Tuckabatchee "on the 3rd Day of September 1752." Wright was wrong. There was no September 3rd that year. By an act of Parliament, Britons went to bed on Wednesday, September 2, 1752, and woke up on Thursday, September 14th. Removing those eleven days corrected a flaw in the old-style Julian calendar, bringing Britain and its colonies into line with the Gregorian calendar used in the rest of Europe. Thomas and Mary Bosomworth arrived in Tuckabatchee on the evening of September 2nd. They "Were very joyfully received," went to their lodgings, and emerged on September 14th to accept the "Compliments" of Tuckabatchee's headmen sitting in the town square. Or at least that is what Thomas's journal suggests. Thomas apparently handled the calendric transition smoothly and without comment, despite the fact that he was in Tuckabatchee, hundreds of miles west of the nearest almanac.[1]

In so doing, Thomas behaved like the vast majority of Britons, whether in the colonies or the mother country. "[T]he introduction of the reformed calendar in colonial America was straightforward, producing little friction and manifesting only minor incompetence," and the transition went just a bit less smoothly in Britain. This success was due, in part, to a pervasive public information campaign. There were any number of ways Thomas and Mary could have learned of the impending change prior to heading off to Creek country. The South Carolina *Gazette* published two articles on the topic over the winter, and a Charleston bookseller advertised almanacs for sale "agreeable to the stile corrected by the late act of parliament." The Bosomworths were still in Georgia at the time—although they may have had access to the *Gazette* since newspapers circulated widely—but John Tobler's "Carolina Almanac" was advertised for sale while they were in Charleston later that spring. And even if the Bosomworths were not in the habit of reading newspapers and almanacs, calendar reform was a common enough topic of conversation in Charleston that the city's residents handled the date shift smoothly despite being under tremendous stress. A devastating hurricane hit the city on September 14th—the day after September 2nd—but the colony's clerks and a Charleston diarist recorded the event under the proper, new-style date. Joseph Wright, the Indian trader, was thus in the distinct minority of Britons who flubbed the calendric transition. That Thomas silently and correctly handled the shift to the new-style calendar simply demonstrates that he—and perhaps also Mary—was habituated to Britain's legal and cultural norms.[2]

That the Bosomworths spent the night separating September 2nd from September 14th at Tuckabatchee, however, shows that they understood not only British temporality but also Creek geography. Given the nature of their Acorn Whistler-related business, Tuckabatchee was exactly the right place for them to be. Tuckabatchee was home to many of Mary's relatives, people closely connected to Malatchi and Coweta, the Bosomworths' power base in Lower Creek country. Tuckabatchee, moreover, was the most influential Upper Creek town in the neighborhood of Acorn Whistler's Little Okfuskee and a rival of its mother town, Okfuskee. As such, Tuckabatchee's support for the Bosomworths' story was both worth having and theirs for the asking. The Bosomworths, in short, were in Tuckabatchee because they knew that political relations in the Creek world were structured by town-based alliances and rivalries. Thomas even expressed British demands via a community-centered idiom, telling Tuckabatchee audiences that Acorn Whistler was executed "for staining the white beloved Town with the Blood of our Friends." The Bosomworths' fluency with the language and strategies of a town-based system of diplomacy demonstrates that they—and, of course, particularly Mary—were habituated to Creek social and cultural norms.[3]

Mary and Thomas, then, could function—even, at times, thrive—in Creek and British worlds. That ability has proven so striking that it has threatened to become the central fact of their historiographical existence, the thing that we remember them for above all else. The Bosomworths appear in our histories as cultural chameleons par excellence, crossers of frontiers, go-betweens, mediators, and middlemen. This scholarly predilection has the unfortunate tendency of obscuring the complexity that characterized each world, homogenizing and flattening colonial experiences into a generic and all-encompassing dichotomy—Creek vs. British—that the Bosomworths could then transcend.

Colonial life was not that simple. Colonists never experienced their home society as featureless and unvarying; they never forgot that there were centers and peripheries, powerful institutions and negotiated relationships. The Bosomworths' various initiatives must be understood in this colonial context. Foregrounding the colonial nature of the Bosomworths' lives allows us to see Creek country and the British empire as the Bosomworths did—as spaces characterized by an inviting mix of hierarchy and fluidity, as homelands rich with traditions that commanded respect but not slavish obedience, as polities saturated with power and resources that could be tapped and exported. For the Bosomworths, moving between Creek country and the British empire was a function of habits and predispositions inculcated by the colonist's need to move within a colonial world. They used their ability to cross political and cultural frontiers as a means toward ends that were firmly grounded in their understanding of the colonial world's possibilities. The story the Bosomworths told about Acorn Whistler most certainly drew on their connections to the Creeks and the British, but that story was—above all else—a colonial story.

Understanding that colonial story requires charting the Bosomworths' evolving place—individually and as a couple—in that world.

We can do so most easily by dipping into their biographies at certain crucial moments: their initial year of marriage; Thomas's early experiences in Georgia; Mary's time first in Pon Pon, South Carolina, and then in Yamacraw, Georgia; and the spring of 1752, as Thomas and Mary had to decide which homeland—England or Creek country—they should go to first. Sampling their biographies demonstrates quite clearly that the colonial claims that they advanced in 1752 were decades in the making.

⌒ MRS. MARY MATTHEWS was joined in marriage to the Reverend Thomas Bosomworth on July 8, 1744. It was his first marriage, but Mary—roughly twenty years Thomas's senior—had out lived two husbands. The wedding ceremony took place in Frederica, Georgia, where Mary, the colony's "Indian Interpretess," occupied a "well built" two-story house and Thomas ministered part-time to the town's garrison and inhabitants. Mary had more extensive holdings in and around Savannah, where Thomas was "appointed to reside," although he spent most of his time in Frederica so as to add "the Allowance for officiating as the Chaplain to the Regiment" to the £50 salary he received as Savannah's minister. Their overlapping residence patterns notwithstanding, Thomas and Mary clearly did not know each other well prior to, in one colonist's words, "this late Surprizing adventure of our Parsons attacking, and carrying the Widow in a Short storm." And thus, when news of the wedding reached Savannah it "appeared so incredible . . . that 'twas looked on as a piece of Merriment and canvass'd as such, among most of their Acquaintance." The "Chattering" had not died down when the Bosomworths arrived in Savannah on August 6th. A year later, a "distress[ed]" Thomas wrote of the "vile & base means [that] have been made use off in order to murther both our Reputations," and it is clear that the Bosomworths remained a topic of conversation for years.[4]

Thomas's typically overwrought rhetoric aside, some of the difficulties the newlyweds faced were simple, garden-variety postwedding adjustments—for example, the inevitable slip-of-the-pen references to "Widow Mathews" (instead of Mrs. Bosomworth) or "Mary Matthews" (instead of Mary Bosomworth). Thomas and Mary, moreover, were hardly shunned socially. Two weeks after arriving in Savannah, "thinking it proper to celebrate their late Nuptials . . . by giving an Entertainment," the Bosomworths borrowed the largest house in town, laid out "all such kind of provisions as this place could afford," and hosted an evening of dining, drinking, and dancing that lasted into "the latest hours." The party was a smashing success. No one got "disordered with Drink," and "nothing happen'd in the whole Company (large as it was) that gave any offense."

Likewise, Mary's Creek relatives showed no signs of ostracizing the pair. Within a few years, in fact, Malatchi and his allies were referring to "our Beloved Man Thomas Bosomworth," a status made possible by Creek women's habit of integrating outsiders into society via marriage. Mary herself was the daughter of one such relationship, and Mary's previous husbands had been English (Jacob Matthews) and Anglo-Creek (John Musgrove). Moreover, since Mary had not spent any significant time in Creek country since at least the mid-1720s, it would have been the rare Creek who was shocked by Mary's choice of an English husband. Thus, acknowledging both the snickering that accompanied Thomas and Mary's May-September marriage and the certainty that some gossips crossed the line into racial invective, it seems clear that the "distress" which Thomas and Mary labored under during their first year of marriage stemmed from something more than "murther[ed]" reputations.[5]

The root cause of their difficulties was that the Bosomworths carried a crushing load of debt contracted as each had tried to profit from the options offered by the colonial world. Mary had exhausted her fortune in a decade's worth of efforts to solidify—and become central to—the relationship between the Creeks and Georgia's de facto leader, General James Oglethorpe. Thomas had moved from position to position and from colony to mother country and back again, each time losing salary and patrons while incurring expenses. Financial salvation in the face of these colonial problems, Mary and Thomas must have realized as they were courting, would most likely come from colonial possibilities—from, that is, leveraging the influence that the combination of Thomas's education and British identity, on the one hand, and Mary's connections and Indian identity, on the other hand, could bring within networks that linked the colonial town of Savannah to Coweta and London. So, as the Bosomworths recovered from the party, they prepared to take the ultimate step available to distressed colonists: "[T]hey were both determined to go to England."[6]

As it turned out, only Thomas went, sneaking aboard a ship in June 1745, one step ahead of a court order seeking money that he did not have. Mary stayed behind, but Thomas's trip was all about her. As he later put it, he went to England "to Claim the Performance of the various Promises" made to "his Wife." The voyage thus combined metropolitan action with colonial referent in a way that owed everything to the colonist's habit of structuring thought, word, and deed around a dialogue with the mother country. That project led Thomas, once he arrived in England, to attach himself to General Oglethorpe's household and to present Oglethorpe with documents asserting Mary's right to both reimbursement for past services and a significant chunk of Georgia real estate. At the same time, Thomas used Mary's Creek heritage in an attempt to smooth things over with Georgia's Trustees and the Society for the Propagation of the Gospel, both of whom were "much surprised at the Return of their Missionary . . . without their Privity or Consent." Thomas acknowledged his "Disobedience," but tried to save his job by claiming that he returned to preserve "the general Peace & Tranquility of the Colony."[7]

The danger? Mary's Creek kinsmen. Thomas had, he told his superiors, married her "the better to enable me to carry on the great Work of promoting [Christian] Knowledge among the Natives of America." The Creeks, though, became outraged at the slanders that colonists hurled at Thomas and Mary after their marriage, and now "threatened to take their own Satisfaction in Case Justice was not done." This claim was utterly ungrounded in colonial reality, but the Bosomworths thought it would resonate in England and thereby provide Thomas with the cover necessary to take a trip that had nothing to do with angry Creeks. Or, put another way, Mary's Indian identity and Creek relations would justify Thomas's presence in England, and Mary's history and influence would allow Thomas access to Oglethorpe's wealth and connections, which an educated Briton like Thomas would put to good use. Being colonial had its privileges.[8]

It is telling, however, that Thomas was unable to make those privileges work to his advantage. His employers ignored his plea for an "Opportunity of Vindicating my Conduct" and appointed a new missionary for Savannah; the Trustees rejected Mary's claims for land and compensation. To be sure, Thomas's trip was not a complete failure. Oglethorpe, in recognition of Mary's past assistance and continuing influence in Creek country, provided Thomas with a £1000 line of credit and favorable letters to people in position to assist the Bosomworths. Mary and Thomas, though, needed cash (not the opportunity to go further into debt) or land that could be converted into cash. And in those crucial respects, Thomas came up short. Moreover, the gains he did realize were offset by very real costs. His "Necessities for Cash" while traveling led him to sign bills of exchange against the hoped-for-reimbursements from the Trustees, and leaving his Savannah flock cost him his position as minister and the salary that came with it. Factor in the reality that the trip severed his ties to patrons among the Trustees and the Society, and it becomes difficult to argue that Thomas had played his family's colonial cards well.[9]

THE STRIKING THING about Thomas's lack of success, though, is that it was not an aberration. He had stumbled down this road before. Thomas was not, to be sure, a failure. He rose too far and too fast to deserve that label, but nor was he a true success. Throughout his life, Thomas displayed a remarkable habit of spying a new opportunity, turning his back on old commitments, and then failing both to prosper as he expected and to convince the Powers That Were that he had acted appropriately.

Thomas was born provincial, not colonial, the son of a Yorkshire landowner of modest means. Testifying to his keen awareness of Britain's social and geographic hierarchies, Thomas pursued London-style cosmopolitanism with a vengeance, acquiring a fine education, using his manners and erudition to cultivate friends and patrons, and relentlessly encouraging those people to advance his prospects. One of those friends, Christopher Orton, brought him to the attention of Georgia's Trustees, and, when Orton became Savannah's minister, the Trustees agreed to pay for Thomas to accompany him to Georgia in 1741. That a man whose "life story can aptly be summarized as a quest to transcend his low social standing and provincialism" would travel to Britain's most marginal North American colony and marry a woman of Creek descent is certainly ironic. More than that, though, it is revealing. Thomas's seemingly odd choices demonstrate how very much colonial life, even at its furthest removes from British norms, remained British-focused. Provincial strivers in Britain effortlessly became colonial wannabes in North America, and provincial strategies morphed seamlessly into colonial initiatives. For Thomas, acquiring a university degree and an Indian wife were part of the same project; he moved to London and Frederica for identical reasons. It is difficult to discern the point at which he ceased being provincial and became colonial.[10]

The smoothness of Thomas's transition to colonial life shows in his unvarying approach to the world. Thomas's life choices were erratic, but reliably, regularly, even religiously so. As Thomas sailed from England, the Trustees told Secretary William Stephens that "Mr. Thomas Bosomworth . . . comes over to be your Clerk." They assured Stephens that, although Thomas's "hand is not perfectly Clerklike," he had a strong "desire to please." Perhaps, but other desires were stronger. Thomas had been in Georgia less than a year before his requests for a more exalted office forced the Trustees to remind him that "assisting . . . Mr. Stephens" was to be "your chief Study." That letter had barely reached Georgia before Reverend Orton's death presented Thomas with a new opportunity. He hastily returned to London and was "admitted into Holy Orders" as an Anglican minister. After intensively lobbying to be appointed Savannah's minister, he returned to Georgia in 1743, carrying with him both the Trustees' reluctant blessing—their first choice fell through—and their explicit instructions that he was "to reside at Savannah." Instead, he settled at Frederica—whose people were, he told his "concern[ed]" superiors, in need of "a shepherd"—and he immediately began asking for advances on his salary. In fact, on June 24, 1744, he wrote a very brief letter to the Society to explain both that he was so ill he could barely hold a pen and that he had drawn once again on his salary.[11]

Exactly two weeks later, he married the Widow Matthews, testifying to both the healing power of ready cash and his own ability to turn on a dime. A year later, after relocating to Savannah and returning the people of Frederica to the ranks of the unshepherded, he was off to England, where his lobbying campaign on Mary's behalf was quintessential Thomas—energetic, heartfelt, ambitious, not entirely unsuccessful, and interrupted by a brief flirtation with the idea of "hazard[ing] my life" on a military expedition to put down the 1745 Jacobite rebellion. When that fixation passed, he came back to Georgia, where he and Mary built a trading post 300 miles up the Altamaha River, used Oglethorpe's credit to buy "a large Cargoe of Indian Goods," and began "a Considerable Indian Trade."[12] And then. . . .

That the list of Thomas's vocational choices could be extended by several paragraphs suggests that he had confused *career* (n.) with *career* (v.). A more charitable interpretation, however, would note two things. In the first place, Thomas had already devoted his life to transformation even before he sailed for Georgia, and the project of acquiring the wealth and manners necessary to achieve gentility in England was daunting enough that anyone undertaking it was well advised to watch for unorthodox avenues of advancement. Second, it is worth acknowledging the catnip-like effects that could ensue when a provincial man-on-the-make suddenly confronted both the possibilities of colonial life and the opportunities inherent in the metropole-colony relationship. We are used to reading that early America was a land of opportunity. Thomas's vocational struggles suggest that, for colonists, opportunity was a double-edged sword.

MARY DID NOT RESPOND to the colonial situation exactly as her third husband did, but anyone looking to answer the "What brought them together?" question could do worse than examine the overlapping ways in which Mary and Thomas positioned themselves within the homeland-periphery relationship. Thomas chose to put that relationship at the center of his life, while Mary had it thrust upon her from the moment of her ca. 1700 birth in Coweta.

Mary's father was a British trader and her mother, as she later put it, "was Sister to the Old Emperor [Brims] of the Same Blood of the Present Mico [Malatchi]." At the age of seven, she remembered being "brought Down by her Father from the Indian Nation, to Pomponne in South Carolina; There baptized, Educated, and bred up in the Principles of Christianity." She was still in Pon Pon a decade later when, during the pan-Indian struggle with South Carolina known as the Yamasee War, she married John Musgrove, Jr., another Anglo-Creek. The next year, the Musgroves accompanied Mary's father-in-law to Coweta as part of the delegation seeking to end Creek-British hostilities. John and Mary's marriage may have been resolemnized in Coweta as a symbol of Creek-British harmony, and it seems likely that they remained there long enough for Mary to deliver her first child in 1718. Sometime soon thereafter, the Musgroves returned to Pon Pon. They remained there until 1732, welcomed another son into their family, and prospered thanks to their ability to combine homemaking, small-scale Indian trading, planting, herding, and government-sponsored Creek diplomacy. It was while living in Pon Pon that Mary became, as her biographer notes, "a woman who expected to succeed in colonial society."[13]

The nature of her life in Pon Pon, though, meant that Mary's version of "colonial society" was powerfully inflected by the fact that she lived on the margins of the Creek homeland. Her family's material success, for example, always involved their Creek kin and connections. John served variously as an interpreter for British diplomats in Creek country, an investigator of Creek-British frontier problems, a commander of British-sponsored Creek war parties against Spanish Florida, and a conduit of British goods and favors to the Musgroves' Creek friends and relatives. He was well paid for these services. The Creek role in the Musgroves' lives at Pon Pon, however, went well beyond the material. Pon Pon was a "multicultural" enclave, the home of British planters, Indian traders, their Anglo-Creek children, and a small community of Creeks who "live[d] on young Musgroves Land." Other Creeks visited regularly enough in the 1720s that British diplomats—worried about everything from Creeks aiding runaway slaves to outbreaks of Anglo-Creek violence—fumed that "these Indians that Live about Pon Pon are very pernicious to our Interest." Pon Pon, it seems, was a Creek colony as much as a British one.[14]

The attachments formed at Pon Pon surfaced repeatedly in Mary's future life, including—most notably—during the Acorn Whistler crisis. Mary's Pon Pon neighbors in the 1720s may have included Lower Creeks from Osochi, the hometown of the men who attacked the Cherokee party on April 1, 1752. Another neighbor was James Welch, a frequent diplomatic partner of John Musgrove and a soldier who served with Mary's brother. By 1752, Welch had married an Estatoe woman and was living in Estatoe, the hometown of the Cherokees killed on April 1. Their reputed killer, Acorn Whistler, stopped at Pon Pon on his way back from Charleston in 1744 and (most likely) in 1752, and several of his Upper Creek followers were captured there after the April 1 attack. Once Acorn Whistler was dead, Thomas Bosomworth spent a night at Pon Pon while returning from Creek country, and after Governor Glen concluded his 1753 Creek conference, Thomas and Mary reacquired the Musgroves' Pon Pon holdings. In a very real way, Mary never left Pon Pon and its people behind.[15]

Even more than relationships to people and place, though, life at Pon Pon solidified Mary's understanding of what was possible when one lived at the intersection of colonial worlds. John's various activities, for example, allowed him to cultivate the British connections that were such a critical component of success in colonial America. At the same time, of course, John and Mary also cultivated connections to the headmen John negotiated with and fought beside, as well as to Mary's Coweta kinsmen. Those Cowetas stopped at Pon Pon on their way to and from Charleston conferences, and they spoke knowledgeably about events in Mary's neighborhood.

These relationships—to powerful Creeks and Britons alike— came together in 1732 when, as Mary later wrote, a group of Creeks who were moving to the future site of Savannah "Request[ed]" that the Musgroves serve as their traders. These Creeks were led by Tomochichi of Apalachicola, the hometown of John Musgrove's uncle. South Carolina's governor gave his "Consent and Approbation," and almost certainly promised the Musgroves a land grant at Yamacraw, on the south side of the Savannah River. There, the Musgroves used their access to "Large Credit and Supplies of Goods . . . from the Merchants in Charles Town" to start a trading house that netted "Large Quantities of Deer Skins," and they began what Mary described as "a very Good Cowpen & Plantation." Trade and agriculture, Creek kinsmen and British patrons, British credit and Creek resources—a family that could draw on those things had every reason to expect prosperity in the Anglo-Creek colonial world. The Musgroves, after all, had done just that at Pon Pon.[16]

⌒ MARY HAD NO REASON to know it at the time, but her experience of unrelieved success at Pon Pon was an aberration. Progress in the colonial world was more typically of the two-steps-forward-one-step-back variety, and while the ability to draw upon British and Creek connections could work wonders, it was just as likely to produce a complicated mix of confusion and bad feelings. Certainly that is what the Musgroves found when Georgia's colonists began arriving in January 1733. Their capital, Savannah, was a short walk from the Creek village at Yamacraw and the Musgroves' trading house. Mary and John were instructed by South Carolina's government to be serviceable to Oglethorpe and his followers, and perhaps the Musgroves—while watching Savannah take shape next to Yamacraw—envisioned replicating Pon Pon's model of Anglo-Creek cooperation and prosperity.

A colonial capital, though, was not an auspicious place to re-create patterns of thought and action developed in an Anglo-Creek frontier enclave. Pon Pon's habits might work for a time and to a degree in Savannah—which was a marginal, ramshackle place—but they would produce many fewer clear-cut successes and many more situations in which progress was married to frustration, proximity to mistrust. For better or worse, however, it likely took Mary some time to recognize her new reality. There was, after all, a great deal about life at Yamacraw in 1733 which looked extraordinarily promising.[17]

Opportunities for financial gain, for example, were thick on the ground. The Georgia colonists offered the Musgroves a regular market for their plantation's meat and produce, and the fact that John and Mary cleared more land than did two Georgia towns suggests that they recognized agriculture's lucrative potential. At the same time, Georgia's officials—grateful for the Musgroves' help with the Creeks—aggressively defended the couple's Indian trading monopoly. In Georgia's first two years, the Musgroves acquired "from the Indians near 12000 Weight of Deer Skin," and in 1735 the Trustees extended the Musgroves' "sole License for Trade with the Indians" beyond the Yamacraw Creeks to Indian communities further up the Savannah River. The Trustees also gave the Musgroves valuable gifts—£20 for Mary; an opulent "Suit of Cloaths" for John—and the Trustees' representatives in Savannah attracted important Indian visitors, who were given food and gifts, which were often purchased from the Musgrove's store. Factor in the 500 acres of land granted to John by the Trustees, and it becomes clear why local gossips could whisper that Mary had "made away with £1600 Currency, the chief of which was in silver and gold." The Musgroves were apparently prospering in Georgia's colonial economy.[18]

That prosperity was intertwined with two other welcome developments: the Musgroves became increasingly close to Georgia's leaders, and the couple's social status rose rapidly. Both Oglethorpe and the Trustees recognized how very useful the Musgroves could be in, as the latter wrote about Mary, "Interpreting for the Indians" and "keeping . . . the Peace with them." Oglethorpe rarely dealt with Indians without summoning a Musgrove, and the couple's ties with him became particularly strong. Mary's modern reputation as the Pocahontas of Georgia stems primarily from this relationship, and while John is not well remembered today he was paid £100 to accompany Oglethorpe and a Yamacraw delegation to London. Even when these opportunities did not work out—for example, John was sometimes too drunk to interpret while in England—they still guaranteed the Musgroves access to the upper levels of Britain's colonial hierarchy. It was, thus, fitting that the Trustees described John as "of the Province of Georgia in America Gentleman," while a minister called Mary "a Sensible well civiliz'd woman." Of course, neither John nor Mary were truly genteel or civilized by British standards, but their status in the colonial world was clearly on the rise. They had become "Mr. & Mrs. Musgrove," a striking recognition of the many ways in which these two Anglo-Creeks had succeeded in the colonial world.[19]

That success was paired with—and dependent upon—similar achievements in the Musgroves' relations with the Creeks. Living near Yamacraw gave John and Mary the opportunity to maintain personal ties to their mothers' people. The Musgroves developed particularly close relationships with the Yamacraw Creeks, an easy

task since, as Mary put it, they were "her Indian Friends and Relations." Some Yamacraws may have followed the Musgroves from
Pon Pon, and others came from Creek country after a Coweta
headman gave three Yamacraw leaders permission "to call the Kindred that love them, out of each of the Creek Towns, that they may
come together and make one Town." One of the three, Stimoio-
che of Osochi, was Yamacraw's head warrior, and his two brothers
left Osochi to become headmen in Yamacraw. Stimoiche died soon
thereafter, but his brothers joined five other Yamacraws in telling a
Georgia official that "We brought our wives and our children here"
to trade "with [John] Musgrove"; when John was in England, they
asked that Mary—"for whose Sake they settled here"—"may trade
by herself." As Mary began shifting her operations from Savannah
to the plantation five miles upriver, the Yamacraws joined her, setting up a new village close enough to Mary that Oglethorpe noted
that two missionaries had "gone up to Tomo-chi-chi Mico and live
with Mrs Musgrove." A decade later, the Yamacraws had moved to
St. Catherine's Island, which the Lower Creeks gave to Mary. She
and Thomas Bosomworth were living there more or less full-time
by the late 1740s, enmeshed in Mary's networks of Creek friends
and the "Indian relations who are allways about her."[20]

In the 1730s, though, Mary's relatives and friends included not
just the ordinary Creeks and local headmen who lived at Yamacraw
but also people back in Creek country who thought of themselves
as national-level leaders. The Musgroves, building on old Pon Pon
ties, developed increasingly close relationships with these important
men. Coweta's headmen, for example, led large delegations to Savannah in 1733, 1735, and 1736. Either John or Mary interpreted for the
resulting conferences, but, more than that, the Musgroves served as
hosts, entertaining the Coweta leaders and their followers for days.
The "near 150 Indians" who came in 1735, for example, stayed near
Mary's plantation (the Cow Pen), and in 1736 "Chigilli Chief of the
Lower Creeks with the Chiefs of 7 Towns and their Attendants to
the number of 60, came down to Mrs. Musgroves Cow Pen," where
they waited for Oglethorpe. By 1740, then, it seemed entirely unre-
markable to Secretary Stephens that "Malatchie went up the River,
with his Attendants, intending to stay a Day or two with" Mary. The

"frequent Resort of these People to her House," combined with "her good Offices in Indian Affairs on many Occasions" and her very real kin ties in Creek country, allowed Mary to have, in Stephens's words, "a very great Influence upon many of them." That "Influence" was one of the perks of living near a colonial capital and being held "in great Esteem [by] the General" who presided over it.[21]

There is no escaping the fact, however, that the benefits Mary enjoyed after moving to the Savannah area came at a steep price emotionally and economically. The emotional price is hinted at in the above paragraphs, in which the story of Mary and John gradually becomes the story of Mary. John Musgrove died of a fever on June 12, 1735. The two Musgrove boys followed their father to the grave within two years. Mary's obvious affection for her husband and her distress at their eldest son's illness leave little room for us to believe that she was anything but utterly devastated by these blows.

At the same time, it became clear that, in the rush of Savannah's early years, the Musgroves had overextended themselves financially. As Mary later put it, they "had but Little Experience of [either] the World" or "the fraudulent Designs of Bad people," and so their fortunes "greatly suffered by giving Large Creditt to sundry Inhabitants and other Persons on publick service." When those people died, fled the colony, or were "not in Circumstances to pay her," Mary was left to write promissory notes to Charleston's merchants for the goods advanced to Savannah's colonists and Indian visitors. By 1737, her situation was dire enough that Oglethorpe could confidently state that Mary would not move back "to Carolina, She owing there a thousand pound[s]." Her position grew even more precarious in the next few years when, during Britain's war with Spain, she "constantly supported at her own Expence, great Numbers of her Friends, and Other War Indians" in their attacks on Spanish Florida, with the result that "her Trade Daily decreased and almost intirely went to Ruin." Add in the fact that her diplomatic duties left her no time to manage her plantation—"neglected & running to Ruin"—and it is clear that Mary suffered a staggering series of reversals. The woman who arrived at Yamacraw as part of a prosperous family was learning that the colonial experience could tear out your heart and empty your wallet.[22]

In the face of these setbacks and tragedies, it was perhaps inevitable that Mary's relations with Georgia's officials would grow evermore fraught. She continued to serve as Oglethorpe's interpreter and advisor, going so far as to accede to his request that she open a trading post at the Forks of the Altamaha River, which the general garrisoned with Georgia rangers. However, Mary's relations with Stephens (who arrived in 1737) were never better than cool, and she had a series of run-ins with lower-level Savannah officials before and after Oglethorpe's 1743 departure from Georgia. These tensions were likely grounded in Mary's growing recognition that her sacrifices were not being adequately compensated, but her 1737 marriage to Jacob Matthews, one of her servants, exacerbated matters. Stephens and his allies never forgot Matthews's lowly origins, accusing him of being "blown up with Pride" because his marriage made him "the greatest Man in this Country," reveling in his failed attempts to exercise "any Sort of Authority or Command" over the Creeks, and slyly referring to "Mrs. Matthews's Cow-Pen" and "Marys house" to highlight Jacob's de facto subordination to his wife. When the Matthewses became leading members of a political faction—the so-called Malcontents—protesting the Trustees' policies, Mary and Jacob rose to the top of the list of colonists who gave the Trustees "great uneasiness."[23]

Oddly enough, the Trustees' fears about Mary came to focus on the very thing that made her so valuable to them: her connections in Creek country. Beginning in the late 1730s, Mary started using those ties to acquire land. In 1738, she received the Yamacraws' tract near Savannah as a gift from Tomochichi and headmen from Osochi and three other Lower Creek towns. At the same time, she committed more resources to her fortified Altamaha River trading post on the very border—"a great way in the Nation"—of Creek country. She and Jacob lived there for months at a time and, after a Spanish force destroyed the buildings just as Jacob was dying in 1742, she and Thomas reclaimed it. Their "Settlement" there consisted of "a very good Dwelling House, outhouses, a large store and Fortify'd the whole round"; the post served as their "principal residence" from 1746 to 1748. Mary's rights there were based on Creek statements of approval rather than a formal cession, but she was still claiming ownership of the site as late as 1760. Well before that point, though, Mary had used "a Grant from the Indians" to claim three of Georgia's Sea Islands, the most valuable of which, St. Catherine's, she and Thomas stocked with slaves and a herd of cattle before moving there in 1748.[24]

These initiatives made the Trustees exceptionally nervous. If Mary wanted to farm, ranch, or trade on land given her by Creeks, that was fine. She was, they reasoned, a Creek, and Creeks could give land to other Creeks. She could not sell that land to other colonists, though, because Creek gifts had no standing in British law; only the Crown or its representatives, not an individual subject, could acquire land directly from Indians. Britons who claimed Creek land which had not first been granted to the king and then regranted to his loyal subjects were calling into question basic tenets of British sovereignty and imperial expansion. Mary was having none of that reasoning, in large part because she had learned the colonial world's lessons entirely too well. As befitted someone who had lived a life defined by the interplay between homeland and periphery, Creek country and British colony, she claimed the right to get land like an Indian but to own it—and, more importantly, to sell it—like a Briton. Any move toward actually selling land, though, was delayed by Jacob's death. It was not until the mid-1740s—and particularly after Thomas Bosomworth returned from England in 1746—that the Trustees' fears were realized, and Mary began aggressively asserting British title to Indian land.

Thomas—and Thomas's debts—certainly played a role in her decision to do so, but it would be a mistake to accord him too much influence in this matter. Mary's years at Yamacraw had primed her to make such a decision. Envisioning the possibility that Creek territory could be transformed into British real estate required recognizing the potential inherent in living on the colonial margins of two homelands. Yamacraw had shown her that huge sums could be made in an Anglo-Creek world. The tracts of Creek land that Mary claimed—what a Georgia governor described as "a large quantity of the best lands on our Sea Coast"—were worth thousands of pounds on the British market, enough to pay off her debts and guarantee her future prosperity. But committing oneself to claiming British title to Creek land required having enough experience with the darker side of colonial life—tragedy and loss; ingratitude and broken promises; hostility and suspicion—to lose faith in official channels, legal niceties, and the men who guarded the former and expounded the latter.[25]

The Bosomworths, after all, were asserting not only that, as Thomas supposedly said, the Creeks were "Sovereigns themselves" but also that Mary and Thomas "could by Law oblige the King to allow" the Creeks to grant land to British subjects. That sort of rhetoric—"incompatible with [Thomas's] Duty as a Subject" and "tending to prove him guilty of Treason"—was "hanging dangerous." It is hard to imagine Mary approving such language while living at Pon Pon in 1725, or after moving to Yamacraw in 1732, or even immediately following John Musgrove's death in 1735. But a dozen years later, Mary wrote that "She at present Labours under every sense of Injury; and Circumstances of Distress; Destitute of even the Common Necessaries of Life, being Insulted, Abused, contemned and Despised by those ungratefull People who are indebted to her for the Blessings they Injoy." She was, by this point, more than ready to use the realities of her colonial position to challenge the British metropole's legal abstractions. In doing so, she might perhaps win some satisfaction for the grief, frustration, and conflict she had experienced while living at Yamacraw.[26]

⌒ ON MAY 20, 1752, Thomas and Mary "arriv'd in Charles Town South Carolina with Intent immediately to proceed for England," where—Mary noted in a June 1st letter to Governor Glen—"I can recover from the Government at Home such Sums as are justly due for my past Services in Georgia." Given Mary's Creek heritage and tense relations with "ungratefull" colonists, her reference to England as "Home" is striking. True, she was the daughter of a Briton, the widow of two others, and the wife of a fourth; true, she had been an almost lifelong "Inhabitant" of Britain's colonies; true, she had repeatedly demonstrated "my Zeal for his Majesty's Service." Mary, though, had never been to her English "Home." Her self-described "Interest and Influence" were in Creek country, where she claimed to have "a rightful and natural Power by the Laws of God and Nature" over the "Chiefs" of the "Nation."

She had, moreover, spent the last half-dozen years wrapping herself ever-more tightly in the mantle of Indian-ness, an identity which she first claimed in print in 1746 and then enhanced with a 1749 reference to her Muskogee name, Coosaponakeesa. All of which is to say that, if Mary was going "Home" in June 1752, she should have been heading west to Coweta, not east to London.[27]

And, of course, that is exactly what transpired: Mary and Thomas went to Creek country in July, with Thomas returning to South Carolina in January 1753 but Mary staying with her mother's people until May. Why, then, did the Bosomworths so viscerally link Mary to England by invoking "Home"? The answer had everything to do with their hope that Mary would be seen as a unique sort of Indian—at once intensely loyal to Britain and impressively powerful in Creek country. Steadfast Britons were a dime a dozen; influential Indians were not hard to find. A person who could plausibly claim to be both, though, was an exceptionally rare—and potentially valuable—commodity. And so Mary wrote of "Home." It was the perfect word for colonists like the Bosomworths who were engaged in their by now second-nature strategy of seeking colonial solutions to colonial problems.

The problems the Bosomworths faced in the late spring of 1752 were easy to see. Most notably, their financial affairs had gone from worrisome to frightful. Mary had continued advancing trade goods to Creeks at the behest of British officers; their failure to repay the loans meant she could not buy more trade goods, forcing her "to forego a most Beneficial Traffic with the Indians." To make matters worse, plans for Mary to leverage her past Creek-related services to Georgia so as to get access to a portion of Britain's gifts for the Creeks fell through. As a result, by 1750, the Bosomworths were being sued for debt by a Savannah mercantile firm and a Frederica widow. Their "Goods and Chattels" on St. Simons Island were seized, and two armed men were posted "where the said Thomas Bosomworth & Mary his Wife then Lodged." No wonder that Mary later remembered that, at this time, they lived as "Prisoners as it were in the Province." When she and Thomas were finally able to leave Georgia in May 1752, they arrived in Charleston only to find that, to satisfy yet another creditor, a bailiff had seized the goods they intended to sell to finance their London trip. Even when they managed to cover that debt, as Mary explained to Glen, Thomas was "hourly liable to be arrested and harrassed by his Creditors whose Demands is not in his Power at present to satisfy." Thomas could eventually leave for Creek country only because Glen issued an official proclamation that "we have taken into our special Protection the said Thomas Bosomworth."[28]

That Glen's decision to protect the said Thomas Bosomworth outraged officials in Georgia points to the other problem facing Mary and Thomas: toxic relations with the leaders of the colony in which they lived. Georgia's officials were certain that, given the "former extraordinary Conduct of these People in respect to these Indians," employing the Bosomworths as agents would "weaken the English Influence among the Indians," "engage us in troublesome Disputes," and "prove very injurious to the Welfare of this Colony." Georgia's leaders had grown increasingly worried about Mary's demands for land, back pay, and reimbursement. The situation came to a head in the summer of 1749 in a very public and very messy Savannah confrontation involving not simply the Bosomworths and Georgia's president and assistants but also Malatchi, dozens of Lower Creeks, and Savannah's militia.[29]

During that brouhaha, Mary spent a night in jail because, in the words of Georgia's official "Proceedings," "She rose to such a pitch of Insolence, as repeatedly to threaten the Lives of some of the Magistrates, and the Destruction of the Colony, through her influence with, and command over the Indians." For his part, Thomas was forced to make a tearful public apology, which he later attributed to his fear of a murderous "Mob" and his "Sense of the Injuries, Injustice, and Tyranny I Suffered; (scarce to be Paralleled under a british Government)." The colony's leaders, for their part, dismissed the Bosomworths as "an Ambitious dissolute and avaricious Family whom the most extraordinary Favors will not satisfy and who may (through their influence with a party of blood thirsty and ignorant heathens if countenanced) bring this Colony into such distressing circumstances as may not be retrieved in many Years." If the Bosomworths hoped to win support at "Home" in 1752, they would have to do it without any help from home.[30]

At the core of the Bosomworths' ever-worsening relationship with Georgia were what the colony's leaders referred to as "Mr. and Mrs. Bosomworth's extravagant and idle Claims of Royalty and Lands." In 1747, Mary invoked her kinship ties to Malatchi's family and began describing herself as the Creeks' "Rightfull and Natural Princess." During the 1749 Savannah confrontation, she promoted herself to "Empress and Queen of the Upper and Lower Creeks," but "Princess" seems to have been the title of choice. Sometimes, as "Sovereign," Mary claimed to "Command" in Creek country, but she was more likely to trot out the "Interest and Influence" phrase she used in her June 1, 1752, letter to Glen. Her 1747 "Memorial," in fact, uses that phrase three times on one page. That Malatchi and his Creek allies sometimes echoed the "Princess" language showed that Mary did, in fact, have an "Interest"—a term Britons used to signify a network of supporters—and the "Influence" it brought within Creek country.[31]

That "Influence" justified her claims to Creek land. In a moment of real anger, she might tell Georgia's leaders "you have not a Foot of Land in this Colony . . . That the very Ground was her's." Such claims, though, were excessively confrontational, unlikely to win support at "Home," and thus counterproductive. Instead, the Bosomworths generally contented themselves with amassing Creek speeches, proclamations, and deeds that supported their title to the three Sea Islands and the Yamacraws' land around Savannah. All such documents were duly witnessed, notarized, and registered, and all mentioned the Creeks' high regard for Mary as the reason that they had "Granted Bargained sold enfeoffed and confirmed" the land to Thomas and Mary "forever." Just to be on the safe side, Mary also made sure that she received Creek authorization, as "our rightful and natural Princess," to travel "over the Great Water." Once there, she was to meet with "the Great King George," and to "Determine, Accomplish and Finish, all Matters and Things" relating to Creek land.[32]

Such documents, of course, were colonial productions for metropolitan consumption, texts meant to be read at "Home" in London, not in Savannah or Charleston. At "Home," the documents' flaws—the marks of headmen who were closely connected to Mary and/or Malatchi and the disconnect between Mary's claims and the reality of Creek political life—would be less noticeable. At "Home," Mary could be at once the Creek princess eager to resolve a delicate issue with Britain's king and the loyal colonist "Desireous and Willing," in her self-description, "to hold What Posesions she is . . . entitled to by the Laws of Nature and Nations, as a Subject of Great Britain." At "Home," Mary and Thomas could hope that the possibilities offered to them by the colonial world would be made real by royal fiat. At "Home," they could finally achieve the goal they had chased since their first weeks of marriage: financial security. If home is where the heart is, then it made a great deal of sense for the Bosomworths to head for "Home."[33]

⌒ BY LATE MAY 1752, then, the Bosomworths were in Charleston preparing to sail for London, carrying with them their Creek deeds and proclamations. And then they learned that Governor Glen was sending an agent to obtain satisfaction for the Lower Creeks' April 1 attack. Thomas and Mary's decision to pursue that assignment and postpone the London trip seems like a classic example of Thomas's *volte-face* approach to the colonial world. In fact, though, the Bosomworths viewed the Creek agency as an unexpected-but-welcome prelude to their voyage "Home." Given both the realities of the Bosomworths' colonial lives and the people involved in the Acorn Whistler crisis, they realized that the best route to London lay through Coweta.

Thus, when Thomas wrote Glen on June 2 to ask for details of the agent's job in the west, he did so with one eye on the east. Thomas was, he told Glen, in need of an "Answer this Evening as I am necessitated to give a final Answer to the Captain of a Vessel with whom I am about to agree for a Passage to England." Likewise, Thomas's questions went well beyond the standard one about "What Services . . . this Government expects Mrs. Bosomworth should perform." He also wanted to know "In what Manner her Services are to be represented to his Majesty in Case of Success," and—only too aware that a trip to London was expensive—he inquired about "What Reward she may expect from this Government in Case every Thing is performed to the Satisfaction thereof." An appalled Georgia official nicely captured what the Bosomworths were hoping for when he noted that Glen "justifies [Mary and Thomas's] extraordinary Claim of Lands here, and has promised him, if he succeeds, a handsome Gratuity, and also to recommend him and his Wife's Services to England."[34]

The Bosomworths, in short, intended to use the prospect of their imminent trip "Home" to pressure a colonial governor into deciding to send them to Creek country where they could perform the "Services" necessary to obtain both the money required to sail to England and the letters of recommendation required to succeed there. It was a complicated strategy, but also a quintessentially colonial one—provided, of course, that the colonists in question could effectively draw on two homelands. And it was a strategy that thrust the Bosomworths into the Acorn Whistler affair. Now, they would need a story.

~ 8

The Colonists' Story

THOMAS AND MARY BOSOMWORTH learned of Acorn Whistler's execution on August 19. Three days later, as they and their Lower Creek allies fretted about the possibly belligerent response of Acorn Whistler's family and community, the Bosomworths heard that a Coweta relative of Acorn Whistler "was sent to bring down his Sons and some of his Relations to talk with them about this Affair." And then, with the possibility of Creek-on-Creek violence hanging in the air and their own lives very much in danger, the Acorn Whistler crisis utterly vanished from Thomas's journal for a week. In its place, Thomas filled page after page with accounts of his dealings with British traders who challenged his authority. Concern about the fallout from Acorn Whistler's death, it seems, led to all sorts of reactions. Malatchi kept a low public profile. A panicked Creek headman killed Acorn Whistler's nephew. And Thomas Bosomworth—who described Acorn Whistler's execution as "a very dangerous and ticklish Point"—vigorously and obsessively defended his status and influence.[1]

That Thomas did so to the exclusion of matters more obviously relevant to his mission was utterly in character. He had a well-developed sense of both insecurity and outrage, and he rarely missed a chance to complain—floridly and at length—of people with "darke Purposes" who sought to "Stigmatize me and my Family" by "Spread[ing] Artifical Mists before the Eyes of Credulous Simplicity." In fact, Thomas and Mary's first communication with Glen after receiving a commission for the Creek agency took the form of a letter complaining about a rumor "calculated to hurt and injure our Characters." Likewise, Thomas's journal of his time as agent opens with entry after entry inveighing against enemies who "throw every Obstacle and Difficulty in our Way that Malice or Envy can invent" by crafting "extravagant Lies and Fictions projected and published with a malicious Intention to taint my Reputation." His rhetoric continued unchanged on the journey to Creek country ("groundless Calumnies and rash Censures"), while in Creek country ("the Teeth of Prejudice and Defamation"), and after he returned to Charleston ("envious and malicious Tongues").

Indeed, once back in South Carolina's capital, Thomas wrote an "Appendix" to his journal so as to "to produce a few Instances of those Prejudices which were preconceived against us, and the determined Combination to oppose us." A published copy covers eleven pages, each chockablock with phrases like "the Rains of Malice and Envy" and "the Wound given to my Character and Reputation which now lies bleeding and unjustly exposed to the World for the gratification of Malice and Envy of those who I doubt not will be ashamed of their Lies and Ignorance." Altogether, it seems entirely appropriate that Reverend Bosomworth's Bible shows three small *x*'s in the margin next to Luke 6:24–26—"Woe to you who laugh now, for you shall mourn and weep." By contrast, the Bible's next section, Luke 6:27–36, is unmarked. The evidence suggests that Thomas was unmoved by its strictures to love your enemies and turn the other cheek. Suffering in silence (Timothy 2:12) was apparently also out of the question.[2]

And yet, having said all of that, it is worth acknowledging that Thomas wore his insecurities on his sleeve because he had much to be insecure about. His habit of responding to life's slings and arrows with volleys of verbiage attested to his knowledge that his situation was so very precarious—indebted; married to an Anglo-Creek; ensconced on the margin of the empire's colonial margin; and estranged from the colonial officials best positioned to help him. Even more than that, though, Thomas lashed out at adversaries real and imagined because he recognized that the colonial initiative by which he and Mary hoped to achieve fortune was (to borrow from his description of Acorn Whistler's execution) "a very dangerous and ticklish" undertaking. Persuading British officials that Mary was a person who could get things done in Creek country would be difficult. Convincing the Creeks that Thomas was a person capable of exercising Britain's power would be a challenge. And then there remained the vexing issue of cajoling Creeks and Britons into agreeing that executing Acorn Whistler was an appropriate way to resolve the impasse created by the April 1 assault. For a colonist, winning approval and preferment from any given metropole was difficult enough, but dealing with two distinct metropoles— each with its own assumptions, agendas, and interest groups—was a daunting proposition. Of course Thomas Bosomworth was nervous.

The Bosomworths' story about Acorn Whistler could never make the anxiety disappear, but that story could reposition things so that weaknesses looked like strengths and liabilities like assets. In this story, the Bosomworths were well placed and politically powerful people willing to deploy their Anglo-Creek knowledge, connections, and influence to negotiate an agreement that advanced Creek and British interests. Of course, for the story to succeed, the Bosomworths would need Mary to become the focus of attention at certain points and Thomas at others. Of course, the Bosomworths would need to persuade both Creeks and Britons that the solution to the April 1 crisis which they were being offered was satisfactory. Of course, the Bosomworths would need to muster all their resources— rhetorical and otherwise—to undermine anyone seeking to cast doubt upon either their legitimacy or the facts undergirding their preferred solution. And, of course, Acorn Whistler had to die.

〜 ON JUNE 1, 1752, Mary wrote to Glen about "my Interest and Influence (authentic Proofs of which I am ready to produce if required) over several [Creek] Chiefs." Three days later, Mary wrote to Glen again, and again waxed parenthetical while referencing "my Interest and Authority in that Nation (which seems to be much disputed)." Those parenthetical phrases reflect Mary's keen awareness that the Bosomworths' story faced significant skepticism in Charleston. Members of South Carolina's government were unenthusiastic about her serving as the colony's agent, and even Glen, her key supporter, was far from steadfast.[3]

True, Glen had nominated Mary for the job on May 27, but the council immediately quashed the idea, conceding only that "Mrs. Bosomworth might be useful & of assistance to an Agent." Glen adopted that proposal, telling Mary on June 2 "that she might be of service to an Agent"; the council read her letters on June 4, but did not change its opinion. As late as June 11, with Thomas now in the picture and Glen making plans for "him & his spouse . . . to proceed on the Affair wherein they are to be employed among the Creek Indians," the governor and council continued to seek someone to ride herd on the Bosomworths by going "up to the Creek Nation as Agent for this Province." Thomas was not appointed agent until the council learned on June 16 that the "Several Gentlemen who had been deemed proper Persons to undertake the said Agency . . . had declined," and the journal entry for that day's council session makes no mention of the new agent's wife. Mary, then, had reason to think that her "Proofs" were "disputed," and thus that the Bosomworths' story might not even be persuasive enough to get them out of Charleston.[4]

After all, for the Bosomworths' story about the Acorn Whistler affair to work, Britain's colonial officials had to be convinced that Mary truly could exercise "Interest and Influence"—or, even better, "Interest and Authority"—in Creek country. Hesitation about employing Mary as agent notwithstanding, the Bosomworths knew that Thomas's chance of being named agent depended on Mary's reputed interest, influence, and authority among the Creeks. Glen, in fact, had repeatedly referred to Mary as "a very proper" agent because of her status as a "near relation to Malatchi," mastery of "the Creek Language," and "Great Influence Among the Chiefs of the Lower Creek Nation." Glen's council saw the same possibilities, and were willing to employ her—although not as the agent—"if she can absolutely engage that the Lower Creeks by her Influence Shall be brought to make a proper Submission, to this Government." Thomas finally became agent, in short, because South Carolina officials looked at him and saw "your Spouse, who is said by her Relation with some of the Head Men to have an Interest in the Creek Nation."[5]

And so, in early June 1752, the Bosomworths did everything they could to encourage the colony's leaders to focus on Mary. That meant, at a minimum, keeping Thomas out of sight. His only public involvement in the Acorn Whistler affair prior to mid-June was to write Glen about what Mary might do as agent. In the set of six questions that Thomas sent Glen on June 2, the first four dealt with the actions of "Mrs. Bosomworth." Thomas only switched from "she" and "her" to "we" and "our" for the last two questions; none of his questions referenced "I" or "my." It comes as no surprise, therefore, to learn that Thomas later referred to himself as the "nominal Agent," a rare moment of self-deprecation that encapsulated the story that the Bosomworths were telling Britons about why South Carolina should sponsor—in the words of a Georgia official—"Mrs. Bosomworth's Embassy."[6]

With Thomas consigned to the background by the Bosomworths' story, Mary was very much a presence in Charleston. She visited Glen and the council unaccompanied by her husband, and began the negotiations by asking Glen "to let her have in Writing the several services proposed for her to perform . . . and she would consider them" before giving her answer; Glen's response was to be sent to "Mrs. Bosomworth." Mary also wrote directly to the governor on two occasions. In these letters, she discussed her own thoughts, actions, and qualifications before mentioning Thomas, who needed to be shielded from his "Difficulties and Distresses." If that was done, Mary suggested, then Thomas could provide Mary-the-agent with "Advice and Cooperation."[7]

Those letters were written in a style that Glen, a habitual self-promoter, certainly would have recognized. Thus, Mary mentioned a long-ago statement from a South Carolina governor that she was "a proper Person to be employed in all Negotiations with that [Creek] Nation," while also making it plain that the Creek initiatives conducted by General Oglethorpe and the British military officers who replaced him in Georgia were "chiefly transacted by my Interest and Influence." Those men relied upon her because, when it came to the leading Creeks, "I have a rightful and natural Power by the Laws of God and Nature." Moreover, Mary told Glen, she was motivated by "my Zeal for his Majesty's Service"—a phrase she repeated in both letters—to persuade the Creeks to make amends for the "high Indignity offered to this Government." In keeping with that zeal, "I have maturely weighed and considered" Glen's demands, and she was not afraid to offer "my Opinion" regarding the difficulty of winning Creek approval. But she was certain of success, provided that "I shall be so farr authorized and empowered to act in this Affair" without "the Interposition of any other Person contrary to my Advice and Opinion."

With all of that established, Mary could gesture—"we will engage"; "we do likewise further engage"; "our Journey"—to her partnership with Thomas. No one in the colonial government could miss, however, that the Bosomworths were hired because of Mary. And no colonial official could doubt that, as Mary wrote, Thomas was "proceeding with me to the Nation," not vice versa. Glen certainly believed that was the case. His instructions to Thomas hinted strongly that "you may probably think proper to carry with you Mrs. Bosomworth," and just in case Thomas did not get the hint, the governor provided a per diem for "you and her." Months later, after Acorn Whistler was executed and Glen had received Thomas's journal, the governor and council's letter to their agent noted that "we are well pleased with the Trouble your Spouse has Taken," but contained not a word of praise for Thomas himself. Glen would later send some kind words Thomas's way, but he also continued to compliment Mary's "Services," which "I truly think . . . are Considerable." Those compliments can be traced back to the Bosomworths' decision to make Mary the public face of their dealings with South Carolina's leaders. Glen's praise for Mary suggests that the story that the Bosomworths told in Charleston in June 1752 had been a smashing success.[8]

In fact, their story worked so well that no one noticed that, while Mary and Thomas were in Charleston, they were resolutely not talking about two subjects of critical importance to their agency. In the first place, the Bosomworths were not talking about the Osochi perpetrators of the April 1 attack. Mary, of course, had strong connections to people from that town going back, perhaps, to her days in Pon Pon. More recently and more concretely, Osochis had been among the leaders of the Creek contingent living with her at Yamacraw, the Cow Pen, and on St. Catherine's Island, and Osochi headmen had publicly approved Mary's 1738 acquisition of the Yamacraw tract, two 1750 documents reconfirming her land claims, and the 1749 and 1750 declarations that she was the Creeks' princess. Mary, in short, had a rich personal and political history with Osochi, a fact that had implications that Creeks immediately recognized. As Chigelly told Thomas and Mary after they arrived in Coweta, "the Offenders were her Relations as well as [Chigelly and Malatchi's], and [she] had as much to say in the Affair as they had, and [Mary and Thomas] must certainly have a Regard for her own Flesh and Blood." Chigelly need not have worried, though, and not just because—as Mary told him—"she had as much Regard for her Friends, and Relations . . . as they could possibly have." More to the point, she and Thomas had no intention of punishing Osochis. That was why the Bosomworths neglected to talk about them in Charleston.[9]

To recognize the telling nature of this omission, recall the deliberations in Coweta and Tuckabatchee over Acorn Whistler's fate. Once Malatchi decided that Acorn Whistler had to die, he immediately called in headmen closely connected to the doomed man's family and community, and a similar thing happened at the Tuckabatchee conference, where Acorn Whistler's execution was legitimized by leaders with ties to Acorn Whistler's family and community. For someone with Mary's connections, then, the Osochi attackers were low-hanging fruit—easy to point out to a prospective patron and relatively easy to pick off. She should have lobbied to become agent by telling Glen that she would use her political and personal ties to Osochi to ensure that the guilty townspeople were punished. But Mary did no such thing. Instead, when dealing with Glen in Charleston, she referenced her ties to Creek leaders in general, and, when specifics were called for, she let Glen mention her kinsman Malatchi. Whether out of loyalty to the Osochis or an insider's sense of Lower Creek realpolitik, Mary and Thomas simply did not mention that "the Offenders" who were to be "delivered into the Hands of this Government" were her kinsmen and allies.[10]

Nor, though, did the Bosomworths talk about Acorn Whistler while they were in Charleston. Raising his name was impolitic, of course. Everyone knew that the Lower Creeks were to blame for the April 1 attack, and Glen had publicly proclaimed Acorn Whistler's innocence. So, when the Bosomworths did reference the tasks they would perform, they used the most general of generalities: "several Maters," "those Matters," "these Matters." To be sure, Thomas and Mary were thinking about ways a specific person might take the fall for matters large and small; as Mary put it, "she had well weighed and considered the Matter before she came from Charles Town." The result of all that weighing and considering? "She for her Part thought it was better that one or two should suffer Death" for the April 1 attack. One or two . . . though, truthfully, one would be better. But there was no need to mention his name in Charleston. Only as the Bosomworths were on their way out of town on July 3 would they pause to send Glen a letter asserting "that neither of us have seen the Acorn Whistler for some Years past."[11]

⌒ GIVEN THAT THE BOSOMWORTHS' STORY centered on the proposition that Acorn Whistler was responsible for the April 1 attack and must suffer the consequences, Mary and Thomas certainly arrived in Coweta on July 24 with Acorn Whistler on their minds. He was not, though, on the tips of their tongues. The Bosomworths could not very well shout that Acorn Whistler must be executed when Glen's instructions to Thomas explicitly and repeatedly blamed the April 1 attack on "the six and twenty Lower Creeks." Glen would need to be presented with a scenario in which his agent acted as instructed before accepting a solution which the governor had not envisioned. Likewise, the Bosomworths could not hope that the Lower Creeks would agree to execute even a problematic Upper Creek like Acorn Whistler without first confronting the possibility that, as Glen's instructions put it, "by the Laws of Carolina all the six and twenty [Osochis] ought to suffer as they were all equally guilty." The Lower Creeks would need to recognize that Glen's idea of "Mercy" was to demand "only" that they "punish with Death some of the most considerable of these twenty-six." Then, Malatchi and his allies might consider offering up an Upper Creek for "Satisfaction." Just as there had been no reason for the Bosom-worths to mention Acorn Whistler until almost the very hour they left Charleston, there was no reason to start talking about him once they arrived in Creek country. Their story about Acorn Whistler required that, for a time, they not talk about Acorn Whistler.[12]

Once in Creek country, then, Thomas and Mary set up a context in which Acorn Whistler could be accused and condemned, but they let others do the verbal dirty work. That strategy explains why Acorn Whistler was not publicly named as "the Cause of all the Mischief" until the August 11 meeting at Malatchi's house, and it further explains why even then it was not the Bosomworths doing the accusing. In fact, a striking aspect of Thomas's journal is that it names many Creeks who spoke out about Acorn Whistler's guilt, but it does not show Thomas and Mary making the same accusation until well after the Creeks had announced their decision. If the journal is to be believed, the Bosomworths insisted that the Creeks provide satisfaction but let the Creeks themselves first raise Acorn Whistler's name and then come to a consensus that he deserved to die.[13]

To be sure, the journal's version of events is too simple by a good deal more than half, but there is an element of truth in its narrative. The Bosomworths secured Acorn Whistler's execution via manipulation, not accusation, a process that at times left their Creek allies in distinctly uncomfortable positions. Malatchi, for example, was quite obviously shocked at the Bosomworths' demand: execute some of the people responsible for the April 1 attack. The Coweta's hesitation and uncertainty strongly suggest that Thomas and Mary had not mentioned Acorn Whistler to him as a possible solution to his newfound problem. And the same goes for August 10th's marathon meeting of Lower Creek headmen, who were utterly unable to agree on a course of action: if the Bosomworths had let it be known that Glen would accept Acorn Whistler's blood for satisfaction, then the headmen might have been spared their all-nighter. Even the events at Malatchi's house on August 11—when the Bosomworths stage-managed Acorn Whistler's accusation by Mary's Osochi relative—suggest that the Lower Creeks were not expecting to hear both that Acorn Whistler was guilty and that killing him would satisfy South Carolina. Malatchi himself needed some time—and some haranguing—to come to terms with the idea. All of which is to say that the Bosomworths kept their Acorn Whistler-related cards close to their chests after they arrived in Creek country.

Such a strategy is not the same thing, to be sure, as sitting back and letting the Creek deliberative process run its course. That the Bosomworths most emphatically did not do. As we have seen, the Bosomworths arrived in Coweta convinced that executing Acorn Whistler would resolve the conflict between Glen's demands and Creek beliefs. They made sure that Hiacpellechi of Osochi was present at the August 11 meeting in Malatchi's house. Mary called Hiacpellechi forwarded, prompted him to tell his story about Acorn Whistler, and then spoke right after him so that, while she never mentioned Acorn Whistler by name, no one could miss the moral of Hiacpellechi's tale. When the Lower Creek headmen could not reach a decision, the Bosomworths threatened to leave Coweta for Okfuskee, where Malatchi knew that the conversation would be about punishing the Osochis, not executing Acorn Whistler. And the Bosomworths then badgered Malatchi to take the step required to make their Okfuskee trip unnecessary. In short, while never explicitly mentioning Acorn Whistler, the Bosomworths did every-thing they could to make sure that he would be killed.

While doing all of that, moreover, the Bosomworths did one other very revealing thing. In a desperate attempt to ensure the viability of their story that Acorn Whistler had to die, they took a sledge-hammer to the reputation of Aleck, a Lower Creek headman who had lived near Mary since the early 1740s. Aleck was from Cusseta, but he had married three Yuchi sisters, and he and his Yuchi fol-lowers established a village at the Forks of the Altamaha and spent time on the Sea Islands and around Frederica. Mary, of course, had a trading post near the Forks, a plantation on the islands, and a house in Frederica, but she and her neighbor Aleck quite obviously did not get along. Aleck later said of Mary's claims to the Forks, "It is not her's. . . . She has no business to go & live there," and in 1749 Georgia's leaders praised Aleck for revealing "the intrigues of the Bosomworths with Malatchee." The Bosomworths' problem with Aleck in the summer of 1752, though, went much deeper than a desire to settle old scores. In July 1752, Aleck was the Lower Creek best positioned to reveal that they were lying.[14]

Aleck, it turns out, had been in South Carolina in early April 1752. He visited Lieutenant Governor William Bull at Sheldon a few days after Acorn Whistler left Bull's plantation. Prior to Aleck's arrival, Bull spent two days with Acorn Whistler's homeward bound Upper Creeks, and he had received two letters from Glen about the April 1 attack. When Aleck talked to Bull, therefore, he certainly learned that South Carolina officials blamed the Osochis, not Acorn Whistler, for the violence. Moreover, the Bosomworths knew that Aleck could learn details about the attack from the Yuchis who had a village ten miles from Bull's plantation. Bull had a long-running relationship with the Yuchi people, two of whom were at Sheldon when Acorn Whistler's party came by on their way to Charleston. Those Yuchis accompanied Acorn Whistler to the capital; one remained with the Upper Creeks until they fled Charleston on April 2. There is no way to know if Aleck talked with either Yuchi, but it seems likely that, at a minimum, he talked to Yuchis who talked with them.[15]

Given Aleck's recent travels in South Carolina, the people he met there, and his fraught history with the Bosomworths, it did not take much imagination to see that Thomas and Mary's story about Acorn Whistler was in real danger once Aleck arrived in Coweta on July 27 and began telling what Thomas called "Stories." And whatever else can be said about the Bosomworths, they did not lack for imagination. They knew a problem when they heard it. But the Bosomworths likewise knew that they could do real damage to Aleck's reputation, and they could hope that, if the messenger was seen as dishonest, then his "Stories" would be dismissed. Trashing Aleck, then, was of a piece with assuring Glen that they had not seen Acorn Whistler for years or ensuring that Hiacpellechi was in Malatchi's house on August 11. Each move was necessary if the Bosomworths' story was to succeed.

And so the Bosomworths wasted no time in striking hard at Aleck. The day Aleck arrived in Coweta, they accused him of being a horse thief and "a Lier." The Cowetas "gave [Aleck] a very severe Reprimand," and Thomas noted that a "very much ashamed" Aleck could only respond "that he was told by the white People to report such and such Stories." A month later, as the Bosomworths waited anxiously for news of Acorn Whistler's execution, Thomas accused Aleck of spreading a British trader's "Talk" that Glen "did not want any of their People to be killed, but that I was very much in Debt and did not know where to go, and so come up with a stoln Talk (as much as to say that I had no Authority for it) and thought to get a little Money for killing the Indians." That sort of thing hit too close to home, and Thomas was happy to record Chigelly's rebuttal: "it was not the first Time that [the trader] and Ellick had made lying Talks together, and he did not think it worth his while to go the Length of the Square to hear what either of them had to say." And just in case that dismissal did not do the trick, Thomas returned to the subject with an October screed against "that ungrateful Villain, Ellick," who "has been one of the chief Instruments made Use of in opposing every thing I have done."[16]

Thomas ended his attacks by asserting that Aleck was "of so little Consequence in the Nation that he is never asked or consulted upon any public Affairs." But the Bosomworths' sustained attempt to make sure that Aleck would not endanger their story about Acorn Whistler suggests otherwise, and Aleck's biography confirms it. Although Thomas worked manfully to obscure the fact, Aleck was on his way to becoming one of the most influential Lower Creeks of his generation. He remained "one of the Headmen of the Euchee and Cussetaw Towns," even while living for months at a time surrounded by British colonists, and he routinely mediated between the Yuchis, the Lower Creeks, and his British neighbors. Not surprisingly, he received regular presents from South Carolina throughout the 1740s, and Georgia's officials and British military officers followed suit in the late 1740s and early 1750s. A few years later, he worked closely with Britain's first Superintendent for Indian Affairs, and he eventually served as the Lower Creeks' spokesman at four British conferences in the 1760s.[17]

The Bosomworths, then had chosen an unlikely victim for their extraordinary campaign of character assassination. Judging from Thomas's constant complaints about slander and obstructionism, the Bosomworths regularly confronted Creeks and colonists who challenged their reputations and their agenda. At no other point, though, did Thomas and Mary subject another Creek—to say nothing of a headman with a sterling reputation and a glittering future—to the sort of sustained personal abuse that they heaped upon Aleck. The Bosomworths may have been happy to undermine an old adversary, but their motivation for mistreating Aleck centered on more immediate needs. They needed the Creeks to believe that Glen would accept the execution of one Little Okfuskee in lieu of a half-dozen Osochis; and they needed to have Acorn Whistler accused and executed without it becoming clear that they were behind either development. Thomas and Mary could see how they could accomplish those things, as long as there was no persuasive Lower Creek counterstory. Aleck, though, had just such a story and the motivation to tell it. If his story found a receptive audience, then the Bosomworths' own story might fail to convince, and they might have to accuse Acorn Whistler themselves. Either outcome would be disastrous. And so the Bosomworths verbally assaulted Aleck to ensure they would not have to do the same to Acorn Whistler. In any good story there was, as Reverend Bosomworth knew, a time to keep silent and a time to speak (Ecclesiastes 3:7).

Thomas and Mary, though, were doing a great deal more in their first month in Creek country than traducing Aleck's reputation and resolutely not talking about Acorn Whistler. Most centrally, they were working to focus Creek attention on Thomas. Doing so, after all, was a critical component of their story. Mary had connections in Creek country—the "interest" she regularly trumpeted—and a degree of influence because of them, but she was no Creek princess. The "Authority" she claimed to possess was mostly a facade, and her assertion of a "rightful and natural Power" wholly so. She had a role to play—more on that below—in the story that the Bosomworths would tell while in Creek country, but that story needed to focus on Thomas because only he could plausibly claim to speak for Britain's imperial officials. The Bosomworths knew that, left to their own devices, the Creek would never execute Acorn Whistler. Mary could not order them to do so, and her "Friends . . . and Relations" were the wrong Creeks to lean on to arrange Acorn Whistler's execution because they were neither members of his clan nor part of

Little Okfuskee's network of friend towns. If the Bosomworths were to get Acorn Whistler executed, therefore, the impetus had to come from outside of Creek society. And the person best positioned to provide that push was—to quote from the title he claimed—"The Reverend Thomas Bosomworth, appointed Agent by Commission from his Excellency James Glen, Esq., his Majesty's Governor of his Province of South Carolina by and with the Advice and Consent of His Majesty's Honorable Council of the said Province."[18]

And so the Bosomworths sought to convince the Creeks that Thomas was a person to take seriously. Doing so required aggressively defending him against the slander of British traders who knew that he was all hat and no cattle, but the Bosomworths also crafted what modern political handlers would label a positive image for Thomas. The Bosomworths, for example, used a £100 advance from Glen to travel in style so as "to make such an appearance in the Nation as may best answer the Ends of the Agency." Thomas, moreover, made it clear to the Creeks that he could provide both gifts—over £400 worth in the first four months of his agency— and less tangible but more substantial rewards. Thus, Glen insisted that Thomas should "acquaint them that your Zeal for his Majesty King George, made you undertake this Service at a Time when you intended . . . going to England." Thomas was delighted to do so, twice telling Malatchi of his delayed trip to England. In so doing, he reminded Malatchi that, once the current crisis was resolved, Thomas would be well positioned to advance the transatlantic initiatives of Malatchi's alter ego, Far Off Mico. By contrast, Thomas managed to neglect the London trip when speaking in Upper Creek country. There, he was content to rely on more tangible markers of status, as he did at September's Tuckabatchee conference, which began when "Mr. Bosomworth first produced his Commission and explained [it] to the Indians. He likewise produced his Instructions under the Seal of the Province."[19]

Those documents, in fact, were the truly critical element in the Bosomworths' efforts to convince the Creeks of Thomas's importance. For generations, British diplomats had arrived in Creek country bearing elaborately sealed and signed pieces of paper. Creeks came to equate these tokens with the belts of shell beads their own diplomats used as a combination emblem of legitimacy, mnemonic device, and gift; travelers who spoke for their people without a belt or its equivalent were generally ignored or ridiculed. Because Thomas bore both a commission and written instructions, he had the right credentials and the ability to claim a title that (as the one quoted above shows) invoked his personal connection to God before going on to reference—in order—governor, king, governor (again), king (again), and council. It was no accident, therefore, that the day after he and Mary arrived in Coweta, Chigelly presented Thomas in Coweta's square by announcing that, in Thomas's words, "I was come upon Business of Importance by Commission from the Governor and beloved Men of Carolina."[20]

Like belts of beads, though, pieces of paper had to be made to speak. Diplomats interpreted and developed the implications of the symbols they brought with them, much as a minister would do when building a sermon around a biblical verse. Thomas, at once "Reverend" and "Agent," was thus on familiar ground when he used his paper credentials to advance the story he wished to tell. Stripped of the flowery rhetoric about "this beloved Paper" and "that great Beloved Seal," Thomas's assertions about his position were clear and straightforward. As he told Chigelly and Malatchi, "I had full Power and Authority for what I said," and "they might depend upon my Talk to be the same as if they heard it from the Governour's Mouth." Thomas repeated the latter point to both the Upper Creeks assembled in Tuckabatchee and the Lower Creeks meeting in Coweta; another Lower Creek conference heard that "I came by Commission from the Governor and acted on his Behalf." Depending on the situation, the implications of that power varied—once, for example, it meant "every white Man in [Creek country] was under my Command"—but the moral of the story never changed: Thomas was Britain's representative in Creek country. As such, he was a person to be reckoned with.[21]

And the Bosomworths made sure that the Creeks noted one more thing about Thomas: he was a friend and kinsman-by-marriage. Thus, immediately after Thomas told Malatchi and Chigelly about his "full Power and Authority," he launched into a description of his "Friendship for their Nation in general and them two in Particular to whom I stood more nearly allied by Blood and natural Affection." Glen's instructions required Thomas to raise the friend/in-law issue, but Thomas did not need any prodding. He hoped Malatchi and Chigelly "were convinced in their own Hearts that I would not advise them to any Thing but what had a manifest Tendency to the Welfare of them and their Posterity," and he noted that "as my Wife (who by the Laws of God and Man is the same as myself) has a great many Friends and Relations among them, the Ties of Blood and Nature laid us both under Obligations to advise them for the best."[22]

It all added up to an image of Thomas as an influential Briton who had real affection for the Creek people. As such, the story that the Bosomworths were telling about Thomas in Creek country closely paralleled the story that they told about Mary in Charleston. Thomas, the Bosomworths insisted in Creek country, had both access to British power and intense personal ties to the Creeks; Mary, the Bosomworths insisted in Charleston, had both access to Creek power and intense personal ties to the British. The Bosomworths' audiences in Creek country and Charleston were meant to understand that Thomas/Mary was influential there and beloved here, and so Thomas/Mary could be counted upon both to speak for them and to represent us.

Was it true? Well, that was another story, but, for those audience members inclined to doubt Thomas/Mary, the Bosomworths could always offer Mary/Thomas. That is, if you think about it, exactly what they did in Charleston. The council objected to having Mary serve as the colony's agent, but they were eventually willing to give the job to Thomas. He was far from their first choice, but he was a well-educated British man who could serve as the public face of a mission whose success depended upon his wife's influence and connections. Hiring Thomas, in other words, allowed the council to tolerate the fact that they needed to rely upon Mary.

As the Bosomworths surely intended, a similar scenario played out in Creek country, only with Mary and Thomas switching places. Creeks who both objected to the demands Thomas made and distrusted his protestations that "Advantages of Education . . . enable me to see more clearly the true Interests of their Nation than perhaps they were capable of themselves" could take comfort from the fact that he was accompanied by Mary, who made a series of speeches in support of Britain's agent. As a Creek woman, Mary had the right to speak out on family-related matters; as a Beloved Woman, Mary had similar rights when it came to national affairs. It seems likely that her talks were every bit as reassuring to skeptical Creeks as Thomas's Yorkshire birthplace, Oxbridge diploma, and general maleness were to Charleston's counselors.[23]

After all, the Lower Creek headmen assembled in Malatchi's house knew that Mary was on solid ground when she claimed that "as she had many Friends and Relations in the Nation . . . it was her duty to speak for their Welfare." They could not have been surprised when a Beloved Woman told them "it was very weak and childish for them to declare that they did not know what was best to be done." For doubting Thomases who found Britain's agent unpersuasive, it was likely reassuring to hear Mary say "That she was a Woman [and] could tell them that it was best to give the Satisfaction demanded." And that was especially true because Mary was not speaking as Creek royalty. Her only threats while in Creek country were linked to Britain's power, not her own. She relied on persuasion, spoke in a "pathetic" manner—Thomas described one of her speeches as "very feeling and affectionate"—and did not pretend to give orders. She was, instead, deploying a culturally resonant social role that would encourage dubious Creeks to acquiesce to Thomas's demands.[24]

In acting in such a way, of course, Mary advanced the Bosomworths' narrative about Thomas, but Mary's actions had the collateral benefit of furthering their story about Acorn Whistler. Consider, for example, Mary's speech to the headmen assembled in Malatchi's house on August 11. Mary took the floor only after Thomas "had used all the Arguments in my Power to convince them of the Necessity of complying" with Britain's demands. She spoke as an influential Creek woman should, underlining the dangers—"they had openly declared War against their best Friends"—of offending Britain. Her message, though, was ostensibly directed not at the Creeks in general or at Acorn Whistler's kinsmen, but at her family, including the guilty Osochis. As she put it, "as those who committed the Crime were her own Relations they must be perswaded she would not speak against her own Flesh and Blood if she was not convinced that it was for the Good of the whole Nation." Mary provided, in short, a kinswoman's perspective on the need to give satisfaction, no matter how painful. Then, at the end of her speech, she summoned Hiacpellechi of Osochi. With the context of self-sacrifice established by Mary, Hiacpellechi named the real mastermind of the April 1 attack and lifted the burden of guilt from Mary's family. The combination of Mary's speech and Hiacpellechi's accusation left Acorn Whistler to be the victim of the satisfaction which Mary had just proclaimed to be a painful necessity "if they thought the Friendship of the English worth preserving."[25]

And then, after the Lower Creek headmen dumped the matter in Malatchi's lap, the Bosomworths followed the same formula to get him to condemn Acorn Whistler. First Thomas spoke: "I hoped he would make no Hesitation in giving the Satisfaction demanded, and I desired to know his final Answer." Then Malatchi and Thomas had many "Disputes," before Mary stepped in: "some of them must suffer Death for Nothing else would make Satisfaction to the English." She ended, once again, with a reference to the British power Thomas could call upon: "it must be done or all the Traders would immediately be ordered out of the Nation." And, once again, it worked: Malatchi told Acorn Whistler's relatives that it was their responsibility to kill him. The Bosomworths had succeeded in convincing the Creeks of both Thomas's influence and Acorn Whistler's suitability as scapegoat. Just as in Charleston, Mary and Thomas had found a way to tell a complicated story in an exceptionally effective manner.[26]

～ A WELL-TOLD STORY brought well-earned rewards. In the late summer and early fall of 1752, as our other storytellers realized that their first stories were in tatters and their second stories were works in progress, the Bosomworths found themselves in an enviable position. They had the luxury of being optimistic and aggressive, not angry (like the Okfuskees) or scared (like Malatchi); they were in control of events and thinking proactively, not blindsided by unforeseen developments (like Glen) or reacting on the fly (ditto). With Acorn Whistler dead, the Bosomworths were free to spend the rest of their time in Creek country strengthening their story and seeking to capitalize on it.

As it became clear that no important Creek interest group was prepared to challenge the Bosomworths' story about why Acorn Whistler had to die, Mary and Thomas added some useful details to that story. Most critically, they began claiming that, as Thomas wrote to Glen, "it was universally allowed by the Evidence of all the white People and Indians in the Nation that the Acorn Whistler was the principal Cause of that Mischief." Put another way, it was not just that Acorn Whistler was guilty but also that everyone agreed he was guilty. Thomas made a very similar comment—"it was universally allowed both by the Indians and white People that the Acorn Whistler was the Cause of that Mischief"—in his journal before launching into his description of the September conference in Tuckabatchee. And then, at that conference, he told the assembled Upper Creeks that "the Lower Creeks . . . Head Men . . . accused the Acorn Whistler as the Cause of all the Mischief. . . . Therefore, if Nothing but Blood would make Satisfaction, he was the Man that ought to suffer."[27]

To buttress those claims, Thomas and Mary presented a new history of the pivotal August 11 meeting in Malatchi's house. The Bosomworths now asserted that Acorn Whistler had been accused, as Thomas said in late September, by "the Lower Creeks . . . Head Men." Thomas, in fact, repeated the claim in January, writing to Glen that, on August 11, "it was the Opinion of the Assembly that [Acorn Whistler] ought to suffer for [the April 1 attack]." He referenced an affidavit by John Ladson, a trader, for proof of this claim. Thomas relied on Ladson's affidavit for support because his journal was already in Glen's possession, and it said nothing about anyone in Malatchi's house beside Hiacpellechi accusing Acorn Whistler of anything. The journal likewise demonstrated that the assembled headmen most certainly had not declared that Acorn Whistler was guilty. And the affidavit? Anyone reading it closely— as Thomas must have hoped that Glen would not—would notice that it did not mention Acorn Whistler. Nor does the affidavit say that anyone in particular was accused at the August 11 meeting, or that the headmen declared anyone to be guilty. It says only that "the whole Assembly" agreed to let Malatchi decide how to resolve this crisis.[28]

The Bosomworths, then, were lying—about the meeting at Malatchi's house; about the degree to which the Creeks were convinced that Acorn Whistler deserved to die; even about the content of the affidavit that was intended to buttress their other lies. But the Bosomworths believed that no one would call them on any of this, and it is easy to see why. As everyone involved in the Acorn Whistler affair adjusted their stories to account for the "fact" that Acorn Whistler was guilty, no one had any incentive to question either the process by which that judgment was reached or the degree to which the Creeks agreed with the decision. In that context, the Bosomworths could lie about Acorn Whistler in the most blatant fashion if they so wished. And, quite obviously, they did so wish, and again it is easy to see why. Thomas and Mary simply could not allow the story of Acorn Whistler's death to become one in which the Lower Creek headmen were stymied by a British demand for the blood of an innocent man and left it all up to Malatchi, who was badgered by the Bosomworths until he gave in. And so the Bosomworths said that the Lower Creek headmen accused Acorn Whistler, decided he had to die, and had their decision ratified by every Creek and Briton in the nation. None of that was true, but truth was not the point. Thomas and Mary were simply putting the finishing touches on their remarkably successful story.

As they did so, the Bosomworths were confident enough about their position to begin focusing on what was, for them, the big picture: their land claims and the evidence they would need to support those claims once they arrived in London. With that in mind, they took time out from September's Tuckabatchee conference to persuade the assembled Upper Creek headmen to sign a paper confirming Mary's title to the Sea Islands and the Yamacraw tract. Naturally, no mention of this transaction made it into the journal Thomas sent Glen. Thomas, though, thought highly enough of the document that, after returning to Charleston, he arranged to have it notarized even before finishing his final report to the governor.[29]

That did not mean, of course, that the Bosomworths intended to slight Glen. Far from it. Glen had to approve the results of the agency for them to get paid, and they very much hoped to get a letter from Glen vouching for their good work and supporting their land claims. And so Thomas made sure to remind Glen of Mary's standing in Creek country, most notably by passing along Malatchi and Chigelly's statement that they had complied with the governor's "Demands" only because of "Mrs. Bosomworth's Interest, and Authority." Thomas also put in his own good word for his wife. He wrote to Glen that "In Justice to Mrs. Bosomworth, I must likewise declare that the Merit of the Whole is chiefly due to her," and noted in his silver-tongued way that "she has undergone Hardships and Fatigues which is scarce credible that a Woman of her Corpalency could ever have endured."[30]

The Bosomworths, though, had real reason to think that Mary's influence was already firmly established in the minds of South Carolina's leaders. Passing along a few Creek statements to the effect that "she had been instrumental in promoting their Happiness" would suffice to confirm the story that the Bosomworths had told about Mary while they were in Charleston. Thomas's reputation was another matter, however. The Bosomworths evidently concluded that one of the real perks of their successful story about Acorn Whistler was that they could rehabilitate Thomas's reputation in Charleston. The Upper Creeks' statement about Mary's land claims was useful, as was the way in which Acorn Whistler's execution could be read as confirming Mary's influence in Creek country. But if Thomas could emerge from the agency with a degree of respectability in the eyes of Britain's rulers, then that would certainly increase the Bosomworths' odds of winning the king's support for their broader claims.[31]

In keeping with the goal of rehabilitating Thomas, Mary almost disappeared from Thomas's journal after the Upper Creeks signed off on Acorn Whistler's execution in late September. Thomas showed her speaking regularly—in public and in private—prior to that, but Mary apparently went mute thereafter. Thomas alone spoke at the October 4 conference in Coweta, and Thomas alone dealt with the necessary last-minute exchanges with Malatchi and Chigelly before sending his journal off to Glen a week later. Even more strikingly, Thomas left Mary behind when he and Malatchi set off to Upper Creek country to seek satisfaction from the Breed Camp Chickasaws for the murder of a British trader. That three-week trip gave Thomas an excellent chance to act as Britain's agent ought to, protecting British honor and defusing a crisis via a mix of diplomacy and threats. The rest of his time in Creek country was spent calming Lower Creeks worried about potential Cherokee war parties and gathering up stolen horses, jobs which his journal suggests he did utterly without Mary's help.[32]

Mary finally resurfaced in his journal in mid-December, and only then because the Creeks asked that she remain in Creek country when Thomas left for Charleston. Thomas was happy to oblige, and only in part because that meant he could claim reimbursement for her per diem expenses for another six months. More to the point, with Mary safely ensconced in Creek country, Thomas could count on having the Charleston spotlight all to himself. If the governor wanted to talk to someone about the agency, it would be Thomas. If the council wanted to know about Creek affairs, they would have to ask Thomas. If letters were to be sent or journals forwarded or accounts turned in, they would all be from Thomas. With Mary in Creek country and Thomas in Charleston, Thomas could truly become Britain's agent to the Creeks.[33]

And viewed from one angle, the strategy worked. By May 1753, Glen would write Thomas "to Commend your Conduct in everything that I commit to your Care. For you not only faithfully follow the directions given you, but upon particular Emergency's that have not been provided for, your Own discretion is a very good Guide." Of course, that sort of written praise from the governor was exactly what the Bosomworths needed to advance their case in London, and Thomas and Mary filed the letter away for future use. They dragged it out in 1754 as part of an epic disgorging of evidence to support the claims of twin petitions to Britain's leaders, one from "Coosapona-keesa Princess of the Upper & Lower Creek Nations" and the other from "Mr. Bosomworth . . . Setting Forth Their Services Amongst the Creek Indians." The former document they had long planned to submit, but until very recently they had no inkling that a petition from Thomas would further their cause in any way. After all, a year before Thomas received his precious letter from Glen, he was saved from debtors' prison only because South Carolina officials needed a front man for his wife's mission. In 1753, by contrast, the Bosomworths could hope that their claims for preferment from London might not have to rest solely on Mary's reputation and past services. Thomas himself had become a potential asset.[34]

⌇ THOMAS'S RISE IN STATUS exemplifies the transformative possibilities available to colonists with the knowledge, connections, and chutzpah necessary to deal with two metropoles at once. That those possibilities were based upon a series of lies told to some of the most powerful men in Creek country and the British empire should not be surprising. Reverend Bosomworth knew that "the truth will set you free" (John 8:32), but Thomas and Mary did not want to be free. They wanted to be financially secure, and to achieve that goal they needed to be not independent but colonial. It would have been idiotic to rail against the colonial condition when colonialism offered them their best chance for wealth. Instead of pursuing freedom, therefore, they made the metropole-colony relationship (in a sense) bipolar, and set themselves up to profit in ways that were unconventional but real.

Insecurity, however, was the rule in the colonial world, and even the best storytellers found it difficult to escape their weaknesses and liabilities for long. The end result was that moments of potential triumph were routinely ruined—in whole or in part—by developments outside of the colonist's control. Chickens came home to roost; houses made of cards collapsed; chinks appeared in the shiniest armor. Not every colonial edifice collapsed in a shower of cliches, of course, but colonists knew that failure was always lurking. The Bosomworths certainly never forgot that, even as their story seemed to sweep all before it. Mary and Thomas were exceptional storytellers, but they also were seeking to overcome daunting liabilities by repeatedly lying to powerful people. They had every reason to be perpetually on edge.

We get a sense of their profound insecurity when a four-day gap suddenly appears in Thomas's journal. On Saturday, December 16, Thomas told a group of Lower Creek headmen that Mary would stay in Creek country for a time and that "as every Thing was now finished that I had in charge . . . I intended in a few Days to leave their Nation to proceed for Charles Town." There is no journal entry for Sunday—as was typical for Reverend Bosomworth—and then a very strange paragraph, one that is worth quoting in full:

> Monday, the 18th. The white People finding I was preparing for my Journey were resolved to create me some fresh Troubles by some lying Reports which were sett on Foot in Regard to the Death of the Indian called the Acorn Whistler, which occasioned me in Hight of Passion to undertake a Journey to the Upper Towns, but as upon cooler Judgement I have Reason to believe that every unprejudiced Man of Sence must be convinced by my Reason already assigned, as to the Cause of the said Indian's Death, I shall pass over in Silence my Journey and Proceedings till I returned to the Cowetas which was Thursday Evening the 21st.

In other words, as Thomas was basking in the job-well-done glow and preparing for his star turn in Charleston, he heard something that made him so angry and worried that he dropped everything and rode 160 miles—from Coweta to Tuckabatchee and back—in three days, before deciding that his story ("my reason already assigned") about Acorn Whistler's death was not truly in any danger. These were not the actions of a confident man.[35]

Thomas did not itemize the "lying Reports" about Acorn Whistler's death, but they clearly concerned what he later described as a "wicked Report . . . that the Acorn Whistler was killed before Malatchi returned from War [on August 3] or any Conference held [on August 10 and 11] or Satisfaction demanded." We can be sure of that because, before Thomas hustled out of Coweta on the morning of December 18, he stopped to take an affidavit from one trader confirming that another trader was saying that "the said Acorn Whistler was killed . . . before the Agent Mr. Bosomworth arrived in the Lower Nation" on July 24. When Thomas arrived in Tuckabatchee the next day, he gathered affidavits from two other traders to the effect that Acorn Whistler was alive in late July and that they learned of his death after August 11. Thomas, in short, rode pell-mell through

Creek country to defend the most basic fact in the Bosomworths' story: Acorn Whistler was executed after they arrived in Coweta.[36]

The image of Thomas riding frantically through a wintry Creek landscape is worth lingering over because it illustrates the fragility of the Bosomworths' story and the shaky fortunes of the people who depended upon it. After all, the fact that Thomas rode to Tuckabatchee to defend was actually a fact: Acorn Whistler had been killed after August 11. Unlike many other "facts" which the Bosomworths peddled, this one was true. With that in mind—and remembering that no one performs injured innocence like a habitual liar whose one truth is doubted—it seems safe to say that the reasons behind Thomas's three-day ride are less interesting than contemplating how very, very concerned the Bosomworths must have been about the many parts of their story that were less-than-firmly grounded in truth. Moreover, it is worth remembering that "The white People" whose "lying Reports" Thomas found so dangerous were Indian traders, members of a profession whose very name was a watchword for dishonesty in the colonies. In rebutting these "lying Reports," then, the Bosomworths were not exactly fighting above their social weight. And yet Thomas treated the traders' lies as if they came from the *beau monde*. If scruffy Indian traders spreading rumors in Upper Creek country represented a crisis, then what would the Bosomworths do when they confronted resistance from within South Carolina's governing elite in Charleston?

The answer became clear in the winter and spring of 1753: flail about. Glen and his council were not the problem. They sent Thomas's papers to the assembly, along with Glen's declaration that "all who understand any thing of these Matters and who Love their Country must Rejoice to see Measures so successfully pursued." The assembly already had in its possession "An Account of the Reverend Thomas Bosomworth amounting to the Sum of Two thousand nine hundred and ninety-five pounds and one shilling, for his services as Agent to the Creek Nation." And there things ground to a halt. The assembly resolved that Thomas's account "ought not to be paid" because Glen had ignored the legislators' written notification that "sending the Agent was contrary to their Opinion." The Bosomworths' financial problems were back.[37]

Thomas was flummoxed by this "non-payment by the Publick." By late March, he was reduced to sending a "Memorial" to the governor and council about his "most calamitous Circumstances" due to the "many Difficulties and Distresses in which your Memorialist is involved in Consequence of the great private Expenses he has been at for the Publick Service of this Province." Another "Memorial" followed three weeks later, this one containing three references to "utter Ruin" along with a statement that he could no longer pay for "his Passage Home to England." His "present Situation," he claimed, was "as calamitous as Imagination can form an Idea of to compleat humane Misery." Somewhere, perhaps, Acorn Whistler was smiling. The Bosomworths' plans were falling apart.[38]

As should be clear by now, however, Thomas and Mary were very proficient at warding off "utter Ruin," even if they likewise struggled to achieve lasting success. Their story about Acorn Whistler could not get them quick access to South Carolina's public funds, but it had won them the support of powerful people. Thus, in the spring of 1753, the council lobbied the assembly on their behalf. In the months that followed, Glen urged Georgia's leaders to find "some Remedy" that would satisfy the Bosomworths' land claims, and he wrote an even more emphatic letter to his superiors in London, calling "Your Lordships particular notice" to a matter "of great importance to the Peace of this Province and of Georgia, I mean the Lands said to be convey'd by the Indians to Mrs. Bosomworth." And then there was Malatchi. When the Creeks met with Glen in late May, the Coweta headman made sure to mention "Mrs. Bosomworth, who is my Sister," on several occasions. He stated unequivocally that the Creeks believed she "was entitled to the Lands she possessed," and he "requested that His Excellency the Governor would be pleased to represent the Case of His Sister Mrs. Bosomworth, concerning the Lands, to the Great King."[39]

As "calamitous" as the Bosomworths' situation may have been in the spring of 1753, then, they were poised to arrive in London— assuming they could round up some money to pay for the trip— bearing powerful statements of support from colonial, imperial, and Native leaders. They had already proven themselves to be very adept at weaving exactly that sort of raw material into a compelling colonial story. Of course, their experience had likewise proven that such narratives were better at staving off failure than grasping success. Still, they had no choice but to continue telling stories about one metropole in the hopes of winning preferment from representatives of a second. It was a colonial strategy that the Bosomworths had raised to the level of an art form. And like most artists, the Bosomworths were much better at producing art—stories, in their case—than at winning critical approval or financial success. The colonies were full of storytellers with similar problems. We could, in fact, do worse than to imagine colonial America as the land of starving artists.

Epilogue

JUNE 5, 1753

*T*HE DAY'S VIOLENCE was unexpected and thus all the more shocking. Malatchi, Red Coat King, and the rest of Governor Glen's Creek visitors left Charleston on June 5, 1753. As the South Carolina *Gazette* reported, they were returning to "their Country, and that Night reach'd Dorchester, where (almost in the Town) a young Fellow, Son to the King, was shot, and his Scalp with part of his Scull carried away." The dead young man was Red Coat King's son; the attacker was—judging from "the usual Token being left near the dead Body"—"a Northern Indian," probably a Shawnee. And, for the Creeks, it was hard to know which detail of the attack was most appalling.[1]

The treatment of the Okfuskee's body was an outrage. As a colonist reported later, "to take part of the Skull (with the Scalp) is the greatest Indignity that can be offered to Indians, and they seldom forgive it." The identity of the victim was also shocking—a man from a leading family who traveled with a party of diplomats and who may himself have borne a title (Estatoe Mico) that attested to his own diplomatic initiatives. And, of course, the location of the assault was hard to stomach. The Creek party was an easy day's walk from Charleston, in the heart of South Carolina's most densely settled area and on the outskirts of the well-established town of

Dorchester. In fact, the Creeks were staying at "Mr. Dow's" plantation, a place the Okfuskees knew well. In 1743, 1745, and 1749, Creek parties that almost certainly included Okfuskees had stayed with the Dowse family, who provided their visitors with "dieting and Liquor," "Pasturage," and "entertaining . . . on the Road." The Dowse plantation was not "White Ground," but it was a familiar place nonetheless. All of which is to say that the militia officer who described the Creeks as "very uneasy" hours after the attack was probably understating matters.[2]

Given that the violence of June 5, 1753, occurred just after the Charleston conference that dealt with the Acorn Whistler crisis, the Dorchester attack necessarily involved all of that crisis's principals. The "Governor set out for Dorchester" the next morning, intent on mollifying the Creeks. The *Gazette* noted that Glen was "attended by the Town Troop of Horse, and a Detachment from the Independent Companies." He was also accompanied by Mary Bosomworth, who served as interpreter for his meetings with the distressed Creeks, and by Thomas, who ran up "Expenses at Dorchester." While in Dorchester, Glen met with "Malatchi and the Creek Indians," telling them that, as Red Coat King remembered it, "when my Son was killed it was the same as if he had been your own Son, and you promised to find out [by] what Nation it was done." The *Gazette* reported that "the Creek Indians were well pleased with his Excellency's Appearance, and they afterwards proceeded on their Journey thoro'ly satisfied." Perhaps they did, but they still sought revenge a few days later when they discovered "4 Northern Indians . . . skulking about" Augusta. A "Gentleman" noted that "Malatchi and his People came to our House" where they "brought in one Fellow alive [who they] had beaten very much, and the scalp with Part of the Skull of one they kill'd." The Creeks took the survivor "to Mr. Rae's," where they "beat him again, and stuck their Knives into his Body, and at last with a Hatchet chopt off his Head."[3]

Malatchi had his reasons for seeking revenge—he believed that his brother and four other Cowetas had recently been killed—but it was Okfuskee's mico who had the best claim to being the driving force behind the Augusta violence: "as they killed my Son we must have Blood for Blood, and we met with two Northerns at Augusta on our own Ground which we killed for Satisfaction." In fact, the killing of Red Coat King's son allowed the Okfuskees and their mico to move themselves and their agenda firmly to the fore. They had left Charleston intent on reminding all and sundry of the enduring power of Creek communities, the continued relevance of bonds of kinship and friendship, and the centrality of Okfuskee for national and international affairs. If their grief over the death of Red Coat King's son had a silver lining, it was that this tragedy made those tasks much easier.[4]

Thus, Red Coat King, who had not spoken during the Charleston meeting despite being repeatedly asked to do so, broke his silence in Dorchester. He made several speeches to the governor, with the result that Glen both promised to help the Okfuskees seek revenge and publicly claimed a familial bond with Okfuskee's leader. And then, when the Creeks arrived in Augusta, not only did Red Coat King reassert Okfuskee's long-standing connection—"our own Ground"—to this town on the trail linking Okfuskee and Charleston, but the Okfuskees likely determined the fate of the two Northern Indians. The Creeks, after all, removed "the scalp with Part of the Skull" of the first man they killed, treating him exactly as the Shawnees had treated Red Coat King's son; and then the Creeks chose to torture and kill their other victim at the house of John Rae, Okfuskee's longtime trader.[5]

The townspeople continued this Okfuskee-centered, locally focused approach to the issues of the day once they returned home. In July, Red Coat King frankly told Glen, "It is of no Use your sending any Peace Talks here without three or four Head Men will come from the Cherokees to my Town, and bring two Northern Indians Slaves with them, which will be the only way to make a good Peace between us and the Cherokees." Okfuskee's mico went on to note, "All the Head Men of the Upper Creeks are to meet at my Town, the Oakfuskees, in three Moons, and then to conclude upon either Peace or War," a message reinforced by a note from Okfuskee Captain—who carried Glen's newly signed commission—stating that "The whole Body of the Upper Creeks are to meet at the Oakfuksees in three Moons, and if Peace is not concluded in that Time we will stay no longer in going to war with the Cherokees which is all from your loveing Son." British traders and other Creeks passed along similar messages about the Okfuskees that fall. And once a Creek-Cherokee peace was eventually finalized, Red Coat King made sure to thank Glen but also to underline the importance of the local by promising that "Nothing in his Power shall be wanting to the great King of the English as long as he lives in the Ockfuskees."[6]

Taken within the context of the four stories about Acorn Whistler's death, the obvious interpretation of the Okfuskees' centrality after June 5, 1753, is that the death of Red Coat King's son returned local issues to prominence while subordinating imperial, national, and colonial agendas. Indeed, the surest indication that Okfuskees found themselves in the driver's seat after June 5, 1753, is the fact that, even though the parallels between that day's events and those of April 1, 1752, were striking, no one commented on them in any way preserved in the extant records. In fact, suddenly, no one was talking about Acorn Whistler at all. He had been a problem, and then (for some) an opportunity; now, he was a nonissue. His family and community were very happy not to talk about him. Malatchi and the Bosomworths also dropped their stories about both the man and the crisis surrounding his death, leaving Acorn Whistler to appear in the records only as the unnamed shadow behind Glen's occasional reference to his own success in convincing Indians of "the Necessity of punishing the guilty in Conformity to the Treaties betwixt them and us." Acorn Whistler had vanished, and no one had more to gain from that fact than the inhabitants of Okfuskee. Of our four storytellers, then, the Okfuskees—the people most discomfited by the Acorn Whistler crisis—had apparently won out in the end.[7]

Since my first book focused on Okfuskee, the Triumphant Okfuskee interpretation has a certain appeal to me, but it relies on a dubious proposition. That reading of events implicitly suggests that it is fine to extend the narrative into the fall of 1753 but that the real story stops there—before 1755 (when Okfuskees found themselves on the losing side of a serious trade dispute with South Carolina), before 1760 (when Okfuskees, led by Red Coat King's other son, killed eleven British traders), before 1773 (when Okfuskees declared that the fire uniting them with Charleston was extinguished), before 1793 (when fourteen Okfuskees were killed or captured by Georgia militiamen), before 1814 (when hundreds of Okfuskees died at the hands of Andrew Jackson's army), before.... You get the point. Pick a different end date and you change the story dramatically. The (apparently) Triumphant Okfuskees who were aggressively promoting their localist vision in the summer of 1753 were Worried Okfuskees by 1755 and Angry Okfuskees by 1760. And those midcentury Okfuskees—whether Triumphant, Worried, or Angry—would have been all but unrecognizable to their bloodied and dispossessed grandchildren. There are, then, many ways to characterize the Okfuskees' experience in the three generations after 1753, but "triumph" is not the word I would choose. Any interpretation that suggests that the Okfuskees emerged victorious from the Acorn Whistler affair seems at once artificial and untenable.[8]

That does not mean, of course, that our other storytellers became winners in the Okfuskees' stead. Glen certainly did not. As Red Coat King mourned the loss of his son, Glen struggled to convince the Creeks "that the said Murder was not committed by any Cherokee," and thus that his Indian alliance still had a future. He succeeded, but his focus on that southern-based alliance left him woefully out of step with the march of Britain's empire. In 1753 and 1754, British officials were growing increasingly concerned over French initiatives in the Ohio Valley, but Glen believed that the French were planning to invade Cherokee country and then fall on South Carolina. As a result, he bragged about his Indian alliance but rebuffed British efforts to mobilize what Lord Halifax described as "His Indians, as he calls them." Even as a British army marched toward France's forces on the Ohio in 1755, Glen made sure that the Catawba and Cherokee warriors remained near South Carolina. When a French and Indian force destroyed Britain's Ohio-bound army, Glen was pilloried. Virginia's lieutenant governor flatly told him that "you are to Judge whether you have done your duty to His Majesty," and Halifax was even harsher, writing that if Glen had acted as he "ought to have done, [General Edward] Braddock's Life and the Honour of His Majesty's Arms . . . would probably have been saved . . . for in that case the Cherokees would have joined our army, and protected it from the Surprize and shamefull Defeat."

The debacle proved once and for all that Glen was too prone to wagering the metropole's future on the periphery's plans to succeed in Britain's new-model empire. "His Indians," his alliance, and his colony dominated his thoughts, an approach to imperial governance that cost him his job and led London's armchair imperialists to denounce his "vile conduct."[9]

Malatchi did a bit better for himself after June 5, 1753, further enhancing his status as the most powerful Creek of his generation. He cast such a long shadow over Creek politics that his son was regularly called "Young Malatchi" and "Young Twin," even though his name was Togulki, not Malatchi, and he was not a twin. But Malatchi died in January 1756, well before his plans for personal power and national unification could come to fruition. He spent the years remaining to him after leaving Dorchester being simultaneously feted by British and French officials eager for the emperor's allegiance and buffeted by his Creek rivals' refusal to see him as anything more than one of several particularly influential Creek leaders. At the time of his death, both the nation and his leadership role within it existed primarily in his mind's eye, and to a great extent his power and his plans accompanied him to the grave, leaving his family and town in a decades' long political eclipse. The modern Creek nation emerged during those dark years, and historians intent on identifying its Father have generally snubbed Malatchi.[10]

As for the Bosomworths, in keeping with the nature of colonial experience, a half-dozen years and a roughly equal number of narrative innovations after leaving Dorchester, they finally resolved their claims for pennies on the dollar. South Carolina's assembly eventually agreed to pay roughly fifty percent of Thomas's final bill, although he never received the money from the colony's treasurer, possibly because it was already spoken for by his creditors. Likewise, the British government eventually agreed to grant the Bosomworths title to St. Catherine's Island, but only if Mary renounced the Yamacraw tract, sold the two other Sea Islands, and accepted the money from that sale as payment for the goods and services she had been providing to British officials for decades. If giving up some property and selling most of the rest to pay off debts owed to you by others does not sound like a clear-cut victory, well, the

Bosomworths "declared themselves perfectly satisfied therewith." Perhaps the realities of the colonial world had taught them to value the bird in the hand? Whatever the case, Mary enjoyed her island for only a few years before dying; Thomas's remarriage to their chambermaid happened—depending on the date of Mary's death—somewhere between quickly and with unseemly haste. And anyone habituated to the Bosomworth-heavy nature of the Georgia records from the 1740s and 1750s will be struck by the speed at which Thomas and Mary faded into colonial obscurity after 1760.[11]

The lesson of June 5, 1753, then, is not that the Dorchester attack changed everything or that it turned losers into winners. Not at all. It is true that the violence at Dorchester allowed certain stories to come to the fore, and it is likewise true that those stories, for a time, furthered some agendas and hindered others. Those developments, though, point us toward process, not product—toward the way life in colonial America worked, not toward the ephemeral stories, temporary solutions, unstable institutions, and mutable structures that littered the colonial world. The events of June 5, 1753, and April 1, 1752—and the relationship between them—remind us of the ordinariness of crisis in colonial America. They remind us of the fluid and unsettled nature of colonial life. They remind us of the weakness of those people who seemed to be most powerful and of the inescapable presence of those people who seemed to be most foreign. They remind us, finally, of what it meant to live in a world that was at once local and imperial, colonial and national.

After all, in the Acorn Whistler affair, the region's most powerful men—Malatchi and Glen—were sucked into a crisis that threatened their ambitions for themselves and their people. Resolving that crisis became incredibly difficult because of the weak nature of their power and the many storytellers who had both their own agendas and the ability to make their voices heard in a meaningful way. In dealing with this reality, Malatchi had to put his neck on the line, and Glen found himself forced to make the best of a solution which was not at all what he had envisioned. And then, when everything finally seemed ironed out and the Creeks were heading home from Charleston, the region's most powerful men found themselves immediately thrust back into another crisis, one which would require new stories and new negotiations with a new set of story-telling stakeholders. Throughout the entire process, people and places that "should" have had little influence on each other were actually intimately entangled. Events were just as likely to be driven by stories from the margins as from a metropolitan center, and even people focused on a transatlantic empire or a nascent nation had to account for the power of the local and the colonial. In such a context, effective leaders were willing to follow, power was regularly whittled down to influence, and solutions to crises ranged from the provisional to the ephemeral.

The Acorn Whistler affair, then, is a particularly evocative example of colonial America's essential nature. And, as such, it is entirely appropriate that our storytellers essentially stopped talking about all things Acorn Whistler as soon as they possibly could. Winners write history, but—to return to my question in the introduction—what of histories where there are no winners? It is all too easy for us to lose track of those stories. No one had a stake in seeing them preserved; no one comes off looking particularly admirable in any of them. And yet, in the end, it is those stories and the ways in which they were told that allow us to understand what it meant to be a contemporary of Acorn Whistler.

Abbreviations

Notes

Acknowledgments

Index

Abbreviations

BPRO-SC   "Records in the British Public Records Office Relating to South Carolina, 1663–1782," edited by W. Noel Sainsbury; 11 reels in the collection of the Georgia Historical Society, Savannah.

CO   Colonial Office, National Archives, Kew, England.

CRSGA   *The Colonial Records of the State of Georgia.* Volumes 1–28 edited by Allen D. Candler, Kenneth Coleman, and Milton Ready (Atlanta and Athens, GA: 1904–1916, 1974–1976). Volumes 29–38 in the microfilm collection of the Georgia Department of Archives and History, Atlanta.

DRIA   *The Colonial Records of South Carolina: Documents Relating to Indian Affairs, 1750–1765,* 2 vols.; edited by William L. McDowell, Jr. (Columbia, SC: South Carolina Department of Archives and History, 1958, 1970).

GT   John T. Juricek, ed., *Early American Indian Documents: Treaties and Laws, 1607–1789. Volume 11: Georgia Treaties, 1733–1763* (Frederick, MD: University Publications of America, 1989).

MPAFD   *Mississippi Provincial Archives: French Dominion,* 5 vols.; edited by Dunbar Rowland, A. G. Sanders, and Patricia K. Galloway (Jackson and Baton Rouge, MS: Mississippi Department of Archives and History, 1927–1932, 1984).

SC-CJ   Journals of South Carolina's Council. South Carolina Department of Archives and History, Columbia.

SC-JCHA   Journals of South Carolina's Commons House of Assembly. For sessions prior to 1736, see "Early State Records: A-1b," from *Records of the States of the United States of America* (Washington, DC: Library of Congress, 1949–1951); for sessions from 1736 to 1757, see *The Colonial Records of South Carolina: The Journals of the Commons House of Assembly,* 12 vols.; edited by J. H. Easterby et al. (Columbia: South Carolina Department of Archives and History, 1951–1983).

SC-UH   Journals of South Carolina's Upper House of Assembly. South Carolina Department of Archives and History, Columbia.

Notes

Prologue

1. For the attack, see SC-CJ, 4/1/1752, pp. 116–118, quotations from 116 ("every one"), 118 ("head"); ibid., 4/3/1752, p. 124 ("destroyed"); Pennsylvania *Gazette*, 4/23/1752 ("sunset," "old"), 4/30/1752 ("volley"); DRIA 1: 211, 345. For the fifth Cherokee, see SC-JCHA, 4/29/1752, p. 260; SC-CJ, 6/16/1752. The fifth victim was not the prisoner, whom South Carolina demanded the Creeks "deliver up . . . if alive" on June 24, well after the fifth Cherokee supposedly died. DRIA 1: 345–346; SC-CJ, 6/24/1752. To complicate matters, the former document says the Creeks "killed four on the spot" (p. 345), as does a letter from late April. It is possible, therefore, that only five Cherokees died—four on April 1, plus the prisoner. For the letter, see DRIA 1: 208–212, especially p. 211; SC-CJ, 4/28/1752, pp. 165–174. Pennsylvania *Gazette*, 4/30/1752 ("Skirmish"); SC-CJ, 4/1/1752, p. 117 (9 p.m.). One description of the attack uses "murder" three times in a single paragraph; DRIA 1: 212.

2. Ibid., 211 ("behind"); Pennsylvania *Gazette*, 4/30/1752. Richard J. Hooker, ed., *The Carolina Backcountry on the Eve of the Revolution: The Journal and Other Writings of Charles Woodmason, Anglican Itinerant* (Chapel Hill: University of North Carolina Press, 1953), 70 ("elegant"). Woodmason states that St. Philips was forty feet tall, with a fifty-foot cupola. A 1770 pamphlet notes that the cupola was topped by "a Lanthorn for the Bells . . . from which rises a Vane in the Form of a Cock"; George Milligen-Johnson, "A Short Description of the Province of South-Carolina," in Chapman J. Milling, ed., *Colonial South Carolina: Two Contemporary Descriptions* (Columbia: University of South Carolina Press, 1951), 111–206, quotation from 143. For Charleston's skyline (including St. Philips), see Robert Olwell, *Masters, Slaves, & Subjects: The Culture of Power in the South Carolina Low Country, 1740–1790* (Ithaca, NY: Cornell University

Press, 1998), 16. St. Philips was on Charleston's north side, near where "The High Way" left the city. See B. Roberts and W. H. Toms, "The Iconography of Charles-Town at High Water" (1739), in Elroy M. Avery, *A History of the United States and Its People*, vol. 3 (Cleveland, OH: Burrows Brothers, 1907), between p. 344 and p. 345; D. Juan de la Cruz, "Plano de Charles Town: capital de la Carolina" [1750?], Kendall Map 29, South Caroliniana Library, University of South Carolina, Columbia.

3. SC-CJ, 4/24/1752, p. 164 ("Sight"); SC-JCHA, 4/29/1752, p. 260 ("Arms"). For reasons discussed below, the assembly reacted in a restrained manner, but even its journal frequently uses "Insult"; see ibid., 5/1/1752, p. 269, and 5/14/1752, p. 357. SC-CJ, 4/24/1752, p. 163 ("outrage"); DRIA 1: 247 ("Path"), 255 ("Nothing"), 259 ("Mischief"), 274 ("Heinousness," "Defiance"), 391–392 (Creeks).

4. For landholding in the area, see Henry A. M. Smith, "Charleston and Charleston Neck: The Original Grantees and the Settlements Along the Ashley and Cooper Rivers," *South Carolina Historical and Genealogical Magazine* 19 (1918): 3–76, map opposite p. 3 and 23–25 (Glen), 27–29 (Elliot), 54–56 (Wragg). DRIA 1: 255 ("Door"); SC-CJ, 4/1/1752, p. 116 (wife, meeting), p. 117 ("half," "gate"). For the location of Glen's house and gate vis-a-vis the main road, see "Plat of Belvedere Plantation," 1790, South Carolina Historical Society, Charleston; Plat, Book CC, p. 337, Register Mesne Conveyance Office, County of Charleston, Charleston, SC. SC-CJ, 4/2/1752, p. 119 ("bodys"), 4/1/1752, p. 118 ("Plantation"). For Wragg, see A. S. Salley Jr., *Death Notices in the South-Carolina Gazette, 1732–1775* (Columbia: Historical Commission of South Carolina, 1917), 24; Wragg Family Papers, 11/466/9, South Carolina Historical Society. George C. Rogers Jr., *Charleston in the Age of the Pinckneys* (Columbia: University of South Carolina Press, 1980 [1969]), 10 ("rice-planting").

5. DRIA 1: 211 ("encamped," "firing"), 233 ("Accident"); Pennsylvania *Gazette*, 4/23/1752 ("School," "Bloodshed").

6. In addition to descriptions written months later, two accounts of the March 31 meeting were recorded at the time: the council minutes from that day (DRIA 1: 224–227), and Glen's April 2 speech (ibid., 228–229). DRIA's versions of the documents are undated, but SC-CJ provides the dates. DRIA 1: 211 ("depend," "believe"), 226 ("Friends"), 229 ("Thing," "Eat," "promised"), 345 ("Brothers").

7. For my own unfortunate contribution to these stories—"Acorn Whistler . . . attacked a Cherokee party then under British protection"—see Joshua Piker, *Okfuskee: A Creek Indian Town in Colonial America* (Cambridge, MA: Harvard University Press, 2004), 59. The finest treatment of the Acorn Whistler affair to date can be found in Steven C. Hahn, *The Invention of the Creek Nation, 1670–1763* (Lincoln: University of Nebraska Press, 2004), 210–218.

8. DRIA 1: 229 ("drinking"); SC-CJ, 4/2/1752, p. 121 ("our People," "they"). DRIA mistranscribes "our People" as "Four People"; ibid., 1: 230. For Acorn Whistler's party, see ibid., 210, 226, 228, 276. For "This was done," see ibid., 229. Glen and his council were referring to Lower Creek responsibility by the evening of April 1; SC-CJ, 4/1/1752, pp. 116–117.

9. See SC-CJ, 3/31/1752, p. 107, for meeting minutes identifying Acorn Whistler as an Upper Creek and mentioning "Eleven other Upper Creeks, his followers," before going on to note "26 more Indians of the lower Creek

nation." For the parties' activities before arriving in Charleston, see DRIA 1: 230, 232, 276, 345, 391; SC-JCHA, 2/20/1753, p. 96. For Sheldon, see William De Brahm, "A Map of South Carolina and a Part of Georgia," in William P. Cumming, *The Southeast in Early Maps*, 3rd ed., revised and enlarged by Louis De Vorsey Jr. (Chapel Hill: University of North Carolina Press, 1998), plate 59c; Mr. Boss, "A map of South Carolina from Savannah Sound to St. Helena's Sound, with the several plantations, their proper boundary lines, their names, and the names of the proprietors included" [1771?], lot 64, Library of Congress, Washington, DC; BPRO-SC, 24: 83.

10. DRIA 1: 232 ("scared"), 234 ("Rate"). For the militia, see SC-CJ, 4/1/1752, p. 117 ("pursuit"), 4/2/1752, p. 118. For de Sausseur, see ibid., 4/6/1752, p. 130 (planter, "fear"); DRIA 1: 235. For the house, see De Brahm, "A Map of South Carolina," lot 10 or lot 28; Boss, "A Map of South Carolina," lot 78 or 79.

11. SC-CJ, 4/1/1752, p. 117 ("utterly"; "Concerned"); DRIA 1: 228–231, 232 ("hanged"). For the Upper Creek who remained in Charleston, see below, chapter 5. For Surreau, see SC-JCHA, 2/28/1753, p. 115, 4/16/1753, pp. 233–234; DRIA 1: 231. As for the movements of the Upper Creeks who fled, the actions of eight (Acorn Whistler, the four men captured at the ferry, and the three men who went to Pon Pon) are documented in SC-CJ, 4/3 and 4/4/1752, pp. 123–128 and in the sources cited in n. 12. All those sources say about the man who vanished, however, is that Acorn Whistler's party met two Yuchis at Bull's house, that one was present at the April 2 meeting with Glen, and that he was not captured at the ferry. He may have gone to the Yuchi village located approximately ten miles south of Bull's house. And the women? Two were in Charleston, and one elected not to stay at the ferry on April 2. A militia officer reported "seven Creek Indians" were at the ferry, and "three got off by Favour of the Night," but colonists often counted only men when discussing the size of Indian groups. It is a reasonable guess, therefore, that the Upper Creeks who "got off" were three men who were accompanied by two women, whose presence went unremarked. I suspect, furthermore, that the "three" Upper Creeks found near Pon Pon were the same three men accompanied by the same unmentioned women. For the Yuchis, see DRIA 1: 232; SC-CJ, 8/23/1750, 7/2/1751. For the women, see DRIA 1: 226, 233; for the officer, see ibid., 231; for Pon Pon, see ibid., 235. The Yuchis had an on-again, off-again relationship with the Creeks. By 1752, they were generally described as Lower Creeks, but there was a Yuchi village in Upper Creek country. Joshua Piker, "To the Backcountry and Back Again: The Yuchi's Search for Stability in the Eighteenth-Century Southeast," in Jason Baird Jackson, ed., *Yuchi Indian Histories before the Removal Era* (Lincoln: University of Nebraska Press, 2012), pp. 189–213.

12. DRIA 1: 232 ("laugh," "resent"), 233 ("Innocent"), 234–235 ("blameless," "starved," "Victuals," "hunt").

13. Ibid., 229 ("King"), 295 ("great"). Jack B. Martin and Margaret McKane Mauldin, *A Dictionary of Creek/Muskogee* (Lincoln: University of Nebraska Press, 2000), 69 *(lak.cv, lak.sv)*. Professor Martin notes that "In spoken Muskogee, the different vowels and consonants would clearly distinguish lakcv from laksv, but the words are similar enough in shape to allow for . . . some kind of word play about Lakcv being a laksv." Jack Martin, e-mail message to author, 10/29/2010.

14. DRIA 1: 228–231 (April 2). SC-CJ, 4/1/1752, pp. 116–117, makes it clear that, prior to the attack, someone gave the British "Information" that "a Party of 26 Creeks were gone in pursuit of the Cherokees." Given that Acorn Whistler made his claims about telling the interpreter of the Lower Creeks' departure while in the interpreter's presence, and given that this interpreter broke the news of the assault to Glen (p. 116), that someone was almost certainly Acorn Whistler.

15. DRIA 1: 276 ("Orders," kinswoman). Hiacpellechi claimed his people met Acorn Whistler "near Savannah River," but the parties actually met at Bull's house, almost one hundred miles east of the river. Hiacpellechi also stated that, while in Charleston, "he (the Acorn Whistler) was the Man that received the Talk from the Governor which they [Hiacpellechi and the other Lower Creeks] did not understand." The Lower Creeks' interpreter, however, was present and on duty when Acorn Whistler "received the Talk" witnessed by Hiacpellechi. As for the half-truth, Hiacpellechi stated that the Lower Creeks "went out purposely in Pursuit of their Enemies, and had no Manner of Intention of going to Charles Town." They may, in fact, have gone to war against the Cherokees, but they quite obviously left the warpath at some point and headed for Charleston. By the time they arrived at Bull's house, they were several hundred miles from Cherokee country, and Glen noted that the Lower Creeks "came by another Road to Charles Town" so as to evade the governor's standing order prohibiting unofficial Indian parties from visiting the capital. For the interpreter see SC-CJ, 3/31/1752, p. 107; SC-JCHA, 2/20/1753, p. 97; ibid., 4/16/1753, p. 233. For these Lower Creeks possibly attacking Cherokees in December 1751, see chapter 1. DRIA 1: 345 ("Road").

Introduction

1. DRIA 1: 334 ("Bussiness"), 335 ("positive"), 339 ("Day," "Tuckabatchees"). For distances, see "A List of Towns & Number of Gun Men in the Creek Nation," in Francis Ogilvie to Thomas Gage, 7/8/1764, Gage Papers, Clements Library, University of Michigan, Ann Arbor; Dunbar Rowland, ed., *Mississippi Provincial Archives, 1763–1766, English Dominion: Letters and Enclosures to the Secretary of State from Major Robert Farmer and Governor George Johnstone* (Nashville, TN, 1911), 95; Baron de Crenay, "Carte De Partie de La Louisiana" (1733), Karpinski Collection, map 450, Huntington Library, San Marino, CA.

2. Mark Twain, "On the Decay of the Art of Lying," http://www.gutenberg .org/cache/epub/2572/pg2572.html, accessed 11/15/12. Twain, of course, was describing lies, which this book treats as a type of story. The stories at this book's center all contain untruths. In some cases, those untruths were both central enough to the story in question and were repeated often enough that it seems fair to say that a given story is a lie and its storyteller a liar. But because that is not true for all of the book's stories, I use "story" as the book's organizing motif. Put another way, in what follows, I will sometimes discuss lies, but this is a book structured around stories. For lies *qua* lies, see Joshua Piker, "Lying Together: The Imperial Implications of Cross-Cultural Untruths," *American Historical Review* 116 (2011): 964–986.

3. SC-CJ 7/28/1744, pp. 428–429. Ibid., 6/21/1744, pp. 348–349 (towns, headmen), 6/27/1744, p. 361 ("5," "Albamas"), 7/28/1744, p. 429 (three Alabamas). BPRO-SC, 21: 392 (July 14); SC-CJ, 7/25/1744, pp. 421–422 (Glen).

4. When Mad Turkey died in 1774, he was living in the Okfuskee village of Chattahoochee; after his death, the Chattahoochees founded a new village, which they named Little Okfuskee. For Mad Turkey, see Joshua Piker, *Okfuskee: A Creek Indian Town in Colonial America* (Cambridge, MA: Harvard University Press, 2004); C. L. Grant, ed., *Letters, Journals and Writings of Benjamin Hawkins*, 2 vols. (Savannah, GA: Beehive Press, 1980), 1: 306 (new village). For Little Okfuskee's location, see Crenay, "Carte." For Acorn Whistler stating "We are Talapussee People," see DRIA 1: 231; see also "A List of Towns & Number of Gun Men in the Creek Nation." For Glen's letter, see SC-CJ, 1/22/1746, p. 26; see also ibid., pp. 25, 27. Until 1752, British calendars started the new year in March; in my citations, I have silently brought the dates into accordance with modern usage. This is worth noting here because Glen's letter referring to Acorn Whistler's visit "last year" was written on January 22, 1745. In our terms, that would be January 22, 1746. I have cited it as such above, but Glen was using a different calendar. So, the 1746 remark about "last year" refers to 1744.

5. DRIA 1: 233 ("called"). "Talisey mico" of Okfuskee never reappeared; Mad Turkey did. See above; SC-CJ, 7/28/1744, p. 429.

6. SC-CJ, 1/22/1746, p. 26 ("sent"), p. 27 ("Talk"); Glen to George Clinton, 9/25/1750 ("Worthless"), box 4, folder 4, George Clinton Papers, Clements Library. DRIA 1: 225 ("observed"), 226 ("do not," "private"), 295 ("as great"), 438 ("greatest"). Glen's reference to "Worthless" does not mention Acorn Whistler specifically, although the context shows that the governor had him in mind; Piker, "Lying Together," 972, n. 15.

7. Account Book of Secretary John Hammerton, 1732–1743, p. 47, in Inventories of Estates, Book LL, 1732–1743, Series S213049, South Carolina Department of Archives and History, Columbia. I learned of this document from the department's senior archivist, Dr. Charles Lesser, who tracked it down based on a few stray (and ultimately misleading) citations that I had culled from a nineteenth-century antiquarian's papers. For Wood, see SC-JCHA, 3/18/1741, pp. 524–525 ("Commissions"). The other headman Wood recommended was "Iffameko an Upper Creek," who the British knew as Dog King; for his connections to Okfuskee and Acorn Whistler, see chapter 5. For the agent and commissions, see Hammerton's Account Book, p. 47; SC-JCHA, 3/25/1741, pp. 561–562; ibid., 6/23/1741, p. 53; ibid., 1/27/1742, p. 355; ibid., 2/24/1752, p. 418. For a Creek referencing Acorn Whistler's commission, see DRIA 1: 278.

8. For Little Okfuskee's population, see section 3. For the size of Acorn Whistler's parties, see SC-CJ, 1/10/1746; DRIA 1: 226. For officials' willingness to meet multiple times with Acorn Whistler, see ibid., 224–230, 233, 276.

9. SC-CJ, 6/27/1744, p. 361 ("two miles"). Ibid., 6/17/1744, p. 339; CO 324/37, f124 ("distress"). SC-CJ, 9/4/1749, p. 584 ("settled").

10. Ibid., 7/28/1744, p. 428 ("Conference"); see also Edmond Atkin to William Lyttelton, 5/20/1756, William H. Lyttelton Collection, Clements Library. South Carolina *Gazette*, 8/13/1744 ("Hostilities"); SC-CJ, 1/25/1745, p. 40 ("uproar"); CRSGA 36: 252. For "ligne," see Anonymous, "Carte de la Riviere Des Cheraquis

ou Grande Riviere avec les tribus," n.d., Karpinski Collection, map 437, Hunting-ton Library. See also another undated and anonymous map, "Carte pour donner une ideé de la positions des Villages Sauvages" in ibid., map 435.

11. SC-CJ, 7/28/1744, p. 429 (goods presented to Acorn Whistler). For a February 12, 1744, letter describing the relation of Acorn Whistler's Tallapoosas to the French see MPAFD 4: 215–224, esp. 223.

12. SC-CJ, 1/22/1746, p. 26; Glen to Clinton, 9/25/1750, Clinton Papers. For Acorn Whistler's 1752 speeches, see DRIA 1: 225–227, 228–231. Ibid., 231 ("Tryffles").

13. DRIA 1: 224 ("Friends"), 225 ("Errand"), 227 ("Presents"). In 1750, John Eycott was licensed to trade in Little Okfuskee; he had been trading in Upper Creek country since at least 1746, but died in June 1751. DRIA 1: 129 (license); SC-CJ, 11/1/1746, p. 177; Wills, Charleston County, South Carolina, W.P.A. Transcripts, vol. 6: 512–513, South Carolina Department of Archives and History.

14. DRIA 1: 229 ("command"), 230 (kick), 232 ("come down"), 276 ("perswaded").

15. SC-CJ, 9/4/1749, p. 583 ("Gang," "Tallapoosas"), p. 584 ("most," "per-suaded"), p. 588 ("could"), p. 589 ("Powder"); BPRO-SC, 23: 449 ("upon"); DRIA 1: 399 ("Hywasse"). For Acorn Whistler's responsibility, see SC-CJ, 9/4/1749, pp. 584, 589; DRIA 1: 399.

16. For Upper Creek efforts to stop Acorn Whistler, see SC-CJ, 9/4/1749, p. 589 ("could not"); DRIA 1: 399. SC-CJ, 5/11/1750 (Cherokees); BPRO-SC, 23: 449 ("hired"); DRIA 1: 339 ("bribed"). See also Glen to Clinton, 9/25/1750, Clinton Papers.

17. SC-CJ, 8/16/1750 ("Intrigues), 9/5/1750 ("Malatche").

18. Ibid.

19. SC-CJ, 9/4/1749; DRIA 1: 399 ("past"); Piker, *Okfuskee*, 47–52.

20. Ibid., 50 (women, "King").

21. SC-CJ, 9/5/1750; CRSGA 7: 341–342; ibid., 26: 194. For Malatchi's actions, see section 2.

22. SC-CJ, 1/22/1746, p. 27 ("return"), 10/31/1752, p. 530 ("White Man"), 11/15/1752 ("Madman"); DRIA 1: 279 ("hott-headed," "ill"), 348 ("dangerous").

Part I. Imperial

1. James Glen to William Lyttelton, 6/9/1756, William Lyttelton Collection, Clements Library, University of Michigan, Ann Arbor. SC-JCHA, 5/8/1754, p. 498; James Abercromby to James Glen, 1/30/1754, in John C. Van Horne and George Reese, eds., *The Letter Book of James Abercromby, Colonial Agent: 1751–1773* (Richmond: Virginia State Library and Archives, 1991), 102; SC-CJ, 6/2/1756, p. 271.

2. BPRO-SC, 27: 64 ("gone"). James Glen to "Honorable Gentlemen & Gen-tlemen of the Assembly" [ca. 1750], p. 1 ("weighty"), South Caroliniana Library, University of South Carolina, Columbia. SC-UH, 5/31/1749 ("Pains," "Indo-lence"); DRIA 2: 83 ("Administration"); SC-JCHA, 5/11/1754, p. 543 ("Justice").

3. W. Stitt Robinson, *James Glen: From Scottish Provost to Royal Governor of South Carolina* (Westport, CT: Greenwood Press, 1996), 15 ("kiss'd).

4. Brendan McConville, *The King's Three Faces: The Rise and Fall of Royal America, 1688–1776* (Chapel Hill: University of North Carolina Press, 2006), chapter 8, esp. p. 220 ("bureaucratic"). Bob Harris, "War, Empire, and the 'National Interest' in Mid-Eighteenth-Century Britain," in Julie Flavell and Stephen Conway, eds., *Britain and America Go to War: The Impact of War and Warfare in Anglo-America, 1754–1815* (Gainesville: University Press of Florida, 2004), pp. 13–40. Troy Bickham, *Savages within the Empire: Representations of American Indians in Eighteenth-Century Britain* (Oxford: Clarendon Press, 2005).

5. Analyses of Glen's political thought often place him within a group of officials concerned with constitutional issues, particularly the relation between Britain and its colonies. In that crowd, however, Glen is better understood as a conservative than a reformer. He hoped to recapture power for the crown, not to rethink the nature of imperial politics. When it came to constitutional issues, Glen was essentially reactive, not creative. He was not, therefore, a member of what David Armitage describes as "a cadre of provincials and imperial officials beyond the metropolis itself" who were reconceiving the British Atlantic "as a single political community." Robinson, *James Glen*, 32–34, 61–66; M. Eugene Sirmans, *Colonial South Carolina: A Political History, 1663–1763* (Chapel Hill: University of North Carolina Press, 1966), 236, 256; Ned Landsman, "Nation, Migration, and the Province in the First British Empire: Scotland and the Americas, 1600–1800," *American Historical Review* 104 (1999): 463–475, esp. 472; Landsman, *From Colonials to Provincials: American Thought and Culture* (Ithaca, NY: Cornell University Press, 2000 [1997]). David Armitage, *The Ideological Origins of the British Empire* (New York: Cambridge University Press, 2000), 9; J. Russell Snapp, "An Enlightened Empire: Scottish and Irish Imperial Reformers in the Age of the American Revolution," *Albion* 33 (2001): 388–403.

1. The Governor

1. For the letters, see Duke of Bedford to James Glen, 3/12/1751, CO 324/38, ff101–102 and ff102–106. For Glen presenting the latter, see SC-CJ, 3/5/1752, p. 57. Glen had shown this letter to the council once before; ibid., 5/28/1751, pp. 114–119. Board of Trade to James Glen, 12/1/1749, in BPRO-SC, 23: 421 ("Irregular"); Lord Commissioners for Trade and Plantations to James Glen, 11/15/1750, ibid., 24: 148–177, quotations from 153 ("Negligence"), 157 ("Inattention"), and 175 ("Duty").

2. Lord Commissioners to James Glen, 12/20/1748, ibid., 23: 280 ("We"). Bedford to Glen, 3/12/1751, CO 324/38, ff101–102; for Glen's response, see Glen to Bedford, 6/23/1751, BPRO-SC, 24: 341–345.

3. William Murray to John Murray, 10/12/1754, American Documents in the Murraythwaite Collection, Scottish Record Office, South Carolina Historical Society, Charleston. Lawrence Henry Gipson, *The British Empire Before the American Revolution, Volume 2: The British Isles and the American Colonies: The Southern Plantations, 1748–1754* (New York: Knopf, 1960 [1936]), 149.

4. For the importance of patronage, see James A. Henretta, *"Salutary Neglect": Colonial Administration under the Duke of Newcastle* (Princeton: Princeton University Press, 1972). For Glen's background, marriage, and patrons, see W. Stitt

Robinson, *James Glen: From Scottish Provost to Royal Governor of South Carolina* (Westport, CT: Greenwood Press, 1996), chapter 1, quotation ("procured") from 14.

5. For Glen's statement about the "Consequence . . . of having the favour and friendship of his Grace the Duke of Bedford," see SC-CJ, 5/27/1749, p. 412. James Glen to Thomas Robinson, 8/15/1754, BPRO-SC, 26: 82 ("distant"); see also James Glen to Thomas Harvey, n.d., Letter Book of James Glen, p. 52, Dalhousie Muniments, Scottish Record Office, microfilm in the Huntington Library, San Marino, CA. James Abercromby to James Glen, 1/16/1755 and 3/8/1753, in John C. Van Horne and George Reese, eds., *The Letter Book of James Abercromby, Colonial Agent: 1751–1773* (Richmond: Virginia State Library and Archives, 1991), 76, 132 ("deserted"). William Murray to John Murray, 4/16/1755 ("Earnestly," "pleased"), Murraythwaite Collection. James Glen to Duke of Bedford, 7/26/1748, BPRO-SC, 23: 166 ("distinguished," "endeavoured"), 167 ("Protection"); James Glen to Earl of Holderness, 12/31/1751, ibid., 24: 387 ("acknowledged"). James Glen to "Dear Sir," ca. 1751, Glen Letter Book, p. 144 ("beg").

6. Ned Landsman, "Introduction: The Context and Functions of Scottish Involvement with the Americas," in Landsman, ed., *Nation and Province in the First British Empire: Scotland and the Americas, 1600–1800* (Lewisburg, PA: Bucknell University Press, 2001), pp. 15–35; Linda Colley, *Britons: Forging the Empire, 1707–1837*, 2nd ed. (New Haven: Yale University Press, 2005), 130; John M. MacKenzie, "Empire and National Identities: The Case of Scotland," *Transactions of the Royal Historical Society* 6th ser., 8 (1998): 215–232; Stephen Conway, *War, State, and Society in Mid-Eighteenth Century Britain and Ireland* (New York: Oxford University Press, 2006), 9, 203. For post-1745 developments, see ibid., 204–205; Kathleen Wilson, *The Sense of the People: Politics, Culture, and Imperialism in England, 1715–1785* (New York: Cambridge University Press, 1995), 174; Harris, *Politics and the Nation*, 149–150; Geoffrey Plank, *Rebellion and Savagery: The Jacobite Rising of 1745 and the British Empire* (Philadelphia: University of Pennsylvania Press, 2005). SC-CJ, 1/17/1746, p. 19 (proclamation). See also ibid., 5/29/1744; SC-UH, 9/17/1746. Glen had particular reason to worry about perceptions of disloyalty since his father had lost his title for being a lukewarm supporter of an earlier Scottish rebellion; Robinson, *James Glen*, 8.

7. Ned C. Landsman, "The Provinces and the Empire: Scotland, the American Colonies and the Development of British Provincial Identity," in Lawrence Stone, ed., *An Imperial State at War: Britain from 1689 to 1815* (London: Routledge, 1994), 258–287. For imperial vs. metropolitan, see Ned Landsman, "Nation, Migration, and the Province in the First British Empire: Scotland and the Americas, 1600-1800," *American Historical Review* 104 (1999): 463–475, esp. 470–473. Eric Richards, "Scotland and the Uses of the Atlantic Empire," in Bernard Bailyn and Philip D. Morgan, eds., *Strangers Within the Realm: Cultural Margins of the First British Empire* (Chapel Hill: University of North Carolina Press, 1991), 67–114, quotation ("overlapping") from 91. For Glen's return to Scotland, see Robinson, *James Glen*; James Glen to the Speaker of the Commons House of Assembly, ca. 1761, James Glen Collection, South Caroliniana Library, University of South Carolina, Columbia. For Glen's Carolina-centered plans, see Robinson, *James Glen*, 104; M. Eugene Sirmans, *Colonial South Carolina: A*

Political History, 1663–1763 (Chapel Hill: University of North Carolina Press, 1966), 296; Mary F. Carter, "James Glen, Governor of Colonial South Carolina: A Study in British Administrative Policies" (PhD diss., UCLA, 1951), chapter 3. For a rosier reading of the impact of Glen's Scottish background on his career, see Alex Murdoch, "James Glen and the Indians," in A. Mackillop and Steve Murdoch, eds., *Military Governors and Imperial Frontiers, c. 1600–1800: A Study of Scotland and Empires* (Leiden: Brill, 2003), pp. 141–159.

8. Conway, *War, State, and Society,* 51. For the 1748 shift and its implications, see Henretta, *Salutary Neglect,* 282–331. For the old-style approach to colonial administration, see letters from the Lord Commissioners to Glen dated 6/27/1745, 5/9/1746, and 5/26/1747, BPRO-SC, 22: 108–110, 156–158, 287–288. Glen to "Dear Sir," c. 1751, Glen Letter Book, p. 144 ("smallest"); Glen to the Duke of Bedford, 7/26/1748, BPRO-SC, 23: 166 ("hopes"). Ian K. Steele, "The Anointed, the Appointed, and the Elected: Governance of the British Empire, 1689–1784," in P. J. Marshall, ed., *The Oxford History of the British Empire, Volume 2: The Eighteenth Century* (New York: Oxford University Press, 1998), pp. 105–127, quotation ("rigour") from 120; Jack P. Greene, "Transatlantic Colonization and the Redefinition of Empire in the Early Modern Era," in Christine Daniels and Michael V. Kennedy, eds., *Negotiated Empires: Centers and Peripheries in the Americas, 1500–1820* (New York: Routledge, 2002), pp. 267–282, quotation ("mode") from 278.

9. Sirmans, *Colonial South Carolina,* 280–282; Robinson, *James Glen,* 52. For Bedford, see CO 324/37, f230 ("Displeasure"), 231 ("Command"). For the Lord Commissioners' first letter, see BPRO-SC, 23: 123–131, quotations from 128 ("dangerous," "attentive"), 129 ("send"). For the next three letters, see ibid., 162–165, quotation ("extraordinary") from 164; ibid., 250–252, quotation ("Papers") from 252; ibid., 276–280, quotation ("difficulty") from 280.

10. SC-JCHA, 11/24/1750, p. 199 ("greatest"); BPRO-SC, 23: 75 ("unanimously"). Glen to the Lord Commissioners, 10/10/1748, in ibid., 203–210 ("Strange"). For the Lord Commissioners' first letter on the Choctaw affair, see ibid., 277–279, quotations from 277 ("equally"), 278 ("Prudence," "Treachery"). For the letter of the following year, see ibid., 420–423, quotation ("Character") from 423. For November 1750, see ibid., 24: 155. The most thorough contemporary investigation of the Choctaw affair is harshly critical of Glen; see Edmond Atkin, "Historical Account of the Revolt of the Chactaw Indians in the late War from the French to the British Alliance and of their Return to that of the French," 1753, Lansdowne Manuscripts #809, British Library, London.

11. For Glen's 1748 dispute with the assembly, see Sirmans, *Colonial South Carolina,* 265–274; SC-JCHA, 6/29/1748, pp. 394–402, quotation ("Sarcasms") from 400; SC-CJ, 6/29/1748, p. 352 ("hasty"). For the letter, see BPRO-SC, 23: 232–245, quotations from 234 ("unhinged"), 236 ("naked").

12. For arenas in which South Carolina's House was especially power hungry, see Jack P. Greene, *The Quest for Power: The Lower Houses of Assembly in the Southern Royal Colonies, 1689–1776* (Chapel Hill: University of North Carolina Press, 1963), 88, 224, 252, 267, 301.

13. SC-JCHA, 1/22/1748, p. 14 ("thousand"); BPRO-SC, 23: 71–82, quotation ("numerous") from 75; ibid., 390 ("History"). Ibid., 24: 168 ("Praise"), 152 ("parallel'd"). Ibid., 25: 131 ("cannot").

14. SC-CJ, 5/29/1744, p. 290 (religion); ibid., 6/26/1744, pp. 357 (king) and 358 ("Councils"). For plans, see BPRO-SC, 23: 81 and 24: 421. Ibid., 23: 71 ("footsteps"). See also SC-JCHA, 6/14/1746, p. 234; James Glen to Thomas Lee, 9/22/1750, in SC-CJ, 11/23/1750; BPRO-SC, 25: 302. SC-UH, 5/31/1749, p. 104 ("Cautious"); BPRO-SC, 25: 71 ("War"). SC-JCHA, 5/22/1750, p. 148 ("beg").

15. For the fall of 1748, see BPRO-SC, 23: 203–245, quotation ("Observations") from 211. For "full," see ibid., 336; for the most thorough report, see SC-UH, 5/31/1749, pp. 82–108. For the Lord Commissioners' letter and Glen's responses, see BPRO-SC, 23: 148–177, 346–364, 389–423. For "ashamed," see ibid., 24: 422.

16. Glen to "My Lords," 7/15/1751, Glen Letter Book, p. 132 ("carefully"); BPRO-SC, 24: 78 ("Invasions"); ibid., 23: 440 ("knowingly"); SC-UH, 4/21/1751, pp. 48–51, quotation ("Seal") from 48. Jonathan Mercantini, *Who Shall Rule at Home? The Evolution of South Carolina Political Culture, 1748–1776* (Columbia: University of South Carolina Press, 2007), chapter 1.

17. For "Mortifying," see BPRO-SC, 23: 442; for "reasonable," see ibid., 24, 149. For encroachments, see ibid., 268–294, quotation from 285 ("fear").

18. Ibid., 23: 421 ("genuine"); for bragging, see ibid., 336–337, 384, and CO 5/389.

19. BPRO-SC, 23: 232–245 (reforms); SC-JCHA, 5/4/1751, p. 397 (constitution).

20. *Journal of the Commissioners for Trade and Plantations from January 1741–2 to December 1749* (London: His Majesty's Stationery Office, 1931); *Journal of the Commissioners for Trade and Plantations from January 1749–1750 to December 1753* (London: His Majesty's Stationery Office, 1932); BPRO-SC, 23: 148–177. The Lord Commissioners ceased writing to Glen seventeen months before a March 1752 policy shift that reduced their correspondence with colonial governors. Even after March 1752, however, the Lord Commissioners communicated directly with other governors, and they starting writing to South Carolina's governor again after Glen left office, sending three letters to Lyttelton in less than a year. For the policy change's effect on imperial records, see Charles M. Andrews, *Guide to the Materials for American History to 1783 in the Public Record Office of Great Britain*, 2 vols. (Carnegie Institute: Washington, DC, 1912–1914), p. 117. For the letters to Lyttelton, see CO 326/18, f105. In March 1753, Glen mentioned receiving a letter from the Lord Commissioners dated June 3, 1752, but Britain's National Archive has no record of the letter, and it does not appear in any published or microfilmed collection; BPRO-SC, 25: 174.

21. Bedford to Glen, 3/12/1751, CO 324/38, ff101–102; Thomas Robinson to Glen, 7/5/1754, BPRO-SC, 26: 72–73; John Pownall to Glen, 1/28/1755, ibid., 151.

22. For the postmortem discussions of Glen's career, see John Pownall to William Lyttelton, 11/7/1757, William Lyttelton Collection, Clements Library, University of Michigan, Ann Arbor. ("want"); Board of Trade to William Lyttelton, 11/9/1757, ibid. ("unaccountable," "steady").

23. For "Plan," see Glen to Thomas Lee, 9/22/1750, in SC-CJ, 11/23/1750; since this volume of SC-CJ is very difficult to read, the quotation is taken from the copy of SC-CJ in CO 5/455, f208. For the plan's origins, see Sirmans,

Colonial South Carolina, 215–216; BPRO-SC, 22: 40–56, esp. 53; SC-JCHA, 7/4/1744, p. 225 ("Settlements"); SC-UH, 4/16/1746.

24. South Carolina *Gazette,* 6/16/1746 ("all"), 6/30/1746; see also SC-CJ, 4/17/1746, pp. 94–96. Glen to Charles McNaire, 12/18/1747, CO 5/373, f26 ("stand"); Atkin, "Historical Account," f47, suggests this letter was backdated. SC-JCHA, 3/12/1747–1748, p. 163 ("Mother"); BPRO-SC, 23: 81 ("perswaded").

25. DRIA 1: 84–86, quotation ("Insurrection") from 85; ibid., 2: 26 ("uniting"). Glen to the Six Nations, SC-CJ, 11/15/1752, p. 12 ("hatchet"). Glen to the Lord Commissioners, 12/?/1751, BPRO-SC, 24: 389–423, quotation ("alive") from 421.

26. Glen to George Clinton, 5/24/1751, DRIA 1: 84–86, quotations ("Chactaws," "different," "Southward") from 85. The DRIA version refers to "the Onis River," but the original refers to "the Ohio River"; see Glen to Clinton, 5/24/1751, box 4, folder 8, George Clinton Papers, Clements Library. Glen to Thomas Lee, 6/7/1750, in SC-CJ, 8/16/1750 ("Cherokees").

27. Glen to the Lord Commissioners, 12/?/1751, BPRO-SC, 24: 389–423, quotations from 403–404.

28. Bedford to Glen, 4/26/1748, CO 324/37, ff207–209, quotation from 207; see also Lord Commissioners to Glen, 7/22/1748, BPRO-SC, 23: 162–165, esp. 162. Lord Commissioners to Glen, 11/15/1750, ibid., 148–177, quotations from 154 ("Advantages"), 156 ("Security"); SC-CJ, 5/20/1751, p. 94 (commission).

29. Glen to Robert Dinwiddie, 6/1/1754, DRIA 1: 524–528, quotation ("come") from 526. Glen to Board of Trade, 12/29/1749, BPRO-SC, 23: 442–453, quotation ("Subjects") from 444.

30. Greene, *Quest for Power,* 316–324; Mercantini, *Who Shall Rule at Home,* chapter 2. Board of Trade to Glen, 12/1/1749, BPRO-SC, 23: 420–424, especially 420–421 ("matters"); SC-CJ, 6/1/1749, p. 458 ("some things"). For the anger of Glen's superiors when he failed to curb the assembly's "many Claims and Privileges . . . relating to Indian Affairs," see Board of Trade to William Lyttelton, 11/9/1757, Lyttelton Collection.

31. For Glen's embrace of the promise made by Acorn Whistler's people "to make the Peace general, when they went home," see above, prologue. Glen to George Clinton, 5/14/1752, in SC-CJ, 5/14/1752, p. 229 ("Easey"). An undated version of this letter appears in DRIA 1: 214; the volume's "Calendar" incorrectly suggests (p. xvi) a date of 10/15/1751. Glen's statement about the difficulties of reconciling northern and southern Indians came while he discussed "the War that [persists] between your People [the Iroquois] and the Creeks." He enclosed a letter to the Iroquois in which he did not bother even mentioning an Iroquois-Creek peace process; Glen to "the Six Nations," in SC-CJ, 5/14/1752, pp. 229–230. Compare this letter's post-April 1 rhetoric about an Iroquois-Creek peace with Glen's pre-April 1 rhetoric in DRIA 1: 206–207. Glen to the Cherokee Nation, 4/5/1752, in DRIA 1: 233–234, quotation ("Surprize") from 234; Glen to the Lord Commissioners, 12/16/1752, BPRO-SC, 25: 130–135, quotation ("Connivance") from 132.

32. SC-CJ, 4/6/1752, p. 134 ("Consideration"). For the thirty-five points, see ibid., 4/23/1752, pp. 159–162; for "Enquiry" and "Insults," see ibid., 162.

33. Abercromby to Glen, 1/25/1752, in Van Horne and Reese, *Letter Book of James Abercromby*, 26 ("disagreeable," "Papers"). Glen received regular shipments of London papers from Abercromby, including a four-month run that likely arrived just as he was writing to the Lord Commissioners; see Abercromby to Glen, 10/7/1751, ibid., 13. Glen to the Lord Commissioners, 12/?/1751, BPRO-SC, 24: 389–423, quotations from 400 ("Person"), 416 ("proper"), 422 ("helped," "Service"). This letter was read by the Lord Commissioners on July 3, 1752; *Journal of the Commissioners for Trade and Plantations from January 1749–1750 to December 1753*, 342.

34. SC-CJ: 3/11/1752, p. 71 ("all," "Original"); 3/12/1752, p. 72 ("unprecedented," "Just"); 3/13/1752, p. 76; 3/20/1752, pp. 97–99; 3/24/1752, p. 101. For Glen's letter, see SC-JCHA, 4/29/1752, pp. 260–262, quotation ("most") from 260.

35. For the assembly's response to Glen, see ibid., 5/1/1752, pp. 268–269, quotation ("dark") from 269. For Glen's concession, see ibid., 5/5/1752, p. 281 ("Prerogative") and pp. 283–284 ("recommend"); for the assembly's reply, see ibid., 5/8/1752, p. 319 ("Government"). Ibid., 5/16/1752, p. 372 ("pursue").

2. The Governor's Story

1. SC-CJ, 1/3/1752, pp. 521–522.

2. For the Lower Creeks' plans, see DRIA 1: 276–277. For Burnett's bills, see SC-JCHA, 1/15/1754, p. 310. See also ibid., 2/5/1754, p. 353 ("Saludy"); DRIA 1: 222. Burnett's house was a regular stopping point for Cherokees and those dealing with them. See ibid., 155–156; SC-JCHA, 3/5/1752, p. 119; "An Account of Monies Paid for the Public by James Glen," 4/23/1761, and Deposition of John Skene, 4/6/1761 ("upon"), both in the James Glen Collection, South Caroliniana Library, University of South Carolina, Columbia.

3. SC-CJ, 1/3/1752, p. 520 ("Crossing"); DRIA 1: 222 ("preparing"). For Lower Creek responsibility, see ibid., 155 ("Coweaters"); SC-CJ, 1/3/1752, p. 520 ("Cowetas"). For "Coweta" as shorthand for "Lower Creek," see MPAFD 5: 74; SC-CJ, 11/15/1751, p. 402; DRIA 1: 394. For Glen blaming the attack on "the Lower Towns People," see DRIA 1: 206–207.

4. For Glen's conversation with Acorn Whistler, see DRIA 1: 226. For "Cowetas, Cowetas," see ibid., 210. For Glen's knowledge that the twenty-six Lower Creeks were Osochis, see ibid., 345; SC-CJ, 11/15/1752, p. 6. Once Glen turned to his second story, he was willing to suggest—as he did in May 1753—that the same Creek party was responsible for both attacks; DRIA 1: 389.

5. SC-CJ, 9/5/1750 ("Behaviour"). For Glen's attacks on Malatchi, see SC-CJ, 1/3/1752, pp. 521–522; DRIA 1: 208 ("Deceivers"), 209 ("Ringleader"); SC-JCHA, 4/29/1752, pp. 260–262.

6. DRIA 1: 209 ("Resentment," "Usage," "Indulgence"), 210 ("base"), 212 ("Brothers"), 345 ("Art," "Blacker," "hear," "Abhorrence"); SC-JCHA, 4/29/1752, pp. 260 ("atrocious"), 261 ("Catalogue"), 262 ("lately").

7. DRIA 1: 208 ("Times"), 233–234 (Cherokees), 234–235 (militia).

8. SC-JCHA, 4/29/1752, p. 261 ("heinous," "smaller," "Censure," "sway"), p. 262 ("small"); DRIA 1: 209 ("Instances," "Ingratitude"), 235 ("regardless"), 234 ("Many"); SC-CJ, 4/24/1752, p. 163 ("barbarously").

9. Glen to the Lord Commissioners, 10/2/1751, BPRO-SC, 24: 126 ("Emperor"). For Glen equating Malatchi and the Lower Creeks, see the awkward shifts between "he" and "they" in SC-JCHA, 4/29/1752.

10. SC-CJ, 1/3/1752, p. 521 ("resentment"), 4/24/1752, p. 163 (council's suggestions); DRIA 1: 207 ("enquire"), 212 (April 28), 234 ("Measures").

11. For the documents Glen presented to the council, see SC-CJ, 5/23/1752, p. 244, and 5/25/1752, pp. 245–258, quotations ("demand," "Excellency") from 258. For the instructions, see ibid., 6/24/1752, pp. 290–296; for the council's suggestions, see ibid., 6/16/1752, pp. 289–290. The item regarding thefts was added in response to letters that Glen presented the council on May 25.

12. DRIA 1: 343–347 (instructions).

13. SC-CJ, 5/27/1752, p. 259 ("with Malatchi"); DRIA 1: 346–347 (instructions).

14. Glen's only letter to the Cherokees between the December attack and the drafting of the agent's instructions was dated April 5, 1752; it did not mention peace with the Creeks. Ibid., 234–235. Glen had last proposed a Creek-Cherokee peace to the Cherokees on November 27, 1751, when he read a draft Cherokee-British agreement to a Cherokee delegation. One article dealt with Glen's plans to restart Creek-Cherokee peace negotiations. The Cherokees did not respond to that proposal; they said "We agree" to most of the other articles. Ibid., 187–196. For the slim prospects for a Creek-Iroquois peace, see SC-CJ, 5/14/1752, p. 229.

15. Seven of the letters were definitely written and sent after the December attack; these are dated 1/29/1752, 2/?/1752, three letters from 7/27/1752, 9/19/1752, and 9/22/1752; BPRO-SC, 25: 3–4, 31–35, 67–80, 84–88, 92–94. The eighth letter focused on Indian affairs and was dated simply "December 1751"; BPRO-SC, 24: 389–423. Glen did not finish and mail it, however, until late January 1752. See ibid., 24: 422; ibid., 25: 3–4; *Journal of the Commissioners for Trade and Plantations from January 1749–1750 to December 1753*, p. 342. Glen to Earl of Holderness, 12/31/1751; BPRO-SC, 24: 387.

16. DRIA 1: 233–234 (Cherokee letter). For Glen meeting the Upper Creeks, see ibid., 231–233, quotation from 232 ("Reason"); SC-CJ, 4/4/1752, pp. 124–128. DRIA 1: 270 (July 24). For Glen's unsent letter, see ibid., 208–212; SC-CJ, 4/28/1752, p. 174 ("might"), 5/25/1752, pp. 257–258. SC-JCHA, 4/29/1752, p. 260–262 (funds).

17. For Glen's letters to the assembly, see SC-JCHA, 4/29/1752, pp. 260–262, 5/7/1752, pp. 296–298, "Satisfaction" quotations from 297, 5/16/1752, p. 372. For the assembly's responses, see ibid., 5/1/1752, pp. 268–269, quotation ("War") from 268, 5/8/1752, pp. 318–319, quotation ("Expence") from 319, 5/14/1752, pp. 356–358, quotation ("Savages") from 357.

18. SC-JCHA, 5/16/1752, p. 372; SC-CJ, 5/25/1752, pp. 257–258 (all quotations).

19. Wilbur R. Jacobs, ed., *The Appalachian Indian Frontier: The Edmond Atkin Report and Plan of 1755* (Lincoln: University of Nebraska Press, 1967 [1954]), 21 ("fit"). For the commissioner, see SC-CJ, 5/25/1752, p. 258, and 5/27/1752, p. 259 ("duty"); Jack P. Greene, *The Quest for Power: The Lower Houses of Assembly in the Southern Royal Colonies, 1689–1776* (Chapel Hill: University of North

Carolina Press, 1963), 313–315, quotation ("disobedience") from 314. For Hyrne, see SC-CJ, 5/27/1752, p. 260 ("fit"), 6/2/1752, p. 260, 6/11/1752, p. 275 ("all"). For Steele, see ibid., 5/27/1752, p. 260, 6/16/1752, p. 289.

20. SC-CJ, 6/16/1752, p. 289; ibid., 5/27/1752, p. 259 ("birth," "Opinion"). DRIA 1: 264–265, quotation ("Necessity") from 264.

21. SC-CJ, 5/27/1752, p. 259 ("Interest"), 6/2/1752, p. 262 ("particularly," "robbing," "Assisting"), 6/4/1752, p. 274 ("Submission"), 6/11/1752, pp. 275–276; DRIA 1: 265–266, quotations from 266 ("difficult," "Advice"), 267–268, 343.

22. All quotations come from Thomas's instructions; DRIA 1: 343–344. For Thomas's financial problems, see chapter 8.

23. CRSGA 25: 413 ("pernicious"); SC-JCHA, 5/26/1749, p. 208 ("Mischief"); SC-CJ, 5/3/1748, p. 248.

24. Glen to "the Chiefs of the Creek Nation," in SC-CJ, 11/15/1752, pp. 5–8. Glen to Lord Commissioners, 12/16/1752, BRPO-SC, 25: 130–135, quotations from 131 ("Gentleman," "minute") and 133 ("Agent"). Glen never sent London a stand-alone version of Thomas's report. Instead, he allowed it be inserted in South Carolina's council journal, and then sent London that year's journal (along with the journals of the Commons House and Upper House, and "An Account of the presents granted by his Most Gracious Majesty for the use of the Indians"). Glen mailed that bundle on July 30, 1753, even though he had received Thomas's report nine months before and even though he sent five letters to his superiors between the time he read the report and the time he sent it out. By contrast, the June 1753 conference minutes, which Glen was eager for his superiors to read, were copied from the council journals, bound together into a separate volume, and put in the mail at the first opportunity, only three weeks after the conference ended. The end result, as Glen surely intended, was that the Lord Commissioners read the June 1753 minutes before Thomas's October 1752 report. *Journal of the Commissioners for Trade and Plantations from January 1749–1750 to December 1753* (London: His Majesty's Stationery Office, 1932), 361, 408, 465; *Journal of the Commissioners for Trade and Plantations from January 1754 to December 1758* (London: His Majesty's Stationery Office, 1933), 34. For editing, compare the conference minutes in DRIA 1: 387–414, esp. 408–411, and CO 5/374, ff157–186, esp. 183.

25. SC-CJ, 10/31/1752, pp. 465–469 (letter), 469–527 (journal). For published versions, see DRIA 1: 268–310 (journal), 347–350 (letter), quotation ("Affairs") from 347. SC-CJ, 11/15/1752, p. 5 ("Satisfaction").

26. Glen to "the Cherokee Indians," SC-CJ, 11/15/1752, pp. 13–15, quotations from 14 ("noted") and 15 ("greatest"). Glen to the Lord Commissioners, 12/16/1752, BPRO-SC, 25: 130–135, quotation ("principle") from 133. Glen to "the Chiefs of the Creek Indian Nation," SC-CJ, 11/15/1752, pp. 5–8, quotations from 6.

27. Glen to the Lord Commissioners, 12/16/1752, BPRO-SC, 25: 130–135, quotations from 132 ("treacherous," "Caution," "promises"). Glen to "the Cherokee Indians," SC-CJ, 11/15/1752, pp. 13–15, quotations from 14 ("pretended"), 14–15 ("Contriver"). Glen to "the Chiefs of the Creek Indian Nation," ibid., pp. 5–8, quotations from 6 ("Master," "Director," "Spring," "Friends") and 7 ("Madman," "Wicked," "Innocent," "Death").

28. Glen to "the Chiefs of the Creek Indian Nation," SC-CJ, 11/15/1752, pp. 5–8, quotations from 6–7. Glen to "the Cherokee Indians," ibid., pp. 13–15.

Glen to Lord Commissioners, 12/16/1752, BPRO-SC, 25: 130–135; Glen to Lord Commissioners, 6/25/1753, ibid., 324–330, quotations from 329–330. When Glen referred to his earlier criticisms of Malatchi, he meant those contained in a 1750 letter rather those in his first story, which he never sent to London.

29. Glen to "the Chiefs of the Creek Nation," SC-CJ, 11/15/1752, pp. 5–8.

30. Glen to "the Cherokee Indians," ibid., pp. 13–15.

31. For quotations in this paragraph and the following one, see Glen to Lord Commissioners, 12/16/1752, BPRO-SC, 25: 130–135.

32. Glen to "the Cherokee Indians," SC-CJ, 11/15/1752, pp. 13–15, quotation from 15. Glen to Lord Commissioners, 12/16/1752, BPRO-SC, 25: 130–135, quotation from 134.

33. For the letters, see SC-CJ, 11/15/1752: Glen to Thomas Bosomworth, p. 5 ("immediately"); Glen to the Creeks, pp. 5–8; Glen to the Catawbas, pp. 9–10; Glen to the Iroquois, pp. 11–12, quotation ("Different") from 11; Glen to the Cherokees, pp. 13–15.

34. SC-JCHA, 2/27/1753, p. 109 ("rejoice").

35. For July 13, see DRIA 1: 269. For Glen's fight with the Lower House, see Terry W. Lipscomb, volume preface, in Lipscomb, ed., *The Journal of the Commons House of Assembly, November 21, 1752–September 6, 1754* (Columbia: South Carolina Department of Archives and History, 1983), xi–xxxv, esp. xii–xv, quotation ("tampering") from xiv.

36. Edmond Atkin, "Historical Account of the Revolt of the Chactaw Indians in the late War from the French to the British Alliance and of their Return to that of the French," f61, 1753, Lansdowne Manuscripts #809, British Library, London; Jacobs, *Appalachian Indian Frontier*, 3–95, esp. 3 (Halifax), 40 ("Regulation," "Direction"), 79 ("future").

37. Atkin's "Account" cited above took the form of a letter dated 1/20/1753. Glen's letter containing his second story was dated 12/16/1752; the Lord Commissioners read it on 3/28/1753. For Glen's letter, see above; for the Lord Commissioners, see *Journal of the Commissioners for Trade and Plantations from January 1749–1750 to December 1753*, p. 408 ("relating").

Part II. National

1. For 1751, see BPROSC, 24: 338; CRSGA 26: 396–397. For 1752, see DRIA 1: 271.

2. Craig Womack, Foreword, in Earnest Gouge, *Totku Mocuse/New Fire: Creek Folktales*, ed. and trans. by Jack B. Martin, Margaret McKane Mauldin, and Juanita McGirt (Norman: University of Oklahoma Press, 2004), pp. ix–xiii, quotation ("They are") from xii; Jack P. Martin, Introduction, in ibid., pp. xvii–xxii. Patricia U. Bonomi, *The Lord Cornbury Scandal: The Politics of Reputation in British America* (Chapel Hill: University of North Carolina Press, 1998), 150–154. Alexander Posey, *Chinnubbie and the Owl: Muscogee (Creek) Stories, Orations & Oral Traditions*, ed. by Matthew Wynn Sivils (Lincoln: University of Nebraska Press, 2005), 36 ("new").

3. For the Lower Creeks' itinerary, see SC-CJ, 4/6/1752, p. 130. For Osochi and Coweta's locations, see H. Thomas Foster II, *Archaeology of the Lower Muskogee Creek Indians, 1715–1830* (Tuscaloosa: University of Alabama Press, 2007),

53, 55, 59–60, 70; Bernard Romans, "A Map of West Florida, part of E. Florida, Georgia, part of South Carolina" (1773), Clements Library, University of Michigan, Ann Arbor. For the Upper Creeks, see DRIA 1: 233, 235 ("Horses"); "At a Congress held at the Fort of Picolata," p. 21 ("Road"), in John Stuart to Thomas Gage, 1/21/1766, Thomas Gage Papers, Clements Library. For Malatchi meeting Acorn Whistler, see DRIA 1: 278. See also ibid., 337.

4. For 1715, see William L. Ramsey, *The Yamasee War: A Study of Culture, Economy, and Conflict in the Colonial South* (Lincoln: University of Nebraska Press, 2008), 151–152. "Journal of Captain Tobias Fitch's Mission from Charleston to the Creeks, 1726," in Newton Mereness, ed., *Travels in the American Colonies* (New York: Macmillan Company, 1916), 176–212, quotation ("Nothing") from 182; BPRO-SC, 13: 98 ("never"); CRSGA 6: 341 ("Agressors"). For the war, see CRSGA 26: 64–65; SC-JCHA, 4/29/1752, p. 261 ("burnt"); DRIA 1: 255 ("slights"), 258 ("hott"). For the Iroquois, see SC-CJ, 3/24/1752 ("Coweta"); DRIA 1: 205 ("Peace"). The scalp was taken near Savannah Town; five months later, Malatchi mentioned the "killing of one of their People on the Town of Savannah." SC-CJ, 3/24/1752; DRIA 1: 277 ("Savannah"). Ibid., 270 ("Friend"), 278 ("no Harm").

5. DRIA 1: 391–393 (1753).

6. Steven C. Hahn, *The Invention of the Creek Nation, 1670–1763* (Lincoln: University of Nebraska Press, 2004).

7. SC-CJ, 11/3/1746.

3. The Emperor

1. For the 1749 peace, see Joshua Piker, *Okfuskee: A Creek Indian Town in Colonial America* (Cambridge, MA: Harvard University Press, 2004), 47–52; SC-CJ, 9/4/1749, pp. 582–583 (Chigelly). For the war, see David H. Corkran, *The Creek Frontier, 1540–1783* (Norman: University of Oklahoma Press, 1967), chapter 8; Kathryn E. Holland Braund, *Deerskins & Duffels: Creek Indian Trade with Anglo-America, 1685–1815* (Lincoln: University of Nebraska Press, 1993), 133. For Malatchi's relations with the French, see SC-CJ, 9/5/1750; CRSGA 6: 341. C. L. Grant, ed., *The Letters, Journals and Writings of Benjamin Hawkins* (Savannah, GA: Beehive Press, 1980), 38 ("captives"); James Adair, *The History of the American Indians*, edited by Kathryn E. Holland Braund (Tuscaloosa: University of Alabama Press, 2005), 274 ("contempt").

2. For Upper Creek involvement in the Cherokee war, see chapter 5; Lachlan McGillivray to James Glen, 4/5/1750, in SC-CJ, 5/7/1750. Ibid., 9/5/1750 ("Brothers," "Twin"); DRIA 1: 64 ("Friends," "Mischief"), 229–230 ("served"). Some Upper Creeks waged a low-level war with the Choctaws, a conflict that Malatchi's people sat out; MPAFD 5: 74, 77–78, 92.

3. SC-CJ, 9/5/1750 ("Behaviour," "Resented"); CRSGA 26: 65 ("check"), 194; DRIA 1: 170 ("Practices," "withdrawing"). MPAFD 5: 74 ("overthrown").

4. White Outerbridge to William Lyttelton, 9/3/1759, Lyttelton Collection, Clements Library, University of Michigan, Ann Arbor; CO 5/70, f89.

5. DRIA 1: 279 ("Life"); 391. GT, 151 ("Skins"). The French noted that Malatchi "trades with [the British] for the things that he needs, which we cannot

supply him." MPAFD 5: 171; see also ibid., 4: 149. Almost two decades later, the Upper Creeks said that, in 1752, Malatchi had stated "the aggressor should die for the good of the Whole to preserve Peace & a good understanding with the English"; "A Talk from the Headmen & Warriors of the Creek Nation," 10/1/1770, in John Stuart to Thomas Gage, 12/13/1770, Thomas Gage Papers, Clements Library.

6. For Malatchi's 1746 speech, see SC-UH, 6/6/1747, p. 14 ("His Father"). Edmond Atkin was present for the 1746 conference at which Malatchi spoke. See SC-CJ, 10/29/1746, 11/1/1746, 11/3/1746; Wilbur R. Jacobs, ed., *The Appalachian Indian Frontier: The Edmond Atkin Report and Plan of 1755* (Lincoln: University of Nebraska Press, 1967), 62 ("understanding"). GT, 151 (1747). For the neutrality movement, see Steven C. Hahn, *The Invention of the Creek Nation, 1670–1763* (Lincoln: University of Nebraska Press, 2004).

7. For Malatchi and the French, see CRSGA 20: 291 ("Intirely"); SC-CJ, 9/4/1749, p. 591 ("Childhood"); CRSGA 26: 194–195 ("closely"); MPAFD 5: 171 ("ally"). For the early 1740s, see CRSGA 4: 466 ("Good-will"), 587 ("Fidelity"); SC-CJ, 6/10/1743, 6/22/1743, 6/23/1743 ("presents").

8. SC-CJ, 10/29/1746, 11/1/1746, 11/3/1746 ("excepted"); SC-UH, 6/6/1747, p. 14 ("consenting"); GT,151 ("cross," "think," "Traders").

9. For military exercises, see South Carolina *Gazette*, 11/3/1746. GT, 151 ("Army," "orders," "Weapons"); CRSGA 27: 233 ("Forces"). For Glen's anger at Malatchi during these years, see chapter 2. SC-CJ, 5/3/1748 ("false"). For Malatchi to Glen, see "The Talk from the Head Men of the Lower Creeks to his Excellency," in SC-CJ, 9/5/1750; this talk is unsigned, but it was given out in Coweta, and the content shows that Malatchi was the speaker.

10. For a convenient summary of Malatchi's complaints, see his 12/7/1747 speech in GT, 148–152, quotations from 150 ("Evidence," "impose," "Paper"), 151 ("French").

11. CRSGA 26: 493 ("Slighted"); ibid., 6: 267 ("Tongues"), 270 ("fraught"), 273 ("foam"). For more "foaming," see ibid., 275. DRIA 1: 405 ("rude"). CRSGA 6: 328 ("Damage"), 289 ("bad Talk"), 295 ("War"). Malatchi described his November 1749 feelings in October 1752, referring to events "above two Years ago"; the Lower Creek in question, Wehoffhee, the Long Warrior of Oconee, traveled to Savannah in November 1749. DRIA 1: 305 ("Years); CRSGA 6: 295–297; "Presents Delivered . . . for the Indians," 11/18/1749, Joseph V. Bevan Papers, folder 5A, item 17, Georgia Historical Society, Savannah; "Presents Delivered to Several Parties of Indians," 8/17/1749–12/21/1749, ibid., item 19.

12. Jack B. Martin and Margaret McKane Mauldin, *A Dictionary of Creek/ Muskogee* (Lincoln: University of Nebraska Press, 2000), 306 ("seeker"); SC-CJ, 10/29/1746; Hahn, *Invention of the Creek Nation*, 195–201. Adair, *History*, 118, translates the Chickasaw version of Opiya Mico as "a far-off, or distant chieftain."

13. GT, 148 ("Commander").

14. For Malatchi's speech, see ibid., 148–152; for Heron telling Malatchi that "your presents will be very acceptable to His Royal Highness" and promising to send the gifts to the prince, see CRSGA 27: 198.

15. CRSGA 25: 409 ("Agent"). GT, 151 ("Abraham"), 153 ("beloved"). For Abraham's status and history, see "The State of the Particular Services of

Abraham Bosomworth" in SC-CJ, 5/28/1751, pp. 115–119, quotation ("Great") from 116; Memorial of Abraham Bosomworth, in SC-JCHA, 5/31/1749, p. 263 ("esteemed").

16. Bedford to Glen, 6/9/1748 ("Agent") in SC-CJ, 5/4/1749; for Glen's reaction, see ibid., 5/27/1749 ("Consequence"). For an invoice of the presents, see ibid., 5/28/1751, pp. 110–114. "The Humble Memorial of Abraham Bosomworth" to the Duke of Bedford, [ca. 1750], CO 5/389, f150 ("afterwards"); CRSGA 25: 419 ("reported"). For the presents Abraham distributed, see CO 5/389, ff135–148.

17. For seeing Mary off, see CRSGA 26: 491–492; ibid., 6: 252–253, 256–257. For the 1749 document, see GT, 179–180, quotations ("authorized," "Majesty") from 180. For 1750, see ibid., 202–205, quotations from 202 ("Complaints"), 203 ("Magistrates," "refused," "Water"); see also ibid., 211–212. DRIA 1: 405 ("advised").

18. For 1747, see GT 148, 151. For Heron's letter, see ibid., 154; for the Lower Creek declaration, see ibid., 155; for the deeds, see ibid., 157–161. For 1749, see ibid., 179. For the 1750 documents, see ibid., 202–210.

19. Alexander Moore, ed., *Nairne's Muskhogean Journals: The 1708 Expedition to the Mississippi River* (Jackson: University of Mississippi Press, 1988), 32 ("hardly"); Dunbar Rowland, ed., *Mississippi Archives, 1763–1766, English Dominion: Letters and Enclosures to the Secretary of State from Major Robert Farmer and Governor George Johnstone* (Nashville, TN: Press of Brandon Printing Co., 1911), 186 ("Competition"). Adair, *History*, 415 ("titles," "empty"); Mark Van Doren, ed., *Travels of William Bartram* (Dover, DE: Dover Publications, 1928), 390 ("executive").

20. CRSGA 6: 289 ("superior"), 296 ("throw"); ibid., 26: 19 ("disown"); DRIA 2: 72 ("Head Men"); Seymour Feiler, ed., *Jean-Bernard Bossu's Travels in the Interior of North America, 1751–1762* (Norman: University of Oklahoma Press, 1962), 152 ("emperor").

21. DRIA 1: 391 ("shoulders").

22. CRSGA 30: 85 (Oglethorpe).

23. GT, 95 (attendees), 239 ("nothing"), 240 ("Great"); DRIA 2: 88 ("little," "Twin," "pleased"). BPRO-SC, 25: 338 (Glen); DRIA 2: 29 ("my People"). Raymond D. Fogelson, "The Context of American Indian Political History: An Overview and Critique," in Frederick E. Hoxie, ed., *The Struggle for Political Autonomy: Papers and Comments from the Second Newberry Library Conference on Themes in American Indian History* (Chicago: The Newberry Library, 1989), 5–29, esp. 15 (jelly).

24. DRIA 1: 229 ("seven"); GT, 224. Adair, *History*, 416 ("independent"). Piker, *Okfuskee*, introduction.

25. Martin and Mauldin, *Dictionary*, 276 (nation), 260 (king), 75 (rule), 260 and 85 (kingdom), 291 (principal chief, president), 150 (white Americans); for *âlki* as a suffix connoting "people," see ibid., 286. William Sturtevant, "Creek into Seminole," in Eleanor Burke Leacock and Nancy Oestreich Lurie, eds., *North American Indians in Historical Perspective* (New York: Random House, 1971), 92–128, quotation ("National Council") from 97. Adair, *History*, 415 ("despotic"); Karen O. Kupperman, *Indians and English: Facing Off in Early America* (Ithaca, NY: Cornell University Press, 2000), 85 (Spaniard).

26. For moieties, see Charles Hudson, *The Southeastern Indians* (Knoxville: University of Tennessee Press, 1976), 234–236.

27. Jerome Courtonne, "List of Headmen of the Creeks," 10/17/1758, Lyttelton Collection ("great"); Adair, *History*, 415 ("bad"). For Acorn Whistler's clan connections, see Hahn, *Invention of the Creek Nation*, 238–239. For Creek and Cherokee clan systems, see Greg Urban, "The Social Organization of the Southeast," in Raymond J. Demallie and Alfonso Ortiz, eds., *North American Indian Anthropology: Essays on Society and Culture* (Norman: University of Oklahoma Press, 1994), 172–198, esp. 174–178.

28. Piker, *Okfuskee*, chapters 1 and 2. For the headmen who received commissions in 1746 supporting Malatchi in 1752, see chapters 4 and 5; For Coweta and Tuckabatchee, see below, chapter 5. Bill Grantham, *Creation Myths and Legends of the Creek Indians* (Gainesville: University Press of Florida, 2002), 117 ("common").

29. CO 5/374, f162 ("would"); for a slightly different version, see DRIA 1: 391.

4. The Emperor's Story

1. DRIA 1: 278.

2. After Malatchi described his conversation with Acorn Whistler, Thomas Bosomworth inserted a sentence saying that the two headmen had heard "the same" talks from Acorn Whistler. In later months, though, when those headmen spoke for themselves, they made no mention of hearing Acorn Whistler's talks. Ibid., 1: 278 ("same"), 291, 303.

3. Ibid., 278.

4. Unless otherwise noted, my description of events in the following paragraphs draws on material cited in the preface and chapter 3. DRIA 1: 278 (August 11) and 305 (October 11). Malatchi invoked ungovernable young men at several points. See CRSGA 27: 232; DRIA 1: 392.

5. DRIA 1: 278 ("Fellows"). The best description of the actions required of a war leader is James Adair, *The History of the American Indians*, edited by Kathryn E. Holland Braund (Tuscaloosa: University of Alabama Press, 2005), 376–378. For women and warriors' power, see ibid., 164. For women as signs of peaceful intent, see SC-CJ, 4/11/1746, pp. 84–85; CRSGA 9: 114–115; ibid., 27: 219, 276; DRIA 1: 324; ibid., 2: 299.

6. DRIA 1: 231–233 (April 4), 235 (April 9; Bull). For gifts, see SC-CJ, 4/4/1752, p. 127; ibid., 6/15/1752, p. 287. Glen ordered more extensive gifts for the Upper Creeks, but corruption by his Commissary General makes it impossible to know if the goods were delivered. See also ibid., 4/1/1752, p. 114; CO 5/374, ff191–223; DRIA 1: 212. Ibid., 339 ("heard").

7. The reference to "good Talks" comes from Thomas Bosomworth's 10/11/1752 letter to Glen; DRIA 1: 348. Thomas suggested that, at the instigation of others, Acorn Whistler sent a "Recantation." If so, the talks were neither preserved nor commented on in any surviving document. For the conversation with Spencer and Nunes, see DRIA 1: 337–338. For Spencer, see ibid., 129; Deposition of Thomas Perriman, 11/23/1759, enclosed in Edmond Atkin to

William Lyttelton, 1/9/1760, Lyttelton Collection, Clements Library, University of Michigan, Ann Arbor. I suggest that the conversation took place in late spring based on Perriman's assertion that Spencer, his employer from 1753 to 1758, spent summers in Augusta. Most traders did the same so that the deerskins from the Creeks' winter hunts would not spoil in the summer heat. For Nunes, see CRSGA 26: 42; DRIA 1: 329. For Mellan, see ibid., 269, 331 ("Houses"), 339. For Blake, see ibid., 339 ("alive"). For the traders' seasonal cycle, see Joshua Piker, *Okfuskee: A Creek Indian Town in Colonial America* (Cambridge, MA: Harvard University Press, 2004), 149–152.

8. For December 1751, see chapter 2. For Glen's letter, see DRIA 1: 206–207. Glen wrote identical letters to the Upper and Lower Creeks on March 17, 1752; he obtained council approval for sending them "to ye Creek Nation" on March 20. SC-CJ, 3/17/1752, 3/20/1752.

9. DRIA 1: 272.

10. Ibid., 274–275.

11. Unless otherwise noted, this paragraph and the preceding one draw on material in DRIA 1: 275–278. Ibid., 308 ("excuse"), 331 ("Square"). In ibid., 276, Mary's speech is described as "publick" due to a mistranscription; see SC-CJ, 10/31/1752, p. 479, for "pathetic." Thomas later wrote of the need "to press Malatchi" for a decision on August 11; DRIA 1: 332. For the Bosomworths putting Acorn Whistler forward as the guilty party, see chapter 8.

12. DRIA 1: 267 (commission), 273, 274 ("Declaration"), 276.

13. For Glen's accusations, as relayed by Thomas, see DRIA 1: 274. For towns that had been designed white/beloved and the limited nature of the protection they offered, see Adair, *History*, 191–193; Mark Van Doren, ed., *Travels of William Bartram* (Dover, DE: Dover Publications, 1928), 313–314. GT, 73 (Chigelly). For the distinction between a temporary truce and an enduring peace, see the contrast between long-term relationships contracted "with deliberation, and formality" and "the usuall method that they who are strangers use in contracting Freindships dureing their Travells"; Alexander Moore, ed., *Nairne's Muskhogean Journals: The 1708 Expedition to the Mississippi River* (Jackson: University Press of Mississippi, 1988), 65–66. For descriptions of the Creeks' 1752 efforts at friend-making in Charleston, see DRIA 1: 211, 229. Ibid., 275 ("Blood").

14. "Mr. Stuart's Journal of His Proceedings," p. 19 ("all") in John Stuart to Thomas Gage, 7/21/1767, Thomas Gage Papers, Clements Library. DRIA 1: 275 ("Relations," "Flesh").

15. GT, 155 ("Prince"). For Osochi in 1749, see Steven C. Hahn, *The Invention of the Creek Nation, 1670–1763* (Lincoln: University of Nebraska Press, 2004), 208. For Osochi's population, see CRSGA 28 (1): 88–89; "A List of Towns & Number of Gun Men in the Creek Nation," in Francis Ogilvie to Thomas Gage, 7/8/1764, Gage Papers. For friend towns, see the discussion of Coweta's ties to Chiaha, which was itself very closely linked to Osochi, in John R. Swanton, *Early History of the Creek Indians and Their Neighbors* (Gainesville: University Press of Florida, 1998 [1922]), 166–170, 230. For resistance by Osochis and their traders when it seemed that some attackers would be executed, see DRIA 1: 284–287.

16. DRIA 1: 278. The quotation regarding "taken care" follows SC-CJ, 10/31/1752, p. 482, and corrects a mistranscription in DRIA.

17. DRIA 1: 278–279.

18. Ibid., 279 ("great").

19. For distances between towns, see "A List of Towns & Number of Gun Men," Gage Papers. DRIA 1: 279 ("Flesh," "Uncle"), 283 ("belonging"). The cover story was plausible enough that a trader heard that "Acorn Whistler had been Killed by one of his own Relations for some difference they had about a Wife"; SC-CJ, 10/31/1752, p. 530.

20. DRIA 1: 278 ("afraid"), 279 ("Danger," "Haste"), 280 ("Miscarriage"), 282 ("drunk," "all"), 288 ("instigate," "Justice," "Speech"), 303 ("Odium").

21. Ibid., 279 ("Danger"), 280 ("immediately").

22. Ibid., 288 ("enraged"), 303 ("white"), 333 ("industrious"), 334–335 (son, "Present"). For the Creek belief that "he who decoyed another to his end, was deemed the occasion of his death, and consequently answerable for it," see Adair, *History of the American Indians*, 184; for Creeks threatening to kill a British agent who was pushing other Creeks to execute three of their townspeople, see the entry for August 8 in "Journal of Joseph Wright's Negotiations with the Lower Creeks, July 20 to August 9, 1758," in Henry Ellis to William Lyttelton, 9/8/1758, Lyttelton Collection.

23. For the Tuckabatchee conference, see DRIA 1: 289–296. Ibid., 291 ("contented"), 292 ("Justice"), 349 ("Grief").

24. Ibid., 297 (meeting), 298 (alcohol, "whatever"). For the Coweta conference discussed in this paragraph and the following one, see ibid., 298–304.

25. Unless otherwise noted, the quotations in this paragraph and the one preceding it come from ibid., 305–306. Ibid., 349, 350 ("Complements").

26. For the last document to link Malatchi to the title Opia Mico, see ibid., 303–304.

27. Ibid., 311, 393 ("Immediately).

28. Ibid., 351 ("Behaviour").

29. Ibid., 351, 392–393 ("One"). For Breed Camp's founding, see James R. Atkinson, *Splendid Land, Splendid People: The Chickasaw Indians to Removal* (Tuscaloosa: University of Alabama Press, 2004), 21–23; for its abandonment, see South Carolina *Gazette*, 3/14/1761 and 6/13/1761. Wilbur R. Jacobs, ed., *The Appalachian Indian Frontier: The Edmond Atkin Report and Plan of 1755* (Lincoln: University of Nebraska Press, 1967 [1954]), 64 ("concern"); DRIA 1: 318 ("younger"). For the Creeks distinguishing the Breed Camp Chickasaws from "us" and "we," see SC-CJ, 9/5/1750.

30. This paragraph and the three that follow draw on Thomas's journal of the Breed Camp trip, particularly DRIA 1: 310–323.

31. For "Friend Town," see "Speeches 3rd, 4th, & 7th of July 1759 before going into Tookybahtchy," p. 4, in Edmond Atkin to William Lyttelton, 11/30/1759, Lyttelton Collection.

32. During the Chickasaw affair, Malatchi started by visiting Coweta's traditional allies in Tuckabatchee. Once he had their support, he took some of their headmen with him to Okchai, the most important Upper Creek town. There, he addressed an Upper Creek meeting, but only about Lower Creek issues; he let Thomas make the British case. When the Upper Creeks agreed to help, Malatchi acted in concert with Okchai's headman over the next week, issuing joint

commands and seconding each other's speeches, sometimes one speaking first, sometimes the other. Only when they arrived at Breed Camp—in a sense, a non-Creek town—did Malatchi speak on his own, and when the party returned to the core Upper Creek towns Malatchi either spoke along with the Okchai headman or not at all. It was not until the Okchai returned home and Malatchi arrived back among his traditional allies at Tuckabatchee that Malatchi again spoke to an assembly by himself.

33. DRIA 1: 322 ("highly"); SC-CJ, 11/15/1752, pp. 5–8 (Glen's letter). See also chapter 2.

34. DRIA 1: 322.

35. South Carolina *Gazette*, 5/28/1753 ("upwards"); CO 5/374, f157 ("happily").

36. DRIA 1: 388–389 (Glen's speech), 390–391 (Malatchi's speech). Malatchi neglected to discuss the December 1751 attack.

37. The quotations in this paragraph come from Malatchi's speech as presented in DRIA 1: 391–392, with the exception of "pretty clear," which is provided by the version in CO 5/374, f162.

38. For the second day, see DRIA 1: 394 ("wise," "punished," "Affair"), 399 ("Acorn Whistler"). For the third day, see ibid., 402.

39. For Malatchi's efforts to win Glen's help in dealing with Georgia, see ibid., 396–397, 404–406, 462; CO 5/374, f175. For Mary, see ibid., ff181–182. For presents, see DRIA 1: 408 ("distribute," "worthy"); CO 5/374, f182. For Glen's praise, see DRIA 1: 397 ("Mouth"), 409 ("Head King"). For other speakers, see ibid., 397 ("any other"), 398 ("chiefly," "Person").

40. For the confrontation, see ibid., 406–408, quotations from 408.

41. CO, 5/374, f182.

42. Ibid. For some Creeks' dissatisfaction with their presents, see DRIA 1: 408–409.

Part III. Local

1. For Little Okfuskee's place vis-a-vis the Choctaw path, see Baron de Crenay, "Carte de Partie de la Louisianne," 1733, Karpinski Collection, map 450, Huntington Library, San Marino, CA. For the trails linking Okfuskee to the Choctaw path, see Bernard Romans, "A Map of West Florida, part of E. Florida, part of South Carolina," 1773, Clements Library, University of Michigan, Ann Arbor. For Okfuskee's relation to the Choctaw trade and the eastern villages, see Joshua Piker, *Okfuskee: A Creek Indian Town in Colonial America* (Cambridge, MA: Harvard University Press, 2004).

2. SC-CJ, 9/4/1749, p. 584 ("settled"). The first reference to Little Okfuskee is Crenay's 1733 "Carte." A reasonably comprehensive 1725 list of Creek towns does not mention Little Okfuskee; a trader referred to "the great Oakfuskees" in 1735, suggesting that a "little" version existed by then. Christian F. Feest, "Creek Towns in 1725," *Ethnologische Zeitschrift Zürich* 1 (1974): 161–175, esp. 163; "Deposition of William Williams," 7/4/1735, in SC-JCHA, 12/15/1736, p. 114.

3. For the French-British struggle in the lower Tallapoosa valley during the 1730s, see MPAFD 1: 258, 415; ibid., 4: 120, 146, 170. For the first map, see

Crenay, "Carte." For Okfuskees' pro-British actions in 1732, see Piker, *Okfuskee*, 21–28. For "ligne qui Separe," see the undated and anonymous "Carte de la Riviere Des Cheraquis ou Grande Riviere avec les tribus," Karpinski Collection, map 437. See also another undated and anonymous map, "Carte pour donner une ideé de la positions des Villages Sauvages," ibid., map 435. "A List of Towns & Number of Gun Men in the Creek Nation," in Francis Ogilvie to Thomas Gage, 7/8/1764, Thomas Gage Papers, Clements Library.

4. For divisional membership, see "A List of Towns & Number of Gun Men in the Creek Nation."

5. A fine recent history of the Alabama mistakenly places Muccolossus in that division; Sheri Marie Shuck-Hall, *Journey to the West: The Alabama and Coushatta Indians* (Norman: University of Oklahoma Press, 2008), 31. For Muccolossus as a Tallapoosa town in the 1750s, see "A List of Towns & Number of Gun Men in the Creek Nation"; Wilbur R. Jacobs, ed., *The Appalachian Indian Frontier: The Edmond Atkin Report and Plan of 1755* (Lincoln: University of Nebraska Press, 1967), 64; The Wolf to William Lyttelton, n.d. [ca. 1757], William Lyttelton Collection, Clements Library, University of Michigan, Ann Arbor; Edmond Atkin to Tallapoosa Headmen, 9/15/1759, and Atkin to Creek Headmen, 9/28–29/1759, both enclosed in Atkin to William Lyttelton, 11/30/1759, Lyttelton Collection; CRSGA 8: 469. James Glen to William Lyttelton, 1/23/1758, Lyttelton Collection ("Chief"); SC-CJ, 11/1/1746 ("other Towns"). DRIA 2: 3 ("mad"); South Carolina *Gazette*, 2/7/1761 ("blame"); Pennsylvania *Gazette*, 7/3/1760 ("proposed").

6. For Little Okfuskee's area, see C. L. Grant, ed., *The Letters, Journals and Writings of Benjamin Hawkins* (Savannah, GA: The Beehive Press, 1980), 293–294, quotations ("low," "broken") from 294. Hawkins does not mention Little Okfuskee because it was abandoned when he wrote. For confirmation that the area he described was the location of Acorn Whistler's town, compare the distances Hawkins discusses with those in a document that does reference Little Okfuskee, "A List of Towns & Number of Gun Men in the Creek Nation." For population, see ibid.; DRIA 1: 225 (Acorn Whistler); John R. Swanton, *Early History of the Creek Indians and Their Neighbors* (Gainesville: University Press of Florida, 1998 [1922]), 436.

7. For the other map showing Acorn Whistler's Little Okfuskee, see Anonymous, "A Map of the Southern Indian District 1764," Clements Library, original in "Colored Maps of Parts of America," collected by George Chalmers, ADD MS 14036, British Library, London. For maps showing some version of "Great Oakfuskee" but not Little Okfuskee, see Anonymous, "Carte de la Riviere Des Cheraquis ou Grande Riviere"; Emanuel Bowen, "A New Map of Georgia, with Part of Carolina, Florida and Louisiana" (1748), in William P. Cumming, *The Southeast in Early Maps*, 3rd ed. revised and enlarged by Louis De Vorsey Jr. (Chapel Hill: University of North Carolina Press, 1998), color plate 18; Gregory A. Waselkov, "Indian Maps of the Colonial Southeast," in Peter H. Wood, Gregory A. Waselkov, and M. Thomas Hatley, eds., *Powhatan's Mantle: Indians in the Colonial Southeast* (Lincoln: University of Nebraska Press, 1989), 292–344, esp. 298. SC-CJ, 2/26/1761, p. 93 ("not Towns"); H. Thomas Foster II, ed., *The Collected Works of Benjamin Hawkins, 1796–1810* (Tuscaloosa: University of

Alabama Press, 2003), 24j (Old Town). For "Ofuckshe," see Grant, ed., *Letters, Journals and Writings of Benjamin Hawkins*, 293–294; for this creek's location across the Tallapoosa River from Little Okfuskee, see the previous note, and Swanton, *Early History*, plate 9. For the reproduction, see ibid., plate 5. Amos J. Wright Jr., *Historic Indian Towns in Alabama, 1540–1838* (Tuscaloosa: University of Alabama Press, 2003), 105, 205 ("source").

8. CRSGA 8: 419–421 ("reckoned," "Fire"). For the villages, see Piker, *Okfuskee*.

9. For moving town fires to Oklahoma, see Douglas A. Hurt, "Defining American Homelands: A Creek Nation Example, 1828–1907," *Journal of Cultural Geography* 21 (2003): 19–43, esp. 26.

5. The Family and Community

1. SC-UH, 1/22/1745, p. 19 (glass). For the 1744 party, see above, introduction; SC-CJ, 6/21/1744, p. 348 ("Chief"). Dog King *(Effa Mico)* was a common title in Creek country, but Eufaula and Okfuskee's Dog Kings were certainly the same person. Okfuskee's Dog King vanishes from the record just as Eufaula's Dog King appears, and both Dog Kings had the same personal name, Chauaway. BPRO-SC, 10: 158, 176, 179; CRSGA 20: 63, 318. For Okfuskee's Dog King, see "Journal of Captain Tobias Fitch's Mission from Charleston to the Creeks, 1726," in Newton Mereness, ed., *Travels in the American Colonies* (New York: Macmillan Company, 1911), 176–212, esp. 202, 206–207; BPRO-SC, 10: 158; ibid., 13: 74, 107, 112; SC-CJ, 4/29/1726, p. 304; ibid., 7/20/1731, p. 117.

2. For the distance between Eufaula and Okfuskee, see Bernard Romans, "A Map of West Florida, part of E. Florida, part of South Carolina," 1773, Clements Library, University of Michigan, Ann Arbor. For 1749, see SC-CJ, 9/6/1749, p. 618; James Adair, *The History of the American Indians*, edited by Kathryn E. Holland Braund (Tuscaloosa: University of Alabama Press, 2005), 290. CRSGA 21: 303 (cattle); ibid., 4: 241 (officer). SC-CJ, 8/15/1739, 8/18/1739.

3. DRIA 1: 227 ("old"); Alexander Moore, ed., *Nairne's Muskhogean Journals: The 1708 Expedition to the Mississippi River* (Jackson: University Press of Mississippi, 1988), 63 ("fires"). In 1752, Acorn Whistler was old enough to have an adult son; DRIA 1: 288.

4. For Glen and Knott, see ibid., 233. For Baxter, see the will of Knott's widow, Isabel, in Wills, Charleston County, South Carolina, W.P.A. Transcripts, vol. 8: 18–19, South Carolina Department of Archives and History, Columbia; "An Account of Sundrys put on Board of Mr. Knotts Trading Boat," 11/9/1750, folder 5, item 23, Joseph V. Bevan Papers, Georgia Historical Society, Savannah; DRIA 1: 289. For Knott's connection to Wood, see Kathryn E. Holland Braund, *Deerskins & Duffels: Creek Indian Trade with Anglo-America, 1685–1815* (Lincoln: University of Nebraska Press, 1993), 44; for Knott's Okfuskee license, see SC-CJ, 9/11/1751, p. 301. Knott gave provisions to "Creek Indians" on 9/11/1749, the same day the Okfuskees left Charleston. SC-JCHA, 3/5/1752, pp. 118–119 ("Provisions," "Road," "Creek"); SC-CJ, 9/11/1749. For the later party and the Okfuskees' part in it, see DRIA 2: 83, 84 ("prevailed"); SC-CJ,

1/23/1756, p. 81. For Bull, see SC-JCHA, 10/12/1743, p. 477; ibid., 12/13/1743, p. 492 ("propose"); ibid., 12/16/1743, p. 507; Wilbur R. Jacobs, ed., *The Appalachian Indian Frontier: The Edmond Atkin Report and Plan of 1755* (Lincoln: University of Nebraska Press, 1967), 64; SC-CJ, 3/21/1744, p. 159 (Fort Bull); ibid., 8/15/1739, 8/18/1739.

5. SC-CJ, 6/21/1744, p. 347; ibid., 6/27/1744, p. 361. For Knott's house, see SC-JCHA, 5/9/1752, p. 331; DRIA 1: 326.

6. For Acorn Whistler's descriptions, see ibid., 226, 229–230.

7. For the Coweta-Okfuskee relationship, see Joshua Piker, *Okfuskee: A Creek Indian Town in Colonial America* (Cambridge, MA: Harvard University Press, 2004), 179–180. For the Coweta and Okfuskee paths, see William DeBrahm, "A Map of the Sea Coast of Georgia & the inland parts thereof extending to the Westward of that part of Savannah Called broad River," 1763, Clements Library, University of Michigan, Ann Arbor. For the Creeks' debate over paths, see Joshua Piker, "'White & Clean' & Contested: Creek Towns, Trading Paths, and Diplomatic Networks in the Aftermath of the Seven Years' War," *Ethnohistory* 50 (2003): 315–347. Upper Creek Headmen to John Stuart, 5/1/1771 ("White"), in John Stuart to Thomas Gage, 8/31/1771, Thomas Gage Papers, Clements Library.

8. For the early 1720s, see BPRO-SC, 10: 158, 178–179. Ibid., 73 (Chigelly), 95 (Long Warrior), 112 (Dog King).

9. CO 5/75, f16 (meetings) and f213 (Cujesse Mico). Piker, *Okfuskee*, 203 (execution).

10. "Presents Distributed to the Micoes, Chieftains & Warriours of the Upper Creek Nation," 5/20/1751, folder 5A, item 30, Bevan Papers. DRIA 1: 348–349 ("Hostages"), 380 (1753).

11. "Speeches 3rd, 4th, & 7th of July 1759," p. 4 (Captain), in Edmond Atkin to William Lyttelton, 11/30/1759, William Lyttelton Collection, Clements Library. For Tuckabatchee as a red town, see C. L. Grant, ed., *The Letters, Journals and Writings of Benjamin Hawkins* (Savannah, GA: The Beehive Press, 1980), 306–307; John R. Swanton, "Modern Square Grounds of the Creek Indians," *Smithsonian Miscellaneous Collections* 85 (Washington, DC: Smithsonian Institution Press, 1931), 6; J. N. B. Hewitt, "Notes on the Creek Indians," edited by John R. Swanton, *Bureau of American Ethnology Bulletin* 123 (Washington, DC: Smithsonian Institution Press, 1939), 123–159, esp. 125–126. Upper Creek Headmen to Stuart, 5/1/1771 ("thence"). SC-CJ, 10/8/1726, pp. 35–44; ibid., 9/5/1750; ibid., 11/1/1746, p. 178. Joseph Hall, "Anxious Alliances: Apalachicola Efforts to Survive the Slave Trade, 1638–1705," in Alan Gallay, ed., *Indian Slavery in Colonial America* (Lincoln: University of Nebraska Press, 2009), pp. 147–184, quotation ("cradle") from 182, n. 78; Grant, ed., *The Letters, Journals and Writings of Benjamin Hawkins*, 468 ("hand"). For a Tuckabatchee with a title that incorporated Coweta's name, see CRSGA 39: 552.

12. "Conferences with Tookybahtchy Mico," pp. 5 (Mad Dog), 9 (emeritus), in Atkin to Lyttelton, 11/30/1759, Lyttelton Collection; for a Tuckabatchee making similar claims during the Acorn Whistler affair, see DRIA 1: 413. For Folutka, see ibid., 231–233, esp. 232 ("Confidence"); SC-CJ, 4/4/1752, p. 127, shows he was a Tuckabatchee.

13. For references to Charleston's white status during the Acorn Whistler crisis, see DRIA 1: 274, 277, 290, 300, 349. Creeks habitually brought outsiders into their polity, a task they generally assigned to white towns; John R. Swanton, "Social Organization and Social Usages of the Indians of the Creek Confederacy," Bureau of American Ethnology *Bulletin* 42 (Washington, DC: Government Printing Office, 1928), 250. "A Treaty of Peace and Commerce held at that Old Town on Ogechee River," 11/6/1777 ("desired"), Henry Laurens Papers, roll 17, South Carolina Historical Society, Charleston. People who "were one fire" were "at home" in each other's towns; Grant, ed., *Letters, Journals and Writings of Benjamin Hawkins*, 135.

14. Tom Hatley, *The Dividing Paths: Cherokees and South Carolinians through the Era of Revolution* (New York: Oxford University Press, 1993), 82 ("kinship"). At least eight of the twelve Cherokees attacked on April 1 were from Estatoe; and since twelve Estatoes had been in Charleston the previous fall the other four may have been as well. DRIA 1: 164, 227–228, 233 ("chiefly"). For Estatoe Mico and the 1749 negotiations, see SC-CJ, 9/6/1749 and 9/11/1749 ("greatest"); Piker, *Okfuskee*, 47–52.

15. SC-CJ, 5/11/1750 ("Lower Creeks"); DRIA 1: 247 ("lost"), 256–257 (trader). For James Beamer, the trader in question, living in Estatoe, see below, n. 17.

16. SC-CJ, 5/22/1750 ("Wife"); ibid., 9/5/1750 ("Town"); DRIA 1: 207 ("Wood"), 216 ("some," "Poor"), 255 (early 1752); Piker, *Okfuskee*, 83–84.

17. For the Chickasaw talk, see DRIA 1: 252; see also ibid., 246–247. The "Fellows" who carried the talk were from "Mr. Beamer's Town." For James Beamer living and trading at Estatoe, see ibid., 249, 250; SC-JCHA, 12/4/1751, p. 513; William Lyttelton to Board of Trade, 10/2/1758, Lyttelton Collection. For 1756, see DRIA 2: 151. This document does not specify the headmen's names, but other documents show that one was Handsome Fellow of Okfuskee. His father was Red Coat King, the father of Estatoe Mico. For the likelihood that Handsome Fellow was not Estatoe Mico, see epilogue. The 1756 document also does not specify where the Okfuskees spoke, stating only that they came to the "Town" of "Mr. Welch." James Welch was Beamer's employee; he married an Estatoe and lived there. For Handsome Fellow, see ibid., 153, 156; Piker, *Okfuskee*. For Welch, see DRIA, 1: 248–249; ibid., 2: 105, 151, 209; Richard Coytmore to William Lyttelton, 2/7/1760, Lyttelton Collection; *Pennsylvania Gazette*, 12/18/1760; *South Carolina Gazette*, 7/7/1766. I am grateful to Professor Tyler Boulware for information regarding Welch. For Beamer's ties to William Thompson, see vol. 9, p. 60, Wills, Charleston County, SC. For Thompson in Okfuskee, see Daniel Pepper, "Some Remarks on the Creek Nation," 1756, Lyttelton Collection; DRIA 2: 372; *South Carolina Gazette*, 6/20/1761. DRIA 1: 247 ("sprinkled").

18. For events in Charleston, see above, preface. Moore, *Nairne's Muskhogean Journals*, 66 ("usuall"); Adair, *History*, 370 ("exchange," "cherish"); DRIA 2: 79 ("Brother"); ibid., 1: 211 (Lower Creeks).

19. For the widespread belief that Acorn Whistler was responsible for the 1749 Hiwassee attack, see introduction; SC-CJ, 5/11/1750 (Cherokee). DRIA 1: 233–234 (Glen).

20. For Glen's neighborhood, see Henry A. M. Smith, "Charleston and Charleston Neck: The Original Grantees and the Settlements Along the Ashley and Cooper Rivers," *South Carolina Historical and Genealogical Magazine* 19 (1918): 3–76, map opposite p. 3, pp. 27–29 (Burnham). For Nicholas's marriage and Mary's family, see A. S. Salley Jr., "William Smith and Some of His Descendants," ibid., 4 (1903): 239–257, esp. 242; Mabel L. Webber, "Death Notices from the South Carolina and American General Gazette, and Its Continuation the Royal Gazette, May 1766–June 1782," ibid., 16 (1915), 34–38, esp. 35, n. 2; vol. 5, pp. 652–663, Wills, Charleston County, SC. Burnham's nieces took possession of the property only after the 1763 wedding of the eldest, Mary. Smith, "Charleston and Charleston Neck," 28; A. S. Salley Jr., *Marriage Notices in the South-Carolina Gazette and Its Successors (1732–1801)* (Baltimore: Genealogical Publishing Company, 1965 [1902]), 23. SC-CJ, 9/6/1749 ("Pasture"); SC-JCHA, 5/3/1750, p. 79 ("entertaining").

21. For the Cherokees in 1749, see SC-JCHA, 2/9/1750, p. 402; ibid., 4/13/1753, p. 215. For Sarah Amory's land at New Market, see South Carolina *Gazette*, 1/3/1743. For New Market's location, see Smith, "Charleston," 13–15; "A Sketch of the Operations Before Charleston," after Sir Henry Clinton's 1780 map, College of Charleston Library, Charleston, SC. For the Amorys' connection to the Indian trade, see South Carolina *Gazette*, 1/13/1743 and 10/24/1745; http://www.archivesindex.sc.gov/onlinearchives/SearchResults.aspx, search term: Amory, John (viewed 5/4/2010). For "Indian Horses" at Amory's in 1740, see John Dart, Order and Account, 1/1/1741, MS 212, Edward E. Ayer Collection, Newberry Library, Chicago, IL. See also SC-JCHA, 5/19/1749, p. 147.

22. For 1748, see SC-JCHA, 6/25/1748, pp. 356–357, 6/28/1748, pp. 369, 374; SC-UH, 6/20/1748. SC-JCHA, 4/13/1753, p. 215 ("died"); DRIA 1: 211 ("rest").

23. Pennsylvania *Gazette*, 10/12/1749; see also Adair, *History*, 111–112.

24. Unless otherwise noted, material in this paragraph and the one preceding it comes from Piker, *Okfuskee*, 49–50. John Stuart's "A Map of Cherokee Country" shows the "Road to the upper Creek Nation" entering Cherokee country at "Hywassee old Town"; this path "winds down the mountains" to Toohtocaugee, an Okfuskee village. Archer B. Hulbert, *The Crown Collection of American Maps*, 22 volumes (Cleveland, OH: A. H. Clark Co., 1904–1930), series 2, vol. 3, pp. 34–35, quotation from 34 ("Road"); Grant, ed., *Letters, Journals and Writings of Benjamin Hawkins*, 303 ("winds"). SC-CJ, 9/4/1749, p. 589 ("Son"), p. 590 ("Women"). Charles Hudson, *The Southeastern Indians* (Knoxville: University of Tennessee Press, 1976), 226 ("hospitality," "social"); John R. Swanton, *Early History of the Creek Indians and Their Neighbors* (Gainesville: University Press of Florida, 1998 [1922]), 250 (village).

25. Sugatspoges, an Okfuskee village, first appears in the records in May 1750; DRIA 1: 128.

26. BPRO-SC, 10: 175–182, quotation from 176 ("delivered").

27. Ibid., 176 ("hear"). For Okfuskee Captain supporting Malatchi's story, see DRIA 1: 291. There are several reasons for thinking that the man who carried the title Mad Warrior in 1746 assumed the title Okfuskee Captain by 1752. In the first place, Okfuskee Captain stated in 1752 that he had signed a 1751 deed.

Two Okfuskees signed that document: Fanni Mico (aka, Red Coat King) and Tustanck Hacho, a title that translates as Mad War Leader. If Okfuskee Captain signed the 1751 deed, then, he did so as Mad Warrior. Relatedly, two years before, Okfuskee's Tustanck Hacho was known as "Captain." Finally, Okfuskee Captain stated in 1753 that he had received a commission from Glen, as Mad Warrior had in 1746. For 1752, see GT, 224–225; Deposition of Joseph Wright, 12/22/1755, Keith Read Collection, box 2, folder 56, Hargrett Library, University of Georgia, Athens. GT, 220 (1751). SC-CJ, 9/6/1749 ("Captain"); DRIA 1: 407 (1753).

28. Grant, ed., *Letters, Journals and Writings of Benjamin Hawkins*, 135 ("fire").

29. Swanton, "Social Organization," 194. For the Yamasee situation, see BPRO-SC, 10: 178–182. For an Okfuskee discussing Cussetas with Cherokees, see A. S. Salley, ed., *Journal of Colonel John Herbert, Commissioner of Indian Affairs for the Province of South Carolina, October 17, 1727–March 19, 1727/8* (Columbia: Historical Commission of South Carolina, 1936), 11. "Journal of Colonel George Chicken's Mission from Charleston, S.C., to the Cherokees, 1726," in Newton Mereness, ed., *Travels in the American Colonies*, (New York: Macmillan Company, 1916), 97–172, esp. 156–157 (plans). For the British building trading posts in Cusseta and Okfuskee, see William L. McDowell Jr., ed., *The Colonial Records of South Carolina: Journals of the Commissioners of the Indian Trade, September 20, 1710–August 29, 1718* (Columbia: South Carolina Department of Archives and History, 1955), 277–278, 304, 306–308; Piker, *Okfuskee*, 25, 215–216, n. 21. For British views of Cusseta, see SC-CJ, 8/24/1725, p. 47, 9/9/1725, pp. 184, 186; "Journal of Captain Tobias Fitch's Mission from Charleston to the Creeks, 1726," in Mereness, ed., *Travels*, 176–212, esp. 184–186, 194–195. For Cusseta's Red Coat King, see SC-CJ, 5/21/1742, 6/8/1743; SC-JCHA, 2/22/1743.

30. For pro-American leanings, see CO 5/79, f160; ibid., 5/80, ff52, 235. For "Friend Towns," see "A Treaty of Peace and Commerce," 11/6/1777, Laurens Papers, and "A Talk from the head Men of the Upper and Lower Creeks," 10/13/1777, ibid. For "relation," see ibid. For Cusseta Tuskeinchau and his relatives, see Grant, ed., *Writings of Benjamin Hawkins*, 16–17, 339; Piker, *Okfuskee*.

31. In 1760, Okfuskees killed Hiwassees in the name of reassuring Charleston, another friend town, of Okfuskee loyalty; ibid., 52–63.

6. The Family and Community's Story

1. DRIA 1: 291.

2. Ibid., 347 (instructions). Glen quoted Red Coat King's statement in a March 20, 1752, letter; ibid., 207. The Okfuskee likely made this comment as part of the 1749 Creek-Cherokee peace effort.

3. Ibid., 207.

4. Ibid., 255 (three), 258 (twelve, "Man"). Tohopeka, the town in Horseshoe Bend, was an offshoot of Okfuskee, and Okfuskees suffered horribly in the battle. See Joshua Piker, *Okfuskee: A Creek Indian Town in Colonial America* (Cambridge, MA: Harvard University Press, 2004), 196–198.

5. DRIA 1: 258 ("sent"), 318 (Red Coat King), 407 ("Home").

6. For the letter and news of the execution arriving in Okfuskee, see ibid., 326, 336. For Ross and Germany's Okfuskee connections, see Piker, *Okfuskee*, 58–59, 140. Ibid., 288 ("enraged," "burnt"), 335.

7. Ibid., 346 (instructions).

8. Ibid., 275.

9. All quotations are from ibid., 289. For forty miles, see ibid., 326.

10. Ibid., 289.

11. For Red Coat King's career, see Piker, *Okfuskee*, chapters 1–2. For South Carolina's use of red coats in the 1740s and 1750s, see SC-CJ, 7/28/1744, 11/22/1746, 7/24/1747, 9/7/1749; SC-JCHA, 4/8/1753, p. 249; Wilbur R. Jacobs, ed., *The Appalachian Indian Frontier: The Edmond Atkin Report and Plan of 1755* (Lincoln: University of Nebraska Press, 1967 [1954]), 85–86; DRIA 2: 265; Seymour Feiler, ed., *Jean-Bernard Bossu's Travels in the Interior of North America, 1751–1762* (Norman: University of Oklahoma Press, 1962), 152–153. DRIA 1: 207 ("Friend").

12. Ibid., 318 ("old Man," "keeping"). For "Old," see SC-CJ, 9/6/1749. For Okfuskee Captain at Tuckabatchee, see above and the version of Thomas's journal in ibid., 10/31/1752, p. 507, where his name appears on a list of Creek participants; the published version of this list (DRIA 1: 296) omits his name.

13. For the speeches by Okfuskee Captain and Acorn Whistler's other relatives, see ibid., 291. SC-CJ, 10/31/1752, p. 507 (title).

14. DRIA 1: 292.

15. Ibid., 318–319.

16. Ibid., 281 ("our Friends"). Thomas did not mention the December 1751 attack to the Creeks, despite Glen's instructions to do so; ibid., 344.

17. SC-CJ, 11/15/1752, pp. 5–8.

18. DRIA 1: 363 (Hiwassee), 367 ("Estertoe"), 507 (Malatchi); SC-CJ, 6/17/1754 ("Warrior"). The DRIA version of the latter document mistranscribes "Cowettas" as "Cowataks" (p. 506). Charles R. Hicks to John Ross, May 4, 1826, John Howard Payne Papers, vol. 7, part 1, p. 13 ("messengers," nineteenth century), Edward Ayer Collection, MS 689, Newberry Library, Chicago, IL. For Cowetas bearing Cherokee titles and vice versa, see DRIA 2: 213; Henry Ellis to William Lyttelton, 2/5/1760, Lyttelton Collection, Clements Library, University of Michigan, Ann Arbor ; Lachlan McGillivray et al., "Talks Regarding Cherokee Disturbances," 2/11/1760, in White Outerbridge to William Lyttelton, 2/12/1760, ibid.; South Carolina *Gazette*, 4/7/1760; "A Talk from the Lower Creeks to John Stuart," 8/19/1772, in John Stuart to Thomas Gage, 11/24/1772, Thomas Gage Papers, Clements Library; CO 5/75, f86.

19. DRIA 1: 410 (list). Thomas also listed each town's headmen together, except the Okfuskees, who he scattered throughout the list; and he classified all thirty of Malatchi's followers as Lower Creeks—rather than distinguishing them by town, as he did for the sixty-nine Upper Creeks—so that their numbers would seem more impressive.

20. Ibid., 397 ("thought"), 410 ("Women"), 412 ("Hopes"). For Fanni Mico's trips to Charleston, see Piker, *Okfuskee*, chapter 1.

21. DRIA 1: 397 (Glen); CO 5/374, f168 (Wolf). The DRIA version of Wolf's speech (1: 397) shows him referring to Malatchi as "King"; the CO version

shows him saying "Malatchi." I use the latter because if Wolf referred to Malat-chi's title, he would have used "mico." Translating that word as "king" fits nicely with Malatchi's goals but does violence to Creek political science. For Hand-some Fellow's first speech, see DRIA 1: 397–398. The speaker is identified only as "Okfuskee Head Warriour," but see Handsome Fellow's speech and title on the conference's third day; ibid., 406. Unless otherwise noted, my discussion of Handsome Fellow's first speech in the paragraphs that follow is drawn from ibid., 397–398.

22. In ibid., 397, Handsome Fellow refers to "the Head Men of our Nation," but the version of this speech in CO 5/374, f168, refers to "the Head Men for our Nation." The latter more accurately captures Handsome Fellow's tone and meaning. Along the same lines, note that Handsome Fellow spoke in Muskogee, which means he certainly did not call Malatchi "the King," even though all ver-sions of this speech put that word in the Okfuskee's mouth. Likewise, he would have referred to the plural Creek leaders as "micos" (*mi:kk-aki*), not "Kings." Jack B. Martin and Margaret McKane Mauldin, *A Dictionary of Creek/Muskogee* (Lincoln: University of Nebraska Press, 2000), 260.

23. For Malatchi's speech, see DRIA 1: 394–397. That speech shows that Handsome Fellow and Malatchi actually agreed on the issue of Cherokee peace. The striking thing about the Okfuskee's speech, therefore, was not his argument about the Cherokees—which echoed Malatchi's at almost every point—but that he felt the need to make it at all. The two headmen were debating precedence, not policy.

24. Handsome Fellow mentioned the current prices for guns, shirts, and shoes; I can, thus, state the reductions he sought on those goods quite precisely. The reductions he sought on the other items are estimates based on a compar-ison between his request and price lists from before and after the 1753 confer-ence. Unfortunately, the extant lists for the pre-1753 period date from the early 1730s while the post-1753 lists date from the late 1750s and early 1760s. I do not, in short, know exactly what the 1753 prices were for many of these items. And to compound the problem, the price lists frequently measured the Creeks' deerskins in different ways (e.g., number of skins vs. pounds of leather), and the same is true for the European goods (e.g., gunpowder sold by the handful vs. by the pound). On the bright side, however, the lists do, at times, explain how to convert from one category to another (e.g., from buckskins to doeskins). Moreover, the lists show that prices for most goods remained relatively stable from the early 1730s to the early 1760s. And, finally, Handsome Fellow's state-ment about the prices charged for guns, shirts, and shoes in 1753 matches up quite well with the prices for those items in the earlier and later lists. All of which is to say that I am confident that the percentages cited are reasonable estimates for each item, and I am certain that my larger point—Handsome Fel-low sought steep price cuts on a wide range of goods—is accurate. Pennsylvania *Gazette*, 7/24/1732; GT, 16–17; "A Schedule of the Rates or Prices of Goods," in Edmond Atkin to William Lyttelton, 8/18/1759, Lyttelton Collection; CO 5/68, f145; CRSGA 28 (2): 118, 121–122.

25. For Glen's speech, see DRIA 1: 398–401.

26. SC-JCHA, 4/29/1752, p. 261 ("gathered"); DRIA 1: 397 ("strict").

27. Ibid., 401–406 (Glen and Malatchi).

28. Ibid., 406 (Handsome Fellow), 408 ("rude").

29. For Okfuskee Captain's speech, see ibid., 407. The version in CO 5/374, f181, provides the phrase "some Accident or other."

30. DRIA 1: 408 (Malatchi), 409 (Bosomworth), 411 (Glen), 413 ("among").

31. Ibid., 407–408.

32. Ibid., 412.

33. For Okfuskee Captain and Glen, see ibid., 413. The new commission was for "Ifa Tustannakee, Head Man of the Offuskees." Okfuskee Captain claimed that title in a letter to Glen. Ibid., 381 (letter), 414 (commission).

34. For Okfuskee demands regarding the Cherokees, see ibid., 379–381. For a change in Okfuskee rhetoric by the fall of 1753, see ibid., 464–465. But note that trade prices continued to be an issue; SC-CJ, 8/18/1755.

35. DRIA 1: 380–381.

Part IV. Colonial

1. Ibid., 266 ("Satisfaction"); SC-CJ, 6/11/1752, p. 276 ("safe").

2. Henry Yonge and William DeBrahm, "A Map of the Sea Coast of Georgia and the inland parts thereof" (1763), British Library, Additional Manuscripts 14036, f15 ; Thomas Wright, "A Map of Georgia and Florida" (1763), in William P. Cumming, *The Southeast in Early Maps*, 3rd ed., revised and enlarged by Louis De Vorsey Jr. (Chapel Hill: University of North Carolina Press, 1998), plate 60. For trading, see Steven C. Hahn, *The Life and Times of Mary Musgrove* (Gainesville: University Press of Florida, 2012), 191.

3. DRIA 1: 328–329 (Thomas), 337 (Nunes), 337–338 (Spencer).

4. Ibid., 268–269.

5. SC-CJ, 6/2/1752; DRIA 1: 276 (August 11), 345–347 (instructions).

6. Unless otherwise noted, my discussion here and in the paragraph above relies on Thomas's journal entry for August 11; ibid., 276–279. For the meeting's location, see ibid., 270, 308–309 ("Private"); Anonymous, "A Ranger's Report of Travels with General Ogelthorpe, 1739–1742," in Newton Mereness, ed., *Travels in the American Colonies* (New York: Macmillan Company, 1916), pp. 218–236, quotation ("Hut") from 220. In general, "a stranger could not distinguish the king's habitation from that of any other citizen, by any sort of splendor or magnificence." A leader's household complex might have four structures—a less prominent family would get by with two or three—but the individual buildings were not large. Mark Van Doren, ed., *Travels of William Bartram* (Dover, DE: Dover Publications , 1928 [1791]), 389 ("stranger"); H. Thomas Foster II, *Archaeology of the Lower Muskogee Creek Indians, 1715–1836* (Tuscaloosa: University of Alabama Press , 2007), 106–110; Cameron B. Wesson, *Households and Hegemony: Early Creek Prestige Goods, Symbolic Capital, and Social Power* (Lincoln: University of Nebraska Press , 2008), 113–122.

7. DRIA 1: 308–309 (affidavit). Thomas evidently recognized this affidavit's weakness because he later had Ladson sign another one affirming that Acorn Whistler was accused at the August meeting. Thomas then argued that the second affidavit proved "that it was the Opinion of the Assembly that [Acorn

Whistler] ought to suffer for" the attack, but Ladson said only that he heard that Acorn Whistler "ought to suffer," not who said or supported it. Thomas's own journal explicitly rejects the notion that the "Assembly" reached a consensus about Acorn Whistler: the headmen left the matter to Malatchi and promised to support "whatever he thought proper to do." Ibid., 277 ("whatever"), 332 ("Opinion"), 340 (Ladson). For the Bosomworths' post hoc efforts to make it seem as if all Creeks agreed that Acorn Whistler was guilty, see chapter 8.

8. Until recently, the literature on Mary has been both broad and exceptionally uneven, with the most comprehensive account of her life appearing in the late Doris Fisher's unpublished dissertation, "Mary Musgrove: Creek Englishwoman" (Department of History, Emory University, 1990). For books that represent dramatic leaps forward analytically and that set a new standard for archival thoroughness, see John T. Juricek, *Colonial Georgia and the Creeks: Anglo-Indian Diplomacy on the Southern Frontier, 1733–1763* (Gainesville: University Press of Florida, 2010); Hahn, *Mary Musgrove*. I am grateful to Professor Hahn for allowing me to read his manuscript prior to its publication.

9. Ralph Bauer and José Antonio Mazzotti, "Introduction: Creole Subjects in the Colonial Americas," in Bauer and Mazzotti, eds., *Creole Subjects in the Colonial Americas: Empires, Texts, Identities* (Chapel Hill: University of North Carolina Press, 2009), pp. 1–57, quotation ("oscillated") from 48; Michael Warner, "What's Colonial about Colonial America?," in Robert Blair St. George, ed., *Possible Pasts: Becoming Colonial in Early America* (Ithaca, NY: Cornell University Press, 2000), pp. 49–70, quotation ("homeward") from 65.

10. CRSGA 30: 191 ("Gentleman"), 196 ("Character").

11. DRIA 1: 265 ("Melancholy"), 327 ("Besieged"), 328 ("Complication"). GT, 141 ("Complaining"). For Thomas's attempts at storytelling, see his two journals and the "Appendix"; DRIA 1: 268–337. For Bosomworth-written histories that detail their situation both prior to becoming Glen's agents and after completing the agency but almost entirely neglect their actions as agents, see ibid., 386, 487–488; SC-JCHA, 2/1/1754, pp. 340–341; CRSGA 26: 484; ibid., 28 (1): 262.

7. The Colonists

1. For Wright's deposition, see http://dlg.galileo.usg.edu/nativeamerican/ jpg/krc037a.jpg accessed 4/29/2011. DRIA 1: 288–289 (Thomas). The unpublished version of the journal likewise shows that Thomas handled the calendar issue without a problem; SC-CJ, 10/31/1752, p. 497. Robert Poole, *Time's Alteration: Calendar Reform in Early Modern England* (London: UCL Press, 1998); Mark W. Smith, "Culture, Commerce, and Calendar Reform in Colonial America," *William and Mary Quarterly* 55 (1998): 557–584.

2. Ibid., 560 (articles), 564–565 (clerks, diarist) 567 ("introduction"); Poole, *Time's Alteration*, chapters 1, 9, and 10. For Tobler, see the South Carolina *Gazette* for April 13, April 20, May 4, May 11, and May 18, 1752. I have been unable to locate the nine issues of the *Gazette* published between May 28 and August 10, 1752. For the hurricane's destruction beginning on "September the 14th, when the Wind in the Afternoon began to blow with great Violence," see George

Milligen-Johnson, "A Short Description of the Province of South-Carolina" (1763), in Chapman J. Milling, ed., *Colonial South Carolina: Two Contemporary Descriptions* (Columbia: University of South Carolina Press, 1951), 128–130, quotation from 128.

3. For Thomas invoking Acorn Whistler's crime against Charleston, see DRIA 1: 290–291, 292. The Bosomworths also had personal, land-related business to raise with the Creeks. It made sense that they do so in Tuckabatchee, where Mary's relatives could be counted on to repudiate a 1751 effort—featuring headmen from Okfuskee and its ally, Okchai—to undermine her title to Georgia land.

4. Steven C. Hahn, *The Life and Times of Mary Musgrove* (Gainesville: University Press of Florida, 2012). Thomas Hawkins, [Numbered Grid of Frederica and details of occupiers], n.d., FEL 1052, part 1, Fellowes Collection, Norfolk Records Office, Norwich, England ("Interpretess," "built"). CRSGA 30: 315 ("appointed"), 330 ("Allowance"); E. Merton Coulter, ed., *The Journal of William Stephens, 1743–1745* (Athens: University of Georgia Press, 1959), 132 ("incredible," "Surprizing," "Chattering").

5. For this paragraph and the one preceding it, see CRSGA 24: 422 ("Widow"); ibid., 27: 7 ("Matthews"); Coulter, *Journal of William Stephens*, 136–137 (party); GT, 209 ("Beloved").

6. Coulter, *Journal of William Stephens*, 132 ("England").

7. CRSGA 28 (1): 259 ("Claim"); ibid., 31: 28 ("surprised"); Thomas Bosomworth to Reverend Bearcroft, 9/3/1745, B12, pp. 682–684, Society for the Propagation of the Gospels in Foreign Parts, London. I am grateful to Professor John Juricek for sending me photocopies of Thomas's SPG letters. For Thomas's time in England, see Hahn, *Mary Musgrove*, chapter 6.

8. Bosomworth to Bearcroft, 9/3/1745. There is no evidence that the Creeks were angry over the Georgia colonists' treatment of Thomas and Mary in 1744 and 1745, and once back in Georgia, Thomas never said they were.

9. Thomas Bosomworth to Reverend Bearcroft, 10/12/1745, Society for the Propagation of the Gospels, B12, pp. 686–687 ("Opportunity," "Cash"). For Thomas's dismissal, see CRSGA 31: 28–30, 33; ibid., 36: 313–314, 316–321. For the Trustees' response to Mary's claims, see GT, 128–129.

10. For Thomas's background, see Hahn, *Mary Musgrove*, 151-158, quotation ("life story") from 151.

11. CRSGA 30: 196 ("Clerk," "hand," "desire"), 253–254 ("assisting"), 260, 330 ("concern"). For Thomas as minister, see ibid., 270 ("admitted"), 279, 284, 315 ("reside"); ibid., 36: 258–260; Thomas Bosomworth to Reverend Bearcroft, 6/24/1744, Society for the Propagation of the Gospels, B12, p. 680.

12. Bosomworth to Bearcroft, 10/12/1745 ("hazard"). CRSGA 28 (1): 260 (trading post).

13. For Mary's memories, see GT, 140–141. Because the evidence is sparse, accounts of this period of Mary's life vary dramatically. My capsule summary relies on Hahn, *Mary Musgrove*, quotation ("expected") from 57, and John T. Juricek, *Colonial Georgia and the Creeks: Anglo-Indian Diplomacy on the Southern Frontier, 1733–1763* (Gainesville: University Press of Florida, 2010). Several documents that I cite below refer to "Edisto," which contemporaries used

interchangeably with "Pon Pon"; see, e.g., the "Ponpon or Edisto River" on William Bull's 1738 [Map of the Southeast], http://hmap.libs.uga.edu/hmap/view?docId=hmap/hmap1738b8.xml, viewed May 20, 2011.

14. For interpreter, see SC-CJ, 8/24/1725; for investigator, see ibid., 8/3/1727 and 9/21/1727. For commander and conduit of goods and services, see ibid., 8/26/1727; BPRO-SC, 13: 84, 113–114, 163; SC-JCHA, 7/15/1731; Public Treasurer's Ledgers, vol. 1, ff62 and 90, South Carolina Department of Archives and History, Columbia. For life at Pon Pon in the 1720s, see Hahn, *Mary Musgrove*, chapter 3, quotation ("multicultural") from 56. For the Creek community there, see SC-UH, 1/5/1722 and 3/8/1722 ("young"). SC-CJ, 9/1/1726, p. 15 ("pernicious"). For Creek-related problems near Pon Pon, see ibid., p. 17; ibid., 10/8/1726, pp. 38–39, 46–47; A. S. Salley, ed., *Journal of Colonial John Herbert, Commissioner of Indian Affairs for the Province of South Carolina, October 17, 1727–March 19, 1727/8* (Columbia: Historical Commission of South Carolina, 1936), p. 21; Clergy of South Carolina to the Secretary of the Society for the Propagation of the Gospel in Foreign Parts, 1/2/1728, http://www.cofc.edu/~speccoll/pdf/SPGSeriesABC.pdf, p. 393, viewed 6/29/2009. Slaves from Pon Pon continued to run to Creek country for years. See BPRO-SC, 12: 116; South Carolina *Gazette*, 10/28/1732 and 6/12/1753; SC-CJ, 7/30/1745.

15. During one of the periodic debates about the Creeks living at Pon Pon, an Osochi headman was appointed to bring his people home; SC-CJ, 10/8/1726, pp. 46–47. For Welch's ties to John Musgrove, see ibid., 8/3/1727, 8/26/1727, and 9/21/1727; Public Treasurer's Ledgers, vol. 1, f90. For Welch serving with George Griffin, Mary's brother, see BPRO-SC, 12: 194; for Welch's ties to Estatoe, see above, chapter 5. For Acorn Whistler's 1744 visit to Pon Pon, see SC-CJ, 9/8/1744 and 1/25/1745. In 1752, Acorn Whistler left Ashley Ferry and arrived at Sheldon. No source describes his route, but the most direct path went through Pon Pon; see William De Brahm, "A Map of South Carolina and a Part of Georgia," in William P. Cumming, *The Southeast in Early Maps*, 3rd ed., revised and enlarged by Louis De Vorsey Jr. (Chapel Hill: University of North Carolina Press, 1998), plate 59c. DRIA 1: 235 (followers), 326 (Thomas). For reacquiring Pon Pon land, see SC-CJ, 7/3/1753, pp. 501–502, and 8/7/1753, pp. 558–564.

16. For Cowetas and Pon Pon, see SC-CJ, 6/30/1721 and 10/8/1726; "Journal of Captain Tobias Fitch's Mission from Charleston to the Creeks, 1726," in Newton Mereness, ed., *Travels in the American Colonies* (New York: Macmillan Company , 1916), 176–212, esp. pp. 211–212. For Mary's comments about 1732, see GT, 141; CRSGA 28 (1): 256 ("Plantation"). Hahn, *Mary Musgrove*, chapters 3–4.

17. SC-CJ, 1/12/1733; CRSGA 28 (1): 256.

18. For the economy during Savannah's early years, see Joshua Piker, "Creeks and Colonists: Re-thinking the Southern Backcountry," *Journal of Southern History* 70 (2004): 503–540. For the Musgroves' land, compare their plantation with Abercorn and Highgate; Robert G. McPherson, ed., *The Journal of the Earl of Egmont: Abstract of the Trustees Proceedings for Establishing the Colony of Georgia, 1732–1738* (Athens: University of Georgia Press, 1962), 306–308. GT, 142 ("Deer Skin"); CRSGA 29: 54 (Mary), 57 ("Suit"), 60 ("License"). Mills Lane,

ed., *General Oglethorpe's Georgia: Colonial Letters, 1733–1743* (Savannah, GA: Beehive Press, 1990), 130 ("made away").

19. For the Musgroves' diplomatic activities, see Hahn, *Mary Musgrove*, chapter 4; Julie Anne Sweet, "John Musgrove: The First British-Creek Mediator of Georgia," *Native South* 2 (2009): 23–50, esp. (for John's drinking) pp. 36, 38. CRSGA 29: 54 ("Interpreting"); ibid., 32: 114 ("Mr. & Mrs."), 186 ("of Georgia"). "Journal of Benjamin Ingham," in Trevor R. Reese, ed., *Our First Visit in America: Early Reports from the Colony of Georgia, 1732–1740*, (Savannah, GA: Beehive Press, 1974), pp. 159–182, quotation ("Sensible") from 175. McPherson, *Journal of the Earl of Egmont*, 67.

20. CRSGA 27: 68 ("Relations"); South Carolina *Gazette*, 5/26/1733 ("Kindred"). For the Osochi brothers, see GT, p. 367, n. 12; Mills, *Oglethorpe's Georgia*, 97 ("wives"); CRSGA 20: 122 ("Sake"). For Mary's Osochi kin, see DRIA 1: 276. For moving upriver, see CRSGA 20: 237, 452; ibid., 21: 77 ("gone"); *The Journal of the Reverend John Wesley*, vol. 1 (New York: Mason and Lane, 1837), 48. For the Bosomworths' home on St. Catherine's Island, see Coulter, *Journal of William Stephens*, 95; William De Brahm, "A map of Savannah River beginning at Stone-Bluff, or Nexttobethell, which continueth to the sea; also, the four sounds Savañah, [Warsaw], Hossabaw, and St. Katharines, with their islands; likewise Neuport, or Serpent River" [1752?], Library of Congress, Washington, DC; Hahn, *Mary Musgrove*, p. 164. For "Indian relations," see the anonymous contemporary margin comments on Hawkins, [Numbered Grid].

21. For the delegations, see South Carolina *Gazette*, 5/26/1733; CRSGA 20: 381–388; GT, 56–57 ("near"); McPherson, *Journal of the Earl of Egmont*, 172 ("Chigilli"). CRSGA 4: 518 ("Resort," "Influence"), 567 ("Malatchie"); ibid., 21: 272 ("Offices").

22. For the deaths, see CRSGA 20: 439; Benjamin Martyn, "A List of all the Lands Granted in the Colony of Georgia in America from the Commencement of the Said Colony to the 24th of June 1749," [1752], CO 5/373, ff77–98, esp. 78 and 83; McPherson, *Journal of the Earl of Egmont*, 292. For Mary's economic situation, see ibid. ("owing"); GT, 142 ("Experience," "suffered," "Circumstances," "Expence," "decreased."); CRSGA 28 (1): 258 ("neglected").

23. CRSGA 23: 219 ("Pride," "greatest"); ibid., 4: 519 ("Authority"); ibid., 4 (Supplement): 158–160 ("Mrs. Matthews's"); GT, 107 ("Marys"). CRSGA 30: 226; for more on the Trustees' worries, see ibid., 223–224, 234, 247; ibid., 36: 275.

24. GT, 86–89 (1738). For Altamaha, see CRSGA 22 (2): 88 ("Nation"); ibid., 25: 235–236; ibid., 4: 319, 511; ibid., 27: 157 ("Settlement"); ibid., 28 (1): 259–260 ("Dwelling"); Edmond Atkin to Henry Ellis, 1/25/1760, pp. 13–14, Henry Ellis Papers, folder 942, item 3, Georgia Historical Society, Savannah; Hahn, *Mary Musgrove*, p. 163 ("principal"). For Mary passing her right to trade at the Forks to Thomas's brother, Adam, see Lilla M. Hawes, ed., "Proceedings of the President and Assistants in Council of Georgia, 1749–1751, Part I" *Georgia Historical Quarterly* 35 (1951): 323–350, esp. 343. For the islands, see CRSGA 25: 235–236 ("Grant"); GT, 156–163.

25. CRSGA 28 (1): 90 ("best").

26. Both here and in the discussion below, my treatment of Mary's land-related initiatives and their legal implications follows the definitive narrative presented

in Juricek, *Colonial Georgia and the Creeks*, chapters 5–7, quotation ("hanging") from 152. CRSGA 27: 193 ("Treason"), 195 ("Sovereigns," "oblige"); ibid., 36: 560 ("Subject"); GT, 144 ("at present").

27. Unless otherwise noted, this paragraph draws on Mary's letter to Glen; DRIA 1: 264–265. SC-JCHA, 2/1/1754, p. 339 (May 20); CRSGA 28 (1): 262 ("arriv'd"). Hahn, *Mary Musgrove*, pp. 166 (1746) and 175 (1749).

28. CRSGA 6: 267, 280, 285–287, 305–306; ibid., 36: 400–401. Ibid., 27: 52–53 (1750). For 1752, see Hahn, *Mary Musgrove*, pp. 190–191; DRIA 1: 264 ("arrested"); James Glen to Provost Marshall, 7/9/1752, Secretary of State, Miscellaneous Records, vol. 21, 1751–1754, p. 498, South Carolina Department of Archives and History, Columbia.

29. CRSGA 26: 402–406.

30. Ibid., 6: 263 ("Insolence"); ibid., 25: 416 ("Ambitious"); ibid., 27: 184 ("Mob"), 185 ("Injuries").

31. Ibid., 36: 408 ("Royalty"). GT, 140 (1747), 142 ("Interest and Influence"). CRSGA 6: 262 ("Empress"), 263 ("Sovereign"). For the Bosomworths describing Mary as "Princess," see GT, 203; CRSGA 26: 466; ibid., 27: 67; ibid., 28 (1): 94. For Creeks referring to Mary as "Princess," see ibid., 27: 16; GT, 179–181, 202–205.

32. CRSGA 6: 264 ("Foot"). For deeds, see GT, 157–162, 205–210, quotation ("Granted") from 206. For Mary as negotiator, see ibid., 202–205, quotations from 203.

33. Once Mary reached London in 1754, she presented the Lord Commissioners for Trade and Plantations with the proclamation authorizing her to resolve the Creeks' land issues; ibid., 234–236, 380, n. 11. For Thomas suggesting to the Board of Trade that satisfying her demands would ensure the safety of the southern frontier, see CRSGA 27: 44–46. For Mary's desire to hold land as a British subject, see GT, 145.

34. DRIA 1: 265 (Thomas); CRSGA 26: 405 (official). Thomas later wrote of "the great Advantage that such a signal Proof of our Zeal for his Majesty's Service properly represented by this Government would be to our Affairs at Home"; DRIA 1: 386.

8. The Colonists' Story

1. For the portion of Thomas's diary that covers the dates in question, see DRIA 1: 282–287; ibid., 280 ("ticklish"), 283 ("Sons").

2. CRSGA 27: 167 ("darke," "Stigmatize," "Mists"). For the early days of Thomas's agency, see DRIA 1: 268–269. For his later rhetoric, see ibid., 271 ("Calumnies"), 307 ("Teeth"), 351 ("Tongues"). For the appendix, see ibid., 326–337, quotations from 329 ("Rains"), 330 ("Prejudices"), 337 ("Wound"). Demeré Family Bible, MS 1702, Georgia Historical Society, Savannah, Georgia; it is impossible to be certain who placed the *x*'s in the margins. I am grateful to Dr. Stan Deaton and the staff at the GHS, who examined the Bible on my behalf.

3. DRIA 1: 266 ("Proofs"), 268 ("disputed").

4. SC-CJ, 5/27/1752, p. 259, 6/2/1752, p. 262, 6/4/1752, p. 274, 6/11/1752, p. 275 ("spouse," "go up"), 6/16/1752, p. 289 ("Gentlemen").

5. DRIA 1: 343–344 ("Spouse"). For Glen's statements about Mary, see SC-CJ, 5/27/1752 ("Malatchi," "proper"), 6/2/1752 ("Language," "Chiefs"); for the council, see ibid., 6/4/1752.

6. Unless otherwise noted, the quotations in this paragraph and the two that follow come from the Bosomworths' letters to Glen; see DRIA 1: 264–266. CRSGA 26: 403 ("Embassy"); ibid., 27: 191 ("nominal").

7. SC-CJ, 6/2/1752; DRIA 1: 264–265 .

8. For Mary's use of the first-person plural to describe the agency, see ibid., 266; for "proceeding," see ibid., 264. Ibid., 343–344 (instructions). SC-CJ, 11/15/1752, p. 5 ("pleased"); CRSGA 27: 21 ("Services").

9. DRIA 1: 275 (Chigelly). For Osochis and Mary's assertions of royalty, see GT, 179, 204, 207, 210.

10. DRIA 1: 266.

11. Ibid., 264–265 ("Maters"; "Matters"), 268 (letter), 275 (Mary).

12. All quotations come from Glen's instructions; ibid., 345–346.

13. For the portion of Thomas's journal that deals with the period from the Bosomworths' arrival in Coweta to the emergence of a consensus about Acorn Whistler's guilt, see ibid., 270–279. Ibid., 276 ("Cause").

14. Edmond Atkin to Henry Ellis, 1/25/1760 ("her's"), Ellis Papers, Georgia Historical Society; CRSGA 6: 283 ("intrigues"). For Aleck's relations with Yuchis, see Joshua Piker, "To the Backcountry and Back Again: The Yuchi's Search for Stability in the Eighteenth-Century Southeast," in Jason Baird Jackson, ed., *Yuchi Indian Histories before the Removal Era* (Lincoln: University of Nebraska Press, 2012), pp. 189–213; for Aleck in the colonies, see Joshua Piker, "Creeks and Colonists: Re-thinking the Southern Backcountry," *Journal of Southern History* 70 (2004): 503–540, esp. 528.

15. For Aleck visiting Bull, see DRIA 1: 235; for Bull's other visitors and the Yuchis with Acorn Whistler, see above, preface. For Glen's letters, see DRIA 1: 235; SC-CJ, 4/6/1752, p. 132. For Bull and his Yuchi neighbors, see Piker, "To the Backcountry and Back Again."

16. DRIA 1: 270–271 (Coweta confrontation), 284–285 (talk and response), 297–298 (October).

17. Ibid. ("Consequence"). For presents from South Carolina, see "The Publick of South Carolina to John Dart", 1741–1742, MS 212, Edward E. Ayer Manuscript Collection, Newberry Library, Chicago; SC-JCHA, 2/24/1742, p. 415, 4/8/1743, p. 374; SC-CJ, 11/22/1746, p. 8, 11/25/1746, p. 10. For Aleck receiving goods from the "King's Magazine at Frederica," see CRSGA 36: 345–347, 359. For Georgia's gifts, see especially items 13–15, 21–22, 26, 28 in box 1, folder 5, Joseph V. Bevan Papers, Georgia Historical Society. For Aleck's dealings with Superintendent Edmond Atkin, see Atkin to Henry Ellis,1/25/1760, Ellis Papers. Edith Mays, ed., *Amherst Papers, 1756–1763: Dispatches from South Carolina, Virginia, and His Majesty's Superintendent of Indian Affairs* (Bowie, MD: Heritage Books, 2009), 111, 117–118; Edmond Atkin to William Lyttelton, 2/5/1760, Lyttelton Collection, Clements Library, Ann Arbor, Michigan; "Conference with Aleck," 2/3/1760, enclosed in ibid. SC-JCHA, 2/24/1742, p. 418 ("Headmen"). For Aleck's status within Cusseta and conferences, see Piker, "To the Backcountry and Back Again."

18. DRIA 1: 298 ("Reverend").

19. Ibid., 265 ("appearance"), 290 ("Mr."), 343–344 ("acquaint"); SC-CJ, 6/11/1752, p. 275 (advance); SC-JCHA, 8/25/1753, p. 299 (gifts) . For England, see DRIA 1: 273, 299. For Thomas failing to tell the Upper Creeks about his postponed trip, see most notably his account of the Tuckabatchee conference; ibid., 289–296, and GT, 224–226.

20. DRIA 1: 270 ("I was"). A generation earlier, Chigelly rejected a Cherokee peace offer because "I see no Present with the Talk"; sending "a small Present" with a peace talk, he said, "is always what is our Custom." SC-CJ, 10/8/1726, p. 39.

21. DRIA 1: 273 ("Seal," "Power," "depend"), 286 ("I came"), 290 (Tucka-batchee), 298 ("Paper," Coweta).

22. Ibid., 273 (Malatchi and Chigelly), 299, 344 (instructions).

23. Ibid., 273 ("Education").

24. Ibid., 275 ("feeling"), 276 (Mary's speech); SC-CJ, 10/31/1752, p. 479 ("pathetic"). DRIA substitutes "publick" for "pathetic," a nonsensical choice of words in context. Two British traders also described Mary's speech as "feeling and pathetic"; DRIA 1: 308.

25. The version of Mary's speech in ibid., 276 places a period after "per-swaded." The quotation I present follows the council journal's version (10/31/1752, p. 480), which more accurately represents the gist of Mary's talk. DRIA 1: 277 ("Friendship").

26. Ibid., 278–279.

27. Ibid., 289 (journal), 291 ("Head Men"), 347 (letter).

28. Ibid., 308 ("whole"), 332 (January). As I discuss above, Thomas had Ladson swear out another affidavit about the August 11 meeting two months later to rectify the flaws (from Thomas's perspective) with his first effort. Even in that latter affidavit, however, Ladson says only that he "heard the Indian called the Acorn Whistler accused . . . and that he . . . ought to suffer for it." Nowhere, in short, did Ladson say that the Lower Creek headmen accused Acorn Whistler, and nowhere did he say that they decided he was guilty. Ibid., 340.

29. GT, 224–226 (paper); DRIA 1: 295–296 (journal entry). For Charleston, see GT, 226; DRIA 1: 326, 350–351.

30. Ibid., 349–350.

31. Ibid., 324 ("Happiness").

32. For the portion of Thomas's journal covering the events discussed here, see Ibid., 296–326. The journal has three throwaway references to Mary during this period: ibid., 296 (falling off a horse), 319 (passing on news about a runaway slave), 322 (giving advice about where to hold a conference). Falling from the horse on September 27 left Mary "very much hurt," but she was up and about by October 4. Thomas never mentioned her "hurt" again, as he would have had she been laid up for weeks. After all, he used Mary's "Hardships and Fatigues" to persuade Glen to send her some gifts for her Creek friends. Ibid., 349–350 (October 4; "Hardships"; gifts).

33. Ibid., 324 (Mary); SC-JCHA, 2/1/1754, p. 341 (per diem).

34. CRSGA 27: 21–22 (Glen's letter). For the petitions, see ibid., 26: 465–502, quotations from 465 ("Princess") and 477 ("Mr."); ibid., 27: 1–22.

35. DRIA 1: 324 (journal), 337–340 (Tuckabatchee). For miles, see Bernard Romans, "A Map of West Florida, part of E. Florida, Georgia, part of South Carolina" (1773), Clements Library.

36. If Acorn Whistler was executed before the Bosomworths arrived, of course, then they could not take credit for convincing the Creeks to make satisfaction for the April 1 attack. DRIA 1: 333 ("wicked"), 337–339 (affidavits), quotation ("killed") from 338.

37. SC-CJ, 2/28/1753, p. 286 ("all who"). SC-JCHA, 2/10/1753, p. 83 ("Account"), 2/27/1753, p. 113 ("sending"), 3/1/1753, p. 127 ("ought"). For the assembly notifying Glen not to send an agent, see ibid., 5/14/1752, pp. 356–358, 5/16/1752, p. 367.

38. DRIA 1: 369 (first memorial); 376–377 (second memorial).

39. SC-UH, 4/14/1753, 4/16/1753, 4/18/1753, 4/19/1753; DRIA 1: 396–397 ("Sister," "entitled"), 404–405, 462 ("Remedy"); BPRO-SC, 25: 337 ("Lordships"); CO 5/374, f181 ("requested").

Epilogue

1. South Carolina *Gazette*, 6/12/1753 (returning, "Token"); SC-CJ, 6/13/1753. DRIA 1: 421–433 (Shawnee); Ian Steele, "Shawnee Origins of Their Seven Years' War," *Ethnohistory* 53 (2006): 657–687.

2. South Carolina *Gazette*, 6/25/1753 ("to take"). No source provides the victim's name, but Red Coat King had at least two sons in the 1753 delegation: Handsome Fellow and the victim. One of Red Coat King's sons bore the title Estatoe Mico during the Okfuskees' 1749 negotiations with the Cherokees. Handsome Fellow dealt with the Cherokees frequently from the mid-1750s to the mid-1770s, but neither he nor any other Okfuskee invoked the title Estatoe Mico after 1749, even when they were interacting with Estatoes; and no source after 1753 refers to Red Coat King having a son other than Handsome Fellow. I think it likely, therefore, that the victim of the 1753 attack was Estatoe Mico. For 1749, see SC-CJ, 9/6/1749, p. 617; for Handsome Fellow's career, see Joshua Piker, *Okfuskee: A Creek Indian Town in Colonial America* (Cambridge, MA: Harvard University Press, 2004). DRIA 1: 462 ("Dow's," "uneasy"). Dowse family accounts for supplies and hospitality provided to Indians traveling to and from Charleston go back to at least 1741; see SC-JCHA, 1/19/1742, p. 316. For the parties referenced here, see ibid., 2/16/1742, p. 376 ("Pasturage"); 1/13/1744, p. 525; 2/12/1745, p. 322 ("dieting"); 5/3/1750, p. 78; 1/11/1754, p. 308 ("entertaining"). The lag time between the dates mentioned in the text and in the notes—e.g., a 1743 party not appearing in the documents until 1744—is due to the slow pace at which South Carolina's government gathered, evaluated, and paid its bills.

3. South Carolina *Gazette*, 6/12/1753 ("Governor," "well pleased"), 6/25/1753 (Augusta); DRIA 1: 380 (Mary, Red Coat King), 414 ("Malatchi"); SC-JCHA, 3/13/1754, p. 420 (Thomas).

4. DRIA 1: 380 ("killed"), 381 (Malatchi).

5. Red Coat King speeches were not recorded, but his reference (ibid., 380) to "my last Talk to [Glen] before [Mrs?] Bosomworth at Dotchester" shows that

he spoke several times. For the Rae family's multigenerational Okfuskee ties, see Piker, *Okfuskee*.

6. Ibid., 380–381 (July letters), 464–465 (reactions to peace). For the fall, see ibid., 378, 381.

7. Ibid., 526 ("Necessity").

8. Piker, *Okfuskee*, 52–53 (1760), 58 (1755), 103 (1793), 187–189 (1773), 196–197 (1814).

9. DRIA 1: 414 ("Murder"), 431. SC-CJ, 8/29/1755, p. 311 ("Judge"); Halifax to William Lyttelton, 8/13/1756 ("His," "ought"), William Lyttelton Collection, Clements Library, University of Michigan, Ann Arbor. Anonymous, "Plan for the Protection of Carolina & Georgia & for the Conquest of Louisiana," 11/16/1756, British Library, Additional Manuscripts, Newcastle Papers, #33029, ff357–371, quotation ("vile") from 359. See also Board of Trade to Lyttelton, 11/9/1757, Lyttelton Collection; John Pownall to Lyttelton, 11/7/1757, ibid.

10. For Malatchi's son, see William Bull to William Lyttelton, 7/24/1758, Lyttelton Collection; White Outerbridge to Lyttelton, 9/3/1759, ibid.; BPRO-SC, 28: 180; South Carolina *Gazette*, 6/13/1761; CRSGA 9: 115–116. DRIA 2: 103 (death). For the most persuasive reading of Malatchi's career within the context of Creek nation-building, see Steven C. Hahn, *The Invention of the Creek Nation, 1670–1763* (Lincoln: University of Nebraska Press, 2004).

11. For a fine summary of Thomas's struggles to win his money from South Carolina, see Terry W. Lipscomb, volume preface, in Lipscomb, ed., *The Journal of the Commons House of Assembly, November 21, 1752–September 6, 1754* (Columbia: South Carolina Department of Archives and History, 1983), xi–xxxv, esp. xxi–xxii. John T. Juricek, *Colonial Georgia and the Creeks: Anglo-Indian Diplomacy on the Southern Frontier, 1733–1763* (Gainesville: University Press of Florida, 2010); Steven C. Hahn, *The Life and Times of Mary Musgrove* (Gainesville: University Press of Florida, 2012) chapter 8. CRSGA 28 (1): 254 ("declared").

Acknowledgments

$\mathcal{I}$ HAVE SPENT EIGHT YEARS working on a book that covers the period between April 1, 1752, and June 5, 1753—a span of one year, two months, and five days. Leaving aside what that ratio of time-spent to time-covered suggests about whether I could survive a project devoted to the *longue durée*, I can confidently state that the only reason the ratio is not more out of whack is that I have been surrounded by exceptionally generous family members, friends, and colleagues. These people have tolerated my enthusiasms, guided my research, refined my thinking, and waded through my prose. They have, in a very real way, made it possible for me to complete this book.

That is especially true in the case of the people to whom this book is dedicated, my wife, Francesca Sawaya, and our daughter, Naima Sawaya. Naima and this book arrived in my life at almost the same time. The baby who slept on my lap while I wrote a book proposal became the toddler who asked "What found in microfilm, Daddy?"; she is now a third-grader with her own enthusiasms and interests. That those include early American history and Indian history has been an unexpected treat, one of the many precious aspects of being her father. Francesca entered my life well before this book—almost exactly twenty years ago, to be precise. She was the center of my world before Acorn Whistler came into our house; she is the center of my world as Acorn Whistler heads out the door.

Turning from my household to our family and friends, I am delighted to have the opportunity to thank my parents (biological and otherwise)—my father, Steve Piker; my mother, Ellie Ryan; my stepfather, John Egan; and my in-laws, Ann Rosa and Fares Sawaya—for all of their love, generosity, and support. I am also profoundly grateful to those members of my extended family who have been such an important part of our lives as I have worked on this book: the Sawayas (Peter, Sherri, Miguel, Matthew, Barbara, Therese, and Marie); the Pikers (Jeff, Tobin, Jill, Tessa, and Max); and the Egan-Portillos (Deirdre, Miguel, Lilianna, and Lucia). And friends! Thanks to Charles and Susanah, John and Jen, Danyelle and Marc, Ari and Lesley, Karl and Chie, Sandie and Bob, Cathy and Rich, Andy and Megan, David and Patty, Julie and Tom, Mark and Gabby, Jean, Wendy, Mary, and all the kids. And a special note of thanks to the extended Banana House family, people I am proud to have called "my Oberlin friends" for over a quarter century.

It is also a pleasure to have the opportunity to thank the many colleagues who have aided my research over the years. That list must begin with the three people who I consider to be my mentors: Dan Usner, the chair of my graduate committee, whose knowledge, friendship, and support I continue to rely upon; Peter Mancall, who has time and again helped me work through knotty professional problems; and Rob Griswold, the chair of my department and the person who, more than anyone, made sure that I had the resources necessary to research and write this book. Others have generously read portions of the book manuscript, written much-appreciated letters of recommendation for fellowships, or provided valuable commentary on papers and essays: Joyce Chaplin, Alan Gallay, Steve Hahn, Ari Kelman, Brett Rushforth, Claudio Saunt, and Susan Sleeper-Smith. I am also grateful to those colleagues who have responded to my questions about book-related matters large and small: David Armitage, George Blanchard, Tyler Boulware, Kathryn Braund, Richard Brown, John Cottier, Dale Couch, Stan Deaton, John Demos, Steve Hahn, Jason Jackson, John Juricek, Cathy Kelly, Charles Lesser, Jack Martin, George Milne, William

Monaghan, Neal Polhemus, Robert Shalhope, Steve Warren, Cameron Wesson, and Don White. Stephen Martin and Jared Mulcare served with distinction as my research assistants.

I would also like to thank the many audiences who have listened to my presentations about Acorn Whistler and offered suggestions for improving the project. I must particularly single out the participants of the 2005 NEH Summer Seminar on "Early American Microhistories," the members of the 2008 Southern Intellectual History Circle, and the students in my 2011 and 2012 graduate seminars. I would also like to express my gratitude to Brian Hosmer and his colleagues at the University of Tulsa and the Gilcrease Museum for inviting me to give the 2012 Cadenhead-Settle Memorial Lecture. More generally, I am grateful to my faculty and graduate-student colleagues in the University of Oklahoma's Department of History for providing such a congenial and engaging work environment. And, of course, I am pleased to have the chance to thank Kathleen McDermott and Andrew Kinney at Harvard University Press as well as Marianna Vertullo for all their hard work on behalf of this book. The two readers recruited by the press to evaluate the manuscript were likewise exceptionally helpful, as was Todd Fagin, mapmaker extraordinaire.

Finally, I would like to acknowledge the generosity of the many institutions that supported this book project. As every historian knows, the most critical institutions are the archives and libraries upon which we depend. I am very grateful for the hospitality, expertise, and hard work of the staffs at OU's Bizzell's Library, the Huntington Library, Britain's National Archives, the British Library, the Clements Library, the Historical Society of Pennsylvania, the American Philosophical Society, the South Caroliniana Library, the South Carolina Department of Archives and History, the South Carolina Historical Society, the College of Charleston Library, the South Carolina Room of the Charleston Public Library, the County of Charleston's Register Mesne Conveyance Office, the Georgia Historical Society, the Norfolk Record Office, the Georgia Department of Archives and History, and the Library of Congress.

I was able to conduct research in those archives thanks to the generous grants provided by the University of Oklahoma's History

Department, vice president for research, Research Council, and College of Arts and Sciences. OU also granted me two sabbaticals, during which I wrote a significant portion of this book. And my research and writing received a critical early boost when the Huntington Library awarded me an NEH-sponsored postdoctoral fellowship. The library remains my intellectual home on the West Coast, and I am grateful to Robert Ritchie, the library's director of research emeritus, and the library's staff and scholarly community. Any views, findings, conclusions, or recommendations expressed in this publication do not necessarily reflect those of the National Endowment for the Humanities.

Index

305